Nature's Mountain Mansion

Wonder, Wrangles, Bloodshed, and Bellyaching from Nineteenth-Century Yosemite

Edited by GARY NOY

University of Nebraska Press
LINCOLN

Acknowledgments for the use of copyrighted material appear on page 349, which constitutes an extension of the copyright page.

The University of Nebraska Press is part of a land-grant institution with campuses and programs on the past, present, and future homelands of the Pawnee, Ponca, Otoe-Missouria, Omaha, Dakota, Lakota, Kaw, Cheyenne, and Arapaho Peoples, as well as those of the relocated Ho-Chunk, Sac and Fox, and Iowa Peoples.

Library of Congress Cataloging-in-Publication Data
Names: Noy, Gary, 1951– editor.
Title: Nature's mountain mansion: wonder, wrangles, bloodshed, and bellyaching from nineteenth-century Yosemite / edited by Gary Noy.
Other titles: Wonder, wrangles, bloodshed, and bellyaching from nineteenth-century Yosemite
Description: Lincoln: University of Nebraska Press, [2022] | Includes bibliographical references.
Identifiers: LCCN 2022014505
ISBN 9781496232519 (paperback)
ISBN 9781496234179 (epub)
ISBN 9781496234186 (pdf)
Subjects: LCSH: Yosemite National Park (Calif.)—Description and travel. | Yosemite National Park (Calif.)—History—19th century—Sources. | BISAC: HISTORY / United States / State & Local / West (AK, CA, CO, HI, ID, MT, NV, UT, WY) | NATURE / Regional
Classification: LCC F868.Y6 N38 2022 | DDC 979.4/4704—dc23/eng/20220414
LC record available at https://lccn.loc.gov/2022014505

Set in Questa by Laura Buis.

No temple made with hands can compare with Yosemite. . . .
Into this one mountain mansion Nature had gathered her
choicest treasures, to draw her lovers into close and
confiding communion with her.

—John Muir, "The Incomparable Yosemite"

CONTENTS

ILLUSTRATIONS

She called it "a trip of a lifetime."

In 1886 Susan Augusta Pike Sanders, who preferred to be called Sue A. Sanders, was selected as an Illinois state delegate to the Grand Army of the Republic's California convention (what they called an "encampment") in San Francisco. Sanders was a notable leader of the Illinois chapter of the Women's Relief Corps, a charity that was the women's auxiliary of the Grand Army of the Republic, a fraternal organization for veterans of the Civil War that campaigned for voting rights for African American veterans, patriotic education, pensions for veterans, and the establishment of Memorial Day as a national holiday.

While prominent in Women's Relief Corps circles, the forty-four-year-old mother of four had rarely traveled far from her home in Delevan, Illinois, a hamlet of eleven hundred souls in the center of the state, south of Peoria. A trip to San Francisco was a magic carpet ride for Sanders. It was a journey she would never forget.

On that trip she kept a travel diary, which was published in 1887 as *A Journey to, on, and from the "Golden Shore."* In addition to attending the convention in San Francisco, she visited Denver, Colorado Springs, Salt Lake City, Flagstaff, Albuquerque, Reno, Sacramento, Oakland, San Jose, Napa Valley, and Yosemite. The trip lasted from July 24 to August 27, 1886. In her journal Sanders is enthusiastic, effusive, and exhaustive in her details. She happily comments on virtually every moment of the memorable 34-day tour. In her 118-page book, there are 175 references to the meals she enjoyed,

157 mentions of trolley cars, more than 300 references to the quality of her lodgings, nearly 150 comments on the comforts (and discomforts) of railroad passenger coaches, and a listing of hundreds of people she met. But there is one moment when Sanders is almost rendered speechless. On Sunday, August 16, 1886, at 3:00 p.m., she has her first glimpse of Yosemite Valley, from Inspiration Point. Unlike her other unrestrained, in-depth accounts, Sanders's comment on her moment of discovery is brief. She is mesmerized: "For a moment all is silence, then comes a sigh of relief and exclamations of wonder and amazement." It was a passionate reaction to which millions of visitors to Yosemite can relate.

For generations, visitors' first impressions of Yosemite have been a curious assortment. While many, such as Sue A. Sanders, have been thunderstruck in that instant, others have viewed the encounter with unease, with a disquieting sense of inadequacy or an unnerving sensation of physical confinement. Yosemite is an emotionally complicated environment. The area of Yosemite National Park is 1,190 square miles, roughly twenty-five times the size of San Francisco, but as author and naturalist Ann Zwinger wrote in 1996, the map is not two-dimensional, as it includes "the senses of time, the waterfalls of the mind."

We have all experienced Yosemite, whether we have been there or not. The image of Yosemite is ingrained in our consciousness from photographs, film, and the written word. Just close your eyes. Think of Yosemite Valley and it will appear. It is more than granite cliffs, thundering waterfalls, and breathtaking views. Yosemite is a symbol, an icon, an inspiration, and a cautionary tale.

For decades observers have been enchanted by and apprehensive about Yosemite. The famous photographer Ansel Adams pondered a vision of the everlasting when he wrote, "Yosemite Valley, to me, is always a sunrise, a glitter of green and golden wonder in a vast edifice of stone and space. . . . At first the colossal aspect may dominate; then we perceive and respond to the delicate and *persuasive* complex of nature."

But there were differing opinions. In 1860, despite his reputation as a relentless promoter of Yosemite Valley, James Mason Hutchings described the valley as "a scene of appalling grandeur." In 1872 travel writer and activist Grace Greenwood noted that in Yosemite "you feel like a magnificent felon, incarcerated in the very fortress of the gods." In 1870 newspaper correspondent Olive Logan was blunt: "The sight of [Yosemite] would not repay one for the suffering involved in getting to it. And the plain truth is that nine out of ten who visit Yo Semite think this, but they will not say what they think." The story of nineteenth-century Yosemite is of a place at once dazzling, demanding, and, for some, deadly.

Yosemite is not only an inspirational setting but a focal point for conquest, criticism, and controversy. *Nature's Mountain Mansion: Wonder, Wrangles, Bloodshed, and Bellyaching in Nineteenth-Century Yosemite* addresses the surprising and sometimes hidden history of Yosemite in that century—a history characterized by profound appreciation for its natural splendor but also bigotry and carnage; travel hardships; poor food and disagreeable lodgings; ill-defined, questionable, and even corrupt government administration; commercial bickering; and heated disputes over the future direction of the extraordinary panorama.

The book's title derives from a statement by John Muir. In the chapter entitled "The Incomparable Yosemite" in his 1912 book *The Yosemite*, Muir rhapsodized, "No temple made with hands can compare with Yosemite. . . . Into this one mountain mansion Nature had gathered her choicest treasures, to draw her lovers into close and confiding communion with her." But the mansion has many rooms, some bright and magnificent, others dark and disturbing. *Nature's Mountain Mansion* presents the inspired, the insipid, and the inexcusable of nineteenth-century reactions to Yosemite. This is not an anthology featuring only romantic word-portraits of the beautiful scenery; it also offers examinations of the grisly and untidy aspects of Yosemite history.

This anthology presents accounts of the remarkable Yosemite experience. From the origin myths and social rituals of the First People, to the aspirations of those who would come to dominate, to the breathless and frequently poignant stories of private discovery, to the sorrowful transitions that mark cultural change, to the angry denunciations of the unscrupulous and negligent, the Yosemite of the nineteenth century emerges.

The readings show tremendous range. There are reports peppered with scientific detail next to personal narratives of gentle poetic lyricism. There are grandiose claims and heart-pounding adventures. There are moments of doubt and cultural exultation. There are instances of genuine rejoicing and bemused resignation. There are accounts of the will to survive and a yearning to understand. There are the voices of pioneering women, provocateurs, disgruntled tourists, soldiers, poets, clergy members, amateur philosophers, and the original inhabitants and their chroniclers. These are tales of wonderment, worry, and whimsy. These are the thoughts of people facing a new reality and struggling to make sense of a fantastic, otherworldly landscape.

The principal source material for this collection is the abundant treasure trove of nineteenth-century letters, diaries, books, journals, letter sheets, and newspaper articles recounting the adventures, intriguing personalities, and impassioned controversies of Yosemite. Some of the documents used in this book have not been published or have been buried in archives for decades. Often these are personal recollections loaded with the prejudices of the participants. Frequently, nineteenth-century historical documentation is repellent to our present-day sensibilities, as the accounts are laden with misspellings, vulgarity, misogyny, racism, and cruelty. However, at times the most informative window into the cultural attitudes of the period is through these odious passages. When used, these selections are presented unedited, as any other approach would be dishonest.

On this historical tour, *Nature's Mountain Mansion* examines the rich lives and ethos of the First Inhabitants, with a focus on their settlement patterns, the impact of disease on their population, and how Native people were perceived by the dominant culture. It considers the dueling perspectives as to Yosemite's geological formation. It also addresses the bloody cultural collision of the Yosemite Valley Native population and the human tsunami of the California gold rush, which led to the most violent episode in Yosemite history—the brutal Mariposa Indian War of 1851–52. This anthology also examines the arrival of tourism in the Yosemite Valley and the ongoing tension arising from private interests, public lands, and dissatisfied visitors. *Nature's Mountain Mansion* considers the influence of and controversies surrounding John Muir, the most famous figure of nineteenth-century Yosemite. This book spotlights growing concerns over the economic exploitation of Yosemite and the fiery debates over who could best administer Yosemite—the State of California or the federal government. Highlighted topics include complaints about accommodations, high prices, and the proliferation of annoying tourists. Finally, the book investigates how mounting numbers of concerned persons were alarmed that Yosemite's spiritual uniqueness was being sullied by crass commercialism and incompetent administration.

So, after some deserved words of gratitude, let's begin with a journey back in time to when the first humans arrived in Yosemite, Nature's "mountain mansion."

ACKNOWLEDGMENTS

My heartfelt appreciation and greatest respect to my friends at the University of Nebraska Press. Bison Books, especially W. Clark Whitehorn, was instrumental in the publication of my very first book—*Distant Horizon: Documents from the Nineteenth-Century American West*—in 1999. It has been a delight to work with him once again, all these many years later.

Extra-special thanks to my friends and colleagues Lynn and Joe Medeiros. *Nature's Mountain Mansion* took its first baby steps in their kitchen. Lynn and Joe graciously took me into their home for a few days as I was recovering from a very bad back problem, and during my stay I began to formulate and outline what would ultimately emerge as this anthology.

Finally, my thanks to all the characters who inhabited Yosemite in the nineteenth century. They were an intriguing lot. Sometimes they were easy to like, occasionally they were despicable, but they were always fascinating.

Nature's Mountain Mansion

1

The Soul of the Ah-wah'-nee

The First People

For tens of thousands of years, Yosemite as we know it today was the exclusive domain of snow and ice, the rush of rivers, gleaming granite, and the natural symphony of rustling leaves, booming thunder, chirping birds, and animal howls. About three thousand years ago, new inhabitants arrived—human beings.

The First People of Yosemite came to a region that featured game and vegetation much like the present, with acorns, pine nuts, deer, and salmon predominant. Archaeology has established three distinctive periods of Native settlement. First was the fifteen-hundred-year Crane Flat phase from 1000 BCE to 500 CE, an era marked by humans hunting with the *atlatl*, or spear-throwing stick. The second was the seven-hundred-year Tamarack phase from 500 to 1200 CE, which saw the development of the stone projectile points used in bows and arrows. The final period prior to European contact in the mid-nineteenth century is known as the Mariposa phase.

In the nineteenth century, the Yosemite region was occupied or visited by various tribal units and nations, including the Miwok, Mono Paiute, Yokuts, Washo, Cassons, and Chukchansi peoples, as well as the clan that resided in Yosemite Valley; they were known as the Awahnichi (alternate spellings are Ahwahnechee and Ahwahneechee). *Ah-wah'-nee,* which means "large or gaping mouth," is the word used by the Native peoples of Yosemite to describe the valley. The Awahnichi and other Yosemite Indians routinely used fire as a management tool, which promoted the spread of the black oak (which provided acorns, an important food and cultural resource) and opened meadows and forests, which aided travel and bolstered defense against surprise attacks.

The actual indigenous population of Yosemite is difficult to determine. In the centuries before their first encounters with Europeans, they repeatedly suffered from pestilence and conflict, which had severe impacts on the number of residents. This led to increased interaction between and consolidation of tribes for survival. These unified community totals were typically low, and the best guess is that by the 1850s the Native population of Yosemite was a few hundred. The earliest nonindigenous visitors reported seeing few, if any, Native people. It does not mean they were not present, but Yosemite Indians may have retreated out of caution to less accessible and less visible areas as they assessed the arrival of the unwelcome trespassers.

With the growing dominance of Anglo-Americans beginning in the 1850s, Yosemite's Native residents were regularly disparaged, displaced, and dispelled.

During the California gold rush, thousands upon thousands of gold seekers swept across the landscape like wildfire, and the official government policy toward the Native people became "extermination." California's first governor, Peter Burnett, made this proclamation in his first annual message to the newly created state legislature in 1851: "That a war of extermination will continue to be waged between the two races until the Indian race becomes extinct must be expected; while we cannot anticipate this result with but painful regret, the inevitable destiny of the [Indian] race is beyond the power and wisdom of man to avert."

Public policy supported this barbarous sentiment. Local governments provided bounties for Indian heads or scalps. At the state level, volunteer militias submitted claims to the California State Treasury for reimbursement of their expenses in "suppression of Indian hostilities" and extermination. Eventually, the federal government reimbursed the state government for the cost of these ghastly efforts.

The Soul of the Ah-wah'-nee

The legal rights of Indians were suppressed. In April 1850 California's new state legislature passed "An Act for the Government and Protection of Indians" that was not remotely close to being protective. Among other actions, the law stated that jurisdiction over complaints between white and indigenous peoples would be granted to a justice of the peace, "but in no case shall a white man be convicted of any offense upon the testimony of an Indian or Indians."

A final provision of the act established a system of Indian "apprenticeship" under which any white person desiring the labor of an Indian child could appear before a justice of the peace and make a petition for the right of custody. Under the law, white residents of the state could obtain the services of any number of Indians males under the age of eighteen and females under the age of fifteen.

In 1860 the apprenticeship provision was revised to allow children to be placed in a master's custody without parental consent. It was also altered to permit "articles of indenture" that authorized the white overseer to have control over the Indian charge for a set period of time: males under fourteen could be detained until the age of twenty-five, and males indentured between the ages of fourteen and twenty could be controlled until the age of thirty. Females could be retained to the age of twenty-five.

It is believed that at least three thousand Indian children were sold into servitude at between $50 and $200 apiece under California's sanctioned "apprentice system."

Indian girls were often sold or kidnapped and forced into sexual slavery. Native women were also frequently kidnapped and forced into prostitution.

The Act for the Government and Protection of Indians remained in effect until 1863, when it was repealed due to President Abraham Lincoln's Emancipation Proclamation. It is uncertain exactly how many Indians were affected by the original 1850 legislation, but historian Robert Heizer estimates that as many as ten thousand Indian children may have been indentured, kidnapped, or sold between 1850 and 1863.

Meanwhile, the federal government engaged in a cynical game of "promises made, promises abandoned." This was most evident in the case of the "Secret Treaties." In 1851 the federal government appointed three commissioners to negotiate treaties with California Indians. By 1852 the commissioners were claiming that eighteen treaties had been negotiated with 139 tribes. The eighteen treaties set aside more than seven million acres of land for use by Native peoples and would fund programs for Indian self-sufficiency. Upon learning of the treaties, the California public was furious. California's legislature instructed the U.S. senators from California to oppose ratification of the treaties.

In February 1852 President Millard Fillmore submitted the eighteen treaties to the U.S. Senate for ratification. The Senate adjourned to a secret session to consider the treaties but failed to ratify any of them. The Senate ordered the treaties to be sealed and kept secret for the next fifty-three years.

The Mariposa Indian War of 1851–52 was a crushing blow to the Native inhabitants. The population surge of the gold rush amplified the mounting pressure on indigenous peoples' settlements. The new rulers decreed that Yosemite Natives were unwanted and undesirable aliens in their ancient homeland. Proponents of Yosemite tourism too often viewed the presence of the besieged and starving Native population as contrary to the blissful Edenic image they were promoting and urged the permanent removal of all indigenous inhabitants of Yosemite. By the end of the nineteenth century, Yosemite Indians were tolerated in the valley but were typically regarded as picturesque adornments for the benefit of visitors. It was not until well into the twentieth century that the rich cultures of the indigenous nations were afforded overdue respect and their history began to be illuminated and honored. And yet, challenges remain. In 2019 the federal government refused tribal recognition for the Southern Sierra Miwok people, which includes descendants of the original inhabitants of Yosemite.

There are relatively few personal narratives of nineteenth-century Yosemite indigenous people that can be considered completely reliable. In the nineteenth century, their recollections were generally recorded, translated, and transcribed by nonindigenous researchers who did not comfortably or completely understand the nuances of Native languages and folkways. As a result, while these contemporaneous narratives are valuable, we cannot fully trust them to represent accurately the opinions and observations of their subjects. Our current portrait of the nineteenth-century Yosemite indigenous population has been primarily derived from archeological studies, historical reexamination, secondary interpretations, a smattering of eyewitness accounts, and the power of Yosemite Indian oral tradition that connects generations and enlightens enduring cultural values and context.

"Innumerable moons and snows have passed."

Galen Clark

Indians of the Yosemite Valley and Vicinity: Their History, Customs and Traditions, 1904

Galen Clark was one of the most prominent figures in Yosemite history. Born in 1814 in Canada, Clark headed to California in 1848. In 1853 he suffered a lung hemorrhage and was informed that he had but a few months to live. Seeking a healthier climate, Clark went to the Sierra Nevada, to a tiny settlement in Mariposa County named Wawona. Recovering his health, Clark established a rest stop called Clark's Station near Wawona and the Mariposa Grove of Giant Sequoias on the main southern road to Yosemite Valley. Seeking protection for the grove and the valley, he wrote letter after letter to friends and members of Congress. He found his greatest supporter in John Conness, a U.S. senator from California, who introduced the bill for the Yosemite Valley Grant Act in 1864. When the valley came under government control, Clark was named the first official "Guardian of the

Grove," a position he held for more than thirty years. He died in 1910 at the age of ninety-five, fifty-seven years after he was given a few months to live. He is buried in Yosemite Valley, at a site he chose, surrounded by sequoia trees that he had planted.

As Guardian of the Grove, Clark gathered information on and impressions of Yosemite Valley from residents and tourists alike. Over a fifty-year span, he researched and obtained valuable information about Yosemite Native culture, including some Yosemite mythology. In 1904 this information was collected in the book *Indians of the Yosemite Valley and Vicinity: Their History, Customs and Traditions*. Chapter 7 of that book examines myths and legends about Yosemite.

In the years that followed, compiling the legends of Yosemite's first people became a cottage industry. There were anthologies from all corners, ranging from highbrow academia to overly romantic popular culture. Often these compendia rehashed or embroidered Clark's earlier efforts. Many of these compilations are considered suspect as to their authenticity. While most are based on good intentions and honest effort, critics have emphasized contradictions, misinterpretations, omissions, misspellings, and contrived stories. Clark himself acknowledged this in *Indians of the Yosemite Valley and Vicinity*, noting that Yosemite Indians were very reluctant to trust a white correspondent and that, as he wrote, "it is probable that most of [the entries] have had at least a foundation in real Indian myths, but many are obviously fanciful in some particulars, and it is impossible to tell how much is of Indian origin and how much is due to poetic embellishment."

Nonetheless, Galen Clark's album of Yosemite Valley myths and legends remains valuable as the collection published in greatest proximity to the nineteenth century and as the most reflective of the stories likely told to nineteenth-century Yosemite visitors.

In the following passage from *Indians of the Yosemite Valley and Vicinity*, Clark recounts the legends of To-tau-kon-nu'-la (El Capitan), Tis-sa'-ack (Half Dome), and Tul-tok'-a-na (the Measuring Worm).

Legend of To-tau-kon-nu'-la and Tis-sa'-ack

Innumerable moons and snows have passed since the Great Spirit guided a little band of his favorite children into the beautiful vale of Ah-wah'-nee, and bid them stop and rest from their long and weary wanderings, which had lasted ever since they had been separated by the great waters from the happy land of their forefathers in the far distant *El-o'-win* (West).

Here they found food in abundance for all. The rivers gave them plenty of *la-pe'-si* (trout). They found in the meadows sweet *ha'-ker* (clover), and sour *yu-yu'-yu-mah* (oxalis) for spring medicine, and sweet *toon'-gy* and other edible roots in abundance. The trees and bushes yielded acorns, pine nuts, fruits and berries. In the forests were herds of *he'-ker* (deer) and other animals, which gave meat for food and skins for clothing and beds. And here they lived and multiplied, and, as instructed by their medicine men, worshipped the Great Spirit which gave them life, and the sun which warmed and made them happy.

They also kept in memory the happy land of their forefathers. The story was told by the old people to the young, and they again told it to their children from generation to generation, and they all believed that after death their spirits would return to dwell forever in that distant country.

They prospered and built other towns outside of Ah-wah'-nee, and became a great nation. They learned wisdom by experience and by observing how the Great Spirit taught the animals and insects to live, and they believed that their children could absorb the cunning of the wild creatures. And so the young son of their chieftain was made to sleep in the skins of the beaver and coyote, that he might grow wise in building, and keen of scent in following game. On some days he was fed with *la-pe'-si* that he might become a good swimmer, and on other days the eggs of the great *to-tau'-kon* (crane) were his food, that he might grow tall and keen of sight, and have a clear, ringing voice. He was also fed on the flesh of the *he'-ker* that he might be fleet of foot, and on that of the great *yo-sem'-i-te* (grizzly bear) to make him powerful in combat.

And the little boy grew up and became a great and wise chieftain, and he was also a rain wizard, and brought timely rains for the crops.

As was the custom in giving names to all Indians, his name was changed from time to time, as his character developed, until he was called Choo'-too-se-ka', meaning the Supreme Good. His grand *o'-chum* (house) was built at the base of the great rock called To-tau-kon-nu'-la, because the great *to-tau'-kons* made their nests and raised their young in a meadow at its summit, and their loud ringing cries resounded over the whole Valley.

As the moons and snows passed, this great rock and all the great rocky walls around the Valley grew in height, and the hills became high mountains.

After a time Choo'-too-se-ka' built himself a great palace *o'-chum* on the summit of the rock To-tau-kon-nu'-la, and had his great chair of state a little west of his palace, where on all festival occasions he could overlook and talk to the great multitude below; and the remains of this chair are still to be seen.

Choo'-too-se-ka' was then named To-tau-kon-nu'-la, because he had built his *o'-chum* on the summit of the great rock and taken the place of the *to-tau'-kons*. He had no wife, but all the women served him in his domestic needs, as he was their great chief, and his wishes were paramount. The many valuable donations which he received from his people at the great annual festivals made him wealthy beyond all personal wants, and he gave freely to the needy.

One day, while standing on the top of the great dome above the south wall of the Valley, watching the great herds of deer,

The Soul of the Ah-wah'-nee

he saw some strange people approaching, bearing heavy burdens. They were fairer of skin, and their clothing was different from that of his people, and when they drew near he asked them who they were and whence they came.

And a woman replied, "I am Tis-sa'-ack, and these are some of my people. We come from *cat'-tan chu'-much* (far South). I have heard of your great wisdom and goodness, and have come to see you and your people. We bring you presents of many fine baskets, and beads of many colors, as tokens of our friendship. When we have rested and seen your people and beautiful valley we will return to our home."

To-tau-kon-nu'-la was much pleased with his fair visitor, and built a large *o'-chum* for her and her companions on the summit of the great dome at the east end of the Valley, and this dome still retains her name. And she tarried there and taught the women of Ah-wah'-nee how to make the beautiful baskets which they still make at the present day; and To-tau-kon-nu'-la visited her daily, and became charmed with her loveliness, and wanted her to remain and be his wife, but she denied him, saying, "I must return to my people," and, when he still persisted, she left her *o'-chum* in the night, and was never seen again. And the love-stricken chieftain forgot his people, and went in search of her, and they waited many moons for his return and mourned his long absence, but they never saw him more.

This was the beginning of a series of calamities which nearly destroyed the great tribe of Ah-wah'-nee-chees. First a great drouth prevailed, and the crops failed, and the streams of water dried up. The deer went wild and wandered away. Then a dark cloud of smoke arose in the East and obscured the sun, so that it gave no heat, and many of the people perished from cold and hunger. Then the earth shook terribly and groaned with great pain, and enormous rocks fell from the walls around Ah-wah'-nee. The great dome called Tis-sa'-ack was burst asunder, and half of it fell into the Valley. A fire burst out of the earth in the East, and the *ca'-lah* (snow) on the sky mountains was changed to water, which flowed down and formed the Lake Ah-wei'-yah [Mirror Lake]. And all the streams were filled to overflowing, and still the waters rose, and there was a great flood, so that a large part of the Valley became a lake, and many persons were drowned.

After a time the Great Spirit took pity on his children, and the dark cloud of smoke disappeared, the sun warmed the Valley again into new life, and the few people who were left had plenty of food once more.

Many moons afterwards there appeared on the face of the great rock To-tau-kon-nu'-la the figure of a man in a flowing robe, and with one hand extended toward the West, in which direction he appears to be traveling. This figure was interpreted to be the picture of the great lost Chieftain, indicating that he had gone to the "happy hunting grounds" of his ancestors, and it is looked upon with great veneration and awe by the few Indians still living in Yosemite.

At about the same time the face of the beautiful Tis-sa'-ack appeared on the great flat side of the dome which bears her name, and the Indians recognized her by the way in which her dark hair was cut straight across her forehead and fell down at the sides, which was then considered among the Yosemites as the acme of feminine beauty, and is so regarded to this day.

Legend of the Tul-tok'-a-na

There were once two little boys living in the Valley of Ah-wah'-nee, who went down to the river to swim. When they had finished their bath they went on shore and lay down on a large boulder to dry themselves in the sun. While lying there they fell asleep, and slept so soundly that they never woke up again. Through many moons and many snows they slept, and while they slept the great rock on which they lay was slowly rising, little by little, until it soon lifted them up out of sight, and their friends searched for them everywhere without success. Thus they were carried up into the blue sky, until they scraped their faces against the moon; and still they slept on.

Then all the animals assembled to bring down the little boys from the top of the great rock. Each animal sprang up the face of the rock as far as he could. The mouse could only spring a hand's breadth, the rat two hands' breadths, the raccoon a little more, and so on. The grizzly bear made a great leap up the wall, but fell back like all the others, without reaching the top. Finally came the lion, who jumped up farther than any of the others, but even he fell back and could not reach the top.

Then came the *tul-tok'-a-na*, the insignificant measuring worm, who was despised by all the other creatures, and began to creep up the face of the rock. Step by step, little by little, he measured his way up until he was soon above the lion's jump, and still farther and farther, until presently he was out of sight; and still he crawled up and up, day and night, through many moons, and at length he reached the top, and took the little boys and brought them safely down to the ground. And therefore the rock was named for the measuring worm, and was called Tul-tok'-a-na.

"He is called savage, I hardly know why."

Jean-Nicolas Perlot
Chercour d'or: Vie et aventures d'un enfant de l'Ardenne, 1897

Mid-nineteenth-century descriptions of Yosemite Native people by white visitors to the valley often overflow with contempt and vicious, racist characterizations. But there are exceptions. There are a few eyewitness accounts of personal encounters with Yosemite Indians that reflect admiration for the indigenous population, evince respect for their traditions and customs, and lament the seemingly inevitable loss of their homeland at the hands of newly arrived gold seekers and aggressive settlers.

An example comes from a twenty-six-year-old Belgian argonaut named Jean-Nicolas Perlot. As did many Europeans during the gold rush, Perlot heard wondrous tales of riches ready and waiting in California. Seeking adventure and instant wealth, Perlot boarded a ship in France in October 1850 and arrived in Monterey, California, in April 1851. A few weeks later, the hopeful gold seeker arrived in the Mariposa/Yosemite region and would remain until 1857. In the 1870s, Perlot would return to Belgium. In 1897 Perlot would publish a memoir entitled *Chercour d'or: Vie et aventures d'un enfant de l'Ardenne* (Gold seeker: Life and adventures of a child of the Ardennes). In his reminiscence, Perlot exhibited a high regard for the indigenous people he encountered in the Yosemite domain. As was common with nineteenth-century recollections, Perlot's overall narrative is embellished and paternalistic, but his admiration for the Native culture is heartfelt and his commentaries are remarkably detailed. Perlot's musings on how indigenous people are misunderstood by the dominant culture constitute the excerpt presented here.

We had built a false idea, certainly, of the Indian when we considered and treated him as a wild beast: he is a being naturally sweet and inoffensive. Having few needs, consequently few desires, he is easy to please. He is called savage, I hardly know why; whether by this word one means a ferocious, unsociable being, or simply being in a state of nature, it belongs in no way to the Indian.

He has, just like us, his customs, his laws, his religion; only, they differ from ours, they constitute at the very least the beginning of civilization, unless they may be the final goal, or else the remnant of an extinct civilization; assuredly, they do not belong to a people who have recently left a state of nature.

Doubtless, there is an institution which forms for so-called civilized peoples one of the bases—some of them say simply the base—of society, and which the Indian does not know: property. Is this a sign of inferiority? I will not decide the question. But who can tell us that the progress of civiliza-

The Soul of the Ah-wah'-nee

tion will not bring us, in this respect, to the point where the Indian is? In the meantime, the latter owes to this ignorance his living in peace with his tribe—and in his family: he does not know law-suits.

His laws and customs proceed from his religious beliefs: the Great Spirit (God) himself is his legislature and his judge; but his action is exerted without any intermediary whatsoever. A theocracy without priests—there, truly is the government of the Indians.

An attentive observer of nature, the Indians see in the mighty phenomena it presents to him, the manifestation of the will of *Nang-Oua*, the Great Spirit, and endeavors to make his conduct conform to it; he obeys him and offers no other worship to him: the precepts of this religion, which the old teach the young, constitute his civil code and his penal code.

If the Indian commits a crime, it is God whom he offends, it is God who will punish him. Others avoid him, for fear of being punished because of him; they leave him in isolation until they are persuaded that by his good works he has succeeded in appeasing the Great Spirit. Thus, the Indian who has fought with another member of his tribe, who refused to share his food with one more feeble than himself, who has broken his bow, his arrows or his fishing tackle, has to exile himself from his tribe and not reappear until the moon has returned to the same phase and to the same point of the sky where it was at the moment of the sin, that is, at the end of the month. Each day of this month, when the moon again passes the point of the meridian where it was at the moment of the sin, the Indian is on his guard, persuaded that the Spirit is going to punish him, by depriving him of health or of food or of sleep; it is ordinarily of this last blessing that he is deprived. . . .

All this refers to the [Indians] of California, . . . when I knew them and associated with them. . . . It could be that today, by virtue of the law of progress, they dress, live, speak, and think like us: they would then have succeeded in becoming civilized, or rather would have exchanged their civilization for ours. If that is the case, alas!, what have they gained?

··

"Survival is a simple concept and a complex act."

··

Kathleen L. Hull

Pestilence and Persistence: Yosemite Indian Demography and Culture in Colonial California, 2009

Kathleen L. Hull is a professor of anthropology and heritage studies at the University of California, Merced. Her expertise is the cultural and demographic impact of colonial encounters on Native people of North America, with a special emphasis on Yosemite Valley Native populations.

In 2009 Hull published *Pestilence and Persistence: Yosemite Indian Demography and Culture in Colonial California*, a groundbreaking study that includes an examination of the adaptability and tenacity of the Awahnichi (or Ahwahneechee) people, the Native inhabitants of Yosemite, both before European contact and after. Hull approached the subject in a novel way. She did not utilize the standard method, which focuses on the individual or regional response to challenges, but on a community reaction as the analytical model. The Awahnichi were periodically threatened by waves of deadly epidemics and physical invasion that swept through the valley for centuries before the arrival of Europeans. Her studies concluded that the Awahnichi survived through perseverance and adaptability. The nation maintained its cultural identity and language even when its people were forced to move away from the Yosemite Valley and intermingle with other bands. The Awahnichi forged relationships and collaborations with other Native people when their own numbers dwindled. And the Yosemite Native people modified and restructured their identity and cultural practices in recognition of the influx

The Soul of the Ah-wah'-nee

and diversity of their expanded community, which now included non-Awahnichi.

In these two passages from *Pestilence and Persistence,* Hull addresses the threats faced by the Awahnichi and describes changes wrought by disease and incursion on Yosemite villages.

Disentangling Colonial Encounters

Survival is a simple concept and a complex act. Day-to-day decisions that affect such endurance draw on the past through experience and look to the future for vindication. But they are executed in a present often fraught with fear and uncertainty. Our lives are dominated by the iterative performance of tasks that provide for our nourishment and protect us from multiple threats to health and happiness. This daily demonstration of purpose and resolve addresses both the mundane and the extraordinary. And in the latter case, the effort to survive requires not only recognizing new enemies but also finding the means to withstand their varied assaults. Some adversaries are overt and make no attempt to hide their intent to control the resources, minds, and bodies of others by coercion or force. Whether they invade in large numbers or small, their will to prevail is fostered by a belief in their right to proceed and is empowered by technology equal to or better than that which they face. Other enemies are more insidious, creeping unseen into communities that awake to the smell of death and the trauma of loss. Such subtle destruction is wrought not at the hands of men with weapons but, rather, by microscopic biological warriors that invade human tissues and organs. In the wake of devastation, these two aggressive forces test both the fortitude of those assaulted and their commitment to their way of life. Survivors are sometimes stronger and often wiser for enduring the experience, but a high price is paid for such wisdom. And the value of the lesson is fully realized only if the knowledge is incorporated into the practices of daily life and if the experience is passed on to future generations through text, story, song, and tradition.

Yosemite Indian history resounds with such experience, and their story of survival provides a lesson to us all. Like other native people throughout North America, the Yosemite Indians faced aggression on both of these fronts in colonial encounters with European people in the late eighteenth and early nineteenth centuries. The first adversary was fatal disease that was inadvertently introduced from a distant colonial outpost. The second was physical incursion into their traditional territory in the central Sierra Nevada of California by men determined to usurp their ancestral claim to the land and its resources. Yosemite Indian population was severely reduced—and their resolve was repeatedly tested—by both of these foes. But they survived these assaults and maintained their traditional ways, as revealed in native oral history, written historical accounts, and archaeological evidence of past lives and people.

Their particular story—encompassing the dual forces of disease and violence—is a microcosm of the process of European colonialism in the Americas, Australia, and the Pacific Islands in the four centuries following Columbus's landfall in the Caribbean in 1492. Colonialism, in this sense, extends well beyond a simple reference to colonies linked to a distant homeland or to the practices and characteristics of colonists in such settings. . . . Rather, it both embraces and symbolizes a systematic global process that refers especially to the spread of European empires, economies, culture, values, diseases, and material goods since the late fifteenth century. Colonialism is a politically charged term, as well as a social process that left a devastating legacy for indigenous people around the world. One need only undertake a cursory review of history to realize that the outcome of colonialism in other places and times was often quite different than that of Yosemite Indians. Many other indigenous peoples did not endure in the face of enemies intent on their disenfranchisement or destruction. Either they did not survive as communities, or they lost their connection to their land and traditions in the wake of one or more colonial assaults. In light of these various histories, we are left to ponder why outcomes were so different when the colonial assaults appear much the same. We are challenged to disentangle the dual assaults of colonialism and understand each in much greater detail to find the answers we seek. And given the relevance of this colonial heritage to past peoples and to modern life, research regarding the role that introduced infectious diseases played in both the process and outcome of colonialism for people such as the Yosemite Indians takes on special significance.

... Given the debate and uncertainty on key issues of timing, magnitude, and cultural consequences of depopulation, the Yosemite Indian story stands as an important example of native experience in the face of colonial-era assaults. While their traditional organization as a small-scale, nonagricultural, and residentially mobile population was far from unique, these characteristics set them apart from nearly all other native groups that have been subject to archaeological assessment of colonial-era depopulation in North America. Thus, the persistence of Yosemite Indians informs our understanding of both native history and culture in North American colonial encounters. Their experience and actions expand our view and thereby help to clarify and define the process of European colonialism itself, as models of colonialism variously ascribe a central role to introduced disease or stress intentionality, colonial power, and native resistance. Preserved in words and objects, the Yosemite Indian story encompasses all of these phenomena and reveals the mechanisms of European colonialism from a native perspective. In so doing, their story underscores the significance of both intentional and unintentional acts and the consequences to indigenous experience and survival in such circumstances.

Hol'-low and He-le'-jah

In the early 1600s, the Awahnichi were living in a world of relative plenty and calm, having maintained their community from one generation to the next through a precipitous decline in population during the previous millennium. They lived in about twenty camps and villages in Yosemite Valley, one of which was Hol'-low (cave). This village was situated near the eastern end of the valley on an open, sunny slope dotted with oak trees and conifers. The nearby creek was shaded by stands of pine and cedar that lined the sandy banks. A large rockshelter decorated with red paintings— from which the village took its name—was present at the edge of an extensive jumble of the huge boulders that had fallen from the cliffs above no more than fifty years before. A few additional boulders, deeply embedded in the surrounding sediments through centuries of deposition, studded the gentle slope below. Here, multiple families lived at least part of each year, occupying a few houses scattered across the flat. Women pounded acorns into flour in the mortars present on two of the larger rocks within the village. At mealtime, food was prepared and consumed in baskets and steatite bowls around household hearths. Robes and baskets, bows and arrows, flaked stone tools, and other implements were manufactured around the hearths and in the open space between the houses. Abundant obsidian and a few chert flakes and tools lost or discarded throughout the flat bear witness to this handiwork. The obsidian may have been acquired through trade with neighbors or procured directly by the Awahnichi through trips to the eastern side of the Sierra in the summer months. The stone and shell beads adorning the baskets and apparel stored in the houses were acquired from trading partners to the west.

By 1800 the world of the Awahnichi was a different place. The descendants of the survivors from the 1600s had faced their own demographic crisis within just one generation— devastating disease transmitted from distant European colonists. As in the past, survivors had made decisions in the wake of population decline that would shape their destiny as individuals and a group in both the short and long term. Survival initially required rebuilding their community through intermarriage with people in the Mono Basin and elsewhere. Although the Awahnichi had interacted with—and perhaps even intermarried among—neighboring people before, interaction now was probably more extensive and profound than at any other time in the recent past. Emigration and intermarriage brought the disparate languages and cultures of the men and women of the western and eastern Sierra together in nearly every household. After more than fifteen years of self-imposed exile elsewhere, reoccupation of Yosemite Valley in the 1800s was tentative at first. By circa 1820, for example, the village of He-le'-jah (mountain lion) was one of perhaps only six camps occupied by the returning Indian people. Located in the central portion of Yosemite Valley, this village was tucked between steep cliffs to the north and the slow waters of the meandering river to the south. A rockshelter that could have provided sanctuary for one family or several adults was present at He-le'-jah, situated on the slope at the lower margin of an oak- and conifer-studded boulder field. It was less than half the size of that at Hol'-low, but it served as shelter for the Indian people living here during the late winter and perhaps at other times of the year. A hearth was situated near the front of the rockshelter to protect the fire from the elements but to keep smoke from filling the small space of the refuge, the ceiling of which was so low that an adult could not stand upright. People worked at tasks out of the elements or in the shade of the shelter during the day and by firelight at night, making arrow points, weaving baskets, and preparing food with handstones and other utensils. Farther back in the shelter, food and gear were stored, and the people made their beds while the fire kept the nighttime chill at bay. And like their ancestors at Hol'-low, these people pounded acorns in one of the dozen mortars present on two boulders in the nearby flat, manufactured stone tools, and traded for shell beads and obsidian.

Thus, in many ways, daily life at He-le'-jah was similar to the routines of more than two hundred years earlier at Hol'-low.

"The villages and camps were sharply divided into two categories."

C. Hart Merriam
"Indian Village and Camp Sites in Yosemite Valley," 1917

C. Hart Merriam (1855–1942) was always fascinated by the outdoors and all living things. At the age of seventeen, Merriam was already so accomplished as a naturalist that he was attached to the famous Hayden Survey of the Rocky Mountain West; the content of more than fifty pages of the expedition's 1873 official government report was authored by Merriam. Although later trained as a medical doctor, Merriam continued his lifelong fascination with biology and ultimately switched to full-time occupation with scientific investigation of the natural world.

During Merriam's long and distinguished career, he was a founder of the National Geographic Society and was elected to the National Academy of Sciences. He was an officer in many scientific organizations, serving as president of the Biological Society of Washington, president of the American Ornithologists' Union, chair of the U.S. Board on Geographic Names, president of the Anthropological Society of Washington, and president of the American Society of Naturalists. Merriam befriended leaders in government and science, including Theodore Roosevelt, Gifford Pinchot, and John Muir.

During his many travels, Merriam became enamored of California, ultimately settling in the Golden State. He also became increasingly interested in documenting the lives of Native people in the West. His voluminous field notes were often the only records of some Indian nations and are considered invaluable historical and anthropological resources. In January 1917 the *Sierra Club Bulletin* published Merriam's article "Indian Villages and Camp Sites in Yosemite Valley." It was a comprehensive and innovative listing of historic Native encampments and communities in the valley and chronicled the richness and diversity of precontact and early-contact Native settlement in Yosemite. The introductory section of the article is presented here.

For ages before its discovery by white men Yosemite Valley was inhabited by Indians. Owing to its isolated position and the abundance of mountain trout, quail, grouse, deer, bear, and other game animals, and of acorns, manzanita-berries, and other vegetable foods, it supported a large population. This is attested not only by the statements of the Indians themselves, but also by the surprisingly large number of villages whose locations have been determined. These were of three kinds: (1) *permanent villages*, occupied the year round, though somewhat depleted in winter; (2) *summer villages*, occupied from May to October, after which the inhabitants moved down into the milder climate of Merced Cañon, where there was little or no snow; and (3) *seasonal camps* for hunting and fishing. The camps were definitely located and each was regularly occupied at a particular season.

It has not always been possible to distinguish between village-sites and camp-sites, but, taken collectively, I have been able, with the help of resident Indians, to locate and name no less than thirty-seven. All of these were in the valley proper, and at least six were occupied as late as 1898. To the list I have added sixteen located in the cañon of the Merced from the Cascades to Ferguson Station, six miles below El Portal, making in all fifty-three villages and camps in a distance of about twenty-two miles; and doubtless there were others which my informants had forgotten.

All of these people belonged to the *Ahwaneéche* or *Ahwah'-nee Mew'-wah*, a subtribe closely akin to the neighboring *Chow-chil'-la Mew'-wah* of Chowchilla Cañon. Their language is the southernmost of the three dialects of the once great *Mé-wuk* family—a family comprising a group of closely related tribes occupying the western foothills and lower slopes of the Sierra Nevada from Cosumnes River south to Fresno Creek.

Origin of the Name Yosemite

In this connection it is interesting to recall how the name Yosemite originated. In the early spring of 1851 the valley was invaded by an Indian-chasing expedition. The word Yosemite, said to be the name of the native Indian tribe, was proposed by Dr. L. H. Bunnell, a member of the expedition, and accepted by the others while still in the valley. During the early fifties there was some controversy between Bunnell and [James Mason] Hutchings as to whether the proper form was *Yo-sem'-i-te* or *Yo-ham'-i-te* (or *Yo-hem'-i-te*). Hutchings was right, *Yo-ham'-i-te* being the name of the band inhabiting a large and important village on the south bank of Merced River at the place now occupied by Sentinel Hotel and its cottages. These Indians hunted the grizzly bear, whose name—*Oo-hoó-ma-te* or *O-ham'-i-te*— gave origin to their own. The tribe next north of the valley called the grizzly *Oo-soó-ma-te*, which doubtless accounts for the euphonious form given by Bunnell and now universally accepted.

Peculiar Classification of the Villages

The villages and camps were sharply divided into two categories—those *north* of Merced River and those *south* of it. This division has a far deeper and more ancient significance than that indicated by the mere position of the villages with respect to the river, for it goes back to the underlying totemic beliefs that form an important part of the religion of this primitive people.

If one of the survivors is questioned as to the location of the villages, he in replying constantly makes use of the terms *inside* and *outside* as denoting one or the other side of the valley; and if the inquiry is pressed a little farther it soon develops that there is a *grizzly-bear* side and a *coyote side*, a *land side (Too-noó-kah)*, and a *water side (Kik-koó-ah)*. This perplexing state of affairs leads to the interesting discovery that after all there are only two sides, but that each of them

The Soul of the Ah-wah'-nee

has four names: that the north side, inside, grizzly-bear side, and land side are one and the same—namely, the side *north* of Merced River; while the south side, outside, coyote side, and water side are only so many different names for the side *south* of Merced River.

The names most commonly used by the Indians themselves for the two sides are *Oo-hoó-mă-tāt ko-tó-wahk* (or *Oo-hoó-mă-te ha-wā'-ah*), the grizzly-bear side, and *Ah-hā'-leet ko-tó-wahk* (or *Ah-hā'-le ha-wā'-ah*), the coyote side—from *Oo-hoó-ma-te*, the bear, and *Ah-hā'-le*, the coyote, respectively.

It is not difficult to see how *Oo-hoó-ma-te*, the bear, an important personage among the early animal-people, might be chosen to represent the land animals; but why *Ah-há-le*, the coyote, should stand for the water-people is not so obvious. For the explanation one must look far back into the mythology of these Indians, in which it appears that before there were any real people in the world *Ah-há-le*, the coyote-man, one of the early divinities of the animal-people, came over the ocean from beyond the sea—for which reason he is ranked with the water-people.

Returning to our more immediate subject, the village and camp sites of Yosemite Valley, it is now easier to understand the grouping employed by the Indians. Indians are naturally methodical, and it is their custom to classify objects and places, and in speaking of them to begin at a fixed point and proceed in orderly sequence. Thus, in seeking the names of animals and plants and of geographic locations, I have several times provoked the undisguised disgust of my informant by not putting my questions in what he or she deemed the proper sequence.

In enumerating the village and camp sites of Yosemite Valley the Indians begin at the upper (or east) end of the north side—the grizzly-bear side—and proceed westerly to *Til-til'-ken-ny* at the lower end of the valley, and then cross the Merced to the south side—the coyote side—and return easterly to the upper end.

Elizabeth H. Godfrey
"Yosemite Indians: Yesterday and Today," 1941

Elizabeth H. Godfrey was a chronicler of Yosemite history for the National Park Service. William C. Godfrey, her husband, was a ranger in Yosemite National Park from 1927 to 1929. During his time in Yosemite, William wrote "Among the Big Trees in the Mariposa Grove" for *Yosemite Nature Notes*, a National Park Service publication. In 1929 he was transferred to Crater Lake National Park, where he served as chief ranger until his death from exposure in November 1930. Following her husband's death, Elizabeth returned to Yosemite, where she was initially a secretary for the Yosemite Museum and later a naturalist until 1945.

Elizabeth Godfrey collected historical material about the valley and wrote articles for *Yosemite Nature Notes*. In 1941 she was instrumental in obtaining and recording the written and audio reminiscences of Cosie Hutchings Mills, daughter of early Yosemite settler James Mason Hutchings. Mills was born in Yosemite Valley in 1867 and is considered the second white child born in the valley.

Also in 1941, Elizabeth Godfrey wrote "Yosemite Indians: Yesterday and Today," an article for *Yosemite Nature Notes* that she based on her study and interviews with Native residents of the park. Her observations are considered trustworthy historical depictions of Yosemite Valley Native life, rituals, and practices from precontact to the mid-twentieth century. Among the aspects of Indian culture that Godfrey examined were the two most associated with the indigenous culture of Yosemite Valley—the preparation and use of acorns and basketry.

Food

Although the Yosemite Indians had neither knowledge of cultivation nor a market place to buy provisions, the food supply furnished by native plants, animals, birds and insects afforded them a varied diet. For meat they killed the deer, small mammals, birds, and caught fish. In addition, there were acorns, berries, pine nuts, edible plants, bulbs, mushrooms, fungi, larvae of ants and other insects in their season. The acorns of the Black Oak, rich in nutritious vitamins, constituted the "staff of life."

Gathering the acorns, storing them in the chuck-ah granary, along with the complicated preparation of acorn mush and bread constituted a laborious and lengthy task that the Indian woman accepted as a matter of routine.

The chuck-ahs in the Museum Garden "Indian Village" constructed by Maggie (Ta-bu-ce) are typical of the granaries employed for storing the acorns. At first glance these huge, cylindrical, basket-like affairs remind one of big, clumsy nests built by some giant bird. Four slender poles of Incense Cedar about eight feet high arranged in a square, and a center log or rock two feet high for the bottom of the chuck-ah, constitute the frame support. The basket-like interior is of interwoven branches of deer brush (Ceanothus) tied at the ends with willow stems and fastened together with wild grapevine. This is lined with dry pine needles and wormwood. The latter supposedly discourages the invasion of insects and rodents, and grows abundantly in the museum region. After the chuck-ah has been filled with acorns gathered in the fall, it is topped with pine needles, wormwood, and sections of Incense Cedar bark that are bound down firmly with wild grapevines to withstand windstorms. The final touch is thatching the exterior with short boughs of White Fir or Incense Cedar, with needles pointing downward to shed snow and rain, and fastening them securely with bands of wild grapevine.

After cracking and shelling the acorns, the spoiled meats were removed, and the kernels pounded into fine yellow meal. Mortar holes in granite are found at every village site. In order to remove the bitter tasting tannin from the meal, leaching was required. In this process the acorn meal was first placed in a previously prepared shallow, hard-packed sand basin. At short intervals water was poured over the mixture, and allowed to seep through the sand. About seven applications of water were necessary to remove the tannin— the last three being increasingly warm.

Three products were obtained from the leaching according to the fineness of the meal: the fine meal served for gruel or thin soup; the middle product for mush[;] and from the coarser material small patties were formed, and baked on hot, flat rocks.

The mush was cooked in a large cooking basket, using the proportion of two quarts of newly leached acorn meal to six or seven quarts of boiling water. Heat was provided for both boiling the water and cooking the mush by gently lowering hot stones into a large cooking basket by means of wooden tongs. When the mush was done, the stones were removed with the tongs and dropped into cold water, so that the mush adhering to them might congeal and when cool be peeled off and eaten.

Basketry

Willow, squaw bush, red-bud, tule-root, red strips of bark from Creek Dogwood, maiden-hair fern, brake fern, wire bunch grass, and other native plants served the Indian woman as material for the many baskets needed to properly perform her domestic tasks. She knew the names of all the basket material plants, their locations, and the proper time for gathering them as well as any botanist.

After gathering the materials, a further knowledge of how to prepare them for weaving was necessary. They had to be peeled, trimmed to correct width, fineness and length, soaked in cold water, boiled or buried in mud, according to her knowledge of the treatment required.

In size, shape, and weave each basket was designed to serve a special purpose. A large conical shaped basket was required for carrying heavy burdens, such as acorns, and was known as the burden basket. Such baskets were supported on the back from a strap passing over the wearer's forehead. There was a large, deep family mushbowl basket around which the family gathered to dip in the acorn mush; a small, closely-woven basket for use in serving food; a tightly woven disc-shaped basket for winnowing wild oats and other seed plants; a seed beater for use in beating seeds into a carrying basket; a dipper basket, which was small and tightly woven for drinking water or manzanita cider; a cradle or openwork basketry—sometimes covered with deer skin for carrying the papoose; special baskets for use in wedding and dance ceremonies, and basket weirs for catching fish.

The twining and coiling methods were used chiefly by Yosemite Indian women in weaving baskets. In the twined basket, the heavy foundation is vertical from the center to the rim, and the woof is of lighter material. In the coiled basket, the heavy foundation is laid in horizontal coils around the basket with the filling running spirally around heavy twigs. Throughout the whole Miwok tribes, practically the only twined baskets made were the burden basket, the triangular scoop-shaped basket for winnowing, the elliptical seed beater, and the baby carrier (hickey). An application of soaproot, which hardens in a thin, brittle sheet, was used to make the burden baskets seed-tight. A scrubbing brush for cleaning the cooking basket was also made of fibers from the dry, outer layers of the soaproot. In weaving the coiled basket, an awl, made chiefly from the bone of a deer, was employed.

Roots of the brake fern were boiled in order to obtain the black material used in designs; red-bud was employed for the red color.

Considering that the Indian woman worked entirely without written rules, the design, color, and the mathematical accuracy of her baskets in entirety represent a work of art. Before commencing a basket she had to know exactly where to place the first stitch of each figure of the design, and as the bowl of the basket continued to flare, the size of each figure had to be correspondingly increased.

> "By the end of the century, Indians had become an important part of the Yosemite experience for the tourists."

Mark Spence

"Dispossessing the Wilderness: Yosemite Indians and the National Park Idea, 1864–1930," 1996

Mark Spence is a historian for the National Park Service and an instructor at Oregon State University. He has written numerous books, articles, and essays on the national parks.

In 1996 Spence wrote an intriguing case study for the *Pacific Historical Review* on Yosemite Indians and their relationship to Yosemite Valley administration. In his article, Spence describes how the state and federal government guardians of the Yosemite Valley (starting during the mid-nineteenth century) sought to make Native American habitation as invisible as possible. The Yosemite Native population was largely relegated to employment as domestic servants or being a tourist attraction in their own homeland, providing a touch of human "wilderness" as an "object of curiosity." In the mid-twentieth century, National Park officials took it a step further by adopting a policy of gradual Indian segregation and removal from Yosemite Valley.

In 1995, prior to its publication, "Dispossessing the Wilderness: Yosemite Indians and the National Park Idea, 1864–1930," was chosen by the editors of the *Pacific Historical Review* as the recipient of the distinguished

W. Turrentine Jackson (Article) Prize recognizing the best article by a graduate student.

Although every area that later became a national park was once utilized or inhabited by American Indians, only Yosemite National Park has ever included a native community within its boundaries. Indeed, Americans are able to cherish their national parks today only because Indians abandoned them involuntarily or were forcibly removed to reservations. Because Indian removal from Yosemite National Park occurred in the first half of this century, and not in the dusty old days of Indian wars and land grabs, the park's early history presents a unique opportunity for examining the basic ideals underpinning American conceptions of wilderness and their close links to ideas about Native Americans. The long presence of Indians in Yosemite is all the more remarkable when compared to the removal and exclusion of Indians from other early national parks like Yellowstone and Glacier, and provides an exceptional case by which to evaluate the policies developed at these and other parks. Such a comparison not only sheds light on Yosemite's unique history, but also demonstrates that the presence of a native community within a national park eventually proved too exceptional for the park service. Consequently, in an effort to hasten the "vanishing" of Yosemite's Indians and bring the park in line with the rest of the national park system, Yosemite officials implemented a program of gradual Indian removal in the 1930s. . . .

Indian employment in Yosemite reflected patterns established throughout the central Sierra Nevada in the years following the gold rush. The massive invasion of miners who poured over the mountains brutally devastated whole Indian societies while the environmental destruction wrought by mining practices undermined seasonal hunting and gathering cycles. Severely weakened and suddenly homeless in their homelands, most of California's shrinking Indian population found the means for survival only in close accommodation with whites. Many Miwok families and individuals moved to where they could eke out a living on the margins of white settlements. Though generally despised and frequently humiliated by whites, their presence was tolerated whenever Indian labor could not easily be replaced by Mexican or Chinese workers. A similar situation developed in Yosemite, but there the Indians got along much better with their white neighbors since the valley did not attract the same rough crowd that congregated in the mining camps. The remoteness of Yosemite also made Indian labor more prized, and because they posed no visible threat to tourists or concessionaires, the Yosemite were left to live in relative peace and allowed to participate in non-Indian society to a degree rarely seen elsewhere in California. The Yosemite's ability to adapt to their new world also made them inconspicuous to state officials, who had taken over Indian policy in California after federal efforts to develop a reservation system in the Central Valley failed in the early 1860s.

Despite the disinterestedness of the state, the presence of Indians in Yosemite proved a matter of considerable interest for many early visitors. The often patronizing affection that early tourists had for the Indians who lived in Yosemite Valley, and the Indians' ability to reciprocate and even exploit these affections, went far toward insuring they would remain in the area long after Yosemite became a national park. As Europeans and Americans had for the previous century-and-a-half, early tourists continued to associate Indians with wilderness and many were delighted to find them still living in Yosemite. Tourists happily recalled being entertained by their native and non-native guides with accounts of Yosemite legends, while other visitors commented excitedly about encounters with local Indians. . . .

The idea that Indians somehow complemented or completed a wilderness scene was also evident in the works of Yosemite's early landscape painters. While images of modern tourists in Yosemite could detract from the sublimity of the landscape, "picturesque" Indians, or Indian-built struc-

The Soul of the Ah-wah'-nee

tures, gave a touch of "native" color to the wilderness and provided a human scale by which to emphasize the grandeur of Yosemite's cliffs and waterfalls. . . .

. . . Indians found other means for profiting from the interest of early tourists in "things Indian." By the early 1870s, individual Indians frequently entertained visitors outside their hotels and charged a penny for a brief dance or song while larger "fandangos," as early Californians called them, may have been held on occasion for the paid entertainment of tourists. The growing popularity of "kodaks" in the late 1880s made photographing Indians another important feature of the Yosemite tourist experience. The Yosemite Indians quickly recognized the marketability of their own "exotic naturalness," and several early tourists made special note of "a very cunning little papoose [who] smiled for a dime a smile." Within a few decades the price for a picture had risen considerably, and one popular basket weaver charged tourists a half dollar to photograph her with her baskets. . . . By the end of the century, Indians had become an important part of the Yosemite experience for tourists, whether as laborers in the tourist industry or as an authenticating aspect of a tourist's encounter with the "wilderness." Likewise, tourists had become an integral part of the Yosemite Indians' lives, and as one frequent visitor [J. Smeaton Chase] to Yosemite commented, a number of Indians were "in the habit of repairing yearly to the Yosemite for the purpose of sharing in the double harvest,—first of the tourists, later of the acorns."

2

"Earth's Undecaying Monuments"
....

Geological Formation

Yosemite is 114 million years old. It looks good for its age.

In geologic time, 114 million years is the blink of an eye, but in human terms Yosemite seems ageless and monolithic. This sense of the eternal is one of Yosemite's greatest virtues and perhaps its most alluring amenity.

In purely scientific terms, however, Yosemite is not timeless, as it has been shaped and reshaped by eons of uplift, scouring, and decomposition. The rock in the region is granitic. The granite structures, called plutons, formed miles deep and rose to the surface during the Late Cretaceous period, after which they were sculpted by erosion and glaciers over the ages.

The most striking feature of the region is Yosemite Valley, the six-square-mile heart and soul of the area. For the last thirty million years, as the acknowledged paradigm proclaims, the valley has been intermittently filled by glaciers. Excepting a few well-known landmarks, such as most of Half Dome and the top of El Capitan, Yosemite Valley as we know it today was scrubbed, pulverized, and polished by a series of glacial juggernauts. As the glaciers retreated, they left behind massive lakes, which, upon evaporating, deposited sediment creating the valley floor.

But in the years before the scientific consensus was established, the inquisitive speculated as to the origin of this granite wonderland. Was it some incomprehensible magic or God's handiwork or a cataclysmic subsidence or the relentless power of the glaciers?

In the late nineteenth century, two influential figures

debated the genesis of Yosemite Valley. One was a renowned professional, California state geologist Josiah Whitney, who argued that in one extraordinary moment the granite shattered, collapsed, and instantly formed the valley. The other was an enthusiastic amateur, the naturalist John Muir, who theorized, based on his extensive studies, that Yosemite Valley was formed by repeated glacial action. Whitney dismissed Muir's conclusion as the uninformed conjecture of a "mere sheepherder," but Muir's theory was ultimately adopted as the orthodox explanation.

> "The bottom of the [Yosemite] Valley sank down
> to an unknown depth . . . owing to its support
> being withdrawn from underneath."

Josiah D. Whitney
The Yosemite Book, 1869

Josiah D. Whitney was appointed the state geologist of California in 1860. Many in the state legislature felt that Whitney's exclusive role should be to discover gold-bearing regions in California. But Whitney was steadfast in following scientific principles, and he conducted extensive surveys and examinations of the entirety of California's geology, including the Sierra Nevada and Yosemite district. Mount Whitney, located in the Sierra Nevada, is the tallest mountain in the contiguous United States and is named in his honor.

Whitney was widely regarded as the ultimate authority on California geology and landforms. Indeed, it was rare for anyone to dispute his conclusions. In 1869 Whitney published *The Yosemite Book*, generally viewed as the last word on all things related to Yosemite's geology. In chapter 3, "The Yosemite Valley," Whitney advanced his theory that Yosemite Valley was formed suddenly as the result of cataclysmic subsidence—in Whitney's words, "the bottom of the Valley sank down to an unknown depth, owing to its support being withdrawn from underneath." Whitney dismissed an alternative theory that Yosemite Valley was formed by glacial action, declaring that glaciers never existed in the valley or anywhere else in the Sierra Nevada.

The Scottish-born naturalist and Yosemite advocate John Muir challenged Whitney's analysis. Muir discovered the first known active glacier in the Sierra Nevada in 1871, chronicled glacier scarring and moraines in Yosemite Valley, and published his studies to acclaim. Whitney arrogantly sniffed his disapproval of Muir and his findings, deriding the naturalist as a "mere sheepherder" and an "ignoramus."

In this passage from the third chapter of *The Yosemite Book*, Whitney explains his theory of the formation of Yosemite Valley.

All will recognize in the Yosemite a peculiar and unique type of scenery. Cliffs absolutely vertical, like the upper portions of the Half Dome and El Capitan, and of such immense heights as these, are, so far as we know, to be seen nowhere else. The dome form of mountains is exhibited on a grand scale in other parts of the Sierra Nevada; but there is no Half Dome, even among the stupendous precipices at the head of the King's River. No one can avoid asking, what is the origin of this peculiar type of scenery? How has this unique valley been formed, and what are the geological causes which have produced these wonderful cliffs and all the other features which combine to make this locality so remarkable? . . .

Most of the great cañons and valleys of the Sierra Nevada have resulted from aqueous denudation, and in no part of the world has this kind of work been done on a larger scale. . . . The eroded cañons of the Sierra, however, whose formation is due to the action of water, never have vertical walls, nor do their sides present the peculiar angular forms which are seen in the Yosemite, as for instance in El Capitan, where two perpendicular surfaces of smooth granite more than 3,000

"Earth's Undecaying Monuments"

feet high, meet each other at right angles. It is sufficient to look for a moment at the vertical faces of El Capitan and the Bridal Veil rock, turned down the Valley, or away from the direction in which the eroding forces must have acted, to be able to say that aqueous erosion could not have been the agent employed to do any such work. . . .

Much less can it be supposed that the peculiar form of the Yosemite is due to the erosive action of ice. A more absurd theory was never advanced, than that by which it was sought to ascribe to glaciers the sawing out of these vertical walls and the rounding of the domes. . . . Besides, there is no reason to suppose, or at least no proof, that glaciers have ever occupied the Valley or any portion of it, . . . so that this theory, based on entire ignorance of the whole subject, may be dropped without wasting any more time upon it.

The theory of erosion not being admissible to account for the formation of the Yosemite Valley, we have to fall back on some one of those movements of the earth's crust to which the primal forms of mountain valleys are due. The forces which have acted to produce valleys are complex in their nature, and it is not easy to classify the forms which have resulted from them in a satisfactory manner. The two principal types of valleys, however, are those produced by rents or fissures in the crust, and those resulting from flexures or foldings of the strata. . . .

If we examine the Yosemite to see if traces of an origin in either of the above ways can be detected there, we obtain a negative answer. The Valley is too wide to have been formed by a fissure; it is about as wide as it is deep, and, if it had been originally a simple crack, the walls must have been moved bodily away from each other, carrying the whole chain of the Sierra with them, to one side or the other, or both, for the distance of half a mile. Besides, when a cliff has been thus formed, there will be no difficulty in recognizing the fact, from the correspondence of the outlines of the two sides; just as, when we break a stone in two, the pieces must necessarily admit of being fitted together again. No correspondence of the two sides of the Yosemite can be detected, nor will the most ingenious contriving, or lateral moving, suffice to bring them into anything like adaptation to each other. . . .

In short, we are led irresistibly to the adoption of a theory of the origin of the Yosemite in a way which has hardly yet been recognized as one of those in which valleys may be formed, probably for the reason that there are so few cases in which such an event can be absolutely proved to have occurred. We conceive that, during the process of upheaval of the Sierra or, possibly, at some time after that had taken place, there was at the Yosemite a subsidence of a limited area, marked by lines of "fault" or fissures crossing each other somewhat nearly at right-angles. In other and more simple language, the bottom of the Valley sank down to an unknown depth, owing to its support being withdrawn from underneath, during some of those convulsive movements which must have attended the upheaval of so extensive and elevated a chain, no matter how slow we may imagine the process to have been. Subsidence, over extensive areas, of portions of the earth's crust, is not at all a new idea in geology, and there is nothing in this peculiar application of it which need excite surprise.

....

"Two years ago, when picking flowers in the mountains
back of Yosemite Valley, I found a book."

....

John Muir
"Yosemite Glaciers," 1871, and "Studies in the Sierra, No. 1," 1874

He was called "John of the Mountains," an immigrant Scotsman fired with enthusiasm for the Sierra Nevada. Some saw him as harbinger of a fresh, long-desired, reverential environmental philosophy, while others viewed him as an irritating, wild-eyed eccentric, but none could doubt his passion and commitment to his beliefs. He was John Muir.

"Earth's Undecaying Monuments"

Arriving in Yosemite in 1868 and instantly enthralled by the natural beauty of the Sierra Nevada, Muir hiked throughout the region, jotting down notes in pencil in a remarkable fashion. It was said that Muir simply opened his notebook and on whatever page appeared he started writing. In 1892 Muir co-founded the Sierra Club and remained its president until 1914. He fought to make Yosemite a national park and unsuccessfully battled against the damming of Hetch Hetchy Valley within the park's boundaries. Arguably, no single individual is as associated with Yosemite as Muir.

But Muir first came to national prominence through his studies of glaciers in the Sierra Nevada and, in particular, the impact of the rivers of ice in carving Yosemite Valley. He questioned Josiah Whitney's thesis that Yosemite Valley was formed suddenly by earth-shattering collapse, and, through his exhaustive studies, Muir argued that Yosemite Valley was the result of eons of "tender snow-flowers" coalescing into formidable glaciers that carved the granite into the breathtaking canyon we know today.

In these two selections, Muir describes his theory of the glacial development of Yosemite Valley. The first is from an article in the *New York Tribune* of December 5, 1871. This essay, entitled "Yosemite Glaciers," was cobbled together from letters to friends and was Muir's first published work. He was paid $200, the equivalent of $4,200 today. The second passage is from Muir's "Studies in the Sierra, No. 1," the first of seven articles published in *Overland Monthly* magazine in 1874–75.

Yosemite Glaciers

Yosemite valley September 28th, 1871. Two years ago, when picking flowers in the mountains back of Yosemite Valley, I found a book. It was blotted and storm-beaten; all of its outer pages were mealy and crumbly, the paper seemed to dissolve like the snow beneath which it had been buried; but many of the inner pages were well preserved, and though all were more or less stained and torn, whole chapters were easily readable. In this condition is the great open book of Yosemite glaciers today; its granite pages have been torn and blurred by the same storms that wasted the castaway book. The grand central chapters of the Hoffman, and Tenaya, and Nevada glaciers are stained and corroded by the frosts and rains, yet, nevertheless, they contain scarce one unreadable page; but the outer chapters of the Pohono, and the Illilouette, and the Yosemite Creek, and Ribbon, and Cascade glaciers, are all dimmed and eaten away on the bottom, though the tops of their pages have not been so long exposed, and still proclaim in splendid characters the glorious actions of their departed ice. The glacier which filled the basin of the Yosemite Creek was the fourth ice-stream that flowed to Yosemite Valley. It was about fifteen miles in length by five in breadth at the middle of the main stream, and many places was not less than 1,000 feet in depth. . . .

Such was Yosemite glacier, and such is its basin, the magnificent work of its hands. There is sublimity in the life of a glacier. Water rivers work openly, and so the rains and the gentle dews, and the great sea also grasping all the world; and even the universal ocean of breath, though invisible, yet speaks aloud in a thousand voices, and proclaims its modes of working and its power; but glaciers work apart from men, exerting their tremendous energies in silence and darkness, outspread, spirit-like, brooding above predestined rocks unknown to light, unborn, working on unwearied through unmeasured times, unhalting as the stars, until at length, their creations complete, their mountains brought forth, homes made for the meadows and the lakes, and fields for waiting forests, earnest, calm as when they came as crystals from the sky, they depart.

The great valley itself, together with all its domes and walls, was brought forth and fashioned by a grand combination of glaciers, acting in certain directions against granite of peculiar physical structure. All of the rocks and mountains and

"Earth's Undecaying Monuments"

lakes and meadows of the whole upper Merced basin received their specific forms and carvings almost entirely from this same agency of ice.

In the beginning of the long glacial winter, the lofty Sierra seems to have consisted of one vast undulated wave, in which a thousand separate mountains, with their domes and spires, their innumerable cañons and lake basins, lay concealed. In the development of these, the Master Builder chose for a tool, not the earthquake nor lightning to rend and split asunder, not the stormy torrent nor eroding rain, but the tender snow-flowers, noiselessly falling through unnumbered seasons, the offspring of the sun and sea. . . .

All classes of glacial phenomena are displayed in the Sierra on the grandest scale, furnishing unmistakable proof of the universality of the ice-sheet beneath whose heavy folds all her sublime landscapes were molded. . . .

. . . When we say that the glacial ice-sheet and separate glaciers *molded* the mountains, we must remember that their molding power upon *hard granite possessing a strong physical structure is* comparatively slight. In such hard, strongly built granite regions, *glaciers do not so much mold and shape,* as *disinter forms already conceived and ripe.* The harder the rock, and the better its specialized cleavage planes are developed, the greater will be the degree of controlling power possessed by it over its own forms, as compared with that of the disinterring glacier; and the softer the rock and more generally developed its cleavage planes, the less able will it be to resist ice action and maintain its own forms. In general, the *grain of a rock determines its surface forms*; yet it would matter but little what the grain might be—straight, curved, or knotty—if the excavating and sculpturing tool were sharp, because in that case it would cut without reference to the grain. Every carpenter knows that only a dull tool will follow the grain of wood. Such a tool is the glacier, gliding with tremendous pressure past splitting precipices and smooth swelling domes, flexible as the wind, yet hard-tempered as steel. Mighty as its effects appear to us, it has only developed the predestined forms of mountain beauty which were ready and waiting to receive the baptism of light.

3

"The Blood-Swollen God"

The Mariposa Indian War and Mariposa Battalion, 1851–1852

Although it is commonly acknowledged that members of the Joseph Walker expedition of 1833 may have been the first non-indigenous people to see Yosemite Valley, it was not until the California gold rush that the area became generally known to the outside world.

Prior to the gold rush, the Sierra Nevada was infrequently visited by Spanish and Mexican authorities, who usually ventured into the mountains only to retrieve stolen horses or apprehend Native Californians fleeing the oppressive mission system.

Starting in 1848, the California gold rush and then the increasing control by Americans fundamentally altered the relationship between the ascendant white population and the Indian community. While the Spanish and Mexican regimes primarily viewed the Native peoples as a cheap dependent labor force and treated them brutally, Indians were still able to retain at least a fragment of their social order and cultural values. Under American rule, however, attitudes toward the First People in California dispensed with any shred of empathy. The Anglo-Americans saw the indigenous people as an unassimilable and bloodthirsty, subhuman obstacle to progress. Governments at all levels made no distinction between Indian nations, clans, tribes, or individuals. Hatred and repression of the Indian was a clear-cut government imperative. A bounty for dead Indians was instituted, and California's first governor, Peter Burnett, stated in an 1851 address to the state Senate that the official Indian policy was "a war of extermination."

The Miwoks and other Native peoples of the Yosemite region were particularly hard hit, as their homelands were almost entirely within the gold-bearing regions of the Sierra Nevada. In search of the elusive yellow metal, argonauts swarmed the Native peoples' territory. The Native Californians had no legal protections and garnered little sympathy from the newly dominant culture that was hell-bent on destroying the "savages." Indian villages were burned, old oak tree groves and stands of conifers were felled, land was routinely fenced or bordered by stone walls, and extensive grazing battered the meadows so critical to the indigenous lifestyle. As the gold rush population skyrocketed, some forty-niners found that feeding and supplying the gold seekers was the only surefire way to prosper in the hyperinflated economy. In the Yosemite area, several former miners turned to farming and raising cattle and horses. When displaced Native people began starving, some of them resorted to stealing livestock and a few engaged in fierce raids against white settlements. This in turn drove the white settlers to even greater abhorrence of the Native Sierran population and led to demands for immediate retribution.

In response, California established a volunteer militia called the Mariposa Battalion. They were authorized to organize a punitive expedition to harass and eliminate the perceived Native threat in the Mariposa and Yosemite region. A particular target was Chief Tenaya and his band of Awahnichi. The result would be the Mariposa Indian War of 1851–52 and the bloodiest chapter of nineteenth-century Yosemite history.

This chapter examines the war from the perspective of participants and critics. It is important to remember that war narratives must be approached with skepticism. It is common for "war stories" of the victors to be self-serving, vainglorious exercises full of romanticized justifications and rationalizations for horrendous acts.

Chapter 3 presents the gory war reports as well as a sober questioning of the Mariposa Battalion's raison d'être. We

"The Blood-Swollen God"

experience the heartbreak of Chief Tenaya as he grieves the death of his youngest son in battle, and we witness the planning of a bloody reprisal after the Mariposa War had supposedly concluded. In early summer 1852, eight miners entered Yosemite Valley despite being warned that the valley remained under Indian control. Three of the miners were killed, the Awahnichi were blamed, and further violence ensued.

"I started for the mountains in pursuit of the Indians who were committing depredations through the country."

Theodore G. Palmer
A Letter to His Father, 1851

After a period of increasing tensions between gold rush miners and the local native population in the San Joaquin Valley and Sierra Nevada foothills, California governor Peter Burnett wished to investigate and resolve the lingering grievances. The efforts proved unsuccessful and ultimately bloody: a trading post operated by James Savage was raided, the trade goods removed, the buildings torched, and three men killed.

In response, Sheriff James Burney of Mariposa organized seventy-seven volunteers into a militia to seek out and destroy the responsible Indian band. James Savage was their guide. On January 11, 1851, Sheriff Burney's expedition reached a camp of four hundred Indians near present-day Oakhurst. The next morning Burney's private army attacked the encampment. The battle lasted three and a half hours. While the Native defenders briefly held the high ground, Burney's men would win the battle, kill forty Indians, and burn their encampment. The militia would suffer six to eight serious casualties, two of which proved fatal.

Sheriff Burney and his followers would retreat after the battle and, four miles distant, hastily construct a fort and wait for reinforcements and supplies. This incident was the beginning of what came to be known as the Mariposa Indian War.

Theodore G. Palmer was a member of Burney's outfit, and on January 16, 1851, he penned an eyewitness account in a letter to his father. This letter was originally published in Lafayette Houghton Bunnell's 1880 book *Discovery of the Yosemite and the Indian War of 1851, Which Led to That Event*, as a means for Bunnell to counter criticism of various details in his narrative.

Hart's Ranch, California, January 16th, 1851

My Dear Father: When I wrote my last letter to you I had fully determined to take a Ranch near Pacheco's Pass, as I informed you, but before three days had passed the report of Jim Kennedy's murder on the Fresno was confirmed, and I started for the mountains in pursuit of the Indians who were committing depredations all through the country and had sworn to kill every white man in it. Four hundred men had promised to go, but at the appointed time only seventy-seven made their appearance. With these we started under the command of Major Burney, Sheriff of Mariposa County, guided by Mr. Jas. D. Savage, who is without doubt the best man in the world for hunting them out.

From his long acquaintance with the Indians, Mr. Savage has learned their ways so thoroughly that they cannot deceive him. He has been one of their greatest chiefs, and speaks their language as well as they can themselves. No dog can follow a trail like he can. No horse endure half so much. He sleeps but little, can go days without food, and can run a hundred miles in a day and night over the mountains and then sit and laugh for hours over a camp-fire as fresh and lively as if he had just been taking a little walk for exercise.

With him for a guide we felt little fear of not being able to find them.

"The Blood-Swollen God"

On Friday morning about ten o'clock, our camp again moved forward and kept traveling until one that night, when "halt! we are on the Indians," passed in a whisper down the line. Every heart beat quicker as we silently unsaddled our animals and tied them to the bushes around us. Commands were given in whispers and we were formed in a line. Sixty were chosen for the expedition, the balance remaining behind in charge of camp.

Savage said the Indians were about six miles off; that they were engaged in a feast. He pointed out their fires, could hear them sing and could smell them, but his eyes were the only ones that could see; his ears alone could hear, and his nose smell anything unusual. Still, there was such confidence placed in him that not one doubted for an instant that everything was as he said.

About two o'clock we started in Indian file, as still as it was possible for sixty men to move in the dark, for the moon had set. For three long hours did we walk slowly and cautiously over the rocks and bushes, through the deepest ravines and up steep and ragged mountain, until within a half mile of the enemy.

Here every one took off his boots, when we again pushed forward to about two hundred yards from the camp. Another halt was called to wait for daylight, while Savage went forward to reconnoitre. He succeeded in getting within ten paces of the Rancharia, and listened to a conversation among them in which his name was frequently mentioned. He found that it was a town of the Kee-chees, but that there were about one hundred and fifty of the Chow-chil-la warriors with them and several of the Chuc-chan-ces. Had he found only the Kee-chees as he expected, we were to surround the Rancharia and take all prisoners, but the presence of so many Chow-chil-las, the most warlike tribe in California, made a change of plan necessary.

Daylight by this time began to appear. We had been lying in our stocking-feet on the ground on the top of a mountain within a few paces of the snow for more than an hour, almost frozen by the intense cold, not daring to move or speak a word.

It was not yet light enough to see the sight of our rifles, when an Indian's head was seen rising on the hill before us. For a moment his eyes wandered, then rested on us, and with a yell like a Coyote he turned for the Rancharia. Never did I hear before such an infernal howling, whooping and yelling, as saluted us then from the throats of about six hundred savages, as they rushed down the hill into the gim-o-sell bushes below.

Our huzzahs could, however, hardly have sounded more pleasant to them, as when finding we were discovered, we charged on their town. Fifty rifles cracked almost instantaneously; a dozen Indians lay groaning before their huts, and many supposed we had undisturbed possession. Our firing had ceased and we were looking around for plunder, when a rifle fired from the bushes below, struck a young Texan, Charley Huston, standing by my side. He fell with a single groan, and we all supposed him dead. My first impression was that I was shot, for I plainly heard the ball strike and almost felt it. This was a surprise that almost whipped us, for not knowing that the Indians had fire-arms, we were only expecting arrows. Before that shot was fired, I had always entertained the idea that I could run about as fast as common men (and I was one of the first in the charge), but by the time I had collected my wandering senses, I was nearly alone; the majority of the party some thirty paces ahead, and running as if they never intended to stop.

Captain Burney and Mr. Savage were on top of the hill using every exertion to make the company halt and form. He had partly succeeded, when a pistol ball struck a man in the face, he fell, but raising himself up said, "if we stay here we will be all shot" and a break was made for the trees.

Still some few remained in rank and others slowly answered to the orders to form, when our Second Lieutenant fell mortally wounded. He was carried off, and every man took his tree.

The Indians had again possession of their Rancharia, and of a slight eminence to the left, and were sending showers of bullets and arrows upon us from three sides. These two points had to be gained even if it cost half our men. Leaving then, enough to guard our present position, the rest of us charged on the hill, took it, stormed the Rancharia, took and burnt it, and returned to our former position with only one man wounded, Wm. Little, shot through the lungs.

The close fighting was now over, for we could not give chase and were forced to lie behind trees and rocks and pick out such as exposed themselves. It was about half past ten when, finding it useless to remain longer, litters were made for the wounded and we started for camp. Then again we had warm work, for all down the pass, the Indians had stationed themselves to fire on us, forcing us to charge on them several times, for while we were in plain sight, they were completely hid behind the gim-o-sell brush.

In our march back, the rear guard was kept at work about as hard as at any time during the morning, but not a single man was hurt, and only one mule was killed.

We moved our camp that night, six miles lower down, where we laid the foundations of a fort and left thirty men to guard it and take care of the wounded.

The rest of us started below the next morning, after burying Lieutenant Skeane, who died in the night.

The Indians acknowledged to eleven men killed, though fifty killed and wounded would be a moderate estimate. Our loss was seven wounded—two mortally. . . .

The force of the Savages consisted of, as near as could be ascertained, four hundred warriors. We burned a hundred wig-wams, several tons of dried horse and mule meat, a great number of bows and arrows, and took six mules. . . .

A large party has started on a second expedition, but I believe I am perfectly satisfied with Indian fighting.

T. G. Palmer

....

"This is not only inhuman and unlawful, but it is bad policy."

....

O. M. Wozencraft
"To the People Living and Trading among the Indians in the State of California," 1851

From the earliest days of European and Anglo-American settlement in California, the Native population was viewed as a dangerous obstacle to progress. Policies to indoctrinate, subdue, and destroy Indian populations were standard. This often violent response intensified during the gold rush and as California attained statehood in 1850.

In preparation for California becoming the thirty-first state, Peter H. Burnett was elected its first governor. He served from 1849 to 1851. In his January 1851 annual message, Governor Burnett commented on the government's relationship with the Native population: "That a war of extermination will continue to be waged between the two races until the Indian race becomes extinct must be expected; while we cannot anticipate this result with but painful regret, the inevitable destiny of the race is beyond the power and wisdom of man to avert. Situated as California is, we must expect a long continued and harassing irregular warfare with the Indians upon our borders and along the immigrant routes leading to the States." Burnett's prediction proved

bloodily accurate. However, not all agreed with a program of warfare and suppression. Alternative avenues
to address the growing hostilities were offered, as there
were voices that called for calm and a peaceful, negotiated resolution of disputes between the Indian nations,
miners, and newly arrived settlers. Most prominent
among these voices was O. M. Wozencraft, who was
appointed by President Millard Fillmore as California's
Indian agent in 1850. A few months after his appointment, Wozencraft, Redick McKee, and George Barbour
were designated as "commissioners" to negotiate treaties with the Indian nations. Wozencraft would serve
as Indian agent/commissioner until 1852. In 1851, in
a report to Commissioner of Indian Affairs Luke Lea,
Wozencraft argued for "adopting a policy toward the
[Native population] dictated by feelings of mercy" and
"treating them kindly."

From information received, as well as from personal observation while travelling among the Indians, and in conformity with the requests made me by the inhabitants, more
particularly the miners, in sections of country occupied by
Indians, it is deemed expedient to publish a communication, advisory of the proper policy to be pursued towards
the Indians, and the laws in relation thereto, that none may
hereafter plead ignorance of the existence of said laws, and
to inform them that those laws will be enforced, in all and
every instance, on those who may become amenable to them.

It would appear that most of the difficulties that unfortu-
nately have occurred between the white and red men have
been owing to an improper and short-sighted policy, or rather
a want of true policy, with these children of the forest. Since
the discovery of gold in this region, the section of country
that was, and is necessarily the homes of the Indians, has
been found rich in the precious metal, and consequently
filled with a population foreign to them; and this has been
done, in most instances, without attempting to conciliate

them or appease them in their grief and anger at the loss of their homes.

I am sorry to say that, in many instances, they have been treated in a manner, were it recorded, would blot the darkest page of history that has yet been penned. Had they even been foreign convicts, possessing as they do, a full knowledge of the evils of crime and the penalties therefor, and received the punishment that had been dealt out to these poor, ignorant creatures, this enlightened community would have raised a remonstrative voice that would have rebuked the aggressor, and caused him to go beyond the pale of civilized man.

Indians have been shot down without evidence of their having committed an offence, and without even any explanation to them of the nature of our laws. They have been killed for practicing that which they, like the Spartans, deemed a virtue; they have been rudely driven from their homes, and expatriated from their sacred grounds, where the ashes of their parents, ancestors, and beloved chiefs repose. The reverential and superstitious feeling of the Indians for the dead, and the ground where they are deposited, is more powerful than that of any other people.

This is not only inhuman and unlawful, but it is bad policy. The Indians of the Pacific are not unlike this great ocean in that respect; they are pacific and very tractable; and, by adopting a policy towards them dictated by feelings of mercy, making due allowance for their ignorance of our habits and institutions, and bearing in mind that their habits and customs are very different from ours, treating them kindly, and with a firm perseverance teaching them the requirements of our laws, permitting them to remain among us, teaching them industrious habits, you will make useful members of the community, instead of the most dangerous and implacable enemies.

In addition to the foregoing direct, atrocious outrages, so frequently perpetrated on the Indians by those claiming to be civilized men, there are those who indirectly cause as much mischief, endangering the lives of the families in the

"The Blood-Swollen God"

community, and finally destroying the Indians as surely, if not as speedily, as the first.

> "We must now chastise these mountain thieves and murderers into submission, or annihilate them."

San Francisco Daily Alta California
"The Indian War," 1851

Commissioner O. M. Wozencraft's plea to treat the Native population with mercy and kindness was overwhelmed by the widely held sentiments supporting retaliation against and subjugation of the California Indian nations. An example of these viewpoints was expressed in the editorial "The Indian War," published by the *San Francisco Daily Alta California* on March 17, 1851, just as the Mariposa Indian War was about to explode.

We have ever been strenuous contenders for a humane and generous policy towards the American aborigines, and are so still. There has been and are abundant reasons capable of being given in favor of a peaceable policy towards these untutored savages, while there remains a hope that the fair overtures of our government through its agents, will have the effect of producing a state of quietness on their part. It would be better to purchase peace with them by fair dealing and generous gifts and annuities than heedlessly rush into a war, the end of which it is not easy to foresee.

But when all reasonable and generous overtures for their pacification have been made in vain, and the resources and business of no small portion of the State are partially or wholly destroyed by the continued and determined hostility of the Indians, then a war at once is better for both races than a state of armed neutrality on our part, which being neither peace nor war, but attended with the colts and horrors of the last without any of the former's advantages, is maintained at the loss of business, property and lives of our people, and serves only to make the savage defy and despise us for a generosity and forbearance which they cannot understand.

We are inclined to think that the time has arrived when a temporizing, delaying, peaceable policy towards the Indians is worse than labor thrown away. From all the accounts which we have been enabled to obtain, by correspondence from the scene of action at the Mariposa from our San José correspondence, and personal intercourse with gentlemen from the troubled section, it seems that there remains scarce a chance for the Commissioners to effect a treaty with the only portion of Indians who have been especially dangerous and troublesome. The rancheros have no alternative but to treat with the whites, and get what they can from the government. But the wild tribes of the mountains, trusting in their position, and under estimating our prowess, will probably decline all treaties, until they are taught by our troops a terrible lesson.

This is a great pity for them and for us. If we could live upon peaceable terms, the Indians, more than the whites, would be gainers. It would retard their certain doom. They must fade away before the Saxon race as the cloud in the west before the light and heat of a greater power. War will no more certainly, but more suddenly complete the annihilation. And to this we have come, as will be perceived by a reference to our San José intelligence. The Indians will now be taught dear bought wisdom.

Taking for granted that Governor McDougal's message to the Legislature is based upon good and sufficient grounds, and information undoubted, the action of the Legislature in at once seconding his appeal, is very commendable. Mariposa county has been for a long time stagnant in business matters in consequence of the Indian depredations and the subsequent condition of affairs. Not only have the miners suffered, and in many cases to the entire ruin of their prospects and hopes. The ranches of the settlers have been broken up, nearly all the horses, mules, and stock generally, stolen and driven into the mountains, and the dwellings of the settlers deserted.

It has come to that pass that no man's life is secure unless he be in company with a strong party. Wagoners, travelers, stragglers, are pretty sure to be cut off, and even stores and houses attacked, and the inmates killed. The U.S. troops and volunteers have been posted near these scenes, but forced to act on the defensive, or rather remain quiescent. This was right so long as a hope remained that the Commissioners would succeed in perfecting peaceable relations between the races. That time, unless our information be erroneous, has passed. We must now chastise these mountain thieves and murderers into submission, or annihilate them.

"No good can be accomplished with the hostile
Indians until they are severely dealt with."

Adam Johnston, Indian Agent
Letter to Luke Lea, Commissioner of Indian Affairs, 1851

In December 1850, as skirmishes between white settlers and Native inhabitants flared in the San Joaquin Valley and Sierra Nevada foothills, Governor Peter Burnett authorized Adam Johnston, a federal Indian agent, to seek resolution of these disputes. Johnston concluded that force would be necessary to subdue the various Indian nations. On March 7, 1851, Johnston reported on his activities to U.S. Commissioner of Indian Affairs Luke Lea.

In 1849 the Bureau of Indian Affairs, known as the Indian Office in the mid-nineteenth century, was reorganized as control transferred from the Department of War to the recently formed Department of the Interior. Lea was Commissioner of Indian Affairs from 1850 to 1853 and supported assimilation of the Native population through a reservation system.

In his March 7, 1851, letter, Indian Agent Johnston describes the churning conditions, events, and attitudes

Mariposa, California

March 7, 1851

Sir: Since my last communication to the department I
have spent most of my time among the Indian tribes of the
San Joaquin valley and those located on the tributaries of
that river, along the western side of the Sierra Nevada.

On my return from a tour through the valley of the
Sacramento, I received information that the Indians
of the San Joaquin valley were exhibiting feelings of
discontent, and occasionally committing depredations
on the persons and property of the whites. The mining
region was threatened, and fears were entertained that
serious consequences would ensue if something was not
immediately done to quiet the Indians, and put a stop to
their thefts, which were becoming daily more frequent and
daring. I was solicited to go to that part of the country at
the earliest possible day. It was thought that a few presents
and fair promises might quiet them for a time—at least
until I could communicate with the department and
obtain instructions for future action. I was then without
funds, and thought the circumstances would justify me
in drawing for a small amount, and accordingly on the
15th day of November, 1850, I negotiated a draft on the
Department of the Interior for the sum of eight hundred
dollars. A few days were occupied in selecting and
purchasing proper articles for presents and in making
other necessary arrangements, previous to leaving
for their location. On the 21st of November I left San
Francisco intending to push as rapidly as possible to the
camp of James D. Savage, situated in the mountains, on
the headwaters of the Mariposa. Mr. Savage has been
for some years with the Indians of California, speaks
the language of several tribes fluently, and possesses

a powerful influence over them. I therefore viewed his camp as the most favorable location for effecting my purpose, and especially for obtaining facilities in opening a communication with the wild Indians of the mountains. Difficulty in obtaining transportation from Stockton to Mariposa delayed me in reaching his camp until the first of December. Mr. Savage was then at another camp or trading post which he had recently established yet further in the mountains, on a river or stream called the Fresno.

I remained at his camp on the Mariposa for a few days; but, as he did not return, I procured an Indian guide and proceeded to the Fresno, where I found him in the midst of numerous wild and rather war-like Indians. The Indians in that region are quite numerous and rather war-like, quite fine looking, especially the "Chowchille" and "Chook-chancy" tribes. The most of them are wild, though they have among them many who have been educated at the missions, and who have fled from their real or supposed oppressors to the mountains. These speak the Spanish language as well as their native tongue, and have intermarried with the wild tribes. Many of the tribes are therefore in a rather doubtful state—rather inclined toward barbarism, than to cherish such ideas of civilization as they may have acquired. This may be said of all the tribes inhabiting the western side of the Sierra Nevada, along the whole valley of the San Joaquin.

Mr. Savage has done much to open communication with the Indians of California, and to keep them on terms of friendship with the Americans. He had often told them before I reached Mariposa, of the Great Father at Washington; that he had sent a man to see them, who would talk with them and make them a few presents. They were therefore expecting me for some time before I reached them. On my arrival on the Fresno the Indians there seemed greatly gratified, and dispatched couriers to the other tribes announcing the fact that I had reached them. I remained on the Fresno several days during which time I had various interviews with the chiefs, braves, and men of authority among their respective tribes, the most powerful of which is the Chouchille. In an interview with the chief of that tribe on one occasion, he said to me:

"This is our country; why do the Americans come here? They are good and brave, but they come upon the land of my people. What do they intend to do? I want to know, and must know, *right now*."

I was not exactly prepared for so imperious a demand, but made such explanations as seemed to satisfy his majesty. After some time he said,

"Heretofore my people did not permit any stranger to pass over our country or stop in it, except Mr. Savage—he made us many presents"; and he added, "If you will make us presents, too, you may remain in our country *awhile*."

I endeavored to explain my mission; told him that the Great Father had sent me to talk with them, and to make them some presents as a token of his friendship and regard for them, but that they must not expect many presents at this time.

At the close of our *talk* the chiefs seemed fully satisfied, and assured me that their people should not steal or commit any depredations on the Americans. At the same time, they told me they should not control others. . . .

My efforts, however, were of no avail, as there was doubtless a general understanding among the various tribes that they should commence a predatory war, at an appointed time, all along the valley of the San Joaquin, if not along the entire base of the Sierra Nevada, from the northern to the southern boundary of the State. As an evidence of this, murders and robberies were committed simultaneously at various points. . . .

Soon after hearing of this outbreak we also discovered that all of the Indians in that vicinity had suddenly disappeared. Every day brought news of thefts and murders in various parts of the valley. This established beyond doubt the fact that a general hostility existed. I had

"The Blood-Swollen God"

obtained information that the Indians declared open war upon the whites, and every day's report confirmed the fact. . . .

On reaching Mariposa we learned that most of the Indians in the valley had hurriedly taken their women and children to the mountains. This is always looked upon as a sure indication of hostilities.

Knowing the meager force of the United States troops here and having no authority to call upon them, I immediately repaired to the seat of government to ask aid from the State.

My communication to the governor (a copy of which I herewith transmit) was laid before the legislature, and that body acted as promptly as possible in furnishing aid and protection to the mining region of this country. Two hundred volunteers, under authority of the State, are at this time encamped within a few miles of this place. They are ordered by the governor to await the arrival of the commissioners, who desire to make an effort for peace before opening the campaign. . . . I fear, however, even if they can be induced to come in, which I doubt, no good can be accomplished with the hostile Indians until they are severely dealt with. In the first place, they are entirely ignorant as to the strength of the Americans. So rapidly have the whites emigrated into this country, that but few of the mountain Indians have any idea of their number. They see the miners among them, and believe the whites have moved their camps from the old camping grounds upon their own. . . . They are now in the valleys and cañons of the mountains, living on animals and provisions plundered from the whites and if not subdued before the snows leave the Sierra Nevada, they will doubtless give the government much trouble, and in all probability a protracted war.

Again: if a treaty could be effected, my opinion is, it will not be respected by either Indians or Americans. The Indians are notoriously treacherous and thievish, and doubtless will continue their depredations. On the other hand, many of the whites in this region have lost either property or friends by the Indians, and openly declare they will shoot down any and all Indians they meet with, whether a treaty be made or not. . . .

I have the honor to remain, your most obedient servant, &c.

Adam Johnston

". . . the most daring robberies and unprovoked murders."

Letter from "M"
"The Indian Expedition," 1851

Once the Mariposa Indian War began, eyewitness accounts of the Mariposa Battalion began appearing. However, few saw them in the beginning. Initially, most participant reports were transmitted as official correspondence to military or political superiors, not to the public. Others battalion members usually waited to describe events more fully in a future book or journal.

One of the earliest public narratives was contained in a letter published by the *San Francisco Daily Alta California* on April 23, 1851. This report was a second-hand chronicle provided by an unnamed correspondent identified only as "M." Subsequently, it was determined that "M" was Judge John G. Marvin, quartermaster of the Mariposa Battalion, who reported information provided by Adjutant Martin B. Lewis and Israel H. Brooks (listed as a lieutenant by "M" but as a corporal in the battalion muster rolls).

The letter by "M" offers details of March–April 1851 encounters between the Mariposa Battalion and various Native bands. Throughout the letter, "M" identifies the chief of the Yosemite Indians, or Awahnichi, as "Yo Semite" or "Yo Semitee"; this is a reference to Chief Tenaya.

"M" also repeatedly mentions the Neuch-Teus, a Yosemite indigenous community that was a Mew'wah band of the Miwok. The letter also provides an early description of the "rancheria of the Yo Semitees"—Yosemite Valley.

San José, April 22, 1851

Messrs. Editors:

I have just had a conversation with Judge Lewis, the Adjutant of Maj. Savage's Battallion of mounted Volunteers, and Lieut. Brooks of the same Battallion, who are recently from the seat of the Indian war in Mariposa County. From them I learn the following particulars: On the 19th of March Major Savage, with Captains Bowling and Dill's Companies started from Camp No. 3 for the head waters of the Merced river to subdue the Yo Semites and Neuch-Teus who refused to come into the treaty made with the tribes in that vicinity by the Indian Commissioners at Camp Frémont. The volunteers after three days march arrived in the neighborhood of the Indians and on the morning of the fourth day surprised the Neuch-Teus and took them prisoners. The march was over rugged mountains and through deep defiles covered with snows and was one of considerable exposure and hardship. The command upon the 21st marched all day and during the night until about 4 o'clock on the morning of the 22d, some forty-five miles, when the troops arrived at the South Fork of the Merced river about seven miles above the rancheria of the Neuch-Teus. During the march the volunteers were without food and marching continually through the snow. Upon arriving at the stream above mentioned, the pack train was left with a guard who succeeded by removing the snow in procuring a few rushes for the animals. The volunteers, after resting a few moments took up the line of march for the rancheria, where they arrived about seven in the morning of the 23d.

This part of the march was exceedingly difficult and dangerous. It lay along a deep canyon and a part of it had to be made through the water and a part over precipitous cliffs covered with snow and ice. Major Savage had with him an Indian boy from the Chowchilla tribe who had married a Neuch-Teus wife who was living in the rancheria at this time. He told the boy that in case the Neuch-Teus attempted to run from the rancheria the whole of them would be killed. The boy was much alarmed at this, went a short distance ahead of the volunteers, and by creeping on his hands and knees through the bushes managed to get within a short distance of the rancheria before being discovered by the Indians. He communicated to them what Savage had told him and finding themselves entrapped surrendered without showing any disposition to fight and without a gun being fired. Almost the first question asked by Pan-Wache, their Chief, was whether Savage was there? When Savage answered in their own language that he was, the Chief came out and met the Major who told the Chief the object for which they had come. The Major told him that he had before said that some day the white people would come for them and that now since his Indians were enemies of the whites he had come to kill them all unless they could consent to live like good Indians.

These Indians as well as most of the tribes on this side of the Sierra's believe in wizards and witches. A man distinguished for his superior knowledge and power is regarded as a wizard. The Major told the Chief that three wizards had been sent to the Indian country by the great wizard of the white men to make the Indians presents, to learn them how to till the soil and live like the whites, and that the great wizard wanted all the Indians to be good and honest and to come out of the mountains and reside on the plains, and that the white people were very numerous, and if the Indians did not do as the three wizards desired the great wizard would tell the white

men to kill all of the Indians. The chief replied that he
had heard at different times the same thing that was now
told him but that he did not believe it was true—since
he (Savage) had come and told him he believed it true
and would go with him. The volunteers having selected
camping ground about two miles from the rancheria,
sent up for the mules, and the next day made preparation
to march against the Yo Semitees, living about twenty-
five miles distant, on the middle fork of the Merced. In
the mean time an Indian courier had been dispatched
by Maj. Savage to the Indians informing them of his
approach to their country and the objects of his mission,
with a request that the chief, Yo Semite, together with
his tribe should come into the camp. The chief obeyed
the summons but brought none of his tribe with him
except two sons. Upon arriving he made many excuses
for not bringing with him his people, among which were
that they were all good Indians—that they never stole
animals nor killed white men—that it was now in the
dead of winter and the snows deep—that they were well
supplied with acorns and living happy and contented.
These Indians, nevertheless, have committed numerous
depredations about Burn's Diggings and Mariposa and
the assertions of their goodness and peaceable intentions
obtained no credence, and the chief and his people were
peremptorily ordered to be in camp within three days.
Major Savage, doubting whether Yo Semitee would obey
the order, started on the morning of the 25th with a part
of his command and three days' provisions for the Middle
Fork. On the way he met the Yo Semitees coming in,
but still doubting whether they were all on the road, he
pushed forward through the snows, and a snow storm, to
the rancheria, taking with him the chief. Upon arriving
there he found a large quantity of acorns put up in cribs
which he destroyed, as well as their huts. He found also
a very old Indian and his wife, the father and mother of
Yosemitee, who had been left behind to perish or to take

care of themselves as best they could. They were living in a cave in which was kindled a small fire, but will doubtless perish during the winter. The Major had a large pile of wood carried to them, and acorns, but they were old, decrepid, and Yo-Semitee remarked that he had thrown them away and must leave them since they could not travel and take care of themselves. . . .

Upon arriving in camp, the Volunteers with the Indians started for the headquarters on the Fresno, on the 29th. The rancheria of the Yo Semitees is described as being in a valley of surpassing beauty, about 10 miles in length and one mile broad. Upon either side are high perpendicular rocks, and at each end through which the Middle Fork runs, deep cañons, the only accessible entrances to the Valley. The forest trees, such as pine, fir, red wood and cedar, are of immense height and size. There is a species of pine tree here from which exudes a sacharine substance nearly resembling in looks and taste brown sugar. The Indians gather and use it as an article for food, and Judge Lewis informs me that excepting a slight piney taste, it cannot be distinguished from common brown sugar. On the first day of April the whole command arrived at the head quarters of the regulars on the Fresno, and the Indians were turned over to the Commissioners. The Commissioners declined treating with them until the Chow-Chillas came in, but furnished them with a supply of food and some clothing.

Judge Lewis and Lieut. Brooks left Camp No. 4 on the Fresno on the 13th of April, upon which day the regulars started for Cassady's on the San Joaquin, and Maj. Savage with his command on an expedition against the Chow-chillas. This, the most powerful of the Indian tribes in California, is believed to have at its command 1,000 warriors. A portion of the Pyanches [Paiutes] from the other side of the Sierras are known to be allied with them and other tribes this side of the mountains. A hard fight is anticipated with them since they have refused all

　　　　　　　　　　"The Blood-Swollen God"

overtures of peace and have committed the most daring robberies and unprovoked murders in the neighborhood of fine and coarse Gold Gulches. Large quantities of snow have fallen since the expedition started, which will render the march exceedingly difficult, and perhaps defeat the ultimate success of the troops. However, the Major and the officers and the men under him will not turn back for any ordinary difficulties, and we may expect soon to hear of the complete subjection of the Chow-chillas. The next treaty will be made with the Indians at some point on the San Joaquin. The best of feeling exists between the regular and volunteer forces, and in the course of a month it is believed that the Indian difficulties will be satisfactorily settled from the Calaveras to the Tulare Lake, opening to miners some of the best mining and agricultural districts in the State. May future success attend the negotiations with the Indians, and the volunteers receive the meed [reward] of praise which they deserve, and the money which they have earned by numerous hardships incident to a border warfare carried on in the snow hills in mid-winter.

M.

"... a shower of huge rocks which came tumbling down the mountain, threatening instant destruction."

Captain John Boling, Mariposa Battalion
Two Letters to the *San Francisco Daily Alta California*, 1851

John Boling was captain of Company B of the Mariposa Battalion. A native of Tennessee, Boling commanded seventy-two men in his company. Following the Mariposa Indian War, Boling was elected sheriff of Mariposa County and served in that role from 1852 to 1856. In 1864 he died of consumption—the common name for tuberculosis in the nineteenth century—at age forty-two.

In these two letters, John Boling describes the 1851 actions of the Mariposa Battalion and the capture of the Awahnichi (usually referred to as the "Yosemite Indians" in contemporary accounts), led by Chief Tenaya. As Tenaya and the battalion neared a Fresno reservation, the Awahnichi escaped and fled to Yosemite Valley. The Mariposa Battalion then reentered Yosemite, captured Tenaya's sons, and killed his youngest son. Tenaya agreed to go back to the reservation. The Yosemite nation under Tenaya would later leave the reservation and melt into the backcountry to join the Mono Paiutes. Subsequently, Tenaya would be detained and then murdered by Mono Paiutes who claimed Tenaya was responsible for the theft of some of their horses.

The first letter is addressed to Major James D. Savage, commanding officer of the two-hundred-member Mariposa Battalion. Despite his lack of military experience, Savage was chosen to lead this state militia unit due to his knowledge of the Yosemite region, his scouting abilities, the political and economic alliances he had forged with local Indian leaders, and his self-proclaimed status as chieftain of the Tularenos Indians, a San Joaquin Valley band.

The second letter was delivered to Indian Commissioner George W. Barbour. In 1850 Barbour, O. M. Wozencraft, and Redick McKee were designated as "commissioners," with their role being to negotiate treaties with the Indian nations. According to their accounts, the three commissioners claimed to have negotiated eighteen treaties with California Indians (none of which was ratified) and discussed and reached agreements for peaceful dispute resolution with the most influential figures from 139 Native communities. Later research has indicated that these numbers were highly inflated and that very few of the agreements were signed by prominent Indian leaders. As historian Gary E. Garrett commented in 1969, "One is left with the conclusion that

Wozencraft, Barbour and McKee used thousands of dollars, months of time, and the services of large military escorts to make treaties not with 139 tribes but with 139 Indians." Other studies have determined that most of California's indigenous people either never encountered the commissioners or were unaware of their activities.

In these letters, the *San Francisco Daily Alta California* spells John Boling's last name as "Bowling," though family records indicate that Boling always spelled and signed his name as "Boling."

San Francisco Daily Alta California, June 12, 1851

Merced River, Yo-Semety Village

May 15, 1851

Major Savage—Sir: On reaching this valley, which we did on the 9th inst. I selected for our encampment the most secluded place that I could find, lest our arrival might be discovered by the Indians. Spies were immediately despatched in different directions, some of which crossed the river to examine for signs on the opposite side. Trails were soon found, leading up and down the river, which had been made since the last rain. On the morning of the tenth we took up the line of march for the upper end of the valley, and having traveled about five miles we discovered five Indians running up the river on the north side. All of my command, except a sufficient number to take care of the pack animals put spurs to their animals, swam the river and caught them before they could get into the mountains. One of them proved to be the son of the old Yo-Semety chief. I informed them if they would come down from the mountains and go with me to the United States Indian Commissioners, they would not be hurt; but if they would not, I would remain in their neighborhood as long as there was a fresh track to be found; informing him at the same time that all the Indians except his father's people and the Chou-Chillas had treated, and that you were then after the Chou-chillas with two companies of volunteers, determined upon chasing them as long as a track could be found in the mountains, and that all the Indians which had been treated with were well satisfied with their situation. He then informed me that we had been discovered by their spies and that we would not have got so close had they have known we could run over the river so quick on horseback, and that if I would let him loose with another Indian, he would bring in his father and all his people by twelve o'clock the next day. I then gave him plenty to eat and started him and his companion out. We watched the others close intending to hold them as hostages until the despatch-bearers returned. They appeared well satisfied and we were not suspicious of them, in consequence of which one of them escaped. We commenced searching for him, which alarmed the other two still in custody, and they attempted to make their escape. The boys took after them and finding they could not catch them, fired and killed them both. This circumstance connected with the fact of the two whom we had sent out not returning, satisfied me that they had no intention of coming in. My command then set out to search for the Rancheria. The party which went up the left towards Canyarthia found the rancheria at the head of a little valley, and from the signs it appeared that the Indians had left but a few minutes. The boys pursued them up the mountain on the north side of the river, and when they had got near the top, helping each other from rock to rock on account of the abruptness of the mountains; the first intimation they had of Indians being near was a shower of huge rocks which came tumbling down the mountain, threatening instant destruction. Several of the men were knocked down, and some of them rolled and fell some distance before they could recover, wounding and bruising them generally. One man's gun was knocked out of his hand and fell seventy feet before

"The Blood-Swollen God"

it stopped, whilst another man's hat was knocked off his head without hurting him. The men immediately took shelter behind large rocks, from which they could get an occasional shot, which soon forced the Indians to retreat, and by pressing them close they caught the old Yo-semity chief, whom we yet hold as a prisoner. In this skirmish they killed one Indian and wounded several others.

You are aware that I know this old fellow well enough to look out well for him, lest by some stratagem he makes his escape. I shall aim to use him to the best advantage in pursuing his people. I send down a few of my command with the pack animals for provisions; and I am satisfied if you will send me ten or twelve of old Pon-watchez' best men I could catch the women and children and thereby force the men to come in. The Indians I have with me have acted in good faith and agree with me in this opinion.

I have the honor to be, very respectfully,

Your most obedient servant,

JOHN BOWLING

San Francisco Daily Alta California, June 14, 1851

Fresno River, May 29, 1851

Sir: You will no doubt have learned from my report of the 12th inst., to Major Savage, that we were at that time in close pursuit of the Yosemitie tribes of Indians, that in a slight brush with them we captured their famous chief, and that at this stage of the proceedings the further success of our proceedings was materially affected from the necessity of having to replenish our stock of provisions, which was at a distance of over one hundred miles from our encampment. Notwithstanding the number of our party being reduced to twenty-two men, by the absence of the detachments necessary to escort with safety the pack train, we continued the chase with such rapidity, that we forced a large portion of the Indians to take refuge in the plains with friendly Indians, while the remainder sought to conceal themselves among the rugged cliffs in the snowy regions of the Sierra Nevada.

Thus far I have made it a point to give as little alarm as possible. After capturing some of them I set a portion at liberty, in order that they might assure the others that if they come in they would not be harmed. Notwithstanding the treachery of the old chief, who contrived to lie and deceive us all the time, his grey hairs saved the boys from inflicting on him that justice which would have been administered under other circumstances. Having become satisfied that we could not persuade him to come in, I determined on hunting them, and if possible running them down, lest by leaving them in the mountains, they should form a new settlement and a place of refuge for other ill disposed Indians, who might do mischief and retreat to the mountains, and finally entice off those who are quiet and settled in the reserve. On the 20th the train of pack animals and provisions arrived, accompanied by a few more men than the party which went out after provisions, and Ponwatchi, the chief of the Nuch-tucs tribe with twelve of his warriors.

On the morning of the 21st we discovered the trail of a small party of Indians traveling in the direction of the Mono's country. We followed this trail until 2 o'clock next day, 22d when one of the scouting parties reported a rancheria near at hand. Almost at the same instant a spy was discovered watching our movements. We made chase after him immediately, and succeeded in catching him before he arrived at the rancheria, and we also succeeded in surrounding the ranch and capturing the whole of them. This chase in reality was not the source of amusement which it would seem to be when anticipated. Each man in the chase was stripped to his drawers, in which situation all hands ran at full speed at least four miles, some portion of the time over and through snow ten feet deep, and in the four mile heat all Ponwatchi gained on my boys was only distance enough to enable them to surround the rancheria while my men ran up in front. Two Indians strung their bows and seized their arrows, when they were told if they did not surrender they would be instantly killed.

They took the proper view of this precaution and immediately surrendered. The inquiry was made of those unfortunate people if they were then satisfied to go with us; their reply was, they were more than willing, as they could go to no other place. From all we could see and learn from those people we were then on the main range of the Sierra Nevada. The snow was in many places more than ten feet deep, and generally where it was deep the crust was sufficiently strong to bear a man's weight, which facilitated our traveling very much. Here there was a large lake completely frozen over, which had evidently not yet felt the influence of the spring season. The trail which we were bound to travel lay along the side of a steep mountain so slippery that it was difficult to get along barefoot without slipping and falling hundreds of yards. This place appeared to be their last resort or place where they considered themselves perfectly secure from the intrusion of the white man. In fact those people appear to look upon this place as their last home, composed of nature's own materials, unaided by the skill of man.

The conduct of Pon-watchi and his warriors during this expedition, entitled him and them to much credit. They performed important service voluntarily and cheerfully, making themselves generally useful, particularly in catching the scattered Indians after surprising a rancheria. Of the Yosemities, few, if any, are now left in the mountains. Our prisoners say they have all gone down to Cypriano's people.

It seems that their determined obstinacy is entirely attributable to the influence of their chief, whom we have a prisoner, among others of his tribe, and whom we intend to take care of. They have now been taught the double lesson, that the white man would not give up the chase without the game, and at the same time, if they would come down from the mountains and behave themselves, they would be kindly treated.

Since I have had those Indians in the service with me, and seen the interest they take in trying to bring all others to terms, taking into consideration the good faith in which they have acted, all the men with me who have been witnesses to their good conduct, are satisfied that if the general government furnishes them promptly, as agreed, and bad-disposed white men are kept from among them, peace and quiet will soon be restored and maintained by the Indians.

I have the honor to be, very respectfully,

Your most obed't serv't,

JOHN BOWLING, *Capt. Comp'y B*

....

"Kill me, sir Captain! Yes, *kill me."*

....

Chief Tenaya's Oration

From Bunnell, *Discovery of the Yosemite and the Indian War of 1851, Which Led to That Event*, 1880

As the Mariposa Indian War unfolded, Chief Tenaya of the Awahnichi became a target of the Mariposa Battalion. Capturing Tenaya was a priority but difficult to achieve. In 1851 Tenaya and his band of seventy-five were apprehended in Yosemite and marched toward a reservation near Fresno. The Awahnichi captives escaped and returned to the Yosemite Valley. The Mariposa Battalion pursued them, reentered the valley, and captured Tenaya's three sons. The youngest son was killed by a soldier. It was reported that Captain John Boling, commander of Company B of the battalion, expressed regret at the killing, but Tenaya was unmoved. According to

"The Blood-Swollen God"

Lafayette Bunnell's account of the incident, the grief-stricken Tenaya remained silent, and "not a single word would he utter in reply; not a sound escaped his compressed lips." Several days later, Chief Tenaya attempted to escape but was wrestled to the ground as he sought to plunge into the river and swim to freedom. Brought before Captain Boling, Tenaya was fearful, angry, and still consumed with grief over the loss of his son.

In this passage from chapter 11 of Bunnell's *Discovery of the Yosemite and the Indian War of 1851, Which Led to That Event*, Tenaya ends his silence, laments his loss, and issues an ominous warning to Boling and his captors.

Chief Tenaya agreed to return to the reservation, but the Awahnichi quickly tired of the restrictions of their confinement and longed for their Yosemite home. Upon Tenaya's promise that he would not disturb white settlers any further, his people were released, and they went to live with the Mono Paiutes. In 1853 Chief Tenaya would be stoned to death by Mono Paiutes who accused him and his Awahnichi of horse theft.

In the earliest days of Yosemite written history, there were various spellings of names and places. Just as "Yosemite" was rendered in various forms, so was "Tenaya." In Lafayette Bunnell's narrative, "Tenaya" is spelled "Ten-ie-ya."

As Ten-ie-ya was brought into the presence of Capt. Boling by Sergt. [Alexander] Cameron, after this attempt to escape, he supposed that he would now be condemned to be shot. With mingled fear of the uncertainty of his life being spared, and his furious passion at being foiled in his attempt to regain his liberty, he forgot his usual reserve and shrewdness. His grief for the loss of his son and the hatred he entertained toward Capt. Boling, who he considered as responsible for his death, was uppermost in his thoughts, and without any of his taciturn, diplomatic style he burst forth in lamentations and denunciations, given in a loud voice and in a style of language and manner of delivery which took us all by surprise. In his excitement, he made a correct use of many Spanish words, showing that he was more familiar with them than he had ever admitted even to Sandino [Native interpreter for the expedition]; but the more emphatic expressions were such as may often be heard used by the muleteers of Mexico and South America, but are not found in the Lexicons. As he approached Capt. Boling, he began in a highly excited tone: "*Kill me*, sir Captain! Yes, *kill me*, as you killed my son; as you would kill my people if they were to come to you! You would kill all my race if you had the power. Yes, sir, American, you can now tell your warriors to kill the old chief; you have made me sorrowful, my life dark; you killed the child of my heart, why not kill the father? But wait a little; when I am dead I will call to my people to come to you, I will call louder than you have had me call; that they shall hear me in their sleep, and come to avenge the death of their chief and his son. Yes, sir, American, my spirit will make trouble for you and your people, as you have caused trouble to me and my people. With the wizards, I will follow the white men and make them fear me." He here aroused himself to a sublime frenzy, and completed his rhapsody by saying: "You may kill me, sir, Captain, but you shall not live in peace. I will follow in your foot-steps, I will not leave my home, but be with the spirits among the rocks, the water-falls, in the rivers and in the winds; wheresoever you go I will be with you. You will not see me, but you will fear the spirit of the old chief, and grow cold."

....

"The valley seemed alive with them—on rocks, and behind trees, bristling like Demons, shrieking the war whoops."

....

Stephen R. Grover
From Carl P. Russell, "Early Years in Yosemite," 1926

Following the incursion of the Mariposa Battalion into Yosemite Valley in 1850–51 as part of the Mariposa

"The Blood-Swollen God"

Indian War, the Yosemite Valley was under government control—according to the white population. The Native population disagreed, particularly the Awahnichi of Chief Tenaya. In early May 1852, a party of eight miners entered Yosemite Valley to search for gold. Among the party were the miners Sherburn (variously spelled "Shurbon" or "Shurborn"), Rose, Aich, Peabody, Babcock, Joseph Tudor, and Stephen F. Grover. Camping near Wawona, the miners encountered a group of Yosemite Indians who cautioned the miners to avoid the valley, as it was still territory controlled by their people. The miners ignored the warning, believing Yosemite Valley was under military protection.

Lafayette Bunnell, who wrote the 1880 book *Discovery of the Yosemite and the Indian War of 1851 Which Led to That Event*, described what followed: "Unsuspicious of danger from an attack, they reached the valley, and while entering it on the old trail, were ambushed by the Indians from behind some rocks at or near the foot of the trail, and two of the party were instantly killed. Another was seriously wounded, but finally succeeded in making his escape."

The two miners killed were Sherburn and Rose. The wounded man was Joseph Tudor, who may or may not have succumbed to his injuries; accounts differ. The Awahnichi were blamed for the deaths.

In retaliation, a detachment of soldiers from Fort Miller on the San Joaquin River entered Yosemite Valley, captured five Indians who were said to be wearing articles of the dead miners' clothing, and executed them by gunshot. Rose and Sherburn were buried in Bridalveil Meadow, and a simple wooden sign marked the spot for many years. In 1920 a large monument to the fallen was planned by the Society of California Pioneers. The impressive memorial was to be about fourteen feet tall, with a nine-by-ten-foot granite block pedestal adorned with ferns and topped by a life-size bronze statue. It was never built.

In 1926 Dr. Carl P. Russell, an ecologist, historian, and National Park Service administrator for thirty-four years, published the narrative of attack survivor Stephen F. Grover. The document had been written years earlier and was in the possession of Galen Clark, the Yosemite "Guardian of the Grove." Grover's reminiscence was in Clark's records until Clark's death in 1910. Galen Clark's papers were then transferred to George Fiske, pioneer Yosemite photographer, and remained in his care until Fiske committed suicide in 1918. Fiske's collection, including Stephen Grover's tale, was then placed in the Yosemite Museum files, where it was unearthed by Russell in 1926 while he was serving as Yosemite National Park's chief naturalist.

Grover's chronicle suffers from inaccurate dates, exaggerations, and confused geographic references, but it is still valuable as an expression of the prevalent attitudes of the dominant culture toward the Native population and as a dramatic record of the incident.

A Reminiscence

On the 27th of April, 1852, a party of miners, consisting of Messrs. Grover, Babcock, Peabody, Tudor, Sherburn, Rose, Aich, and an Englishman whose name I cannot now recall, left Coarse Gold Gulch in Mariposa County, on an expedition prospecting for gold in the wilds of the Sierra Nevada Mountains. We followed up Coarse Gold Gulch into the Sierras, traveling five days, and took the Indian trail through the Mariposa Big Tree Grove, and were the first white men to enter there. Then we followed the South Fork of the Merced River, traveling on Indian trails the entire time.

On reaching the hills above Yosemite Valley, our party camped for the night and questioned the expediency of descending into the Valley at all. Our party were all opposed to the project except Sherburn, Tudor, and Rose. They overpersuaded the rest and fairly forced us against our will, and we finally followed the old Mariposa Indian trail on the morning of the 2nd of May, and entering the Valley on the East side of the Merced River, camped on a little opening, neat bend in the River free from any brush whatever, and staked out our pack mules by the river. I, being the youngest of the party, a mere boy of twenty-two years, and not feeling usually well that morning, remained in camp with Aich and the Englishman to prepare dinner, while the others went up the Valley, some prospecting, and others hunting for game. We had no fear of the Indians, as they had been peaceable, and no outbreaks having occurred, the whites traveled fearlessly wherever they wished to go. Thus, we had no apprehension of trouble. To my astonishment and horror I heard our men attacked, and amid firing, screams, and confusion, here came Peabody, who reached camp first, wounded by an arrow in his arm and another in the back of his neck, and one through his clothes, just grazing the skin of his stomach, wetting his rifle and ammunition in crossing the river as he ran to reach camp. Babcock soon followed, and as both men had plunged through the stream that flows from the Bridal Veil Falls in making their escape, they were drenched to the skin. . . .

The Indians gathered around as near as they dared to come, whooping and yelling, and constantly firing arrows at us. We feared they would pick up the rifles dropped by our companions in their flight, and turn them against us, but they did not know how to use them. As we were very hard pressed, and as the number of Indians steadily increased, we tried to escape by the old Mariposa trail, the one by which we entered the Valley, one of our number catching up a sack of a few pounds of flour and another a tin cup and some of our outer clothing and fled as best we could with the savages in hot pursuit. We had proceeded but a short distance when we were attacked in front by the savages who had cut off our retreat. Death staring at us on almost every hand, and seeing no means of escape, we fled to the bluff, I losing my pistol as I ran. We were in a shower of arrows all the while, and the Indians were closing in upon us very fast;

the valley seemed alive with them—on rocks, and behind trees, bristling like Demons, shrieking their war whoops, and exulting in our apparently easy capture. We fired back at them to keep them off while we tried to make our way forward[,] hugging the bluff as closely as possible. Our way was soon blocked by the Indians who headed us off with a shower of arrows, (two going through my clothing, one through my hat which I lost), when from above the rocks began to fall on us and in our despair we clung to the face of the bluff, and scrambling up we found a little place in the turn of the wall, a shelf-like projection, where, after infinite labor, we succeeded in gathering ourselves, secure from the falling rocks, at least, which were being thrown by Indians under the orders from their Chief. The arrows still whistled among us thick and fast, and I fully believe—could I visit that spot even now after the lapse of all these years—I could still pick up some of those flint arrow points in the shelf of the rock and in the face of the bluff where we were huddled together. . . .

We were crowded together beneath this little projecting rock, (two rifles were fortunately retained in our little party, one in the hands of Aich and one in my own), every nerve strung to its highest tension, and being wounded myself with an arrow through my sleeve that cut my arm and another through my hat, when all of a sudden the Chief just below us, about fifty yards distant, suddenly threw up his hands and with a terrible yell fell over backwards with a bullet through his body. Immediately, the firing of arrows ceased and the savages were thrown into confusion, while notes of alarm were sounded and answered far up the Valley and from the high bluffs above us. They began to withdraw and we could hear the twigs crackle as they crept away.

It was now getting dusk and we had been since early morning without food or rest. Not knowing what to expect we remained where we were, suffering from our wounds and tortured with fear till the moon went down about midnight;

"The Blood-Swollen God"

then trembling in every limb, we ventured to creep forth, not daring to attempt the old trail again; we crept along and around the course of the bluff and worked our way up through the snow, from point to point, often feeling the utter impossibility of climbing farther, but with an energy born of despair, we would try again, helping the wounded more helpless than ourselves, and by daylight we reached the top of the bluff. A wonderful hope of escape animated us though surrounded as we were, and we could but realize how small our chances were for evading the savages who were sure to be sent on our trail. Having had nothing to eat since the morning before, we breakfasted by stirring some of our flour in the tin cup, with snow, and passing it around among us, in full sight of the smoke of the Indian camps and signal fires all over the valley.

Our feelings toward the "Noble Red Man" at this time can better be imagined than described.

Starting out warily and carefully, expecting at every step to feel the stings of the whizzing arrows of our deadly foes, we kept near and in the most dense underbrush, creeping slowly and painfully along as best we could, those who were best able carrying the extra garments of the wounded and helping them along; fully realizing the probability of the arrow tips with which we were wounded having been dipped in poison before being sent on their message of death. In this manner we toiled on, a suffering and saddened band of once hopeful prospectors. . . .

Traveling on thus for five days, we at last reached Coarse Gold Gulch once more, barefooted and ragged but more glad than I can express. An excited crowd soon gathered around us and while listening to our hair-breadth escapes, our sufferings and perils, and while vowing vengeance on the treacherous savages, an Indian was seen quickly coming down the mountain trail, gaily dressed in war paint and feathers, evidently a spy on our track, and not three hours behind us. A party of miners watched him as he passed by the settlement. E. Whitney Grover, my brother, and a German cautiously followed him. The haughty Red Man was made to bite the dust before many minutes had passed.

My brother Whitney Grover quickly formed a company of twenty-five men, who were piloted by Aich, and started for the Valley to bury our unfortunate companions. They found only Sherburn and Tudor, after a five days march, and met with no hostility from the Indians. They buried them where they lay, with such land marks as were at hand at that time. I have often called to mind the fact that the two men, Sherburn and Tudor, the only ones of our party who were killed on that eventful morning, were seen reading their Bibles while in camp the morning before starting into the Valley. They were both good men and we mourned their loss sincerely. . . .

Years afterward, in traveling at a distance and amongst strangers, I heard this story of our adventures repeated, as told by Aich, and he represented himself as the only man of the party who was not in the least frightened. I told them that "I was most thoroughly frightened, and Aich looked just as I felt."

Stephen F. Grover, Santa Cruz, California

....

"A party of miners, after the news came in,
went in pursuit of the Indians."

....

Lieutenant Tredwell Moore
Reports to Captain E. D. Townsend, 1852

The primary source of information concerning the Mariposa Indian War is Lafayette Houghton Bunnell's 1880 book *Discovery of the Yosemite and the Indian War of 1851, Which Led to That Event*. However, Bunnell's narrative has been called into question for being self-absorbed and occasionally inaccurate. Other chronicles of the war provide alternative descriptions of the events that counterbalance Bunnell's account.

"The Blood-Swollen God"

Among them are reports submitted by Lieutenant Tredwell Moore to Captain E. D. (Edward Davis) Townsend in 1852. Seymour Tredwell Moore was born in Ohio and graduated from West Point in 1847. In 1851–52, Moore was serving with the Second Infantry in Mariposa County, where he led troops into Yosemite Valley and helped construct Fort Miller on the San Joaquin River, northwest of Fresno. In June and July 1852, Lieutenant Moore unsuccessfully pursued Chief Tenaya in the Sierra Nevada. Moore's reports to Townsend are reproduced here. In November 1851, Townsend was assigned to the U.S. Army's Pacific Command as assistant adjutant general.

Bunnell's version of events could not be contrasted to Moore's reports had it not been for the dogged research of historian Thomas C. Fletcher in his 1987 study *Paiute, Prospector, Pioneer: The Bodie–Mono Lake Area in the Nineteenth Century*. Fletcher scoured U.S. Army records in the National Archives and discovered Moore's reports in long-forgotten correspondence files.

In the years following the Mariposa Indian War, Moore was promoted several times until he achieved the brevetted rank of brigadier general during the Civil War, when he was tasked with suppressing possible insurrections by Confederate sympathizers in Nevada. Townsend served in California until 1856, when he was transferred to Washington DC for the remainder of his career. During the Civil War, Townsend was the principal executive officer in the Department of War and a trusted advisor to President Lincoln and Secretary of War Edwin Stanton. In 1869 Townsend was promoted to brigadier general and became an adjutant general in the U.S. Army, a rank he held until his retirement in 1880. Townsend was responsible for the establishment of Fort Leavenworth, Kansas, as a military prison.

Hd Qrs Fort Miller, Cal.

June l2th, 1852

Sirs

Information was received at this post a few days since, that the Indians on the head waters of the Merced had made an attack on eight white men who were "prospecting" the south fork of that river. Three of the whites were killed, and two were severely wounded. A party of miners, after the news came in, went in pursuit of the Indians. They did not succeed in overtaking them but have I believe recovered the bodies of the killed. The Indians who committed the murders belong to the Yo-sem-i-ties, of whom complaint was made to the Genl. Comds. last winter. They have committed many robberies, but have until this last act, refrained from murder. I will start in pursuit of them on Monday next, and endeavor not only to punish the Indians who were engaged in committing the murder, but also to remove the tribe to the reservation set aside for them by the commissioners last year. Qr. Masters funds will be necessary to carry on the Expedition. Enclosed you will find requisitions for funds and stores, which please submit to the General Comds. as early as convenient.

Capt. E. D. Townsend

Ass. Adj. Genl.

Benicia, Cal.

I am sir very respectfully

Your obt Srvt

T. Moore

Report of July 8, 1852

Head Quarters Camp Steele [Little Yosemite Valley]

"The Blood-Swollen God"

Near the Head Waters of the Merced

July 8th, 1852

Sir

I have the honor to report that, I arrived at my present
encampment on the Head Waters of the Merced on the
20th of June, immediately on my arrival scouting parties
were sent to scour the country in all directions. Many
deserted "Rancherias" were found, but no Indians. The
friendly Indians we had with us as guides are of the
opinion that the entire tribe had crossed the Sierras. Major
Savage with a party of Indians struck a fresh trail heading
from the valley towards the head waters of the San
Joaquin, his provisions giving out he was obliged to return.
On the lst I took with me a party of twelve men and taking
Major Savage's trail soon came to a heavy trail. This we
continued to follow. And on the morning of the 4th crossed
the main ridge of the Sierra. I encamped about noon and
sending out scouts I received information that there was
a "Rancheria" some four miles distant, by dividing my
party I was enabled to take them so completely by surprise
that before they were able to move they were entirely
surrounded. Twenty-one prisoners were taken—six men,
the remainder women and children—one of the prisoners
acknowledged that they saw the murders of the whites
on the Merced, but denied having participated in it. A
number of trinkets together with some clothing was found
which fully implicated their participation in the division
of the murdered men's property, if not in the murder.
The men I then ordered to be shot which was done on the
morning of the 5th. From the women taken I have learned
that it was a general thing and that nearly the entire tribe
was present at the murder. Lieut. McLean started for Yo
Semity Valley on the 1st with ten men with instructions
to destroy the "Rancherias" and provisions there, he
succeeded in finding a large quantity of acorns which were

destroyed. One of his men (Riley) was severely wounded receiving two arrow shots on the night of the 4th while on post as sentinel. Lieut. McLean arrived this morning, having accomplished the destruction of as much property and provisions as could be found. Riley the wounded man died last night. Mr. Crosby will hand you requisition which please submit to the Genl. Commanding at your earliest opportunity.

Capt. E. D. Townsend

Ass. Adjt. Genl.

Pacific Division

San Francisco, Cala.

I am Sir

Very Respectfully

Your obdt Servt.

T. Moore

1st Lt. Infantry

Comdg. Expedition

Report of July 9, 1852

Hd. Qrs. Camp Steele

July 9th, 1852

Sir

From information received from the Indian women taken a few days since, I have determined to follow the Yosemities across the Sierras, into the Mono country. The Yo semitis are on friendly terms with the Monos and have fled to this country thinking that the whites will not follow them across the snow. A few families are yet scattered in the vallies high up in the mountains, but are making their way as rapidly as possible to the Mono territory. The squad taken on the 4th was one of these detached parties.

"The Blood-Swollen God"

The Indians inform me that mules can be taken across the mountains without much difficulty—In connection with this I would state that my command is so small, that I cannot with prudence detach men from it to guard the pack train. This up to the present, has not been necessary, but my farther movement in the mountains will require that the train have a small escort for the safe transmission of supplies. I would respectfully suggest that a small detachment of dragoons be sent to me for that purpose—I would also state that the necessity of detaching two and three men as scouts, without other arms than muskets, has led me to think that a few six shooters would be of service for parties of this nature. Enclosed I transmit a requisition for ten which I hope will meet the approbation of the Genl Comdg

Capt. E. D. Townsend

Ass. Adj. Genl.

Pacific Division

San Francisco, Cal.

I am Sir very respectfully

Your obt servt.

T. Moore

Lt. In'try

4

"The Lark at Heaven's Gate Sings"

Initial Encounters, 1850–1859

The first well-documented visit to Yosemite by nonindigenous persons was during the Mariposa Indian War of 1851–
52. This military campaign saw Anglo-Americans first attach
the name "Yosemite" to the valley. The Yosemite Valley indigenous population referred to the magnificent granite chasm
as "Ah-wah'-nee," or "place of the open or gaping mouth."
Yosemite, which was spelled in various creative forms, was
a misunderstanding or corruption of the Southern Miwok
term *yohhe'miti* or the Central Miwok word *yos s e'meti*—
both of which translate as "those who kill." Their usage was
referring to the Awahnichi, the resident clan in the Yosemite Valley, who were a feared traditional enemy.

With the finale of the Mariposa Indian War, visitation by
civilian Anglo-Americans commenced. The tourists were
only a trickle for many years, due to the challenging journey and the lack of accommodations. Today as many as five
million throng to Yosemite annually, but from 1855 to 1865
the *total* number of visitors was about 650. Even by the end
of the nineteenth century, sightseers still numbered only a
few thousand per year.

In 1854 John Capen "Grizzly" Adams trapped grizzlies for
display in his bizarre Mountaineer Museum in San Francisco.
In 1855 ardent Yosemite promoter and hotelier James Mason
Hutchings led the first tourist party to Yosemite Valley. One
member of the Hutchings company, artist Thomas Ayres,
created the first published illustrations of the breathtaking
gorge. Astonished readers and editors questioned whether
they were realistic depictions or tall tales.

As word spread of the remarkable landscape, rudimentary toll roads and horse paths led toward the valley. It normally took days of hard, sometimes dangerous, travel to reach Yosemite. In 1857 the first hotel was constructed there, but it was little more than a covered shelter devoid of creature comforts. A handful of other lodgings followed, equally rustic. It was not until 1859 that the first white person, James Lamon, took up permanent year-round tenancy in Yosemite Valley.

These early encounters with Yosemite spawned written narratives that followed a distinctive pattern. Virtually every description of the initial glimpse of the valley was filled with a sense of awe, a gasping incredulity at the majesty of the great granite cathedral. The expressions of amazement were often reverential, with exuberant and flowery prose and poetry struggling to adequately express the author's feelings of wonderment at what they emotionally proclaimed as God's glorious creation. Occasionally, usually in conjunction with the worshipful tone but sometimes independently, a persnickety traveler would grumble about the trip or whine about the poor food and housing. But, in all but a tiny minority of cases, the faultfinders noted that the transcendent vista of the Yosemite Valley was well worth the physical demands of visiting.

> "I then proposed . . . that we give the valley the name
> Yo-sem-i-ty, as it was suggestive, euphonious,
> and certainly *American*."

Lafayette Houghton Bunnell

*Discovery of the Yosemite and the Indian War of 1851,
Which Led to That Event*, 1880

In 1851 Dr. Lafayette Houghton Bunnell was a member of the Mariposa Battalion, a local volunteer militia that was charged with finding Native American tribal leaders involved in recent raids on Anglo-American settlements in the region. That search for the indigenous leaders, undertaken by the Mariposa Battalion and led by James Savage, is believed to be the first authenticated visit to the Yosemite Valley by nonindigenous persons. Subsequently, Bunnell led additional expeditions into the valley and named many of its geographic landmarks. Lafayette Bunnell also served in the Civil War as a surgeon for the Thirty-Sixth Wisconsin Volunteer Infantry. In 1880 Bunnell wrote *Discovery of the Yosemite and the Indian War of 1851, Which Led to That Event*. These selections from chapters 3 and 4 of that book describe Bunnell's first glimpse of the majestic Yosemite Valley (a moment Bunnell notes filled him with "a peculiar exalted sensation") and the discussion of Bunnell and other members of the Mariposa Battalion regarding a name for the valley they claimed to have "discovered" in March 1851. These events occurred while the Mariposa Battalion was in the midst of a military campaign to detain any remaining Native inhabitants of Yosemite Valley and destroy their food stores.

Chapter 3

We suddenly came in full view of the valley in which was the village, or rather the encampments of the Yosemities. The immensity of rock I had seen in my vision on the Old Bear Valley trail from Ridley's Ferry was here presented to my astonished gaze. The mystery of that scene was here disclosed. My awe was increased by this nearer view. The face of the immense cliff was shadowed by the declining sun; its outlines only had been seen at a distance. . . . That stupendous cliff is now known as "El Capitan" (the Captain), and the plateau from which we had our first view of the valley, as Mount Beatitude [known as Old Inspiration Point today].

It has been said that "it is not easy to describe in words the precise impressions which great objects make upon us." I cannot describe how completely I realized this truth. None but those who have visited this most wonderful valley, can even imagine the feelings with which I looked upon the view

"The Lark at Heaven's Gate Sings"

that was there presented. The grandeur of the scene was but softened by the haze that hung over the valley,—light as gossamer—and by the clouds which partially dimmed the higher cliffs and mountains. This obscurity of vision but increased the awe with which I beheld it, and as I looked, a peculiar exalted sensation seemed to fill my whole being, and I found my eyes in tears with emotion.

During many subsequent visits to this locality, this sensation was never again so fully aroused. It is probable that the shadows fast clothing all before me, and the vapory clouds at the head of the valley, leaving the view beyond still undefined, gave a weirdness to the scene, that made it so impressive; and the conviction that it was utterly indescribable added strength to the emotion. It is not possible for the same intensity of feeling to be aroused more than once by the same object, although I never looked upon these scenes except with wonder and admiration.

Chapter 4

After relating my observations from the "Old Bear Valley Trail," I suggested that this valley should have an appropriate name by which to designate it, and in a tone of pleasantry, said to Tunnehill [Sgt. Benjamin Tannihill], who was drying his wet clothing by our fire, "You are the first white man that ever received any form of baptism in this valley, and you should be considered the proper person to give a baptismal name to the valley itself." He replied, "If whisky can be provided for such a ceremony, I shall be happy to participate; but if it is to be another cold water affair, I have no desire to take a hand. I have done enough in that line for tonight." Timely jokes and ready repartee for a time changed the subject, but in the lull of this exciting pastime, some one remarked, "I like Bunnell's suggestion of giving this valley a name, and to-night is a good time to do it." "All right—if you have got one, show your hand," was the response of another. Different names were proposed, but none were satisfactory to a majority of our circle. Some romantic and foreign names were offered, but I observed that a very large number were canonical and Scripture names. From this I inferred that I was not the only one in whom religious emotions or thoughts had been aroused by the mysterious power of the surrounding scenery.

As I did not take a fancy to any of the names proposed, I remarked that "an American name would be the most appropriate"; that "I could not see any necessity for going to a foreign country for a name for American scenery—the grandest that had ever yet been looked upon. That it would be better to give it an Indian name than to import a strange and inexpressive one; that the name of the tribe who had occupied it, would be more appropriate than any I had heard suggested." I then proposed "that we give the valley the name of Yo-sem-i-ty, as it was suggestive, euphonious, and certainly *American*; that by so doing, the name of the tribe of Indians which we met leaving their homes in this valley, perhaps never to return, would be perpetuated." I was here interrupted by Mr. Tunnehill, who impatiently exclaimed: "Devil take the Indians and their names! Why should we honor these vagabond murderers by perpetuating their name?" Another said: "I agree with Tunnehill;—the Indians and their names. Mad Anthony's plan for me! Let's call this Paradise Valley." In reply, I said to the last speaker, "Still, for a young man with such *religious tendencies* they would be good objects on which to develop your Christianity." Unexpectedly, a hearty laugh was raised, which broke up further discussion, and before opportunity was given for any others to object to the name, John O'Neal, a rollicking Texan of Capt. Boling's company, vociferously announced to the whole camp the subject of our discussion, by saying, "Hear ye! Hear ye! Hear ye! A vote will now be taken to decide what name shall be given to this valley." The question of giving it the name of Yo-sem-i-ty was then explained; and upon a *viva voce* vote being taken, it was almost unanimously adopted. The name that was there and thus adopted by us, while seated around our camp fires, on the first visit

"The Lark at Heaven's Gate Sings"

of a white man to this remarkable locality, is the name by which it is now known to the world.

....

".. . cheek by jowl with our friend El Capitan."

....

Warren Baer

"A Trip to the Yosemite Falls," 1856

One of the earliest tourist parties in Yosemite Valley visited in July 1856. The following month, on August 5, the *Mariposa Democrat* published the following account of the trip. It is one of the first comprehensive descriptions of Yosemite Valley. The article was unsigned, but it is generally believed that the author was Warren Baer, the editor of the newspaper and a member of the party. Baer's florid description of the many landmarks in Yosemite Valley followed the pattern of these first narratives—personal wonderment coupled with a romantic, almost mystical narrative. Warren Baer is credited with naming the Nevada Fall in Yosemite Valley.

In this selection Warren Baer describes the party's first glimpse of the valley and their wonderment at seeing the waterfalls, the rocky crags; experiencing the powerful silence; and encountering the myriad other delights found in the "immensity of the grandness."

We came suddenly, abruptly in view of the Valley; and then commenced our descent of the mountain, following a narrow and winding trail, until we reached the plain below. There was no danger in our path, and if there had been, we would not have regarded it, for our eyes were riveted upon the scenery that was imperceptibly spreading and brightening as we descended the trail. . . . There was a break in the timber before us, which afforded a full view of the Valley. We hope no one will attribute to us designing motives, to draw travel through this country, or treat our description of the Valley as the ravings of a wild enthusiast,—because we have no other object in view than to make known to those afar off, who may have never heard of this Valley, what a wilderness of majestic beauty they have yet to explore within the limits of our own State.

As though the enchantress of the woods had suddenly waved her magic wand o'er the mountains, was this fairy scenery opened to our view. Thrilling sensations of awe pervaded our senses, which, as we approached, gradually subsided into pleasurable emotions of wonder and delight, similar to those produced upon the soul by distant music echoing amid the hills and valleys in the quiet hours of midnight. Through the blue haze that lingered o'er the scene, we traced the bold outlines of the towering peaks of the distant range of the Sierra Nevada; while before us, or rather beneath us, spread the verdant Valley of the Yosemite, encased in lofty and picturesque walls of granite, and fertilized by the transparent waters of the Middle Fork of the Merced River. As we approached, the blue haze grew fainter and thinner, seeming to fade from the rocks we neared, only to thicken in density on the more distant summits, that ever and anon were opening to our gaze. Vainly, with attentive mind, we endeavored to catch the first sound of animated nature. We saw the cascade leaping from its precipitous terminus into the depths below. We knew that the river was flowing beneath us. Yet we heard not the voice of either. Hushed was the cooing of the grouse, and still was the moan of the turtledove. The spell of silence was flung o'er stream and hill, and we appeared like intruders into the realm of Nature's secret repose. In contemplating the grandeur of the scene, the imagination recoils back upon itself, content to follow the reach of vision, completely paralyzed by the magnitude of the expanding vista. Down, down we go, twisting, winding with the path, until we reach the meadow below. And now we first hear the gentle roar of the river, and feel the freshening breeze of the Valley. Glorious Spring was here, quickening Nature with her smiling presence, and lulling her to repose with her sportive zephyrs, sighing through the trees; while around, above,

"The Lark at Heaven's Gate Sings"

and before us—anywhere and everywhere—was written the majesty of God; and our hearts bowed in all humility to the magnitude of his greatness. Change, the handmaid of Time, was most impressively on the face of the stupendous precipices, and by the crumbling ruins scattered near their base. When first entering the Valley, the mind becomes stupefied by the immensity of the grandness to which it is opposed. Soon it begins to admire points of beauty in the rocks, or in the trees growing from the crevices of their perpendicular sides. And thus commencing with small objects, it slowly and gradually arrives at a contemplation of some particular height, and finally meditates upon their combined grandeur, blended in one universal harmony of perfect sublimity. Thus we rode along, glancing from summit to summit of towering rocks, until proceeding for about a mile and a half up stream, we came opposite the falls of what has been inappropriately called the Cascade of the Rainbow [today's Bridalveil Fall]. We say this not to reflect upon the judgment of the gentleman who has ventured to bestow this fanciful name upon one of the most attractive cascades of the Valley. But inasmuch as the falls in the Valley are never of the magnitude of a cataract, and all reflect rainbows at certain hours of the day, the name might be promiscuously applied to all the cascades separately. This fall of water is nearly opposite to the famous giant of the valley, El Capitan. The stream of water which supplies it, rises in the ridge of mountains that divides the South from the Main Fork of the Merced River, and is one of the latter's tributaries. The volume of water running over the precipice will average, in summer, about three cubic feet per second, and is precipitated in an unbroken sheet of spray, and without an opposing obstacle, to a depth of 928 feet below, where the stream unites with the river, after coming through a narrow channel for a distance of three hundred yards. Viewed from any quarter or point of the horizon, this cascade is very attractive. To our mind, it resembles a cambric veil, of ample folds, of the finest texture, the purest whiteness, and fringed with silver fleece or silken floss. Sitting beside the cherry trees, at some fifty yards from the falls, we were singularly struck with the graceful motion of the water in its descent, when pressed by the breeze. Its foldings and unfoldings—its wavings and its twistings—its contractings and expandings—possess an irresistibly attractive fascination, beyond any object on which we have ever gazed, and one, too, from which the eyes are drawn with the greatest reluctance. At night, when our trip recurs to our mind, we muse on its loveliness, until we again hear the noise of its waters in their fall, and see the rainbows that follow its wanderings through the air, in its downward search for the earth and the Valley. We make bold to call it the Bridal Veil; and those who may have the felicity to witness the stream floating in the embrace of the morning breeze will acknowledge the resemblance, and perhaps pardon the liberty we have taken in attempting to apply so poetical a name to this Queen of the Valley. Nearly opposite to the Bridal Veil stands the Monarch of the Vale, the El Capitan of the Yosemite Tribe. It is the terminus of a ridge of mountains, standing out in bold relief, with perpendicular front, and rising to an elevation of 3100 feet above the level of the river that roars at his base. His stern and prominent front is the first to greet the eye of the visitor. He almost seemed to frown on us as we passed near his base; and on his bleached and rugged visage, the last beams of the setting sun linger with affectionate warmth. This monster of rocks stands on the left-hand side of the Valley as you go up the stream, and adjoining him looms up, with a broad, oval top, the Signal Rock, on which the Yosemites lit their signal fires in the hour of danger. The El Capitan projects further out towards the middle of the Valley than any of his kindred, and eclipses all of them for huge proportions and lofty bearing, and is some three hundred feet higher than the Signal Rock. Opposite the Signal Rock stand three sharp-pointed peaks, almost in the position of a triangle. They are jagged, and change their shape and location when viewed from different points. They are the Three Brothers; and further up the Valley, beyond them, and slightly thrown back or in the rear of the Brothers, are the Twins or Two Sisters. They cannot be mistaken, for though, when looking down through the Valley, they seem as a single rock, yet when nearly fronting them, they present two sharp projecting points, and are worthy of attention from the great resemblance they bear to each other.

The Yosemite Falls now make their appearance on the lefthand side of the Valley as you follow up the stream; while directly opposite these Falls stands the Pyramid Rock [Sentinel Rock], which, when seen from a distance, is shaped and squared like a pyramid, but when viewed from its front, presents a flat, smooth surface. . . . We stopped for the night, and prepared our supper, which we ate with a hearty good relish; and after tracing the dim white line of the Yosemite Falls, . . . and bowing in silent reverence to the Pyramid on the South, we closed our eyes for the night, and joyfully greeted the morning sun, which, when we awoke, was cheek by jowl with our friend El Capitan.

> "We sat down to drink in the varied beauties of
> this intoxicating and enchanting scene."

James Mason Hutchings
"The Musical Name—Yo Semite," 1886,
and "California for Waterfalls!," 1855

During the nineteenth century, the greatest promoter of the commercial prospects of Yosemite Valley was James Mason Hutchings. He became intimately tied to Yosemite Valley as both advocate and entrepreneur. After immigrating to the United States from his native England in 1848, his future would change in July 1855. In that month Hutchings led the second (and first well-documented) tourist trip into Yosemite Valley. Soon afterward he became one of the earliest Anglo-American settlers in the valley. Hutchings operated an inn, was a frequently requested tour guide, and was an indefatigable campaigner for Yosemite. James Mason Hutchings described Yosemite Valley as a "singular and romantic valley" that he urged visitors to "enjoy . . . with luxurious zest."

Hutchings published his *Hutchings' Illustrated Magazine* from 1856 to 1860. Its pages frequently extolled the valley's beauty. In 1860 Hutchings published *Scenes of Wonder and Curiosity in California*, which was primarily a tourist guide to Yosemite. In 1886 he wrote *In the Heart of the Sierras*, a classic description of the virtues of the valley. Sadly, in 1902, while visiting Yosemite Valley, Hutchings was tossed from his buggy when his horse reared, and he died of a head injury.

Two selections from Hutchings's writings are presented here. The first, from *In the Heart of the Sierras*, describes the naming of Yosemite Valley and the correct pronunciation and spelling of the valley's appellation (Hutchings refers to today's commonly accepted spelling of "Yosemite" as "the present slovenly way of spelling it"—Hutchings preferred "Yo Semite.") The second is a passage from the *San Francisco Daily California Chronicle* of August 18, 1855. It is essentially a reprint of an earlier article published by the *Mariposa Gazette* on August 9, 1855. The article is an account of the Hutchings-led second tourist party to visit Yosemite Valley.

The Musical Name—Yo Semite

Its meaning is, according to the very best authorities, *a large, or full-grown, grizzly bear*; and is pronounced Yo Sem-i-tee. The old Indian name was Ah-wah-nee, and the tribe which inhabited it—the remote ancestors of Ten-ie-ya—were Ah-wah-nee-chees, the origination or signification of which is still veiled in mystery. All these considerations, and other proposed names meriting attention, were fully discussed at this opportune juncture, but "Yo Semite," the one suggested by Dr. L.H. Bunnell, was finally adopted by an almost unanimous vote.

"The Lark at Heaven's Gate Sings"

From an intelligent Indian, whose life the writer was once instrumental in saving, and from whom many interesting facts concerning his race have been obtained, and will be given in due season, he received the following[:]

Legendary Tradition concerning "Yo Semite"

A band of the Ah-wah-nee-chees, then a tribe numbering over one thousand, was encamped among the oaks near the foot of Indian Cañon; when, early one morning, an athletic chief determined upon going to Mirror Lake (called by them "Ke-ko-too-yem," or Sleeping Water, and "Ah-wi-yah") for the purpose of spearing a number of its delicious trout. On threading his way among the bowlders that strewed the ground, and when passing one of the largest, he was suddenly met by an enormous grizzly bear. The abruptness of this unexpected meeting must have been interpreted by the grizzly as an unjustifiable intrusion upon his ursine privileges and domain, as he immediately declared it a *casus belli*, by an instantaneous and ferocious attack upon the Indian. Unprepared as the young chief was for such an unequal encounter, he resolved upon standing his ground, and doing his best, as nobly as he could, so that the children of Ah-wah-nee might see that the valorous blood of their ancestors was still flowing in the veins of their descendants. The dead limb of a tree, lying near, provided him with a weapon of defense, and with it he dealt out heavy and lusty blows upon the head of his antagonist; and, although badly lacerated and torn by the teeth and claws of the infuriated brute, the Indian courageously held to the uneven contest, until the eyes of bruin began to glaze in the cold glare of death; and "victory had perched upon the banners" of the chief. The astonished Indians, in admiring acknowledgment of the unexampled prowess of the dauntless Ah-wah-nee-chee, thence forth called him "Yo Semite" in honor of his successful and great achievement. This well-won cognomen was eventually transmitted to his children; and, finally, to the whole tribe; so that the "Yo Semites" were known, and feared, by all the Indians around their wildly defensive habitation.

It is apparent from Dr. Bunnell's statement that the signification of "Yo Semite" was not generally known to the battalion; nor was there any uniformity in its general pronunciation, even among the Indians themselves, some calling it Oo-soom-i-tee, others Oo-hum-i-tee, Yo-hum-i-tee, Yo-hem-i-tee, and still others Yo-ham-i-tee, while Bullack, the oldest of the Yo Semites now living, calls it Ah Hum-a-tee-all, however, having the same meaning. . . .

Before fully closing these inquiries, it may not be inappropriate to consider why preference is given here to the construction of the word *Yo Semite* with a capital S on its second syllable. It is this: Dr. Bunnell, to whom the world is indebted for the choice and adoption of this euphonious name, so gave it to the writer, some thirty years ago, and before the present slovenly way of spelling it came into practice. It is true, Dr. Bunnell, in his valuable work, "The Discovery of the Yosemite," has fallen into that habit; but, when asked his reasons for making the change, replied, "I allowed the printer to follow his own way of spelling it. Yours, however, is the correct one, and I must give you credit for keeping up its pure orthography, that being the construction given to it, and agreed upon, at our first camp-fire in Yo Semite in 1851." The Act of Congress making the donation of the valley to the State, so gives it.

California for Waterfalls!

From Mr. Hunt's store, we kept an east-of-north course, up the divide between the Fresno and Chowchilla valleys; thence descending towards the South Fork of the Merced river, and winding around a very rocky point, we climbed nearly to the ridge of the Middle or main fork of the Merced, and descending towards the Yo-Semity valley, we came upon a high point, clear of trees, from whence we had our first view of this singular and romantic valley; and, as the scene opened in full view before us, we were almost speech-

"The Lark at Heaven's Gate Sings"

less with wondering admiration at its wild and sublime grandeur. "What!" exclaimed one at length, "have we come to the end of all things?" "Can this be the opening of the Seventh Seal?" cries another. "This far, very far, exceeds Niagara," says a third.

We had been out from Mariposa about four days, and the fatigue of the journey had made us weary and a little peevish, but when our eyes looked upon the almost terrific grandeur of this scene, all, all was forgotten. "I never expected to behold so beautiful a sight!" "This scene alone amply repays me for the travel!" "I should have lost the most magnificent sight that I ever saw had I not witnessed this!" were exclamations of pleasurable surprise that fell from the lips of all, as we sat down to drink in the varied beauties of this intoxicating and enchanting scene.

On the north side stands one bold, perpendicular mountain of granite, shaped like an immense tower. Its lofty top is covered with great pines, that by distance become mere shrubs. Our Indian guides called this the "Capitan." It measures from the valley to its summit about two thousand eight hundred feet.

Just opposite this, on the south side of the valley, our attention was first attracted by a magnificent waterfall, *about seven hundred feet in height.* It looked like a broad, long feather of silver, that hung depending over a precipice; and as this feathery tail of leaping spray thus hung, a slight breeze moved it from side to side, and as the last rays of the setting sun were gilding it with rainbow hues, the red would mix with the purple, and the purple with the yellow, and the yellow with the green, and the green with the silvery sheen of its whitened foam, as it danced in space.

On rushed the water over its rocky bed, and as it reached the valley, it threw up a cloud of mist that made green and flourishing the grass and flowers, and shrubs, that slumbered at the mountain's base—while towering three thousand feet above the valley, stood the rugged and pine covered cliffs that, in broken and spiral peaks, girdle in the whole.

Passing further up the valley, one is struck with the awful grandeur of the immense mountains on either side—some perpendicular, some a little sloping. One looks like a light-house, another like a giant capital of immense dimensions—all are singular, and surmounted by pines.

Now we crossed the river, and still advancing up the valley, turned a point, and before us was an indescribable sight—a waterfall *two thousand two hundred feet in height*—the highest in the world. It rushes over the cliffs, and with one bold leap falls one thousand two hundred feet, then a second of five hundred feet more, then a third of over five hundred feet more—the three leaps making two thousand two hundred feet.

Standing upon the opposite side of the valley, and looking at the tall pines below, the great height of these falls can at a glance be comprehended.

About ten miles from the lower end of the valley, there is another fall of *not less than fifteen hundred feet.* This, with lesser falls and a lake, make the head of the Yo-Semity Valley, so that this valley is about ten miles in length, and from a half to one mile in width; and although there is good land enough for several farms, it cannot be considered upon the whole as a good farming valley. Speckled trout, grouse and pigeons are quite numerous.

....

"The picture is photographed on the tablets
of my memory in indelible colors."

....

James Henry Lawrence
"Discovery of the Nevada Fall," 1884

James Henry Lawrence was a member of one of the ear-liest tourist parties to Yosemite, visiting the valley in August 1855. As were many during the gold rush years, Lawrence was not a California native son. Born in Massachusetts in 1831, Lawrence arrived in California in the

"The Lark at Heaven's Gate Sings"

fateful year of 1849, after serving as a teenage soldier during the 1846–48 war with Mexico.

Settling in Mariposa, James H. Lawrence would eventually become a lawyer, a newspaper editor, and a politician. He was a leader of the California Democratic Party and served as a state senator representing Mariposa, Stanislaus, and Merced Counties from 1867 to 1871. Lawrence would also be arrested and acquitted on a homicide charge, abandon his wife and young daughter, and die "in a state of mental collapse" in 1901.

In this October 1884 article from *Overland Monthly* erroneously titled "Discovery of the Nevada Fall" (Lawrence's tourist party did not "discover" Nevada Fall nor were they the first to describe it), Lawrence recounts the rapturous moment when his ten-member company first beheld the Yosemite Valley.

It was nearly sunset before we reached what is now termed "Inspiration Point." Here we had our first view of Yosemite. There it lay before us in all its beauty, an oasis walled in by towering cliffs; a virgin meadow threaded by a silvery stream and girdled with a zone of granite[,] an emerald in a setting of gray. It was a grand view, worth the whole journey; and we would have liked to linger and watch it fade away through the hazy twilight till it was lost in the somber uniformity of night, but we had no time to lose. "It's about four miles to the foot of this little hill," said Haughton, "and it will be as much as we can do to make it before dark. We must repack and cinch those mules for keeps. From here to the foot of the hill, though not exactly dangerous, is liable to be troublesome in the night time. In fact, it's safe to say it's the roughest you ever saw." . . .

We made our camp temporarily on the north side of the river, at the lower end of the valley, just below the base of the grand old cliff now known as Tutockanulah and El Capitan. . . .

How still it was! Only the least bit of a breeze stirring tree leaves and whispering in the tree tops. A gentle, soft murmuring rose and fell with the variable wind.

"That comes," said Haughton, "from a waterfall on a stream the other side of the river—a tributary of the Merced. At this low stage of water its volume is very small, and it breaks into a cloud of spray long before it gets to the bed of the stream below." We had no names for the different falls at that time, but this one described by our guide and afterwards visited by us was the Bridal Veil, otherwise known as the Pohono, or "Spirit of the Evil Wind"—a dreadful name to attach to a waterfall that never did anybody any harm. . . .

As surmised by Haughton, it was only a wreath of spray, which hung pendant and gracefully swinging with the breeze. The great Yosemite Fall was a thing of the past. It had left its impress on the naked rocks in a broad stain, but a meager, trickling, straggling stream, lazily crawling down the face of the seamed cliff, and wiggling among the jagged rocks below, was all that was left of the grand fall, which, with its roaring and thundering, strikes terror to the soul of the tourist who ventures near it during the spring or earlier summer months. . . .

One evening, after a series of dare-devil escapades for no particular purpose, except to demonstrate how near a man can come to breaking his neck and miss it, some one suggested an expedition up the main river, above the valley. . . .

It looked like a perilous undertaking, and there were some doubts as to the result; nevertheless, the conclusion was to see how far we could go. Away up, up, far above us, skirting the base of what seemed to be a perpendicular cliff, there was a narrow belt of timber. That meant a plateau or strip of land comparatively level. If we could only reach that, it was reasonable to suppose that we could get around the face of the cliff. "Then we will see sights," was the expression of one of the trio. . . .

But to reach the plateau—that was the problem. It was a fearful climb. Over and under and around masses of immense rocks, jumping across chasms at imminent risk of life and limb, keeping a bright lookout for soft places to fall, as well as for the best way to circumvent the next obstacle, after about three hours wrestling, "catch as catch can," with that grim old mountain side, we reached the timber. Here, as we had surmised, was enough of level ground for a foothold, and here we took a rest, little dreaming of the magnificent scene in store for us when we rounded the base of the cliff. . . .

The oft-quoted phrase, "A thing of beauty is a joy forever," was never more fully realized. The picture is photographed on the tablets of my memory in indelible colors, and is as fresh and bright to-day as was the first impression twenty-nine years ago. To the tourist who beholds it for the first time, the Nevada Fall, with its weird surroundings, is a view of rare and picturesque beauty and grandeur. The rugged cliffs, the summits fringed with stunted pine and juniper, bounding the cañon on the southern side, the "Cap of Liberty" standing like a huge sentinel overlooking the scene at the north, the foaming caldron at the foot of the fall, the rapids below, the flume where the stream glides noiselessly but with lightning speed over its polished granite bed, making the preparatory run for its plunge over the Vernal Fall, form a combination of rare effects, leaving upon the mind an impression that years cannot efface. But the tourist is in a measure prepared. He has seen the engravings and photographic views, and read descriptions written by visitors who have preceded him. To us it was the opening of a sealed volume. Long we lingered and admiringly gazed upon the grand panorama, till the descending sun admonished us that we had no time to lose in making our way campward. . . .

Our evenings were pleasant and sociable. Around the cheerful camp-fire we discussed the grandeur of our surroundings and the possibilities of the future. It was unanimously agreed that for beauty and sublimity of scenery the valley was without a peer: as people from all parts of the world visited Niagara Falls, and our own countrymen made the European tour for the special purpose of viewing the wonders of the Alps, why should not this wonder-land attract thousands from the Atlantic States and Europe, when its fame should become world-wide?

....

"... after great fatigue and some swearing,
we reached the summit."

....

Mariposa Gazette
"The Yo Semity Valley," 1855

The first non-Native visitors to Yosemite generally had two reactions. First, the valley and surrounding landscape constituted a breathtaking natural wonder, and second, it was a grueling trudge to get there.

An early account of the difficulties and dangers of a trip to Yosemite was published in the *Mariposa Gazette* on October 11, 1855. The *Mariposa Gazette* was founded in 1854 and claims to be "California's oldest weekly newspaper of continuous publication." Without question, it is an essential resource chronicling early Yosemite history.

In this passage, the intrepid visitors explore the Yosemite Valley on foot.

Nature made the lovely spot, and kept from it the "dross" which alone induces man to despoil. Embowered in the mountains in its wildness and beauty, it seems desecration for civilization to intrude upon its loveliness. . . .

After examining all, or rather as much of the beauties as our time would allow; our party proceeded up the South Fork of the river to see the main falls [Vernal Fall]. We mounted our steeds, and proceeded up some two and a half miles; where we dismounted and proceeded on foot two miles more.

As you go up, the southern valley narrows by degrees until within two miles of the falls, when it assumes the form of a cañon. Like the lower cliffs, the rocks have fallen, and the passage up the river is very difficult. We reached the falls about noon, and in nearing it, beheld the pool where the water collects after its descent. It is an ellipsis, or nearly so, and about one hundred feet in length. The water falling a distance of three hundred and fifty feet is broken into spray upon the rocks, and is collected in this pool prior to its tortuous passage through the Cañon. A constant mist spreads several hundred yards around, irrigating vegetation, which is remarkably green in the vicinity of the falls. Large boulders have fallen and been rolled up in huge masses by the water on either side of the river, and apparently without any soil, is growing upon them the real "Kentucky Blue Grass," covering the spaces and uneven surfaces between the rocks with mats, which renders it dangerous to proceed, except on "all fours"; otherwise the visitor might fall between the rocks, and be lucky to escape with a sound neck-bone. Our party went around on the side of the falls, and sat under the mist. . . .

The water is icy cold, and the spray as it would envelope us, caused us to draw tight our coats around us. After lunching, and allowing ourselves to take a lingering look at a sight so beautiful, we prepared for returning. Here allow me to state that our party made no effort to go beyond these falls; but I have learned that other parties have explored the river higher up, and they assert that above these falls is another, grander if possible, falling from a greater height [Nevada Fall], and that the vicinity is wilder and more picturesque than in the valley. I give the information for what it is worth, not having seen it myself. Our descent to our animals was slow and tedious. On our route we passed a large boulder, which from its appearance, has recently been detached from the mountains and fallen nearly to the bed of the stream. It weighs many thousand tons, and on the lower side we registered our names, and for that reason it may be known as "register rock." I would advise parties visiting this fall, to keep near the boulders and timber. If they attempt to go too high up from the river they will be encompassed by rocks on the way side, and if they go too near the river they will find themselves in a swamp, and in danger of meeting a "grizzly." . . .

After passing up the north fork of the river, a very fine

view of the peaks is to be seen. The most prominent object at this point is Capitol Rock [North Dome]. It is a large bluff surmounted by a dome, rising regularly to the height of one hundred feet. To the right, is seen another dome, which is partially fallen away, and on the side next to the valley presents an uneven perpendicular appearance [Half Dome]. In this valley are several small lakes or ponds, through which the river runs. They abound in fish, and are resorted to by every variety of water fowl.

There is some good land in this valley, and a large amount of good grazing. We penetrated some four or five miles up this valley, but were compelled to return on account of the rugged state of the cañon. Like the other valley, it gradually narrows, until the river passes through a narrow channel, hemmed in on both sides by high cliffs.

The next day being Sunday, our party rested from its labors. Monday was spent in a general hunt, in company with a party from Big Oak Flat, who came into the valley the day before. In the evening the song and jest passed right merrily, and all seemed pleased with their visit. Next day we moved to the foot of the valley, preparatory to our final exit. We determined to try a new route home, and left the valley by the trail passing on the north side of the river. About a mile and a half below the valley, the trail leaves the river and begins to ascend the mountains. The ascent is steep and dangerous, but after great fatigue and some swearing, we reached the summit.

. . . .

". . . the everlasting walls of the Yohemity . . ."

. . . .

Thomas A. Ayres

"A Trip to the Yohamite Valley," 1856

Born in 1816 in New Jersey, Thomas Almond Ayres was trained as a draftsman in Minnesota. He joined the California gold rush in 1849. For the next seven years, Ayres traveled throughout California. In 1855 he was with the first recognized tourist party to visit Yosemite

"The Lark at Heaven's Gate Sings"

and is widely considered to be the first artist to sketch the extraordinary valley. He also produced a highly regarded panorama of the valley that was displayed in Sacramento. In 1857 Ayres went to New York City to exhibit his work, and also in that year he received a commission from *Harper's Magazine* to provide additional depictions of California for a series of articles. In 1858, while on a voyage from Southern California to San Francisco, Ayres died when his ship sank in a storm on April 26, 1858.

In August 1856 Ayres wrote an article for the *San Francisco Daily Alta California* that recounted his adventures as a member of the first tourist party to Yosemite Valley, in 1855. Place-names and spellings for Yosemite Valley landmarks were not firmly established when Ayres wrote his article, and the names he uses vary from those of today: "Cascade of the Rainbow" is today's Bridalveil Fall; "South Dome" is Half Dome; "High Falls" is Yosemite Falls; "Lower Falls of the Middle Fork" is Vernal Fall; "Upper Falls" is Nevada Fall; and, most noticeably, Ayres spells Yosemite as "Yohemity." "Yohamite" was the spelling offered by the *Daily Alta California*.

This passage begins as the party leaves Coulterville, a major way station about fifty-five miles west of Yosemite Valley.

June 25th—A very perceptible change in the temperature has taken place since leaving Coulterville, owing to our increased altitude. The vegetation, also, has a spring appearance—beautiful flowers in bloom upon every side—while at Coulterville and the region below, everything green has disappeared in the summer drought of California. Mounting our animals, we soon reached "Crane Flat," a large meadow surrounded by the lofty forest, and adorned with brilliant flowers. Here the trail leads to the right, leaving the divide to the left, and descending into the waters of Cascade Creek and its tributaries. Ascending and descending several steep spurs and crossing several streams, we finally caught a glimpse of the everlasting walls of the Yohemity . . .

. . . The first object that attracts our attention is the Cascade of the Rainbow, descending into the valley on our right from a height of nine hundred and twenty eight feet. The water comes over the sharp granite edge of the precipice, then descending, is broken into fleecy forms, sometimes swayed hither and thither by the wayward winds; at other times the sun lights up its spray with all the colors of the rainbow, hanging like a prismatic veil from the sombre cliff. The surrounding peaks are riven into varied forms, most picturesque in their outlines, contrasting beautifully with the emerald meadows and masses of pines, cedars and oaks at their base. . . .

As we proceeded onward we were held in silent awe by the sublime proportions of "El Capitan," or the Chieftain of the Yohemity—a cliff of granite lifting its awful forms on the left to the height of three thousand one hundred feet—a sheer precipice jutting into the valley. Upon the opposite side of the valley (which is here only three-fourths of a mile in width) immense cliffs also occur, their serrated pinnacles piercing the very skies, and forming with El Capitan the colossal "Gateway of the Merced." . . .

Looking from the edge of the grove in rear of the house, we obtain a full view of the High Falls, which are the great feature of the valley as far as waterfalls are concerned. The valley is here a mile and a half in width, the river of the valley flowing near the middle, with meadows and groves upon either hand, while the cliff beyond rises to the height of three thousand feet. The water is seen flashing over the cliff at the height of two thousand five hundred feet, and at one bound reaches the granite shelf fifteen hundred feet below—hanging like a fleecy cloud from the precipice, from which dart masses of foam, gleaming like rockets in their perilous fall; gathering themselves upon the immense granite floor, the waters descend by a succession of cascades (the lower one being six hundred feet), finally reach the valley and unite with the river below. Every hour of the day varies the effect of light and shade upon the cliff, which rises with picturesque out-lines, surmounted with sentinel pines, dwindled in their majestic proportions to mere straws by the height and dis-tance, while ever and anon comes the roar of the cataract falling upon the ear, now in fitful lower tones—the lonely voice—the solitary hymn of the valley. . . .

Leaving camp, we rode up the valley some three miles, and turning to the right, crossed the broad delta where the waters of the middle and south forks unite with those of the valley. Here we tied our animals and proceeded on foot. . . . After an arduous walk, we saw the waters of the fall gleam-ing between the trees[,] and passing a huge mass of gran-ite, upon which many visitors have inscribed their names with charcoal, we reached an immense mass of granite cov-ered with moss, from which we obtained a fine view of the "Lower Falls of the Middle Fork.["]

For picturesque beauty, together with the surrounding combinations of rocks and trees, this waterfall excels; yet it is the least in height, being not more than two hundred feet perpendicular. It comes over the cliff in a broad sheer, retaining its form until lost in the pool below. Crawling along the sloping edge of the cliff, drenched with spray, we passed the falls and reached the Arch Rock beyond. Here the rocks overhang some seventy-five feet, forming a magnificent area, its recesses adorned with exquisite ferns and mosses—one of Nature's own temples, not made with hands—while the cataract below fills it with the melody of many waters. One of our companions climbed over the cliff to obtain a view of the upper cliff beyond—a feat having too much of the terri-ble for me to undertake. . . .

The general view of the Upper Falls from the shelf by which we reached them, is grand, as it embraces the surrounding peaks. Commencing at the extreme left, the South Dome rises with its bare granite columns fifteen hundred or two thousand feet above the surrounding cliffs, . . . while imme-diately to the left of the falls a peak rises bare and abrupt in the height of a thousand feet above the edge of the precipice. Above and beyond the falls the mountains are lost in the distance, their ragged outlines softened by dark masses of pines and firs, the scene altogether having a wild, Alpine grandeur, sublimely beautiful. . . .

Upon another occasion we rode down the valley some six miles, and crossing the picturesque ford where the Mariposa trail enters the valley, ascended the mountain, reaching a point on the trail some fifteen hundred feet above the river. From here the traveler obtains the most complete general view of the entire valley. Far below [lie] its green meadows and beautiful groves of oaks and pines, the river at intervals gleaming amid the forest and winding like a serpent through the valley, while the surrounding walls of granite lift their awful forms, contrasting their stern sublimity with the beauty spread at their feet. To the right descends the Cascade of the Rainbow in all its beauty, giving life and expression to the scene, while the Two Domes bound the dim distance. All, all is as Nature has made it, fresh and beautiful from the hand of the Creator.

"... so utterly incompetent to do justice to my subject."

Reverend Samuel D. Simonds or Reverend Eleazer Thomas
"The Yo-hem-i-ty Valley and Falls," 1856

On October 8, 1856, the *Country Gentleman,* a New York agricultural magazine, published a description of the Yosemite Valley. This account is considered the first extensive account of the valley published on the East Coast.

The article was reprinted from the *California Christian Advocate,* a Methodist Episcopal Church newspaper based in San Francisco since 1851. The writer of the commentary is not specified, but the editors of the *California Christian Advocate* in 1856 were Reverend Samuel D. Simonds and Reverend Eleazer Thomas, one of whom was likely the author.

The *Country Gentleman*'s description of the valley spurred public interest in Yosemite back East. In 1857 artist Thomas Ayres displayed his landscape illustrations of the valley, the earliest known drawings of Yosemite Valley, at the American Art Union in New York City. The demand for reproductions of Ayres's works was enormous. The same year, author T. Addison Richards included Yosemite Valley in his landmark *Appletons' Illustrated Hand-book of American Travel*. Richards gushed that "the scenery of this valley . . . is perhaps the most remarkable in the United States, and perhaps in the world."

The editor of the California Christian Advocate thus speaks of a visit to the Yo-hem-i-ty valley and falls. The description is graphic and interesting; if correct, as we have no reason to doubt it is, we do not see but they must rank with the most striking natural wonders on the Atlantic slope of the continent, if not as superior to many of them.

The Yo-hem-i-ty valley is located—as nearly as I can judge without a map—in the north-western part of Mariposa county. It was first discovered in 1851, by a company of soldiers in pursuit of a tribe of Indians, who having committed numerous depredations, such as driving horses and cattle, and carrying various kinds of plunder there, were followed, and about seventy including the chief, were taken captive. I was informed that the purport of the name is Grizzly Bear Valley, but a gentleman says it means High Valley. The true signification must be learned from the Indians, of whom a few remain here, but I did not see any of them.

It was visited by a party in 1854, and by several parties in 1855. Many more will go this year. I think it will ultimately become a place of great resort.

It is said to be about eight miles long, and will probably average a mile in width. Much of it produces most excellent grass, which in places grows three or four feet high.

There is a considerable quantity and variety of wild fruit; I saw strawberries, raspberries, gooseberries and currants.

It is inclosed on both sides by stupendous mountains, mostly of solid granite; their average height is estimated at 3,000 feet. The sides, in most places are a little sloping, but in some quite perpendicular, and indeed in not a few places, the top seems to project several feet. These ranges run nearly parallel, and are pretty nearly in a straight line. Besides the average height, there are many cliffs and peaks which ascend much higher, some of them, it is thought nearly 4,000 feet.

The most remarkable cliff, called *El Capitan*, is on the north-east side of the river, and can be seen very plainly from the mountain on which I stood on Thursday evening. I judge it to be about a mile long at the base, is somewhat narrow towards the top, which is 3,100 feet above the valley. The rock is solid granite, about perpendicular, and in many places as smooth as a plastered wall. Not a tree, shrub, nor spire of grass can find a place to take root on it.

The Captain—There he stands in all his glory. I almost think he could bear up the world on his shoulders. Really strange! Though it might be considered rude to gaze in any other captain's face so intently, yet I cannot help but gaze at him. What a magnificent sight.

The next most remarkable object we saw, is a peak on the other side of the river, a little farther up. This is probably 3,500 feet, and runs up to so sharp a point that I think no one could ascend within a thousand feet of the top from any place, without exposing himself to imminent danger. Should one fall over one of these precipices, there would be no possibility of stopping short of about 3,000 feet. It is frightful to contemplate such an event. Being the first minister of our denomination that ever visited this place, the privilege of naming this peak was granted to me, so I called it "the Giant Pillar [Cathedral Rock]."

Still farther up there are two cliffs, one on each side of the river, called the north and south domes. The former is a most beautiful rock, the top of which looks like a perfect dome—the part resembling which ascends probably 500 feet above the cliff which supports it, and possibly would measure a mile in circumference at the base. The south dome [Half Dome] is not so perfect, as in the lapse of time, one slab or block after another has fallen off, till about one-fourth is gone. If this were perfect they would be almost alike. This is 3,200 feet high. I have seen many steep mountains, cliffs, and peaks, both in the Atlantic states and in this, but never any thing like these; none that could begin to compare with them.

... We visited the three upper falls; the upper and highest is said to be 2,600 feet; a little below this there is another, but much smaller fall; and again below this another of about 700 feet.

The volume of water is not large, but the fall, considering its height, is one of the most remarkable natural curiosities in the world. The next fall [Nevada Fall] we visited is on the main branch of the river, and in some respects is the most noted. The chasm, through which the river passes, is about 100 feet wide; and the stream itself is about fifty feet. It falls about 300 feet. The third fall [Illilouette Fall] is on the South Fork, and is said to be 700 feet. The fourth is at the lower end of the valley—the one I saw on Thursday evening. It is called the Cascade of the Rainbow [Bridalveil Fall], because of the beautiful rainbow seen in the spray when the sun shines through it, and is 928 feet. We did not go very near to these two, but had a fine view from a distance.

They are all indescribably beautiful. It is supposed there are still others which have not yet been discovered; and besides these, there are more than half a dozen cascades which pour their limpid waters over these tremendous precipices, several of which come from the tops of some of the highest cliffs, and fall nearly perpendicular, almost 3,000 feet. The North Fork runs directly through a small lake [Mirror Lake], which in time of high water covers about two acres. Several of these streams unite at or near the head of the valley, and form the surpassingly-beautiful Merced river. I use this adjective in describing this river because it is as clear as crystal; and at this place has never been sullied by dirt from the miner's tom or rocker. There are many speckled trout, and I suppose other kinds of fish in it. Of game—there are bear, deer, squirrels, grouse, ducks, cranes, pigeons, snipe, etc. The valley is ornamented with beautiful flowers; I saw some varieties here which I think I never saw before. There are many other things worthy of note, which I have neither time nor ability to describe. I never before felt so anxious to write, and so utterly incompetent to do justice to my subject. Of all the scenery I have ever witnessed, I never saw anything so magnificent. Often, while gazing with amazement on the huge mountains and stupendous falls, I repeated the passage of Scripture:—"Great and marvelous are thy works, Lord God Almighty." Never before was I so deeply impressed with the omnipotence and wisdom of Deity.

"...5 gallons whisky..."

Hutchings' California Magazine
"The Necessaries of Life," 1859

Although a journey to Yosemite became less difficult as the nineteenth century progressed, it was never easy. Visiting Yosemite Valley and environs could take days, if not weeks, and required significant expenditures of time and money. However, the rewards upon arrival were inestimable.

In the October 1859 edition of *Hutchings' California Magazine*, editor and publisher James Mason Hutchings described the psychic compensation for the effort—the first view of Yosemite Valley: "When the inexpressible 'first impression' had been overcome and human tongues had regained the power of speech, such exclamations as the following were uttered—'Oh! now let me die, for I am happy.' 'Did mortal eyes ever behold such a scene in any other land?' 'The half had not been told us.' 'My heart is full to overflowing with emotion at the sight of so much appalling grandeur in the glorious works of God!' 'I am satisfied.' 'This sight is worth ten years of labor,' &c., &c."

Nonetheless, it took considerable sweat and frustration to reach that point. In the same issue of *Hutchings' California Magazine*, Hutchings reprinted a tongue-in-cheek sidebar from the *Mariposa Star* newspaper listing "the necessaries of life" required for a party of four to travel to Yosemite. Clearly, alcohol was a priority.

As the Yo-Semite Valley seems to be the great point of attraction to parties recreating, it may not be amiss to give, from the *Mariposa Star*, the following amusing list of provisions that four persons deemed necessary on such a trip!—

A party recently left Joe's store at Mormon Bar for the Valley, and a friend of the *Star* furnishes the following statistics—showing the amount of "the necessaries of life" which is required for an eight day's trip in the mountains:

8 lbs potatoes.

1 bottle whisky.

1 bottle pepper sauce.

1 bottle whisky.

1 box tea.

9 lbs onions.

2 bottles whisky.

1 ham.

11 lbs crackers.

1 bottle whisky.

½ doz. sardines.

2 bottles brandy, (4th proof.)

6 lbs sugar.

1 bottle brandy, (4th proof.)

7 lbs cheese.

2 bottles brandy, (4th proof.)

1 bottle pepper.

5 gallons whisky.

4 bottles whisky (old Bourbon.)

1 small keg whisky.

1 bottle of cocktails, (designed for a "starter.")

"The *fall* of the Yosemite, so called, is a humbug."

Horace Greeley

An Overland Journey from New York to San Francisco in the Summer of 1859, 1860

For most early travelers, their introduction to Yosemite Valley was a transcendent, almost religious experience, but not all visitors were enamored of the majestic valley. Case in point: Horace Greeley.

In the summer of 1859, Horace Greely, crusading reformer and editor of the nationally influential *New York Tribune*, embarked on a tour of the American West. Greeley visited developing western communities such as Denver, Salt Lake City, Sacramento, and San Francisco, as well as many spots in between. His observations were dispatched to the *New York Tribune* and were published for an eager audience. In 1860 Horace Greeley collected his impressions and published *An Overland Journey from New York to San Francisco in the Summer of 1859*. This book served as a vehicle for Greeley to promote the construction of a transcontinental railroad, but it was popular for his trenchant commentaries on the places and people he encountered.

In mid-August 1859, Horace Greeley entered Yosemite Valley. Although he came to admire Yosemite as "the most unique and majestic of nature's marvels," his original opinion was far from favorable. Greeley grumbled that the horseback journey was a "weary, interminable ride"; his toes "had sprained and swelled"; the lodging was "rude" and uncomfortable; he was so tired he could not eat; and he deprecated the "foolish names" others had given Yosemite landmarks, such as the Two Sisters (known today as Cathedral Spires), which Greeley belittled as "maladroit and lackadaisical." Horace Greeley found the waterfalls unimpressive, especially Yosemite Falls. As he readily acknowledged, he was visiting in August when the snowmelt had subsided and some falls generally fade to a trickle, but, nevertheless, he complained.

Descent into the Yosemite is only practicable at three points— one near the head of the valley, where a small stream makes in from the direction of the main ridge of the Sierra, down which there is a trail from the vicinity of Water River, Utah—a trail practicable, I believe, for men on foot only. The other two lead in near the outlet, from Mariposas and Coulterville respectively, on opposite banks of the Merced, and are practicable for sure-footed mules or horses. We, of course, made our descent by the Mariposas trail, on the south side of the little river which here escapes from the famous valley by a cañon which water alone can safely, if at all, traverse, being shut in by lofty precipices, and broken by successive falls.

My friends insisted that I should look over the brink into the profound abyss before clambering down its side; but I, apprehending giddiness, and feeling the need of steady nerves, firmly declined. So we formed line again, and moved on.

The night was clear and bright, as all summer nights in this region are; the atmosphere cool, but not really cold; the moon had risen before seven o'clock, and was shedding so much light as to bother us in our forest-path, where the shadow of a standing pine looked exceedingly like the substance of a fallen one, and many semblances were unreal and misleading. It was often hard to realize that the dark, narrow current-like passage to the left was our trail, and not the winding, broader, moonlighted-opening on the right. The safest course was to give your horse a free rein, and trust to his sagacity, or self-love for keeping the trail. As we descended by zigzags the north face of the all but perpendicular mountain our moonlight soon left us, or was present only by reflection from the opposite cliff. Soon, the trail became at once so steep, so rough, and so tortuous, that we all dismounted; but my attempt at walking proved a miserable failure. I had been riding with a bad Mexican stirrup, which barely admitted the toes of my left foot; and continual pressure on these had sprained and swelled them, so that walking was positive torture. I persevered in the attempt, till my companions insisted on my remounting, and thus floundering slowly to the bottom. By steady effort, we descended the three miles (four thousand feet perpendicular) in two hours, and stood at night by the rushing, roaring waters of the Merced.

That first full, deliberate gaze up the opposite height! can I ever forget it? The valley is here scarcely half a mile wide, while its northern wall of mainly naked, perpendicular granite is at least four thousand feet high—probably more. But the modicum of moonlight that fell into this awful gorge gave to that precipice a vagueness of outline, an indefinite vastness, a ghostly and weird spirituality. Had the mountain spoken to me in audible voice, or began to lean over with the purpose of burying me beneath its crushing mass, I should hardly have been surprised. Its whiteness, thrown into bold relief by the patches of trees or shrubs which fringed or flecked it wherever a few handfuls of its moss, slowly decomposed to earth, could contrive to hold on, continually suggested the presence of snow, which suggestion, with difficulty refuted, was at once renewed. . . .

To my dying day, I shall remember that weary, interminable ride up the valley. We had been on foot since daylight; it was now past midnight; all were nearly used up, and I in torture from over twelve hours' steady riding on the hardest trotting horse in America. Yet we pressed on, and on, through clumps of trees, and bits of forest, and patches of meadow, and over hillocks of mountain *debris*, mainly granite bowlders of every size, often nearly as round as cannon balls, forming all but perpendicular banks to the capricious torrent that brought them hither—those stupendous precipices on either side glaring down upon us all the while. How many times our heavy eyes—I mean those of my San Francisco friend and my own—were lighted up by visions of that intensely desired cabin—visions which seemed distinct and unmistakable, but, which, alas! a nearer view proved to be made up of moonlight and shadow, rock and trees, into which they faded one after another. . . .

At length the *real* cabin—one made of posts and beams and whip-sawed boards, instead of rock, and shadow, and moonshine—was reached, and we all eagerly dismounted, turning out our weary steeds into abundant grass, and stirring up the astonished landlord, who had never before received guests at that unseemingly [*sic*] hour. (It was after one A. M.). . . .

The *fall* of the Yosemite, so called, is a humbug. It is not the Merced River that makes this fall, but a mere tributary trout brook, which pitches in from the north by a barely once-broken descent of two thousand six hundred feet, while the Merced enters the valley at its eastern extremity, over falls of six hundred and two hundred and fifty feet. But a river thrice as large as the Merced, at this season, would be utterly dwarfed by all the other accessories of this prodigious chasm. Only a Mississippi or a Niagara could be adequate to their exactions. I readily concede that a hundred times the present amount of water may roll down the Yosemite Fall in the months of May and June, when the snows are melting from the central ranges of the Sierra Nevada, which bound this abyss on the east; but this would not add a fraction to the wonder of this vivid exemplification of the divine power and majesty. At present, the little stream that leaps down the Yosemite, and is all but shattered to mist by the amazing descent, looks like a tape-line let down from the cloud-capped height to measure the depth of the abyss. The

Yosemite Valley (or Gorge) is the most unique and majestic of nature's marvels, but the Yosemite Fall is of little account. Were it absent, the valley would not be perceptibly less worthy of a fatiguing visit. . . .

Perhaps the visitor who should be content with a long look into the abyss from the most convenient height, without braving the toil of a descent, would be wiser than all of us; and yet that first glance upward from the foot will long haunt me as more impressive than any look downward from the summit could be.

I shall not multiply details, nor waste paper in noting all the foolish names which foolish people have given to different peaks or turrets. Just think of two giant stone-towers, or pillars, which rise a thousand feet above the towering cliff which form their base, being styled the "Two Sisters [Cathedral Spires]!" Could anything be more maladroit and lackadaisical? "The Dome" [Half Dome] is a high, round, naked peak, which rises between the Merced and its little tributary from the inmost recesses of the Sierra Nevada already instanced, and which towers to an altitude of over five thousand feet above the waters at its base. Picture to yourself a perpendicular wall of bare granite nearly or quite one mile high! . . . I know no single wonder of nature on earth which can claim superiority over the Yosemite. Just dream yourself for one hour in a chasm nearly ten miles long, with egress, save for birds and water, but at three points, up the face of precipices from three thousand to four thousand feet high, the chasm scarcely more than a mile wide at any point, and tapering to a mere gorge, or canyon, at either end, with walls of mainly naked and perpendicular white granite, from three thousand to five thousand feet high, so that looking up to the sky from it is like looking out of an unfathomable profound—and you will have some conception of the Yosemite.

"The Lark at Heaven's Gate Sings"

5

"Sermons in Stone"

John Muir

The grandest monuments of Yosemite are the granite monoliths that dominate the valley. We all know their names—El Capitan, Half Dome, Cathedral Spires, Liberty Cap, Glacier Point, and their granitic kinfolk. When coupled with the dazzling necklace of cascades tumbling from the Yosemite Valley rim, the visual and emotional sensation is unforgettable.

Many people, however, believe that the treasured monuments should also include a human—the naturalist and conservationist John Muir. There was a universe of desire and deed in the Scottish-born, Wisconsin-raised Muir. He was a writer, naturalist, booster, botanist, glaciologist, rover, teacher, sheepherder, fruit grower, sawmill operator, inventor, husband, father, and a passionate advocate celebrating the wilderness.

Most observers would agree with the assessment of the John Muir Birthplace Trust in his hometown of Dunbar, Scotland, which states that Muir was on "a lifelong journey, both physical and spiritual, of exploration, revelation, hardship and wonder. His introduction to Yosemite Valley, California, resulted in his campaign to preserve wilderness for wilderness' sake. This led to the establishment of the world's first national park system. Today he is remembered as a pioneer of the modern conservation movement."

But the legacy of John Muir is controversial and complicated. Almost from the very second Muir emerged on the scene, he was the subject of both criticism and adulation. While many viewed him as the "Father of the National Parks" and a righteous apostle of environmental preservation whose lyrical, transcendent prose epitomized pioneering conservation beliefs in his era, nearly as many regarded John Muir in a negative light. Critics considered his enthusiastic embrace and promotion of the natural world as eccentric and harmful to commercial development. Professional geologists dismissed Muir's theories on the glacial development of Yosemite Valley as odd and downright amateurish. Denigrators noted Muir's friendships and working alliances with supporters of eugenics and white supremacy. Some commentaries on the history of environmental advocacy argue that Muir's preservation ethic, while designed to benefit society at large, plainly favored the educated and prosperous urban tourist over the working class, the poor, and people of color. Others concluded that Muir was elitist for supposedly endorsing an image of the ideal natural landscape as being largely devoid of human habitation, save for temporary visitors. Some were uncomfortable with Muir's willingness to affiliate with corporate interests, such as railroads, to foster the national parks as sanctuaries of "concocted wilderness," as the historians Robert V. Hine and John Mack Faragher have labeled the approach. And more than a few were deeply troubled by Muir's racially offensive references to Native Americans and African Americans in his journals, articles, and books.

In part, this last rebuke gained particular currency in July 2020, when Michael Brune, then executive director of the Sierra Club, the environmental organization which Muir cofounded in 1892, issued a statement that denounced Muir's "derogatory comments about Black people and Indigenous peoples . . . [that] continue to hurt and alienate Indigenous people and people of color who come into contact with the Sierra Club." Scholars have addressed John Muir's racial attitudes for decades. In most cases, historians have attributed Muir's racial characterizations to childhood imprinting from an abusive, racist father or as a product of nineteenth-century cultural norms or determined that his groundbreaking efforts to preserve the integrity of natural ecosystems outweigh and

"Sermons in Stone"

atone for any racist declarations. Many have maintained that, as Muir aged, his racial perspectives evolved into a more enlightened point of view.

John Muir defenders and detractors both have a point. Even his most ardent supporters would acknowledge that John Muir was occasionally susceptible to misjudgment and mistakes. He was a product of his nineteenth-century milieu, a world rife with blatant and casual racism and hard-hearted personal attack, and his words and actions must be placed within that context, as unpleasant as that may be. It is indisputable that John Muir used racial characterizations that are odious to present sensibilities. It is undeniable that Muir caustically attacked those who disagreed with his philosophy, lambasting them as "temple destroyers, devotees of ravaging commercialism, [who] seem to have a perfect contempt for Nature."

But even the harshest cynics would concede that Muir's incomparable writing was influential and thought-provoking. Naysayers must admit that his activism was effective, gaining the ear of the mighty and applying pressure to the levers of power.

And both sides of the equation must certainly recognize that John Muir was an equal opportunity critic. The common denominator of his annoyance was impatience with and antagonism toward those who did not share his enthusiasm for wilderness or his environmental ethic. Opponents and roadblocks were skewered regardless of class, culture, or creed.

John Muir was always forthright, but he was not an easy fellow to know. He was always a bit mysterious. Perhaps this was best expressed by his oldest daughter, Wanda. In 1939 Linnie Marsh Wolfe, in the process of writing her 1946 biography *Son of the Wilderness: The Life of John Muir*, interviewed Wanda. "If you had known him," Wanda recalled, "you would have seen only one side of him, and he had many sides. No two people—even his closest friends ever had quite the same idea of him."

John Muir is best judged by his influence and impact. Despite his flaws, Muir has inspired generations to be mindful and protective of our precious wild lands so that we may always have a place to connect with our ancient heritage and refresh our spirits. And Yosemite was always his spiritual home. For that reason alone, Muir deserves a separate section in this anthology.

In this chapter are examples of John Muir's evocative prose from the 1860s to the end of the nineteenth century. In these selections, Muir describes his first summer in the Sierra Nevada, Yosemite in the spring and winter, his astounding adventure on a frozen waterfall, and his solitary wanderings, which fostered his bonding with the vitality of the natural world.

....

"The west is flaming in gold and purple, ready
for the ceremony of the sunset, and back I go to camp
with my notes and pictures, the best of them printed
in my mind as dreams."

....

John Muir
"The Yosemite," 1869

In 1911 John Muir's *My First Summer in the Sierra* was published. Based upon Muir's original trail journals and drawings, the book recounts Muir's trek in the Sierra Nevada from June to September 1869.

First arriving in Yosemite in 1868, John Muir was hired in 1869 to supervise a flock of two thousand sheep at the headwaters of the Merced and Tuolumne Rivers, the two streams that flow into Yosemite Valley and Hetch Hetchy Valley. Muir's journal chronicles not only his experiences with the sheep but also his fascination with the Sierran flora and fauna, his adventures climbing mountains, and his reverence for the "Yosemite temple"— Yosemite Valley.

In this July 20, 1869, entry from "The Yosemite," which is chapter 5 of *My First Summer in the Sierra*, Muir attempts to describe the physical and emotional experience of the Yosemite Valley, but, as he notes, "it is easier to feel than to realize, or in any way explain Yosemite grandeur."

My First Summer in the Sierra

July 20 [,1869].—Fine calm morning; air tense and clear; not the slightest breeze astir; everything shining, the rocks with wet crystals, the plants with dew, each receiving its portion of irised dewdrops and sunshine like living creatures getting their breakfast, their dew manna coming down from the starry sky like swarms of smaller stars. How wondrous fine are the particles in showers of dew, thousands required for a single drop, growing in the dark as silently as the grass! What pains are taken to keep this wilderness in health,—showers of snow, showers of rain, showers of dew, floods of light, floods of invisible vapor, clouds, winds, all sorts of weather, interaction of plant on plant, animal on animal, etc., beyond thought! How fine Nature's methods! How deeply with beauty is beauty overlaid! the ground covered with crystals, the crystals with mosses and lichens and low-spreading grasses and flowers, these with larger plants leaf over leaf with ever-changing color and form, the broad palms of the firs outspread over these, the azure dome over all like a bell-flower, and star above star.

Yonder stands the South Dome [Half Dome], its crown high above our camp, though its base is four thousand feet below us; a most noble rock, it seems full of thought, clothed with living light, no sense of dead stone about it, all spiritualized, neither heavy looking nor light, steadfast in serene strength like a god. . . .

Sketching on the North Dome. It commands views of nearly all the valley besides a few of the high mountains. I would fain draw everything in sight,—rock, tree, and leaf. But little can I do beyond mere outlines,—marks with meanings like words, readable only to myself,—yet I sharpen my pencils and work on as if others might possibly be benefited. Whether these picture sheets are to vanish like fallen leaves or go to friends like letters, matters not much; for little can they tell to those who have not themselves seen similar wildness, and like a language have learned it. No pain here, no dull empty hours, no fear of the past, no fear of the future. These blessed mountains are so compactly filled with God's beauty, no petty personal hope or experience has room to be. Drinking this champagne water is pure pleasure, so is breathing the living air, and every movement of limbs is pleasure, while the whole body seems to feel beauty when exposed to it as it feels the camp-fire or sunshine, entering not by the eyes alone, but equally through all one's flesh like radiant heat, making a passionate ecstatic pleasure glow not explainable. One's body then seems homogeneous throughout, sound as a crystal.

Perched like a fly on this Yosemite dome, I gaze and sketch and bask, oftentimes settling down into dumb admiration without definite hope of ever learning much, yet with the longing, unresting effort that lies at the door of hope, humbly prostrate before the vast display of God's power, and eager to offer self-denial and renunciation with eternal toil to learn any lesson in the divine manuscript.

It is easier to feel than to realize, or in any way explain Yosemite grandeur. The magnitudes of the rocks and trees and streams are so delicately harmonized they are mostly hidden. Sheer precipices three thousand feet high are fringed with tall trees growing close like grass on the brow of a lowland hill, and extending along the feet of these precipices a ribbon of meadow a mile wide and seven or eight long, that seems like a strip a farmer might mow in less than a day. Waterfalls, five hundred to one or two thousand feet high, are so subordinated to the mighty cliffs over which they pour that they seem like wisps of smoke, gentle as floating clouds, though their voices fill the valley and make the rocks tremble. The mountains, too, along the eastern sky, and the domes in

"Sermons in Stone"

front of them, and the succession of smooth rounded waves between, swelling higher, higher, with dark woods in their hollows, serene in massive exuberant bulk and beauty, tend yet more to hide the grandeur of the Yosemite temple and make it appear as a subdued subordinate feature of the vast harmonious landscape. Thus every attempt to appreciate any one feature is beaten down by the overwhelming influence of all the others. And, as if this were not enough, lo! in the sky arises another mountain range with topography as rugged and substantial-looking as the one beneath it—snowy peaks and domes and shadowy Yosemite valleys—another version of the snowy Sierra, a new creation heralded by a thunder-storm. How fiercely, devoutly wild is Nature in the midst of her beauty-loving tenderness!—painting lilies, watering them, caressing them with gentle hand, going from flower to flower like a gardener while building rock mountains and cloud mountains full of lightning and rain. Gladly we run for shelter beneath an overhanging cliff and examine the reassuring ferns and mosses, gentle love tokens growing in cracks and chinks. Daisies, too, and ivesias, confiding wild children of light, too small to fear. To these one's heart goes home, and the voices of the storm become gentle. Now the sun breaks forth and fragrant steam arises. The birds are out singing on the edges of the groves. The west is flaming in gold and purple, ready for the ceremony of the sunset, and back I go to camp with my notes and pictures, the best of them printed in my mind as dreams. A fruitful day, without measured beginning or ending. A terrestrial eternity. A gift of good God.

....

"Winter has taken Yosemite, and we are snowbound."

....

"In the Yo-Semite: Holidays among the Rocks," 1872

John Muir's interests were wide-ranging but always focused on one central theme—the value and necessity of wildness. His writings often concentrated on the changing seasons and the astounding transitions of the Yosemite Valley, from snowbound to verdant to the dying gasps of autumn. Muir wrote of the winter of 1871 in an article headlined "In the Yo-Semite: Holidays among the Rocks," published March 13, 1872, in the *New York Weekly Tribune*. That was a winter, Muir observed, when the snowflakes were "steady, exhaustless, innumerable."

Yosemite Valley, January 1st, 1872. Winter has taken Yosemite, and we are snowbound. The latest leaves are shaken from the oaks and alders; the snow-laden pines, with drooping boughs, look like barbed arrows aimed at the sky, and the fern-tangles and meadows are spread with a smooth cloth of snow. . . .

The 20th of November first brought us signs of winter. Broad, fibrous arcs of white cloud, spanned the valley from wall to wall; grand, island-like masses, bred among the upper domes and brows, wavered doubtfully up and down, some of them suddenly devoured by a swoop of thirsty wind; others, waxing to grand proportions, drifted loosely and heavily about like bergs in a calm sea, or jammed and wedged themselves among spiry crests, or, drawing themselves out like woolen rolls, muffled the highest brows sometimes leaving bare summits cut off from the walls with pine tops atop, that seemed to float loose as the clouds. Tissiack [Half Dome] was compassed by a soft, furry cloud, upon which her dome seemed to repose clear and warm in yellow light. At the end of these transition days, the whole company of valley clouds were marshaled for storm; they fused close, and blended, until every seam and bay of blue sky was shut, and our temple, throughout all of its cells and halls, was smoothly full. Rain and snow fell steadily for three days, beginning November 24th, giving about four feet of snow to the valley rim. The snow line descended to the bottom of the valley on the night of November 25th, but after-rains prevented any considerable accumulation. . . .

This three days' chapter of rain was underscored by a seam

of sunshine half a day in width, beneath which darkness began to gather for a chapter of snow; heavy cloud-masses rolled down the black-washed walls, circling cathedral rocks and domes, and hiding off all the upper brows and peaks. Thin strips of sunshine slid through momentary seams that were quickly blinded out. The darkness deepened for hours, until every separating shade and line were dimmed to equal black, and all the bright air of our gulf was sponged up, and fastened windless and pulseless in universal cloud. "It's bound to snow," said a mountaineer to me, as he gazed into the heavy gloom, "bound to snow when it gathers cloud material gradual as this. We'll have a regular old-fashioned storm afore long." Scarce had he delivered himself of this meteorological prophecy, ere the beginning flakes appeared, journeying tranquilly down with waving, slow-circling gestures, easy and confident as if long familiar with the paths of sky. Before dark they accomplished a most glorious work of gentle, noiseless beauty. Twelve inches of snow fell during the night and when morning opened our temple, there was more of beauty than pen can tell—from meadow to summit, from wall to wall, every tree and bush, and sculptured rock was muffled and dazzled in downy, unbroken, undrifted snow. Transparent film-clouds hung in the open azure or draped the walls, the gray granite showing dimly through their fairy veil. This after-storm gauze is formed when vapor is made by sun-rays upon exposed portions of the wet walls, which is of higher temperature than the air with which it drifts into contact. . . .

On November 28th came one of the most picturesque snow storms I have ever seen. It was a tranquil day in Yosemite. About midday a close-grained cloud grew in the middle of the valley, blurring the sun; but rocks and trees continued to caste [sic] shadow. In a few hours the cloud-ceiling deepened and gave birth to a rank down-growth of silky streamers. These cloud-weeds were most luxuriant about the Cathedral Rocks, completely hiding all their summits. Then heavier masses, hairy outside with a dark nucleus, appeared, and foundered almost to the ground. Toward night all cloud and rock distinctions were blended out, rock after rock disappeared, El Capitan, the Domes and the Sentinel, and all the brows about Yosemite Falls were wiped out, and the whole valley was filled with equal, seamless gloom. There was no wind and every rock and tree and grass blade had a hushed, expectant air. The fullness of time arrived, and down came the big flakes in tufted companies of full grown flowers. Not jostling and rustling like autumn leaves or blossom showers of an orchard whose castaway flakes are hushed into any hollow for a grave, but they journeyed down with gestures of confident life, alighting upon predestined places on rock and leaf, like flocks of linnets or showers of summer flies. Steady, exhaustless, innumerable. The trees, and bushes, and dead brown grass were flowered far beyond summer, bowed down in blossom and all the rocks were buried. Every peak and dome, every niche and tablet had their share of snow. And blessed are the eyes that beheld morning open the glory of that one dead storm. In vain did I search for some special separate mass of beauty on which to rest my gaze. No island appeared throughout the whole gulf of the beauty. The glorious crystal sediment was everywhere. From wall to wall of our beautiful temple, from meadow to sky was one finished unit of beauty, one star of equal ray, one glowing sun, weighed in the celestial balances and found perfect.

....

"Now is the birth-time of leaves; the pines are retassled,
and the oaks are sprayed with young purple.
Spring is fully committed."

....

"Yosemite in Spring," 1872

The arrival of spring in the Yosemite Valley was always an exciting moment for John Muir. The emergence of the new or sleeping flora and fauna, the rush of swollen waterfalls, and the symbolism of rebirth and renewal was thrilling to the Scottish naturalist. In July 1872 Muir wrote "Yosemite in Spring" for the *New York Tribune*. In addition to his account of the hopeful blossoming of a new season, Muir described a powerful and ominous earthquake cluster that shook the valley. For weeks, he declared, Yosemite Valley was "atremble" with "subterranean thunders."

Yosemite Valley, May 7th, 1872. . . . This Yosemite portion of the Sierra Nevada mountains still yields supple compliance to the time and rhyme of earthquakes, and most of our one-score-and-ten inhabitants are over-satisfied with their uncountable abundance, and at every new burst of shockwaves, and subterranean thunders, declare that it is "full time them goings on down there were lettin' up," for though founded on a rock, some of us consider our houses insecure, and fear they sink fast by our native shore. Since the severe opening shocks of March 26th, the valley has not been calm for a single day. About the middle of April the earthquakes and rumblings became so gentle that they were found only by those who sought for them, and it was generally believed among us that our rocking domes were about to return to trustworthy solidity and fixedness, but a few days ago they were all atremble again. . . .

We have all become philosophers, deep thinkers. Instead of wasting breath when we meet on the green of meadows or brightness of the sky, we salute by great shakes, solemnly comparing numbers and intensities. What care we for the surface of things. Our thoughts go far below to the underground country where roll the strange thunders, and the waves to which our mountains are a liquid ocean and a sky. Half believing, we paint hypothetic landscapes of the earth beneath, volcanic fountains, lakes, and seas of molten rock fed by a thousand glowing rivers. Amazons of gurgling, rippling fire flowing in beveled valleys, or deep Yosemite cañons, with a glare of red falls and cascades, with which our upper valley, in all its glory, will not compare. . . .

Now is the birth-time of leaves; the pines are retassled,

and the oaks are sprayed with young purple. Spring is fully committed. Ferns are a foot high, willows are letting fly drifts of ripe seeds. Balm of Gilead poplars, after weeks of caution, have launched their buds full of red and leaves of tender glossy yellow. Cherries, honeysuckles, violets, bluets, buttercups, larkspurs, gilias, are full of bloom of leaf and flower. Plant-odor fills the valley in light floating clouds and mists; it covers the ground and trees, the chaparral and tabled rocks, coming in small flakes from the impartial snow. Standing on the smooth, plushed meadows, bossed here and there with willows, and browned along the edge with dead ferns, the yellow spray of white-stemmed poplars is seen against the purple of oaks and the high green groves of pine, back of which rise purple and gray-rock walls fringed with glossy green live-oak, spotted with the yellow and orange of mistle-toe. The scents and sounds and forms of Yosemite spring-time are as exquisitely compounded as her colors. . . . The abundant snows of our compassing mountains are freely melted into flooded streams. Beside the five principal falls of the valley—Pohono [Bridalveil Fall], Illouette [Illilouette], Vernal, Nevada and Yosemite—there are at present fed from the universal snows a large number of smaller cascades and falls, which come down on steps from a few feet to thousands of feet in height. The best known of these are the Big and Lit-tle Sentinel [Sentinel Falls], Cascades, the Bachelor's Tears, and the Virgin's Tears [Ribbon Fall]—magnificent weepers both of them. El Capitan is softened with a most graceful lit-tle stream that steals confidingly over his massive brow in a clear fall of more than a thousand feet. Seen at the right time the whole breadth of this fall is irised almost from top to bottom. But of all the white outgush of Yosemite waters, the Upper Yosemite Fall is the greatest. . . .

Seen from up the valley . . . a cross-section five or six hun-dred feet in length is most gorgeously irised throughout—not as a motionless arc, but as a living portion of the fall with ordinary forms and motions of shooting rockets and whirling sprays of endless variety of texture transformed to the sub-

"Sermons in Stone"

stance of rainbow melted and flowing. At this Upper Yosemite Fall, and also at the Middle Yosemite Fall, magnificent lunar bows may be found for half a dozen nights in the months of April, May, June, and sometimes July. If the weather continues sunful, the falls will speedily attain to highest development. . . . Tourists will find no difficulty procuring bread and smiles—bread at three dollars a day smiles free—both articles in abundance, and excellent in quality.

"I concluded not to attempt to go nearer, but did, nevertheless, against reasonable judgment."

"The Treasures of the Yosemite," 1890

As years passed and John Muir grew more celebrated and influential, his writings became a mixture of elegant nature writing, personal reminiscence, and advocacy.

By the late 1880s, Muir was greatly concerned about the impact in Yosemite of meadow overgrazing, sequoia harvesting, and the general commercial exploitation and overuse of the Yosemite Valley. He convinced prominent political, economic, and cultural leaders to support his blueprint for placing the region surrounding Yosemite Valley under federal protection. An important ally was Robert Underwood Johnson, editor of the *Century Magazine*. Muir and Johnson were convinced that, unless there was immediate action, Yosemite's natural and spiritual resources would continue to be abused beyond any hope of renewal.

As legislation was being considered in the U.S. Congress to incorporate the peaks, meadows, lakes, and ecosystem of the Yosemite high country into a national park, Muir wrote two persuasive articles on Yosemite for the *Century Magazine* extolling the beauty and value of a future Yosemite National Park. One of these articles was "The Treasures of the Yosemite," published in August 1890. The commentary was a combination of lobbying and Muir's revisiting of his experiences in Yosemite Valley.

When "The Treasures of the Yosemite" was published, it generated a national response. Public support for federal protection of the Yosemite region grew. On September 30, 1890, Representative Lewis E. Payson, a Republican from Illinois, introduced H.R. 12187. The bill was entitled "An Act to Set Apart a Certain Tract of Land in the State of California as a Forest Reservation." The legislation would grant exclusive jurisdiction over the area to the secretary of the interior, essentially establishing a national park. The State of California would still retain control over the Yosemite Valley and Mariposa Grove. The act was passed by both houses of Congress on the day it was introduced and signed into law the next day, October 1, 1890, by President Benjamin Harrison.

In this passage from "The Treasures of the Yosemite," Muir expresses his awe at the splendor and strength of Yosemite Falls and recalls his harrowing attempt to examine an ice cliff at the falls.

All the wide, fan-shaped upper portion of the basin is covered with a network of small rills that go cheerily on their way to their grand fall in the valley, now flowing on smooth pavements in sheets thin as glass, now diving under willows and laving their red roots, oozing through bogs, making tiny falls and cascades, whirling and dancing, calming again, gliding through bits of smooth glacier meadows with sod of Alpine agrostis mixed with blue and white violets and daisies, breaking, tossing among rough boulders and fallen trees, flowing together until, all united, they go to their fate with stately, tranquil air like a full-grown river.... The total descent made by the stream from its highest sources to its confluence with the Merced in the valley is about 6000 feet, while the distance is only about ten miles, an average fall of 600 feet per mile. The last mile of its course lies between the sides of sunken domes and swelling folds of the granite that are clustered and pressed together like a mass of bossy cumulus clouds. Through this shining way Yosemite Creek goes to its fate, swaying and swirling with easy, graceful gestures and singing the last of its mountain songs before it reaches the dizzy edge of Yosemite to fall 2600 feet into another world, where climates[,] vegetation, inhabitants, all are different. Emerging from this last cañon the stream glides, in flat, lace-like folds, down a smooth incline into a small pool where it seems to rest and compose itself before taking the grand plunge. Then calmly, as if leaving a lake, it slips over the polished lip of the pool down another incline and out over the brow of the precipice in a magnificent curve thick sown with rainbow spray. . . .

To me it seemed nerve-trying to slip to this narrow foot-hold and poise on the edge of such a precipice so close to the confusing whirl of the waters; and after casting longing glances over the shining brow of the fall and listening to its sublime psalm, I concluded not to attempt to go nearer, but did, nevertheless, against reasonable judgment. Noticing some tufts of artemisia in a cleft of rock, I filled my mouth with the leaves, hoping their bitter taste might help to keep caution keen and prevent giddiness; then I reached the lit-tle ledge, got my heels well set, and worked side-wise twenty or thirty feet to a point close to the out-plunging current. Here the view is perfectly free down into the heart of the bright irised throng of comet-like streams into which the whole ponderous volume of the fall separates a little below the brow. So glorious a display of pure wildness, acting at close range while one is cut off from all the world beside, is terribly impressive.

About forty yards to the eastward of the Yosemite Fall on a fissured portion of the edge of the cliff a less nerve-trying view may be obtained, extending all the way down to the bottom from a point about two hundred feet below the brow of the fall, where the current, striking a narrow ledge, bounds out in the characteristic comet-shaped masses. Seen from here towards noon, in the spring, the rainbow on its brow seems to be broken up and mingled with the rushing comets until all the fall is stained with iris colors, leaving no white water visible. This is the best of the safe views from above, the huge steadfast rocks, the flying waters, and the rainbow light forming one of the most glorious pictures conceivable.

The Yosemite Fall is separated into an upper and a lower fall with a series of falls and cascades between them, but when viewed in front from the bottom of the valley they all appear as one. . . .

A wild scene, but not a safe one, is made by the moon as it appears through the edge of the Yosemite Fall when one is behind it. Once after enjoying the night-song of the waters, and watching the formation of the colored bow as the moon came round the domes and sent her beams into the wild uproar, I ventured out on the narrow bench that extends back of the fall from Fern Ledge and began to admire the dim-veiled grandeur of the view. I could see the fine gauzy threads of the outer tissue by having the light in front; and wishing to look at the moon through the meshes of some of the denser portions of the fall, I ventured to creep farther behind it while it was gently wind-swayed, without taking sufficient thought about the consequences of its swaying back to its natural position after the wind pressure should be removed. The effect was enchanting. Fine, savage music sounded above, beneath, around me; while the moon, apparently in the very midst of the rushing waters, seemed to be struggling to keep her place, on account of the ever-varying form and density of the water masses through which she was seen, now darkened by a rush of thick-headed comets, now flashing out through openings between them. I was in fairyland between the dark wall and the wild throng of illumined waters, but suffered sudden disenchantment. . . . Down came a dash of spent comets, thin and harmless-looking in the distance, but desperately solid and stony in striking one's shoulders. It seemed like a mixture of choking spray and gravel. Instinctively dropping on my knees, I laid hold of an angle of the rock, rolled myself together with my face pressed against my breast, and in this attitude submitted as best I could to my thundering baptism. The heavier masses seemed to strike like cobblestones, and there was a confused noise of many waters about my ears—hissing, gurgling, clashing sounds that were not heard as music. The situation was easily realized. How fast one's thoughts burn at such times! I was weighing the chances of escape. Would the column be swayed a few inches away from the wall, or would it come yet closer? The fall was in flood, and not so lightly would its ponderous mass be swayed. My fate seemed to depend on a breath of the "idle wind." It was moved gently forward, the pounding ceased, and I once more revisited the glimpses of the moon. But fearing I might be caught at a disadvantage in making too hasty a retreat, I moved only a few feet along the bench to where a block of ice lay. Between the ice and the wall I wedged myself, and lay face downwards until the steadiness of the light gave encouragement to get away. Somewhat nerve-shaken, drenched, and benumbed, I made out to build a fire, warmed myself, ran home to avoid taking cold, reached my cabin before daylight, got an hour or two of sleep, and awoke sane and comfortable, better, not worse, for my wild bath in moonlit spray. . . .

Throughout the winter months the spray of the upper Yosemite Fall is frozen while falling thinly exposed and is deposited around the base of the fall in the form of a hollow truncated cone, which sometimes reaches a height of five hundred feet or more, into the heart of which the whole volume of the fall descends with a tremendous roar as if pouring down the throat of a crater. In the building of this ice-cone part of the frozen spray falls directly to its place, but a considerable portion is first frozen upon the face of the cliff on both sides of the fall, and attains a thickness of a foot or more during the night. When the sun strikes this ice-coating it is expanded and cracked off in masses weighing from a few pounds to several tons, and is built into the walls of the cone; while in windy, frosty weather, when the fall is swayed from side to side, the cone is well drenched, and the loose ice-masses and dust are all firmly frozen together. The thundering, reverberating reports of the falling ice-masses are like those of heavy cannon. They usually occur at intervals of a few minutes, and are the most strikingly characteristic of the winter sounds of the valley, and constant accompaniments of the best sunshine. While this stormy building is in progress the surface of the cone is smooth and pure white, the whole presenting the appearance of a beautiful crystal hill wreathed with folds of spray which are oftentimes irised. But when it is wasting and breaking up in the spring its surface is strewn with leaves, pine branches, stones, sand, etc., that have been brought over the fall, making it look like a heap of avalanche detritus.

After being engulfed and churned in the stormy interior of the crater the waters of the fall issue from arched openings at the base, seemingly scourged and weary and glad to escape, while belching spray spouted up out of the throat past the descending current is wafted away in irised drifts to the rocks and groves.

Anxious to learn what I could about the structure of this curious ice-hill, I tried to climb it, carrying an ax to cut footsteps. Before I had reached the base of it I was met by a current of spray and wind that made breathing difficult. I pushed on backward, however, and soon gained the slope of the hill, where by creeping close to the surface most of the blast was avoided. Thus I made my way nearly to the summit, halting at times to peer up through the wild whirls of spray, or to listen to the sublime thunder beneath me, the whole hill sounding as if it were a huge, bellowing, exploding drum. I hoped that by waiting until the fall was blown aslant I should be able to climb to the lip of the crater and get a view of the interior; but a suffocating blast, half air, half water, followed by the fall of an enormous mass of ice from the wall, quickly discouraged me. The whole cone was jarred by the blow, and I was afraid its side might fall in. Some fragments of the mass sped past me dangerously near; so I beat a hasty retreat, chilled and drenched, and laid myself on a sunny rock in a safe place to dry.

"A Near View of the High Sierra," 1894

An outgrowth of John Muir's formidable 1890 articles for the *Century Magazine* was not only the establishment of Yosemite National Park but also the public's hunger for more Muir writings. In 1894 the Century Company, under the direction of *Century Magazine* editor Robert Underwood Johnson, published *The Mountains of California*, John Muir's observations on the flora, fauna, and aesthetics of California's mountains, with a special focus on the Sierra Nevada and Yosemite.

In this excerpt from the chapter "A Near View of the High Sierra," Muir recalls an 1870s outing with two artists in search of "a landscape suitable for a large painting" in the backcountry of Yosemite. Muir describes his delight in shepherding the first excursion of these two novices into the wilderness, their "feasting" on the view, and Muir's decision to leave them for three days to climb nearby Mount Ritter, a 13,149-foot peak just outside Yosemite's southeast boundary.

Muir begins by recounting his 19-mile hike from Mount Lyell, at 13,115 feet the highest peak within the Yosemite National Park borders, to Yosemite Valley, where he encounters the artists.

On the head waters of the Tuolumne, is a group of wild peaks on which the geologist may say that the sun has but just begun to shine, which is yet in a high degree picturesque, and in its main features so regular and evenly balanced as almost to appear conventional—one somber cluster of snow-laden peaks with gray pinefringed granite bosses braided around its base, the whole surging free into the sky from the head of a magnificent valley, whose lofty walls are beveled away on both sides so as to embrace it all without admitting anything not strictly belonging to it. The foreground was now aflame with autumn colors, brown and purple and gold, ripe in the mellow sunshine; contrasting brightly with the deep, cobalt blue of the sky, and the black and gray, and pure, spiritual white of the rocks and glaciers. Down through the midst, the young Tuolumne was seen pouring from its crystal fountains, now resting in glassy pools as if changing back again into ice, now leaping in white cascades as if turning to snow; gliding right and left between granite bosses, then sweeping on through the smooth, meadowy levels of the valley, swaying pensively from side to side with calm, stately gestures past dipping willows and sedges, and around groves of arrowy pine; and throughout its whole eventful course, whether flowing fast or slow, singing loud or low, ever filling the landscape with spiritual animation, and manifesting the grandeur of its sources in every movement and tone.

Pursuing my lonely way down the valley, I turned again and again to gaze on the glorious picture, throwing up my arms to inclose it as in a frame. After long ages of growth in the darkness beneath the glaciers, through sunshine and storms, it seemed now to be ready and waiting for the elected artist, like yellow wheat for the reaper; and I could not help wishing that I might carry colors and brushes with me on my travels, and learn to paint. In the mean time I had to be content with photographs on my mind and sketches in my note-books. At length, after I had rounded a precipitous headland that puts out from the west wall of the valley, every peak vanished from sight, and I pushed rapidly along the frozen meadows, over the divide between the waters of the Merced and Tuolumne, and down through the forests that clothe the slopes of Cloud's Rest, arriving in Yosemite in due time—which, with me, is *any* time. And, strange to say, among the first people I met here were two artists who, with letters of introduction, were awaiting my return. They inquired whether in the course of my explorations in the adjacent mountains I had ever come upon a landscape suitable for a large painting; whereupon I began a description of the one that had so lately excited my admiration. Then, as I went on further and further into details, their faces began to glow, and I offered to guide them to it, while they declared that they would gladly follow, far or near, whithersoever I could spare the time to lead them. . . .

I led them out of the valley by the Vernal and Nevada Falls, thence over the main dividing ridge to the Big Tuolumne Meadows, by the old Mono trail, and thence along the upper Tuolumne River to its head. This was my companions' first excursion into the High Sierra, and as I was almost always alone in my mountaineering, the way that the fresh beauty was reflected in their faces made for me a novel and interesting study. They naturally were affected most of all by the colors—the intense azure of the sky, the purplish grays of the granite, the red and browns of dry meadows, and the translucent purple and crimson of huckleberry bogs; the flaming yellow of aspen groves, the silvery flashing of the streams, and the bright green and blue of the glacier lakes. . . .

After feasting awhile on the view, I proceeded to make camp in a sheltered grove a little way back from the meadow, where pine-boughs could be obtained for beds, and where there was plenty of dry wood for fires, while the artists ran here and there, along the river-bends and up the sides of the cañon, choosing foregrounds for sketches. After dark, when our tea was made and a rousing fire had been built, we began to make our plans. They decided to remain several days, at the least, while I concluded to make an excursion in the mean time to the untouched summit of [Mount] Ritter. . . .

Next morning, the artists went heartily to their work and I to mine. Former experiences had given good reason to know that passionate storms, invisible as yet, might be brooding in the calm sun-gold; therefore, before bidding farewell, I warned the artists not to be alarmed should I fail to appear before a week or ten days, and advised them, in case a snow-storm should set in, to keep up big fires and shelter themselves as best they could, and on no account to become frightened and attempt to seek their way back to Yosemite alone through the drifts. . . .

All my first day was pure pleasure; simply mountaineering indulgence, crossing the dry pathways of the ancient glaciers, tracing happy streams, and learning the habits of the birds and marmots in the groves and rocks. Before I had gone a mile from camp, I came to the foot of a white cascade that beats its way down a rugged gorge in the cañon wall, from a height of about nine hundred feet, and pours its throbbing waters into the Tuolumne. I was acquainted with its fountains, which, fortunately, lay in my course. What a fine traveling companion it proved to be, what songs it sang, and how passionately it told the mountain's own joy! Gladly I climbed along its dashing border, absorbing its divine music, and bathing from time to time in waftings of irised spray. Climbing higher, higher, new beauty came streaming on the sight: painted meadows, late-blooming gardens, peaks of rare architecture, lakes here and there, shining like silver, and glimpses of the forested middle region and the yellow lowlands far in the west. . . .

In these bits of leafiness a few birds find grateful homes. Having no acquaintance with man, they fear no ill, and flock curiously about the stranger, almost allowing themselves to be taken in the hand. In so wild and so beautiful a region was spent my first day, every sight and sound inspiring, leading one far out of himself, yet feeding and building up his individuality.

Now came the solemn, silent evening. Long, blue, spiky shadows crept out across the snow-fields, while a rosy glow, at first scarce discernible, gradually deepened and suffused every mountain-top, flushing the glaciers and the harsh crags above them. This was the alpenglow, to me one of the most impressive of all the terrestrial manifestations of God. At the touch of this divine light, the mountains seemed to kindle to a rapt, religious consciousness, and stood hushed and waiting like devout worshipers. Just before the alpenglow began to fade, two crimson clouds came streaming across the summit like wings of flame, rendering the sublime scene yet more impressive; then came darkness and the stars. . . .

The dawn in the dry, wavering air of the desert was glorious. Everything encouraged my undertaking and betokened success. There was no cloud in the sky, no storm-tone in the wind. Breakfast of bread and tea was soon made. I fastened a hard, durable crust to my belt by way of provision, in case I should be compelled to pass a night on the mountain-top; then, securing the remainder of my little stock against wolves and wood-rats, I set forth free and hopeful.

How glorious a greeting the sun gives the mountains! To behold this alone is worth the pains of any excursion a thousand times over. The highest peaks burned like islands in a sea of liquid shade. Then the lower peaks and spires caught the glow, and long lances of light, streaming through many a notch and pass, fell thick on the frozen meadows. The majestic form of Ritter was full in sight, and I pushed rapidly on over rounded rock-bosses and pavements, my iron-shod shoes making a clanking sound, suddenly hushed now and then in rugs of bryanthus, and sedgy lake-margins soft as moss. Here, too, in this so-called "land of desolation," I met cassiope, growing in fringes among the battered rocks. Her blossoms had faded long ago, but they were still clinging with happy memories to the evergreen sprays, and still so beautiful as to thrill every fiber of one's being. Winter and summer, you may hear her voice, the low, sweet melody of her purple bells. No evangel among all the mountain plants speaks Nature's love more plainly than cassiope. Where she dwells, the redemption of the coldest solitude is complete. The very rocks and glaciers seem to feel her presence, and become imbued with her own fountain sweetness. All things were warming and awakening. Frozen rills began to flow, the marmots came out of their nests in boulder-piles and climbed sunny rocks to bask, and the dun-headed sparrows were flitting about seeking their breakfasts. The lakes seen from every ridge-top were brilliantly rippled and spangled, shimmering like the thickets of the low Dwarf Pines. The rocks, too, seemed responsive to the vital heat—rock-crystals and snow-crystals thrilling alike. I strode on exhilarated, as if never more to feel fatigue, limbs moving of themselves, every sense unfolding like the thawing flowers, to take part in the new day harmony.

1. Overhanging Rock at Glacier Point was a favorite location for photographs. The figure nonchalantly taking in the view is John Muir. From the stereograph *Hanging Rock. Glacier Pt {Yosemite Falls}, [no.] 60 [graphic]*, unknown photographer, ca. 1900. Courtesy of the California History Room, California State Library, Sacramento, "Journey of John Muir," ID: Hanging Rock, Stereo-3005.

2. The Hutchings House Hotel, in the shadow of the towering Sentinel Rock. From the stereograph *Sentinal [sic] Rock*, Martin Mason Hazeltine, artist and publisher, ca. 1876–78. Courtesy of the California History Room, California State Library, Sacramento, ID: Hutchings Hotel and Sentinel Rock, Stereo-3981.

3. (*opposite top*) The Wawona Hotel, near the Mariposa Grove. *Wawona Hotel, Yosemite National Park*, unknown artist, ca. 1900. Courtesy of the California History Room, California State Library, Sacramento, ID: Wawona Hotel 2014-0700.

4. (*opposite bottom*) The Stoneman House Hotel, named for Major General George Stoneman, quartermaster of the Mormon Battalion and a Civil War cavalry officer. The Stoneman House stood in the Yosemite Valley from 1887 until 1896, when it was destroyed by fire. *Stoneman House, Yosemite Valley #3983*, photograph by Isaiah West Taber, ca. 1890. Courtesy of the California History Room, California State Library, Sacramento, ID: Stoneman House 2008-0059.

5. Leidig's Hotel. Built by George F. Leidig in 1869, Leidig's Hotel stood in the Yosemite Valley until 1888, when it was demolished following the completion of the nearby Stoneman House. *Laddeig's [sic] Hotel*, from a stereograph by John P. Soule, ca. 1870. Library of Congress, Prints and Photographs Division, Washington DC [LC-DIG-stereo-1s01121].

6. (*opposite*) The Wawona Tree. The tunnel through this giant sequoia was cut in 1881 by the Yosemite Stage and Turnpike Company as a tourist attraction. The tree fell in 1969 under a massive load of snow. *Wawona, diam. 30 ft., Mariposa Grove, #376*, photograph by George Fiske, ca. 1885. Found in *Fiske's Photographs of Yosemite and Big Trees—Summer and Winter*, page 30. Courtesy of the California History Room, California State Library, Sacramento, ID: Wawona 2010-6371.

7. (*opposite top*) Visitors relaxing on the porch of La Casa Nevada, a Yosemite Valley hotel operated by Albert and Emily Snow until the early 1890s. Thundering in the background is Nevada Fall. *Snow's Hotel and Nevada Fall, Yosemite Valley, Cal. No. 288*, from a stereograph published by John James Reilly, ca. 1885. Courtesy of the California History Room, California State Library, Sacramento, ID: Yosemite, Stereo Collection, Reilly, J. J.: No. 2—Stereo-0903.

8. (*opposite bottom*) Early camping in Yosemite was often a group affair, requiring much planning and myriad supplies. Frequently visitors brought such items as brass beds, bookcases, and kegs of whiskey. From "Harringtons' Yosemite Camping Party Photographs, 1901 [18 views]," photograph by George Clifford Matthews, 1901. Courtesy of the California History Room, California State Library, Sacramento, ID: Camping cao759.

9. (*above*) A campground at the base of Yosemite Falls, ca. 1900. From "Harringtons' Yosemite Camping Party Photographs, 1901 [18 views]," photograph by George Clifford Matthews, 1901. Courtesy of the California History Room, California State Library, Sacramento, ID: Camping cao760.

10. Until the early twentieth century, the only means by which to visit and travel in Yosemite were by foot, in a wagon or stagecoach, or by horse or mule. From the stereograph *South Dome and Clouds' Rest, Rising One Mile above the Valley, Yosemite, California, U.S.A.*, published by Strohmeyer and Wyman, ca. 1894. Courtesy of the California History Room, California State Library, Sacramento, ID: South Dome and Clouds' Rest—Stereo-4137.

11. From the beginnings of nineteenth-century Yosemite tourism, women were regular visitors. The demands of the journey and the rustic nature of the outing afforded women opportunities for personal freedom and independence not commonly available. From the stereograph *Yosemite Falls from Glacier Point Trail, California, U.S.A.*, published by Strohmeyer and Wyman, ca. 1894. Courtesy of the California History Room, California State Library, Sacramento, ID: Yosemite Falls from Glacier Point Trail—Stereo-4135.

12. A family portrait of Yosemite Valley Native Americans, ca. 1875. Gustav Fagersteen, artist and publisher, from the stereograph *American Indians, Portrait*, ca. 1875. Courtesy of the California History Room, California State Library, Sacramento, ID: American Indians, Portrait—Stereo-2530.

Ma-ha-la of the Yosemite Band.

13. Ma-ha-la may have been the name of the woman pictured, and like other
Native Americans of Yosemite, she surely felt the negative impacts of the
arrival of the Euro-American culture in the nineteenth century. Through
violence and subjugation, Yosemite Indians saw their numbers and influence
wane. *Ma-ha-la of the Yosemite Band, 271*, photograph by George Fiske, ca.
1885. Found in *Fiske's Photographs of Yosemite and Big Trees—Summer and
Winter*, page 8. Courtesy of the California History Room, California State
Library, Sacramento, ID: Ma-ha-la 2010-6328.

14. (*opposite*) A favored setting for Yosemite photographers in the nineteenth century was Overhanging Rock at Glacier Point. Subjects crept out to the edge of the granite table despite the daunting realization that from the edge of the rock to the Yosemite Valley floor was a precipitous drop of three thousand feet. *Overhanging Rock at Glacier Pt., 3200 ft., 287*, photograph attributed to George Fiske, ca. 1895. Courtesy of the California History Room, California State Library, Sacramento, ID: Photo: Yosemite Valley: Glacier Point, 2015-1149.

15. (*above*) George Anderson, shown here perched on the rim of Half Dome, became the first known human to scale the great granite knob, achieving that feat in 1875. *Yosemite Valley, View from the Rim of Half Dome*, photograph attributed to Alfred Judkins Perkins, ca. 1880. Image shows negative deterioration. Courtesy of the California History Room, California State Library, Sacramento, ID: Photo: Yosemite Valley 2008-0053.

16. (*opposite top*) The Yosemite Valley from the Mariposa Trail in 1865. This image is from a so-called "Mammoth Print." When printed, this photograph measured seventeen by twenty-one inches. *From the Mariposa Trail*, photograph attributed to Carleton Watkins, ca. 1865. Courtesy of the California History Room, California State Library, Sacramento, ID: View 1—Yosemite Valley—2010-0587.

17. (*opposite bottom*) Vernal Fall and Liberty Cap in 1870. Vernal Fall was named by Lafayette Bunnell of the Mariposa Battalion in 1851. The waterfall's Native name was Yan-o-pah. *Vernal Fall (350 feet high) and Cap of Liberty, 4600 feet above the Valley, #1212*, from a stereograph published by John P. Soule, ca. 1870. Courtesy of the California History Room, California State Library, Sacramento, ID: Vernal Fall—Stereo 4122.

18. (*above*) Although accessible only about half the year, Glacier Point was a preferred spot from which to view the majestic Yosemite Valley. In this image, a band of 1880s sightseers drink in the spectacular panorama of Half Dome, Liberty Cap, Vernal Fall, and Nevada Fall. *Vernal and Nevada Falls from Glacier Point*, photograph by Isaiah West (I. W.) Taber, ca. 1880. Plate in the album California Views, page 36. Courtesy of the California History Room, California State Library, Sacramento, ID: Glacier Point—2009-1296.

19. The most famous resident, interpreter, and enthusiastic advocate for Yosemite Valley and Yosemite National Park was John Muir. In this evocative photograph from 1900, Muir contemplates his beloved valley from Artist Point. From the stereograph *View from Artists Pt., Yosemite Valley, [no.] 30 [graphic]*, unknown photographer, ca. 1900. Courtesy of the California History Room, California State Library, Sacramento, "Journey of John Muir," ID: Artists Point—Stereo 2991.

20. James Lamon's cabin in Yosemite Valley. Lamon is considered the first nonindigenous permanent resident in Yosemite Valley. Arriving in the early 1860s, Lamon was a farmer who provided fruit, vegetables, and hay for visitors to the valley. *Lamon's Cabin,* from a stereograph by John Soule, ca. 1870. Library of Congress, Prints and Photographs Division, Washington DC [LC-DIG-stereo-1s01104].

21. John Conness, U.S. senator from California (1863–69) and author of the Yosemite Valley Grant Act of 1864. *John Conness*, photograph by Matthew Brady, ca. 1865. From the Brady-Handy Photograph Collection, 1855–65, Library of Congress, Prints and Photographs Division, Washington DC [LC-DIG-cwpbh-01372].

22. El Capitan, the great granite monolith of the Yosemite Valley. *El Capitan, reflected 3,300 feet,* photograph attributed to Isaiah West (I. W.) Taber, ca. 1880. Plate in the album California Views, page 8. Courtesy of the California History Room, California State Library, Sacramento, ID: El Capitan—001393478.

23. Nevada Fall on the Merced River plunges 594 dramatic feet to the Yosemite Valley floor. The local Miwok called the waterfall Yo-wy-we, which translates as "squirming waterfall." In this photograph from 1900, the figure second from the left is John Muir. From the stereograph *Nevada Falls Y.V. 617 ft., [no.] 52 [graphic]*, unknown photographer, ca. 1900. Courtesy of the California History Room, California State Library, Sacramento, "Journey of John Muir," ID: Nevada Falls—Stereo 3000.

24. Galen Clark and George Fiske. Clark (*left*) was named the first official "Guardian of the Mariposa Grove," a position he held for more than thirty years. Fiske (*right*) was an early and prominent photographer in Yosemite. *Galen Clark and George Fiske*, photograph by Arthur C. Pillsbury, published by Velox, ca. 1897. Courtesy of the California History Room, California State Library, Sacramento, ID: Galen Clark and George Fiske—2008-0041.

25. James Mason Hutchings was the greatest promoter of the Yosemite Valley as a tourist attraction that ever lived. *J.M. Hutchings of Yo Semite*, photograph published by Isaiah West (I. W.) Taber, ca. 1890. Courtesy of the California History Room, California State Library, Sacramento, ID: J. M. Hutchings of Yo Semite—2008-0047.

26. Members of the California State Geological Survey, 1863. *Left to right:*
Chester Averill, William M. Gabb, William Ashburner, Josiah Whitney,
C. F. (Charles Frederick) Hoffman, Clarence King, and William Brewer.
The Immortal Few, photograph by Silas Selleck, ca. 1863. Courtesy of the
California History Room, California State Library, Sacramento,
ID: California State Geological Survey—1990-1757.

27. In the summer of 1859,
the famous newspaper
publisher Horace Greeley
took a journey from New
York to San Francisco.
On his itinerary was
Yosemite Valley. Greeley
found some aspects of
Yosemite underwhelming.
*Horace Greeley [between
1855 and 1865],* from the
Brady-Handy Photograph
Collection, 1855–65,
Library of Congress, Prints
and Photographs Division,
Washington DC [LC-
BH82-23 A—cwpbh 00704.]
Image shows negative
deterioration.

28. Joseph LeConte (*center, standing*) was a physician, geologist, conservationist, and a professor at the University of California, Berkeley. He was an ardent proponent of Yosemite, which he first visited in 1870 with his students (shown here). *Great Yosemite Fall, 2634 Feet High.* Courtesy of the California History Room, California State Library, Sacramento, ID: Great Yosemite Fall—2011-1255.

29. Born Sara Jane Clarke, this writer would adopt the name "Grace Greenwood" in both her professional and personal life. Greenwood was a prolific commentator of her era and wrote many travel articles on the wonders of the American West. She found Yosemite Valley somewhat intimidating. *Grace Greenwood*, daguerreotype by Albert Sands Southworth and Josiah Johnson Hawes, ca. 1850. Courtesy of the George Eastman Museum, ID: 1974.0193.0067.

30. The celebration marking the completion in July 1875 of the Mariposa Road into Yosemite Valley. The attendees are gathered in front of the Coulter and Murphy Hotel (formerly the Hutchings House Hotel). *Completion of Mariposa Road Celebration.* Courtesy of the Yosemite Research Library, National Park Gallery (Yosemite), National Park Service, ID: RL_01705.

31. (*opposite top*) The Twenty-Fourth Infantry on mounted patrol in Yosemite in 1899. From 1891 to 1914, Yosemite National Park was administered by the U.S. Army until the establishment of the National Park Service. Some years the troops on patrol were the crack African American units known as the "Buffalo Soldiers." *24th Mounted Cavalry, Yosemite,* photograph by Celia Crocker Thompson, 1899. Courtesy of the Yosemite Research Library, National Park Gallery (Yosemite), National Park Service, ID: RL_05701.

32. (*opposite bottom*) Among the army units that patrolled Yosemite National Park prior to the establishment of the National Park Service was the Ninth Cavalry, here posing on the Fallen Monarch in the Mariposa Grove of Giant Sequoias. *Troop D on Fallen Monarch, Yosemite.* Courtesy of the Yosemite Research Library, National Park Gallery (Yosemite), National Park Service, ID: RL_19829.

33. (*above*) The "Big Tree Room" in the Hutchings House Hotel. This lounging area was constructed around a massive incense cedar. Today, the hotel is long gone but the tree stump still remains. *Big Tree Room.* Courtesy of the U.S. National Park Service, National Park Gallery (Yosemite), Negative Number: RL_14442, ca. 1886.

34. For many tourists, their entry into Yosemite Valley was aboard a stagecoach. It was a bumpy, frequently uncomfortable journey with a spectacular reward at the end. This stagecoach is on the Wawona Road, today's Highway 41. *Horse Stage on Wawona Road*, unknown photographer, ca. 1895. Courtesy of the Yosemite Research Library, National Park Gallery (Yosemite), National Park Service, ID: mpd0009.

35. (*opposite top*) In 1868 journalist John Shertzer Hittell wrote *Yosemite: Its Wonders and Its Beauties*, which is considered one of the earliest guidebooks to Yosemite (some consider it the first). It featured hand-tipped (hand-pasted) original photographic prints by the eccentric photographer Eadweard Muybridge. *John Shertzer Hittell*, ambrotype by William Shew, ca. 1855–60. Courtesy of the Bancroft Library, University of California, Berkeley, ID: BANC PIC 19xx.495-Case—brk00040498_8a.tif.

36. (*opposite bottom*) Yosemite Valley attracted celebrities almost from the beginning of its emergence as a tourist destination in the mid-1850s. In this photograph, flamboyant showman P. T. Barnum (*standing, second from left*) visits Yosemite Falls with his entourage. *Yo-Semite Fall, (2634 feet high) from near Sentinel House, P.T. Barnum and Party*, from a stereograph by John P. Soule, ca. 1870. Library of Congress, Prints and Photographs Division, Washington DC [LC-DIG-stereo-1s01078].

Cabin in Yo. Val. 1864

37. (*opposite top*) John Muir's own drawing of his cabin in Yosemite Valley, 1869. Muir arrived in Yosemite in 1868 and was hired to manage the sawmill operated by James Mason Hutchings. *Yosemite National Park—Historic Houses, etc.—John Muir's Cabin in Yosemite Valley, 1869*, drawing by John Muir, 1869. John Muir Papers, Holt-Atherton Special Collections and Archives, University of the Pacific Library, © 1984, Muir-Hanna Trust, ID: MuirFiche5Frame0244.tif.

38. (*opposite bottom*) A fashionable group of visitors lounging beside the Merced River at Camp Grove, ca. 1880. *The Yo Semite Falls from Camp Grove, 3174*, from a stereograph by Carleton Watkins, ca. 1880. Courtesy of the California History Room, California State Library, Sacramento, ID: Yosemite Falls—Stereo 3029.

39. (*above*) In the winter months, transportation in Yosemite Valley was often confined to skis, more commonly called snowshoes in the nineteenth century. In this photograph, Elmira Morrill Fiske, the wife of the celebrated Yosemite photographer George Fiske, enjoys the snowy landscape as the family cat hitches a ride. *Mrs. Fiske on Skis*, photograph by George Fiske, ca. 1890. Courtesy of the Yosemite Research Library, National Park Gallery (Yosemite), National Park Service, ID: YM_12906.

40. John Muir in 1872. By 1872 Muir had achieved recognition as a leading Yosemite naturalist. *John Muir Portrait*, photograph by Henry William Bradley and William Herman Rulofson, ca. 1872. John Muir Papers, Holt-Atherton Special Collections and Archives, University of the Pacific Library, © 1984, Muir-Hanna Trust, ID: MSS048.f23-1248.tif.

41. In 1871 Ralph Waldo Emerson, world-famous philosopher, poet, and Transcendentalist, visited Yosemite Valley. During this visit, the sixty-eight-year-old Emerson met with an ardent admirer, the thirty-three-year-old John Muir. Their encounter was a contrast in enthusiasm and manner. *Ralph Waldo Emerson/L. Grozlier, 1859.* Library of Congress, Prints and Photographs Division, Washington DC [LC-DIG-pga-01425].

42. About twenty miles north of Yosemite Valley and within the national park boundaries is Hetch Hetchy Valley. John Muir considered Hetch Hetchy Valley the "remarkably exact counterpart" of Yosemite Valley. Following the passage of the Raker Act in 1913, Hetch Hetchy Valley was dammed to provide water for San Francisco. If you were standing on this spot today and the reservoir were full, you would be under three hundred feet of water. *Hetch-Hetchy Valley, Sierra Nevada Mts., Calif.*, panoramic photograph by Matt Ashby Wolfskill, 1911. Library of Congress, Prints and Photographs Division, Washington DC [pan 6a19572 //hdl.loc.gov/loc.pnp/pan.6a19572].

43. Oliver Lippincott (*left*) and Edward E. Russell (*right*) driving the first automobile to enter Yosemite Valley, June 24, 1900. They are pictured at Mirror Lake. Courtesy of the U.S. National Park Service, National Park Gallery (Yosemite), Negative Number: RL_18970. Original in the Los Angeles County Museum of Natural History.

44. Group portrait in front of Yosemite Falls, ca. 1880. This photograph of unnamed visitors was taken by Gustav Fagersteen, who had a studio near the Cosmopolitan Bathhouse and Saloon in Yosemite Valley. Courtesy of the U.S. National Park Service, National Park Gallery (Yosemite), Negative Number: RL_13774.

45. The Reverend Thomas Starr King. In 1860 King visited Yosemite Valley and wrote eight letters to the *Boston Evening Transcript* describing the valley and the Sierra Nevada. These letters were especially credible due to his reputation as a respected chronicler of mountain landscapes. *Thomas Starr King.* Courtesy of the California History Room, California State Library, Sacramento, ID: Photo: King, Thomas Starr—1993-0631, ca. 1860.

6

"Enter These Enchanted Woods, You Who Dare"

Reverie and Rusticity, 1860–1869

Yosemite in the 1860s was experiencing growing pains. But as the valley and environs became better known to the public, the fear of potential exploitation of the Yosemite Valley by shoddy, privately controlled moneymaking attractions swelled.

Visiting Yosemite remained a trial, requiring days of uncomfortable travel on rough roads and saddle sore–inducing excursions on horseback. For most visitors, however, the rewards of a Yosemite encounter far outweighed the inconvenience. Upon arrival, tourists could lodge in a growing number of modest hotels offering poor to passable meals. Sightseers might spy Charles Weed snapping the first photographs of Yosemite or recognize artists, such as Albert Bierstadt, who were reimagining the valley on enormous canvases.

Yosemite enthusiasts feared that the majestic valley might suffer the fate of Niagara Falls in western New York State; the waterfall area had been transformed into a tacky carnival of tourist traps, hucksters, and unchecked construction. In 1864, in part to forestall the development of another Niagara, the federal government ceded the Yosemite Valley and Mariposa Grove of Giant Sequoias to the State of California with the Yosemite Valley Grant Act. This legislation, introduced by U.S. senator John Conness of California, instituted state jurisdiction of the valley but did not provide funding or administration. However, this pathbreaking action established the principle that government should protect areas of natural beauty and prevent commercial misuse.

The State of California soon created the Yosemite Park Commission. However, after it initially denied private claims in Yosemite Valley, it was later criticized as inefficient and probably in the pocket of special and private interests.

In the immediate aftermath of the Civil War, the United States was enamored with expansionism and exceptionalism—the concept that the country was fulfilling the old dream of Manifest Destiny and, compared to the rest of the world, that everything in America was grander and more glorious. Yosemite became the natural quintessence of this new perspective. Yosemite was no longer just a beautiful valley; it was now a divine temple to American ideals of growth and national splendor.

In the last few years of the 1860s, Yosemite encountered several turning points that ultimately shaped its future. The first was in 1868, when John Muir paid his first visit to Yosemite Valley. The second was the publication of the first Yosemite guidebook illustrated with photographs. The third was a series of surveys and studies detailing the remarkable landscapes outside of Yosemite Valley, most notably Hetch Hetchy Valley. And finally, with the 1869 completion of the transcontinental railroad, the ultimate symbol of nineteenth-century American empire-building, a rail spur was extended from Sacramento to Stockton, easing travel to Yosemite for the budding tourist population.

"The ninth Symphony is the Yo-Semite of music."

Thomas Starr King
"A Vacation among the Sierras, No. 6," 1861

When Yosemite Valley became gradually more accessible in the 1860s, bands of intrepid visitors made the journey to the majestic valley, although the numbers remained small—fewer than a thousand visitors from 1855 to 1864. The trip still required days on horseback and a willingness to "rough it." Those who made the commitment were frequently overwhelmed by the experience, dazzled by the breathtaking beauty, and usually noted a frustrating inability to satisfactorily describe the Yosemite Valley.

In 1860 the Reverend Thomas Starr King, a thirty-six-year-old Unitarian Universalist minister from Boston, became pastor of San Francisco's First Unitarian Church. That summer King visited Yosemite and the Sierra Nevada and wrote eight letters to the *Boston Evening Transcript* chronicling his adventure.

King's letters were published only a few years after the first nonindigenous people visited Yosemite. Few accounts of the valley had filtered to the East Coast, and often they were dismissed as exaggerations or tall tales. However, the reverend's letters were considered especially credible. Reverend King had gained a reputation as a respected observer of mountain landscapes due to his 1859 book *The White Hills: Their Legends, Landscapes, and Poetry*, which was about the White Mountains of New Hampshire.

King was a passionate advocate for California remaining in the Union during the Civil War. He embarked on an extensive lecture tour to promote his cause. Exhausted, King died unexpectedly of diphtheria and pneumonia in 1864 at the age of forty. From 1931 to 2009, a statue of Thomas Starr King was one of California's two representatives in National Statuary Hall, located inside the U.S. Capitol. In 2009 King's statue was replaced by one of Ronald Reagan.

In his sixth letter to the *Boston Evening Transcript*, Reverend King offers his impressions of the Yosemite Valley. Letter Six was written in December 1860 and published in the *Boston Evening Transcript* on January 26, 1861.

Letter Six, San Francisco, December 1860

The Yo-Semite Valley

Dear Transcript: The Yo-Semite valley is a pass about ten miles long, which, at its eastern extremity, splits into three narrower notches, each of which extends several miles, winding by the wildest paths into the heart of the Sierra Nevada chain. For seven miles of the main valley, which varies in width from three quarters of a mile to a mile and a half, the walls are from two thousand to nearly five thousand feet above the road, and are nearly perpendicular. The valley is of such irregular width, and bends so much and often so abruptly, that there is great variety and frequent surprise in the forms and combinations of the overhanging rocks, as one rides along the bank of the stream. The patches of luxuriant meadow with their dazzling green, and the grouping of the superb firs, two hundred feet high, that skirt them, and that shoot above the stout and graceful oaks and sycamores, through which the horse path winds, are delightful rests of sweetness and beauty amid the threatening awfulness,— like the threads and flashes of melody that relieve the towering masses of Beethoven's harmony. The ninth Symphony is the Yo-Semite of music. The Merced, which flows through the main aisle we are speaking of, is a noble stream a hundred feet wide and ten feet deep. It is formed chiefly of the streams that leap and rush through the narrower notches above referred to, and it is swollen also by the bounty of the marvellous waterfalls that pour down the ramparts of the wider valley. The sublime poetry of Habakkuk [a Biblical prophet] is needed to describe the impression and perhaps the geology of these mighty fissures: *Thou didst cleave the earth with rivers.*

Now let us descend from "Inspiration Point" by a very steep trail to the level of the Merced, and ride up between the cliffs to such rude hospitality as the isolation of the region may afford. If our readers don't like the title, "Inspiration Point" they are welcome to the Indian name of that perch, on the Mariposa trail, Open-eta-noo-ah. I would tell them what it means, if I knew. The first portion of it, "Open" is certainly appropriate, as we look down into the granite-lined abyss.

At the foot of the break-neck declivity of nearly three thousand feet by which we reach the banks of the Merced, we are six miles from the hotel, and every rod of the ride awakens wonder, awe and a solemn joy. First, we come within the sound of a sweet and steady thunder which seems to pour from heights at our right hand. The trees allow only glimpses of the wall, but not the cause of the continuous music. Soon we cross a fair sized rivulet that flows merrily athwart the trail; then another, and another, and another, each of them large enough for a quartz-mill stream. Again and again we meet and ford them. There are a dozen such, and soon in a wider opening among the trees we see the parent stream. But it is no prosaic water. It is a gush of splendor, a column of concentrated light from heaven. Of course, we turn our horses' heads straight toward it. Soon we dismount, and clamber over the boulders and debris around which its dishevelled strands are briskly leaping. The rich bass deepens as we rise, and before long we are in a cloud of spray.

Not a very "gentle" rain, however, as our soaked clothes soon attested. I did not stay long amid the glories of the flashing iridescence, for I wished to stand by the wall itself and look up. So I pushed ahead through the blowing rainbows, and soon reached the smooth-faced rampart. I was entirely safe now from the spray, which fell forty feet in front upon the boulders, and I could look up steadily, with no mist in the eyes except what the wonder of the picture stimulated. I am not going to describe it. The ponderous and the sentimental adjectives shall be undisturbed in my Worcester's Dictionary, which has come to me "around the Horn." The wall is here about a thousand feet high, for a distance of an eighth of a mile. It sags in the centre, and there, eight hundred feet over my head, was the curve of the cataract, as it pours from the level stream for its unbroken descent of a sixth of a mile. Not a single projection from the wall, or bulge in it, is there to fret or mar the majesty and freedom of the current. It was probably fifteen feet wide where it started its descent; it kept its curve and a concentrated life for some three hundred feet; and then gravitation got hold of it, shook it apart, and made it tumble headlong through the air for five hundred feet more, scattering millions of pearls, and whole sheets of filmy mist, to be smitten with splendor by the sun.

This cascade is called "The Bridal Veil." A worse name might be given to it. In fact a worse name was given to it; for I find that in 1856 it was christened "Falls of Louise" by some explorers, in honor of "the first lady of our party that entered the valley." Thank Heaven, the cataract wouldn't stand this nonsense; and it seemed to me to be pleading with us to have the "Bridal Veil" folly thrown aside, that it might be known forever by its Indian baptism, "Pohono." As I think of it, I lose quickly the impression of the widening of its watery trail before it struck the rocks to strike thunder from them; I do not dwell, either, on the fascinations of its evermelting and renewing tracery, nor on the brilliance of the Iris-banners that are dyed into its leaping mists and flying shreds; I can recall for my supreme delight only the curve of the tide more than eight hundred feet aloft where it starts off from the precipice, and the transparency of its "vitreous brink" with the edge now and then veiled with a little curling, dusty vapor when the wind blew hard against it, but generally tinged with a faint apple-green lustre. Thus, before we had been twenty minutes in the Yo-Semite valley, we were at the foot of a fall as high and more beautiful than the celebrated Staub[b] ach [waterfall in Switzerland], the highest in Europe.

Still we have five miles of horseback riding to the hotel. Is there such a ride possible in any other part of the planet? Nowhere among the Alps, in no pass of the Andes, and in no cañon of the mighty Oregon range, is there such stupendous rock-scenery as the traveller now lifts his eyes to. . . .

After leaving the nook in which the Pohono tumbles, we found ourselves soon under a cliff twice as high. We were obliged to turn our heads back, to see its crest, two thousand feet of sheer height above us. The first view was so terrible that I supposed this must be the most striking scenery in all the valley, and I was greatly astonished at learning the absolute measurement of the precipice. Opposite this cliff, on the left or northerly bank of the river, stood the sublime rock called "El Capitan" or the Chieftain—a Spanish rendering of the Indian name "Tu-toch-ah-nu-lah," a sachem of one of the early tribes. This wonderful piece of natural masonry stands at an angle with the valley, presenting a sharp edge and two sides in one view. And how high, think you? 3,817 feet! Can't we honestly put an exclamation point there? Remember, too, that it stands straight. There is no easy curve line as in the sides of the White Mountain Notch—to a picture of which I lift my eyes as I write in my library. In fact, the monstrous mass beetles a little. You can stand on the summit and drop a plumb-line to the base. I called it just now a piece of natural masonry; but the word is inaccurate. The immense escarpment has no crack or mark of stratification. There is no vegetation growing anywhere on it, for there is no patch of soil on either front, and no break where soil can lodge and a shrub can grow. It is one block of naked granite, pushed up from below to give us a sample of the cellar-pavement of our California counties, and to show us what it is that our earthquakes joggle. But on one face the wall is weather stained, or lichen-stained with rich cream-colored patches; on the other face it is ashy grey. A more majestic object than this rock I expect never to see on this planet. Great is granite, and the Yo-Semite is its prophet!

. . . [A]s we approach the hotel and turn toward the opposite bank of the river, what is that

Which ever sounds and shines,
A pillar of white light upon the wall
Of purple cliffs aloof descried?

That, reader, is the highest waterfall in the world, the Yo-Semite cataract, 2500 feet in its plunge, dashing from a break or depression in a cliff 3200 feet sheer! Of course, we must not commence a description of it here. It won't run dry—at least the memory of it will not—before another letter can be written. With its music in our ears we will go into the Shanty-Hotel, and ask for rooms, and water, and a meal. The hotel is a two story institution about fifty feet long, and fifteen feet deep. The front is clap-boarded; the back wall is common cotton cloth. The hall upstairs is not finished off into chambers, but has spaces of eight feet square divided by cotton screens, within which beds without sheets are laid upon the bare floor. There are two rooms below which have beds on posts, and furniture for ladies. But what care we for rooms and furniture, when the windows are open, and we look out upon that opposite wall and the marvellous cascade, whose glorious music floods the air?

K.

....

"I have seen some of the finest scenery of Switzerland, the Tyrol, and the Bavarian Alps, but I never saw any grander than this."

....

William H. Brewer

Up and Down California in 1860–1864

William Henry Brewer (1828–1910) started his professional career as a professor of chemistry at Washington and Jefferson College in Pennsylvania. However, just two years into his tenure, Brewer's wife and infant son died. Emotionally devastated, he sought personal and professional change. In 1860 Brewer accepted a post as chief botanist on the staff of Josiah Whitney, California's first state geologist. Brewer was chosen to lead the field teams for the State Geologic Survey, authorized by the

California legislature in 1860. The book *Up and Down California in 1860–1864* (1930), a compilation of Brewer's journals and reports, provided important insights not only into Whitney's geological surveys but into California society as well. The book, essentially a journal, is not merely a scientific study but also a story of the surveyor's enjoyment and appreciation of the remarkable terrain. After four years with Whitney's office, Brewer returned to the East Coast and became a professor of agriculture at Yale, his alma mater, where he then taught for nearly forty years.

In this passage from the June 21, 1863, entry in *Up and Down California in 1860–1864*, Brewer describes the approach to the Yosemite Valley and, upon arrival, his thoughts on the extraordinary landforms. Brewer concludes that the Yosemite Valley "is not only the greatest natural curiosity in this state, but one of the most remarkable in the world."

Yosemite Valley

June 21, 1863

The trail grew rougher, across canyons, over hills. At last we crossed a hill, and a view of a portion of the valley burst upon us in all its beauty—the valley far below us, its peaks rising still higher than we were. We descended into the valley, passed the Bridal Veil Fall, and camped beneath the enormous precipice called Tu-tuc-a-nu-la [El Capitan]. The next day we crossed the river and went up the valley about three miles, and camped directly in front of the great Yosemite Fall. We see it continually when we are in camp; it is the first thing we see in the gray dawn of morning, the last thing at night.

I will give a general description of the valley, without following the order in which the points were visited. Yosemite (pronounced *Yo-sem´-i-tee*) Valley is not only the greatest natural curiosity in this state, but one of the most remarkable in the world. It is on the Merced River, about sixty miles from the plain. (It is on a branch and marked *Yohamite* on your maps.) The stream is so large that it cannot be forded here. I tried it two days ago, but although in the best place, my horse was carried off his feet. We had to swim, and got a good wetting, so you can see that there is plenty of water. Below, the river runs in a narrow canyon; here, it widens out and is the Yosemite Valley proper—six or seven miles long, and about a mile wide, and over four thousand feet above the sea. The trails to it lead over the mountains.

We descend into the valley by a terribly steep hill—we have to descend nearly three thousand feet within four or five miles. We strike the level bottom, green and grassy, and pass up. The Bridal Veil Fall is in front (called also *Pó-hono*). It is a stream larger than Fall Creek at Ithaca, and falls *clear* at one leap over eight hundred feet! Some measurements make it 950 feet. The stream entirely dissolves in spray, which sways back and forth with the breeze, like a huge veil. It is vastly finer than any waterfall in Switzerland, in fact finer than any in Europe.

Now the valley begins to assume its characteristic and grand features. By the Pohono Fall rises the Cathedral Rock, a huge mass of granite nearly 4,000 feet high; while opposite is Tutucanula, a bluff of granite, rising from this plain perpendicularly 3,600 feet (we made it over 3,500 by our measurements). It rises from the green valley to this enormous height without any talus at the foot. You cannot conceive the true sublimity of such a cliff. It is equivalent to piling up *nine* such cliffs as the entire height of the walls of the ravine at Taughannock Falls [in the Finger Lakes region of New York].

We pass up the valley to our camp. South of us rises the Sentinel Rock, like a spire, 3,100 feet above us. There are the Three Brothers, the highest 3,443 feet above the valley, and in front the great Yosemite Fall, of which more anon. . . .

The Merced River, however, comes down the central canyon. Here, between precipices of at least two thousand feet, nearly perpendicular, are two falls—the Vernal Fall, or Piwyac, and the Nevada, or Yowiye—the former four hundred feet high, the latter over six hundred feet. The quantity of water is large, so you may well imagine that they are sublime. The lower fall, Piwyac, is easily reached by a trail, and by ladders which carry us up to the top. Not so the Nevada Fall—that is more difficult—but we went up to measure it, to see if the heights previously given were exaggerated. We had a rough climb, but were amply repaid by the fine views. But few visitors ever attempt it.

But the crowning glory of the valley is the Yosemite Fall. . . . The stream, fed by melting snows back, is a large sized mill-stream, say fifteen feet wide and two or three deep at the top of the fall. It comes over the wall on the north side of the valley, and drops 1,542 feet the first leap, then falls 1,100 more in two or three more cascades, the entire height being over 2,600 feet! We measured it yesterday. I question if the world furnishes a parallel—certainly there is none known. . . .

The view from the top was magnificent. The valley, over half a mile—in fact over three thousand feet—below us, its green plain spotted with trees which seemed flat bushes, the river winding through it, the granite domes around, and last of all, the snowy peaks of the higher Sierra just beyond, rising several thousand feet higher—all conspired to form a scene of grandeur seldom met with. I have seen some of the finest scenery of Switzerland, the Tyrol, and the Bavarian Alps, but I never saw any grander than this.

"The premises shall be held for public use, resort and recreation; shall be inalienable for all time."

Senator John Conness and the U.S. Congress
The Yosemite Valley Grant Act, 1864

As Yosemite garnered increasing public notice during the early 1860s, the rush to capitalize on the valley's moneymaking potential concerned an increasing number of observers. Critics of unregulated economic growth in Yosemite worried that the valley would suffer the fate of New York's Niagara Falls, a natural wonder that, in the words of English travel writer Isabella Bird in 1856, had devolved into "a great fungus-growth of museums, curiosity-shops, taverns, and pagodas with shining tin cupolas." Fearful that Yosemite would metamorphose into an overly commercialized tourist trap unbecoming of the awesome splendor of the landscape, activists undertook efforts to control development through legislation.

On March 28, 1864, U.S. senator John Conness of California introduced Senate Bill 203—ultimately known as the Yosemite Valley Grant Act—which would grant to the State of California the Yosemite Valley and the Mariposa Grove of Giant Sequoias.

That act did not establish the national park—that would come later, in 1890—but it did inaugurate the concept that protecting places of natural beauty should be a national priority, an idea that ultimately led to the founding of the first national park, at Yellowstone, in 1872. In the eyes of Congress, the act had the added benefit that no money was appropriated in support of the bill, no supporting legislation provided for federal administration of the areas, and jurisdiction was left to California.

The Yosemite Valley Grant Act passed both houses of Congress after only a few hours of debate, and on June 30, 1864, during the depths of the Civil War, it was signed into law by President Abraham Lincoln.

The following presents a portion of Senator John Conness's passionate Senate floor argument of May 17, 1864, urging passage of the bill and the final legislation signed by President Lincoln.

Senator John Conness of California

May 17, 1864

Congressional Globe, Senate, 38th Congress, 1st Session

I will state to the Senate that this bill proposes to make a grant of certain premises located in the Sierra Nevada moun-

"Enter These Enchanted Woods, You Who Dare"

tains, in the State of California, that are for all public purposes worthless, but which constitute, perhaps, some of the greatest wonders of the world. The object and purpose is to make a grant to the State, on the stipulations contained in the bill, that the property shall be inalienable forever, and preserved and improved as a place of public resort, to be taken charge of by gentlemen to be appointed by the Governor, who are to receive no compensation for their services, and who are to undertake the management and improvement of the property by making roads leading thereto and adopting such other means as may be necessary for its preservation and improvement. It includes a grant of a few sections of ground upon which one of the celebrated big tree groves of that state is located, of which most Senators doubtless have heard. The trees contained in that grove have no parallel, perhaps, in the world. They are subject now to damage and injury; and this bill, as I have before stated, proposes to commit them to the care of the authorities of that State for their constant preservation, that they may be exposed to public view, and that they may be used and preserved for the benefit of mankind. It is a matter involving no appropriation whatever. The property is of no value to the Government.

An Act of June 30, 1864, 38th Congress, 1st Session, Public Law 159, 13 stat 325, Authorizing a Grant to the State of California of the "Yo-Semite Valley," and of the Land Embracing the "Mariposa Big Tree Grove"

Be it enacted by the Senate and House of Representatives of the United States of America, in Congress assembled, That there shall be, and is hereby, granted to the State of California, the "Cleft" or "Gorge" in the Granite Peak of the Sierra Nevada Mountains, situated in the county of Mariposa, in the State aforesaid, and the headwaters of the Merced River, and known as the Yosemite Valley, with its branches and spurs, in estimated length fifteen miles, and in average width one mile back from the main edge of the precipice, on each side of the Valley, with the stipulation, nevertheless, that the said

State shall accept this grant upon the express conditions that the premises shall be held for public use, resort, and recreation; shall be inalienable for all time; but leases not exceeding ten years may be granted for portions of said premises. All incomes derived from leases of privileges to be expended in the preservation and improvement of the property, or the roads leading thereto; the boundaries to be established at the cost of said State by the United States Surveyor-General of California, whose official plat, when affirmed by the Commissioner of the General Land Office, shall constitute the evidence of the locus, extent, and limits of the said Cleft or Gorge; the premises to be managed by the Governor of the State, with eight other Commissioners, to be appointed by the Executive of California, and who shall receive no compensation for their services.

Sec. 2. *And be it further enacted*, That there shall likewise be, and there is hereby, granted to the said State of California, the tracts embracing what is known as the "Mariposa Big Tree Grove," not to exceed the area of four sections, and to be taken in legal subdivisions of one-quarter section each, with the like stipulations as expressed in the first section of this Act as to the State's acceptance, with like conditions as in the first section of this Act as to inalienability, yet with the same lease privileges; the income to be expended in the preservation, improvement, and protection of the property, the premises to be managed by Commissioners, as stipulated in the first section of this Act, and to be taken in legal subdivisions as aforesaid; and the official plat of the United States Surveyor-General, when affirmed by the Commissioner of the General Land Office, to be the evidence of the locus of the said Mariposa Big Tree Grove.

Shortly after the legislation was signed by President Abraham Lincoln, California governor Frederick F. Low issued a proclamation taking possession of the Yosemite Valley and Mariposa Grove of Giant Sequoias and appointed a board of commissioners to manage these lands.

"Enter These Enchanted Woods, You Who Dare"

The first commissioners included Frederick Law Olmsted, nationally prominent landscape architect; Josiah D. Whitney, California state geologist; William Ashburner, member of the California Geological Survey and professor of mining; I. Ward Raymond, a well-known merchant whose advocacy letters to Senator Conness influenced the legislation; Erastus S. Holden, a druggist and the mayor of Stockton; Alexander Deering, lawyer and future judge; George W. Coulter, miner, merchant, and founder of Coulterville; and Galen Clark, future "guardian" of the Yosemite Valley and Mariposa Grove from 1866 to 1897.

The enabling legislation that led to the creation of Yosemite National Park was a long journey, one that lasted for more than four decades. From 1864 to 1906, state and federal acts and resolutions defined the parameters and functions of government administration of Yosemite.

While the National Park Service has identified several dozen critical laws that have influenced Yosemite through the years, the four most important nineteenth-century legislative actions regarding the "origin" of Yosemite National Park were as follows:

- Yosemite Valley Grant Act of 1864 ("An Act authorizing a Grant to the State of California of the Yo-Semite Valley, and of the Land embracing the Mariposa Big Tree Grove." *U.S. Statutes at Large*, 1864, volume 13, chapter 184, p. 325 [S. 203; Public Act No. 159]).

- The 1890 establishment of Yosemite National Park ("An act to set apart certain tracts of land in the State of California as forest reservations." *U.S. Statutes at Large*, 1890, volume 26, chapter 1263, pp. 650–52 [H.R. 12187]). Sections 1 and 2 of this act concern Yosemite National Park, while section 3 establishes General Grant National Park, now part of Kings Canyon National Park, and a portion of Sequoia National Park.

- California's 1905 regranting of Yosemite Valley and the Mariposa Grove to the federal government ("Act of the Legislature of the State of California, Approved March 3, 1905, Regranting to the United States of America the Yosemite Valley and the land embracing the 'Mariposa Big Tree Grove.'" *Statutes of California* [1905], p. 54).

- The March 1905 congressional acceptance of California's return of these natural wonders ("Joint Resolution Accepting the recession by the State of California of the Yosemite Valley Grant and the Mariposa Big Tree Grove in the Yosemite National Park." *U.S. Statutes at Large*, 1905, volume 33, part 1, Resolution No. 30, p. 1286 [S.J.R. 115; Public Resolution No. 29]).

The March 5, 1905, congressional resolution was brief and confusing. It lacked detail, so questions arose. On July 1, 1905, the *San Francisco Call* published "The Yosemite Muddle," an editorial that addressed concerns held by many. The *Call* asserted that there was long-standing uncertainty about Yosemite's boundaries and that the resolution did not provide any clarity. While supporting the noble aim of federal dominion over the Yosemite region, the newspaper noted that the congressional statement offered "not a word about the Yosemite Valley or the acceptance of its recession." Furthermore, the editorial continued, "to add to the muddle, the Big Tree Grove is not in the Yosemite National Park at all, but is inclosed by the Sierra Forest Reserve. When the next Congress meets it will be in order for some one to draw an acceptance of the recession, properly describing the valley and the grove. Just how the title and text of the resolution got divorced no one seems to know. It appears to be one of the curiosities of legislation."

On June 11, 1906, a second congressional resolution was passed, and it provided the specifics the *San Francisco Call* craved. It was entitled "Joint Resolution Accepting the recession by the State of California of the

"Enter These Enchanted Woods, You Who Dare"

Yosemite Valley Grant and the Mariposa Big Tree Grove, and including the same, together with fractional sections five and six, township five south, range twenty-two east, Mount Diablo meridian, California, within the metes and bounds of the Yosemite National Park, and changing the boundaries thereof," per U.S. *Statutes at Large*, 1906, volume 34, part 1, Resolution No. 27, pp. 831–32 (H.J.R. 118; Public Resolution No. 27).

> ". . . an unspeakable suffusion of glory created
> from the phoenix-pile of the dying sun."

Fitz Hugh Ludlow
"Seven Weeks in the Great Yo-Semite," 1864

As visitation to Yosemite Valley increased during the 1860s, the most enthusiastic and exasperated tourists were often artists and writers, who struggled to depict or describe Yosemite in all its glory.

In 1863 painter Albert Bierstadt and writer Fitz Hugh Ludlow visited Yosemite for the first time. Bierstadt painted what were commonly called "Great Pictures," that is, large-scale paintings that toured the country attracting critical attention, wealthy patrons, and well-heeled buyers. Yosemite Valley became the creative axis for Bierstadt as he produced grand paintings of the breathtaking setting. Ludlow was an author and journalist who was well known for his 1857 autobiographical book *The Hasheesh Eater*, an account of his altered state of consciousness due to zealous consumption of hashish, a cannabis extract.

Bierstadt and Ludlow spent seven weeks in Yosemite, which the latter recounted in a June 1864 article for the *Atlantic Monthly*. Ludlow noted that he christened their camp in Yosemite Valley "Camp Rosalie," after "a dear absent friend of mine and Bierstadt's." Rosalie was Ludlow's wife. Just as Bierstadt was instantly smitten with the valley's grandeur, he was also infatuated with the beautiful and flirtatious Rosalie, whom Bierstadt would later marry.

Following the 1863 visit to Yosemite, Bierstadt completed his first painting of the valley: *Looking Down the Yosemite Valley, California*. This five-by-eight-foot canvas established Bierstadt's reputation as America's preeminent creator of monumental paintings. He became one of the most famous artists of the nineteenth century.

Ludlow died in 1870 from the cumulative effects of excessive drug use, pneumonia, and tuberculosis. He was thirty-four years old.

In this passage from "Seven Weeks in the Great Yo-Semite," Ludlow describes his and Bierstadt's initial glimpse of Yosemite Valley from Inspiration Point and his exaltation of the beauties of the mountain cathedral, a vision of "a new heaven and a new earth into which the creative spirit had just been breathed."

Our dense leafy surrounding hid from us the fact of our approach to the Valley's tremendous battlement, till our trail turned at a sharp angle and we stood on "Inspiration Point." That name had appeared pedantic, but we found it only the spontaneous expression of our own feelings on the spot. We did not so much seem to be seeing from that crag of vision a new scene on the old familiar globe as a new heaven and a new earth into which the creative spirit had just been breathed. I hesitate now, as I did then, at the attempt to give my vision utterance. Never were words so beggared for an abridged translation of any Scripture of Nature.

We stood on the verge of a precipice more than three thousand feet in height,—a sheer granite wall, whose terrible perpendicular distance baffled all visual computation. Its foot was hidden among hazy green *spiculæ*—they might be tender spears of grass catching the slant sun on upheld aprons of cobweb, or giant pines whose tops that sun first gilt before he made gold of all the Valley. . . .

"Enter These Enchanted Woods, You Who Dare"

First, . . . there projected boldly into the Valley from the dominant line of the base a square stupendous tower that might have been hewn by the diamond adzes of the Genii for a second Babel-experiment, in expectance of the wrath of Allah. Here and there the tools had left a faint scratch, only deep as the width of Broadway and a bagatelle of five hundred feet in length; but that detracted no more from the unblemished four-square contour of the entire mass than a pin-mark from the symmetry of a door-post. A city might have been built on its grand flat top. And, oh! the gorgeous masses of light and shadow which the falling sun cast on it,— the shadows like great waves, the lights like their spumy tops and flying mist,—thrown up from the heaving breast of a golden sea! In California at this season the dome of heaven is cloudless; but I still dream of what must be done for the bringing-out of Tu-toch-anula's coronation-day majesties by the broken winter sky of fleece and fire. The height of his precipice is nearly four thousand feet perpendicular; his name is supposed to be that of the Valley's tutelar deity. He also rejoices in a Spanish *alias*,—some Mission Indian having attempted to translate by "*El Capitan*" the idea of divine authority implied in Tu-toch-anula.

Far up the Valley to the eastward there rose far above the rest of the sky-line, and nearly five thousand feet above the Valley, a hemisphere of granite, capping the sheer wall, without an apparent tree or shrub to hide its vast proportions. This we immediately recognized as the famous To-coy-æ, better known through [Carleton] Watkins's photographs as the Great North Dome. . . .

What was he who stood up before Tis-sa-ack [Half Dome] and said, "Thou art dead rock!" save a momentary sojourner in the bosom of a cyclic period whose clock his race had never yet lived long enough to hear strike? What, too, if Tis-sa-ack himself were but one of the atoms in a grand organism where we could see only by monads at a time,—if he and the sun and the sea were but cells or organs of some one small being in the fenceless *vivarium* of the Universe?

Let not the ephemeron that lights on a baby's hand generalize too rashly upon the non-growing of organisms! As we thought on these things, we bared our heads to the barer forehead of Tis-sa-ack. . . .

Let us leave the walls of the Valley to speak of the Valley itself, as seen from this great altitude. There lies a sweep of emerald grass turned to chrysoprase by the slant-beamed sun,—chrysoprase beautiful enough to have been the tenth foundation-stone of John's apocalyptic heaven. Broad and fair just beneath us, it narrows to a little strait of green between the butments that uplift the giant domes. Far to the westward, widening more and more, it opens into the bosom of great mountain-ranges,—into a field of perfect light, misty by its own excess,—into an unspeakable suffusion of glory created from the phœnix-pile of the dying sun. Here it lies almost as treeless as some rich old clover-mead; yonder, its luxuriant smooth grasses give way to a dense wood of cedars, oaks, and pines. Not a living creature, either man or beast, breaks the visible silence of this inmost paradise; but for ourselves, standing at the precipice, petrified, as it were, rock on rock, the great world might well be running back in stone-and-grassy dreams to the hour when God had given him as yet but two daughters, the crag and the clover. We were breaking into the sacred closet of Nature's self-examination. . . .

During our whole stay in the Valley, most of us made it our practice to rise with the dawn, and, immediately after a bath in the ice-cold Merced, take a breakfast which might sometimes fail in the game-department, but was an invariable success, considered as slapjacks and coffee. Then the loyal nephew of the Secesh governor and the testamentary guardian of the orphan mules brought our horses up from picket; then the artists with their camp-stools and color-boxes, the sages with their goggles, nets, botany-boxes, and bug-holders, the gentlemen of elegant leisure with their naked eyes and a fish-rod or a gun, all rode away whither they listed, firing back Parthian shots of injunction about the dumpling in the grouse-fricassee.

"Enter These Enchanted Woods, You Who Dare"

Sitting in their divine workshop, by a little after sunrise our artists began labor in that only method which can ever make a true painter or a living landscape, *color*-studies on the spot; and though I am not here to speak of their results, I will assert that during their seven weeks' camp in the Valley they learned more and gained greater material for future triumphs than they had gotten in all their lives before at the feet of the greatest masters.

"Such tide of feelings, such stoppage of ordinary emotions comes at rare intervals in any life."

Samuel Bowles
Across the Continent, 1865

In the first decade of visitation to Yosemite Valley, it was common for observers to extol the extraordinary landscape in religious terms. Partly, this was the result of many of the earliest accounts being penned by members of the clergy, but secular witnesses were just as often moved to flights of spiritual enchantment. Such was the case with Samuel Bowles, editor of the influential *Springfield Republican* newspaper in Massachusetts.

In the summer of 1865, Bowles traveled through the states and territories of Kansas, Nebraska, Colorado, the Dakotas, Utah, California, Oregon, and Washington. His traveling companions included Speaker of the House Schuyler Colfax and editors of the *Chicago Tribune* and *New York Tribune*. Bowles collected his observations and commentaries in the 1865 book *Across the Continent: A Summer's Journey to the Rocky Mountains, the Mormons, and the Pacific States, with Speaker Colfax*.

The *Springfield Republican* was an abolitionist newspaper and an inspiration for the developing Republican Party. As editor, Bowles strove not only to chronicle daily occurrences but to also be a force in the moral and literary life of the community. It is not surprising, therefore, that Bowles's description of the Yosemite Valley includes words such as "worship," "majesty," "Infinite Creator," "religion," and "God." Samuel Bowles even remarks that being in Yosemite Valley was akin to being "under the ruins of an old Gothic cathedral, to which those of Cologne and Milan are but baby-houses."

In *Across the Continent*, the musings of Bowles are presented in the form of letters. An 1866 appraisal from the *North American Review* states that the letters read as if "they were addressed to a circle of friendly readers, and with almost the familiarity and directness of private correspondence."

In this excerpt, Bowles offers his thoughts on Yosemite Valley, cleverly comparing prominent features to those on the East Coast with which his audience would be more familiar.

Letter 22. The Yosemite Valley and the Big Trees

Yosemite Valley, California, August 11 [1865]

The Yosemite! As well interpret God in thirty-nine articles as portray it to you by word of mouth or pen. As well reproduce castle or cathedral by a stolen frieze, or broken column, as this assemblage of natural wonder and beauty by photograph or painting. The overpowering sense of the sublime, of awful desolation, of transcending marvelousness and unexpectedness, that swept over us, as we reined our horses sharply out of green forests, and stood upon high jutting rock that overlooked this rolling, upheaving sea of granite mountains, holding far down its rough lap this vale of beauty of meadow and grove and river,—such tide of feeling, such stoppage of ordinary emotions comes at rare intervals in any life. It was the confrontal of God face to face, as in great danger, in solemn, sudden death. It was Niagara, magnified. All that was mortal shrank back, all that was immortal swept to the front and bent down in awe. We sat till the rich elements of beauty came out of the majesty and the desolation, and then, eager

"Enter These Enchanted Woods, You Who Dare"

to get nearer, pressed tired horses down the steep, rough path into the Valley.

And here we have wandered and wondered and worshiped for four days. Under sunshine and shadow; by rich, mellow moonlight; by stars opening double wide their eager eyes; through a peculiar August haze, delicate, glowing, creamy, yet hardly perceptible as a distinct element,—the New England Indian summer haze doubly refined,—by morning and evening twilight, across camp fires, up from beds upon the ground through all the watches of the night, have we seen these, the great natural wonders and beauties of this western world. Indeed, it is not too much to say that no so limited space in all the known world offers such majestic and impressive beauty. Niagara alone divides honors with it in America. Only the whole of Switzerland can surpass it, no one scene in all the Alps can match this before me now in the things that mark the memory and impress all the senses for beauty and for sublimity.

The one distinguishing feature is a double wall of perpendicular granite, rising from a half a mile to a mile in hight, and inclosing a valley not more than half a mile in width on the average, and from ten to fifteen miles in length. It is a fissure, a chasm, rather than a valley, in solid rock mountains; there is not breadth enough in it for even one of its walls to lie down; and yet it offers all the fertility, all the beauties of a rich valley. There is meadow with thick grass; there are groves of pine and oak, the former exquisite in form and majestic in size, rising often to two hundred and two hundred and fifty feet; there are thickets of willow and birch, bay trees and dogwood, and various flowering shrubs; primrose and cowslip and golden rod and violet and painted cup, more delicate than eastern skies can welcome, make gay garden of all the vacant fields now in August; the aroma of mint, of pine and fir, of flower loads the air; the fern family find a familiar home everywhere; and winding in and out among all flows the Merced River, so pure and transparent that you can hardly tell where the air leaves off and the water begins, rolling rapid over polished stones or soft sands, or staying in wide, deep pools that invite the bather and the boat, and holding trout only less rich and dainty than the brook trout of New England. The soil, the trees, the shrubs, the grasses and the flowers of this little Valley are much the same in general character and variety as those of your Connecticut River valleys; but they are richer in development and greater in numbers. They borrow of the mountain fecundity and sweetness; and they are fed by summer rains as those of other California valleys rarely are.

Now imagine,—can you?—rising up, sheer and sharp, on each side of this line of fertile beauty, irregularly-flowing and variously-crowned walls of granite rock, thrice as high as your Mounts Tom and Holyoke, twice as high as Berkshire's Graylock. The color of the rock is most varied. A grayish drab or yellow is the dominant shade, warm and soft. In large spots, it whitens out; and, again it is dark and discolored as if by long exposure to rain and snow and wind. Sometimes the light and dark shades are thrown into quick contrast on a single wall, and you know where the Zebra and Dr. Bellows' church [a nineteenth-century New York church designed in a "striped" Italian Romanesque style] were borrowed from. More varied and exquisite still are the shapes into which the rocks are thrown. The one great conspicuous object of the Valley is a massive, two-sided wall, standing out into and over the meadow, yellowish-gray in color, and rising up into the air unbroken, square, perpendicular, for full three-quarters of a mile. It bears in Spanish and Indian the name of the Great Jehovah [El Capitan]; and it is easy to believe that it was an object of worship by the barbarians, as it is not difficult for civilization to recognize the Infinite in it, and impossible not to feel awed and humbled in its presence. . . .

The highest rock of the Valley is a perfect half-dome, split sharp and square in the middle, and rising almost a mile or near five thousand feet,—as high as Mount Washington is above the level of the sea,—over the little lake which perfectly mirrors its majestic form at its foot. Perfect pyramids take their places in the wall; then these pyramids come in families, and mount away one after and above the other, as "The Three Brothers." "The Cathedral Rocks" and "The Cathedral Spires" unite the great impressiveness, the beauty and the fantastic form of the Gothic architecture. From their shape and color alike, it is easy to imagine, in looking upon them, that you are under the ruins of an old Gothic cathedral, to which those of Cologne and Milan are but baby-houses. . . .

Over the sides of the walls pour streams of water out of narrower valleys still above, and yet higher and far away, rise to twelve and thirteen thousand feet the culminating peaks of the Sierra Nevadas, with still visible fields of melting snows. All forms and shapes and colors of majesty and beauty cluster around this narrow spot; it seems created the home of all that is richest in inspiration for the heroic in life, for poetry, for painting, for imaginative religion.

"It should . . . be made the duty of the Commission to prevent a wanton or careless disregard on the part of anyone entering the Yosemite."

Frederick Law Olmsted
"Draft of the Preliminary Report upon the Yosemite and the Big Tree Grove," 1865, and "The Great American Park of the Yosemite," 1868

The Yosemite Valley Grant Act of 1864 ceded authority over the Yosemite Valley and Mariposa Grove of Giant Sequoias to the State of California, and Governor Frederick Low appointed a commission to oversee management of the grant. Among its members was forty-three-year old Frederick Law Olmsted, a landscape architect who had recently settled in the Yosemite region as superintendent of the Mariposa Mining Estate. Olmsted was already a known figure for his work in designing New York City's Central Park, then under construction.

Olmsted's plan for Central Park required massive alteration of the landscape. Ultimately, five million cubic feet of soil and rocks had to be removed from the site, tons of gunpowder were used to clear the area, and more than twenty thousand workers manipulated the topography. It was assumed that Olmsted would advocate a similar plan for Yosemite Valley, much to the approval of entrepreneurs such as James Mason Hutchings, who had already built a hotel in the valley and was charging tourists to enter Yosemite.

But Olmsted surprised them. In a detailed report about Yosemite and the Mariposa Grove, Olmsted promoted leaving Yosemite largely untouched, with the exception of building better roads. He argued for strict regulations to protect Yosemite from continuing assaults by the "bad taste, playfulness, carelessness, or wanton destructiveness of present visitors." Yosemite, Olmsted believed, should not be an isolated refuge for the wealthy but public lands freely accessible to all.

On August 9, 1865, Olmsted read his report to an assembly in Yosemite Valley. It met with immediate disapproval from the other commissioners. Originally intended for presentation to the state legislature, the report was snubbed and shelved. A handwritten draft of the report in the hand of Henry Perkins, Olmsted's secretary, was buried in the archives and quickly gathered dust. At the end of 1865, Olmsted returned to New York.

Largely forgotten until the twentieth century, Olmsted's draft report then resurfaced as an insightful early proclamation of the values of the environmental preservation movement embodied in the national parks.

But, unlike his report, Olmsted's endorsement of Yosemite's appeal did not disappear from public view. On June 18, 1868, an Olmsted letter to the *New York Evening Post* was published. Entitled "The Great American Park of the Yosemite," the missive reinforced Olmsted's belief that Yosemite constituted "the greatest glory of nature."

"Draft of the Preliminary Report upon the
Yosemite and the Big Tree Grove"

It is the will of the nation as embodied in the act of Congress that this scenery shall never be private property, but that like certain defensive points upon our coast it shall be held solely for public purposes. . . .

That when it shall become more accessible the Yosemite will prove attraction of a similar character and a similar source of wealth to the whole community, not only of California but of the United States, there can be no doubt. It is a significant fact that visitors have already come from Europe expressly to see it, and that a member of the Alpine Club of London having seen it in summer was not content with a single visit but returned again and spent several months in it during the inclement season of the year for the express purpose of enjoying its winter aspect. Other foreigners and visitors from the Atlantic states have done the same, while as yet no Californian has shown a similar interest in it.

The first class of considerations referred to then as likely to have influenced the action of Congress, is that of the direct pecuniary advantage to the commonwealth which under proper administration will grow out of the possession of the Yosemite, advantages which, as will hereafter be shown, might easily be lost or greatly restricted without such action.

A more important class of considerations, however, remains to be stated. These are considerations of a political duty of grave importance to which seldom if ever before has proper respect been paid by any government in the world but the grounds of which rest on the same eternal base of equity and benevolence with all other duties of republican government. It is the main duty of government, if it is not the sole duty of government, to provide means of protection for all its citizens in the pursuit of happiness against the obstacles, otherwise insurmountable, which the selfishness of individuals or combinations of individuals is liable to interpose to that pursuit.

It is a scientific fact that the occasional contemplation of natural scenes of an impressive character, particularly if this contemplation occurs in connection with relief from ordinary cares, change of air and change of habits, is favorable to the health and vigor of men and especially to the health and vigor of their intellect beyond any other conditions which can be offered them, that it not only gives pleasure for the time being but increases the subsequent capacity for happiness and the means of securing happiness. The want of such occasional recreation where men and women are habitually pressed by their business or household cares often results in a class of disorders the characteristic quality of which is mental disability, sometimes taking the severe forms of softening of the brain, paralysis, palsy, monomania, or insanity, but more frequently of mental and nervous excitability, moroseness, melancholy or irascibility, incapacitating the subject for the proper exercise of the intellectual and moral forces.

It is well established that where circumstances favor the use of such means of recreation as have been indicated, the reverse of this is true. For instance, it is a universal custom with the heads of the important departments of the British government to spend a certain period of every year on their parks and shooting grounds or in travelling among the Alps or other mountain regions. This custom is followed by the leading lawyers, bankers, merchants and the wealthy classes generally of the empire, among whom the average period of active business life is much greater than with the most nearly corresponding classes in our own or any other country where the same practice is not equally well established. . . .

But in this country at least it is not those who have the most important responsibilities in state affairs or in commerce, who suffer most from the lack of recreation; women suffer more than men, and the agricultural class is more largely represented in our insane asylums than the professional, and for this, and other reasons, it is these classes to which the opportunity for such recreation is the greatest blessing.

If we analyze the operation of scenes of beauty upon the mind, and consider the intimate relation of the mind upon the nervous system and the whole physical economy, the action and reaction which constantly occur between bodily and mental conditions, the reinvigoration which results from such scenes is readily comprehended. Few persons can see such scenery as that of the Yosemite and not be impressed by it in some slight degree. All not alike, all not perhaps consciously, and amongst all who are consciously impressed by it, few can give the least expression to that of which they are conscious. But there can be no doubt that all have this susceptibility, though with some it is much more dull and confused than with others.

The power of scenery to affect men is, in a large way, proportionate to the degree of their civilization and the degree in which their taste has been cultivated. Among a thousand savages there will be a much smaller number who will show the least sign of being so affected than among a thousand persons taken from a civilized community. This is only one of the many channels in which a similar distinction between civilized and savage men is to be generally observed. The whole body of the susceptibilities of civilized men and with their susceptibilities their powers, are on the whole enlarged.

But as with the bodily powers, if one group of muscles is developed by exercise exclusively, and all others neglected, the result is general feebleness, so it is with the mental faculties. And men who exercise those faculties or susceptibilities of the mind which are called in play by beautiful scenery so little that they seem to be inert with them, are either in a diseased condition from excessive devotion of the mind to a limited range of interests, or their whole minds are in a savage state; that is, a state of low development. The latter class need to be drawn out generally; the former need relief from their habitual matters of interest and to be drawn out in those parts of their mental nature which have been habitually left idle and inert.

But there is a special reason why the reinvigoration of those parts which are stirred into conscious activity by natural scenery is more effective upon the general development and health than that of any other, which is this: The severe and excessive exercise of the mind which leads to the greatest fatigue and is the most wearing upon the whole constitution is almost entirely caused by application to the removal of something to be apprehended in the future, or to interests beyond those of the moment, or of the individual; to the laying up of wealth, to the preparation of something, to accomplishing something in the mind of another, and especially to small and petty details which are uninteresting in themselves and which engage the attention at all only because of the bearing they have on some general end of more importance which is seen ahead.

In the interest which natural scenery inspires there is the strongest contrast to this. It is for itself and at the moment it is enjoyed. The attention is aroused and the mind occupied without purpose, without a continuation of the common process of relating the present action, thought or perception to some future end. There is little else that has this quality so purely. There are few enjoyments with which regard for something outside and beyond the enjoyment of the moment can ordinarily be so little mixed. The pleasures of the table are irresistibly associated with the care of hunger and the repair of the bodily waste. In all social pleasures and all pleasures which are usually enjoyed in association with the social pleasures, the care for the opinion of others, or the good of others largely mingles. In the pleasures of literature, the laying up of ideas and self-improvement are purposes which cannot be kept out of view.

This, however, is in very slight degree, if at all, the case with the enjoyment of the emotions caused by natural scenery. It therefore results that the enjoyment of scenery employs the mind without fatigue and yet exercises it; tranquilizes

"Enter These Enchanted Woods, You Who Dare"

it and yet enlivens it; and thus, through the influence of the mind over the body, gives the effect of refreshing rest and reinvigoration to the whole system. . . .

Thus without means are taken by government to withhold them from the grasp of individuals, all places favorable in scenery to the recreation of the mind and body will be closed against the great body of the people. For the same reason that the water of rivers should be guarded against private appropriation and the use of it for the purpose of navigation and otherwise protected against obstruction, portions of natural scenery may therefore properly be guarded and cared for by government. To simply reserve them from monopoly by individuals, however, it will be obvious, is not all that is necessary. It is necessary that they should be laid open to the use of the body of the people.

The establishment by government of great public grounds for the free enjoyment of the people under certain circumstances, is thus justified and enforced as a political duty.

Such a provision, however, having regard to the whole people of a state, has never before been made and the reason it has not is evident.

It has always been the conviction of the governing classes of the old world that it is necessary that the large mass of all human communities should spend their lives in almost constant labor and that the power of enjoying beauty either of nature or of art in any high degree, requires a cultivation of certain faculties, which is impossible to these humble toilers. Hence it is thought better, so far as the recreations of the masses of a nation receive attention from their rulers, to provide artificial pleasure for them, such as theatres, parades, and promenades where they will be amused by the equipages of the rich and the animation of crowds. . . .

The main duty with which the Commissioners should be charged should be to give every advantage practicable to the mass of the people to benefit by that which is peculiar to this ground and which has caused Congress to treat it differently from other parts of the public domain. This peculiarity consists wholly in its natural scenery.

The first point to be kept in mind then is the preservation and maintenance as exactly as is possible of the natural scenery; the restriction, that is to say, within the narrowest limits consistent with the necessary accommodations of visitors, of all artificial constructions and the prevention of all constructions markedly inharmonious with the scenery or which would unnecessarily obscure, distort or detract from the dignity of the scenery.

In addition to the more immediate and obvious arrangements by which this duty is enforced there are two considerations which should not escape attention.

First: the value of the district is in its present condition as a museum of natural science and the danger, indeed the certainty, that without care many of the species of plants now flourishing upon it will be lost and many interesting objects be defaced or obscured if not destroyed. . . .

Second: it is important that it should be remembered that in permitting the sacrifice of anything that would be of the slightest value to future visitors to the convenience, bad taste, playfulness, carelessness, or wanton destructiveness of present visitors, we probably yield in each case the interest of uncounted millions to the selfishness of a few individuals. . . .

It is but sixteen years since the Yosemite was first seen by a white man, several visitors have since made a journey of several thousand miles at large cost to see it, and notwithstanding the difficulties which now interpose, hundreds resort to it annually. Before many years if proper facilities are offered, these hundreds will become thousands and in a century the whole number of visitors will be counted by the millions. An injury to the scenery so slight that it may be unheeded by any visitor now, will be one of deplorable magnitude when its effect upon each visitor's enjoyment is multiplied by these millions. But again, the slight harm which the few hundred visitors of this year might do, if no care were taken to prevent it, would not be slight if it should be repeated by millions.

At some time, therefore, laws to prevent an unjust use by individuals, of that which is not individual but public property must be made and rigidly enforced. The principle of justice involved is the same now that it will be then; such laws as this principle demands will be more easily enforced, and there will be less hardship in their action, if the abuses they are designed to prevent are never allowed to become customary but are checked while they are yet of unimportant consequence.

It should, then, be made the duty of the Commission to prevent a wanton or careless disregard on the part of anyone entering the Yosemite or the Grove, of the rights of posterity as well as of contemporary visitors, and the Commission should be clothed with proper authority and given the necessary means for this purpose.

"The Great American Park of the Yosemite"

To the Editors of the Evening Post:

With the early completion of the Pacific Railroad there can be no doubt that the Park established by act of Congress as a place of free recreation for the people of the United States and their guests forever, will be resorted to from all parts of the civilized world. Many intelligent men, nevertheless, have hardly yet heard of it, and hence an effort to give an account of the leading qualities of its scenery may be pardoned, however inadequate it is sure to be.

The main feature of the Yo Semite is best indicated in one word as a chasm. It is a chasm nearly a mile in average width, however, and more than ten miles in length. The central and broader part of this chasm is occupied at the bottom by a series of groves of magnificent trees, and meadows of the most varied, luxuriant and exquisite herbiage, through which meanders a broad stream of the clearest water, rippling over a pebbly bottom, and eddying among banks of ferns and rushes; sometimes narrowed into sparkling rapids and sometimes expanding into placid pools which reflect the wondrous heights on either side. The walls of the chasm are generally half a mile, sometimes nearly a mile in height above these meadows, and where most lofty and nearly perpendicular, sometimes over jutting. At frequent intervals, however, they are cleft, broken, terraced and sloped, and in these places, as well as everywhere upon the summit, they are overgrown by thick clusters of trees. . . .

Banks of heartsease and beds of cowslips and daisies are frequent, and thickets of dogwood, alder and willow often fringe the shores. At several points streams of water flow into the chasm, descending at one leap from five hundred to fourteen hundred feet. One small stream falls, in three closely consecutive pitches, a distance of two thousand six hundred feet, which is more than fifteen times the height of the falls of Niagara. In the spray of these falls superb rainbows are seen.

At certain points the walls of rock are ploughed in polished horizontal furrows, at others moraines of boulders and pebbles are found; both evincing the terrific force with which in past ages of the earth's history a glacier has moved down the chasm from among the adjoining peaks of the Sierras. Beyond the lofty walls still loftier mountains rise, some crowned by forests, others in simple rounded cones of light, gray granite. The climate of the region is never dry like that of the lower parts of the state of California; even when, for several months, not a drop of rain has fallen twenty miles to the westward, and the country there is parched, and all vegetation withered, the Yo Semite continues to receive frequent soft showers, and to be dressed throughout in living green. . . .

Flowering shrubs of sweet fragrance and balmy herbs abound in the meadows, and there is everywhere a delicate odor of the prevailing foliage in the pines and cedars. The water of the streams is soft and limpid, as clear as crystal, abounds with trout and, except near its sources, is, during the heat of the summer, of an agreeable temperature for bathing. . . .

The other district, associated with this by the act of Congress, consists of four sections of land, about thirty miles distant from it, on which stand in the midst of a forest composed of the usual trees and shrubs of the western slope of the Sierra Nevada, about six hundred mature trees of the giant Sequoia. Among them is one known through numerous paintings and photographs as the Grizzly Giant, which probably is the noblest tree in the world. Besides this, there are hundreds of such beauty and stateliness that, to one who moves among them in the reverent mood to which they so strongly incite the mind, it will not seem strange that intelligent travellers have declared that they would rather have passed by Niagara itself than have missed visiting this grove. . . .

By no statement of the elements of the scenery can any idea of that scenery be given, any more than a true impression can be conveyed of a human face by a measured account of its features. It is conceivable that any one or all of the cliffs of the Yosemite might be changed in form and color, without lessening the enjoyment which is now obtained from the scenery. . . .

There are falls of water elsewhere finer, there are more stupendous rocks, more beetling cliffs, there are deeper and more awful chasms, there may be as beautiful streams, as lovely meadows, there are larger trees. It is in no scene or scenes the charm consists, but in the miles of scenery where cliffs of awful height and rocks of vast magnitude and of varied and exquisite coloring, are banked and fringed and draped and shadowed by the tender foliage of noble and lovely trees and bushes, reflected from the most placid pools, and associated with the most tranquil meadows, the most playful streams, and every variety of soft and peaceful pastoral beauty.

The union of the deepest sublimity with the deepest beauty of nature, not in one feature or another, not in one part or one scene or another, not in any landscape that can be framed by itself, but all around and wherever the visitor goes, constitutes the Yo Semite[,] the greatest glory of nature. No photograph or series of photographs, no paintings ever prepare a visitor so that he is not taken by surprise, for could the scenes be faithfully represented the visitor is affected not only by that upon which his eye is at any moment fixed, but by all that with which on every side it is associated, and of which it is seen only as an inherent part. For the same reason no description, no measurements, no comparisons are of much value. Indeed, the attention called by these to points in some definite way remarkable, by fixing the mind on mere matters of wonder or curiosity presents the true and far more extr[a]ordinary character of the scenery from being appreciated.

"It is very beautiful—considerably
more beautiful than the original."

Mark Twain

Letter 24 to the *San Francisco Daily Alta California*, 1867

Yosemite was always a magnet for the monumental landscape painters of the era. Artists such as Albert Bierstadt, Thomas Hill, William Keith, and Thomas Moran helped define how the astonishing landscape was seen and interpreted. Their depictions would influence state and federal policies regarding the Yosemite region as well. Foremost among the painters was Bierstadt, who was the first of this quartet to be linked to the Yosemite Valley.

While the works of these artists were generally praised, some people viewed the paintings as unrealistic and exaggerated. For instance, detractors contended that the peaks were unnaturally jagged, or the foliage was too lush, or the rivers were an abnormally luminous hue.

As a case in point, in 1867 LeGrand Lockwood, railroad financier and officer of the New York Stock Exchange, commissioned Bierstadt to produce a Yosemite Valley work. The finished product, an enormous canvas nine and a half feet tall and fifteen feet wide, was entitled *The Domes of the Yosemite*. The painting was displayed in

"Enter These Enchanted Woods, You Who Dare"

New York and evoked both accolades and acerbic criticism. Some felt *The Domes of the Yosemite* was Bierstadt at his most inspiring and accomplished, while others echoed the judgment of *New York Tribune* art critic Clarence Cook, who dismissed the painting as clumsy, pretentious, and with "little accurate knowledge of nature."

Weighing in was a visitor to New York named Samuel Clemens, the "Special Travelling Correspondent" of the *San Francisco Daily Alta California* who began using the pseudonym "Mark Twain" early in his career. In early 1867, Twain convinced the *Daily Alta California* to provide $1,250 to pay his fare on the sidewheel steamship *Quaker City* for a tour of Europe, the Middle East, and the Holy Land. This expedition would result in Twain's *The Innocents Abroad* (1869), the book that would propel Twain to international celebrity.

As Twain traveled to New York City, he sent dispatches on his adventures to an eager audience in San Francisco. Readers often had to wait weeks for Twain's correspondence to reach the City by the Bay due to the slow pace of mail delivery at the time. In Letter 24, written in New York City on June 2, 1867, and published by the *Daily Alta California* on August 4, 1867, Twain recalls his initial reluctance to view *The Domes of the Yosemite* and offers his mixed review of the colossal painting. Five days after writing this letter, Twain would board the *Quaker City* and embark on the journey that would change his life forever.

New York,

June 2d, 1867.

"THE DOMES OF THE YOSEMITE"

That is the name of Bierstadt's last picture. The art critics here abused it without stint when its exhibition began, a month ago. They ridiculed it so mercilessly that I thought it surely could not be worth going to see, and so I staid away. I went to-day, however, and I think it is very well worth going to see. It is very beautiful—considerably more beautiful than the original.

You stand twelve hundred feet above the valley, and look up it toward the east, with the North Dome on the left and the South Dome on the right. The rugged mountain range beyond the latter sweeps round to the right and shuts up the valley, and, springing up among the clouds in the distance, you see one or two great peaks clad in robes of snow. Well, the bird's-eye view of the level valley, with its clusters of diminished trees and its little winding river, is very natural, and familiar, and pleasant to look upon. The pine trees growing out of clefts in a bold rock wall, in the right foreground, are very proper trees, and the grove of large ones, in the left foreground, and close at hand, are a true copy of Nature, and so are the various granite boulders in the vicinity.

Now, to sum up the picture's merits, those snow-peaks are correct—they look natural; the valley is correct and natural; the pine trees clinging to the bluff on the right, and the grove on the left, and the boulders, are all like nature; we will assume that the domes and things are drawn accurately. One sees these things in all sorts of places throughout California, and under all sorts of circumstances, and gets so familiar with them that he knows them in a moment when he sees them in a picture. I knew them in Bierstadt's picture, and checked them off one by one, and said "These things are correct—they all look just as they ought to look, and they all belong to California." But when I got around to the atmosphere, I was obliged to say "This man has imported this atmosphere; this man has surely imported this atmosphere from some foreign country, because nothing like it was ever seen in California." I may be mistaken, for all men are liable to err, but I honestly think I am right. The atmospheric effects in that picture are startling, are full of variety, and are charming. It is more the atmosphere of Kingdom-Come than of California.

The time is early morning; the eastern heavens are filled with shredded clouds, and these afford the excuse for the dreamy lights and shadows that play about the leftward precipices and the great dome—a rich blending of softest purple, and gray, and blue, and brown and white, instead of the bald, glaring expanse of rocks and earth splotched with cloud-shadows like unpoetical ink-blots which one ought to see in a Californian mountain picture when correctly painted. Some of Mr. Bierstadt's mountains swim in a lustrous, pearly mist, which is so enchantingly beautiful that I am sorry the Creator hadn't made it instead of him, so that it would always remain there. In the morning, the outlines of mountains in California, even though they be leagues away, are painfully bold and sharp, because the atmosphere is so pure and clear—but the outlines of Mr. Bierstadt's mountains are soft and rounded and velvety, which is a great improvement on nature.

As a picture, this work must please, but as a portrait I do not think it will answer. Portraits should be accurate. We do not want feeling and intelligence smuggled into the pictured face of an idiot, and we do not want this glorified atmosphere smuggled into a portrait of the Yosemite, where it surely does not belong. I may be wrong, but still I believe that this atmosphere of Mr. Bierstadt's is altogether too gorgeous.

Mark Twain

....

"The great attraction of Yosemite is the crowding of
a multitude of romantic, peculiar, and grand
scenery within a very small place."

....

John Shertzer Hittell

Yosemite: Its Wonders and Its Beauties, 1868

As awareness of Yosemite grew and sightseeing became less problematic, demand for reliable tourist information developed. Guidebooks were published as early as 1860, but they were text only. In 1868 John Shertzer Hittell published *Yosemite: Its Wonders and Its Beauties*, which is generally considered the first guidebook to feature photographs. The images were taken by the eccentric photographer Eadweard Muybridge. The twenty photographs were hand-pasted, or "tipped," into individual copies of the book. As a result, the pages in Hittell's book are "cockled," meaning they have a rippled or wavy appearance.

Yosemite: Its Wonders and Its Beauties borrowed heavily from other Yosemite chronicles of the time, including descriptions by Josiah D. Whitney, Samuel Bowles, Horace Greeley, and Thomas Starr King. What makes the fifty-nine-page guidebook unique is the photographs, which provided genuine visual representation of the fabled valley, rather than artists' interpretive engravings or drawings.

Hittell was an intriguing figure as well. Born in Pennsylvania in 1825, he graduated with a master of arts degree from Miami University in Ohio at the age of eighteen. He became a lawyer soon afterward. Following a health setback, Hittell left Ohio to become a forty-niner by joining the California gold rush. He took a crack at mining but failed. By 1853 Hittell had become a member of the *San Francisco Daily Alta California* editorial staff, and he remained there for the next twenty-five years. Over his long career, Hittell wrote many books on history, mining, religion, and politics. He was considered an expert on California industries and natural resources and was fluent in multiple languages, including Latin, Greek, German, and French.

In this excerpt from *Yosemite: Its Wonders and Its Beauties*, Hittell describes the "General Features" of Yosemite Valley and offers tips for tourists.

Yosemite Valley is generally regarded by travelers who have visited it, and have seen many of the most noted scenes in other countries, as one of the greatest, if not *the* greatest of the natural wonders of the world. Niagara, the Mammoth Cave, the Giant's Causeway, the views from Mount Diablo, Mount Shasta, Mount Washington, Ben Lomond, or from any peak of the Alps, are rated as far inferior by those whose ability, taste and observation give authority to their judgment. There is more to see in Switzerland than in this one little valley, but if a fair comparison is to be made by taking into account the whole region of the Californian Alps, from the Mokolumne [sic] to Kern River, a distance of a hundred miles, the Helvetian Alps will be as much inferior as the Staubbach is to the grand Cataract of the Sierra Nevada is. The great attraction of Yosemite is the crowding of a multitude of romantic, peculiar and grand scenes within a very small space. One of these waterfalls, one of these vertical cliffs, half a mile high, one of these dome or egg-shaped mountains, or the chasm itself, as a geological curiosity, would be worthy of worldwide fame; but at Yosemite there are eight cataracts, five domes, a dozen cliffs, several lakes and caverns, and numberless minor wonders, besides the big-tree groves near by, and a score of mountains that reach an elevation varying from 13,000 to 15,000 feet, including the highest peak of the United States, within sight. The cataract of the Staubbach, of Switzerland, reputed to be the highest waterfall of the Old World, is only nine hundred feet high, and that of Tequendama, in New Grenada [sic], which had the first place in the New World before the discovery of the Yosemite, is only six hundred and fifty. The largest and highest works of human art dwindle into insignificance when compared in bulk or elevation with the tremendous precipices of Yosemite. The elevation of Cheops pyramid is four hundred and ninety-eight feet, and the highest cathedral spires are those of Strasb[o]urg, four hundred and sixty-six feet, Vienna, four hundred and forty-one feet, and of Rome, four hundred and thirty-two feet. They would be lost in the unnoticed talus of Tutucanula, which rises to 3,800 feet, or of Sentinel Rock, which ascends to 3,000.

Yosemite Valley is situated one hundred and forty miles east of San Francisco, on the western slope of the Sierra Nevadas, thirty miles west of their summit, at an elevation of 4,060 feet above the sea. The general course of the valley is nearly east and west, its length about eight miles, and the width of the level bottom land from half a mile to a mile. The walls are of granite, varying in height from 1,200 to 4,700 feet, in many points vertical, and in all very steep, so that there is no place where a wagon can enter it, only two where horses can get in, and there with much difficulty, and half a dozen others where men can clamber out. The two sides of the valley are crooked, and nearly parallel to each other, suggesting the idea that they were torn apart from each other, and have not changed much in outline since. At the base of the walls on each side is a talus or slope (of rocks and dirt which have fallen from above). The angle of this talus is from twenty-five to forty degrees, the height from one hundred to four hundred feet, generally two hundred. The main material is rock, covered in most places with a stony soil, and elsewhere bare, showing here small fragments of rock, and there immense masses, with great passages under their projecting edges. The bare rocks of the talus are largest in the Toloolewack cañon. The color of the walls is yellowish on the north side of the valley, and blue or gray on the south.

The Merced runs nearly in the middle of the valley, is sixty feet wide, from three to eight feet deep in July, and the surface is generally from five to ten feet below the surface of the valley. The river is clear and the current lively; the descent in the eight miles of valley being about fifty feet. The water is never warm enough for comfortable bathing, but there are some ponds which get warm in the summer.

A party intending to go to Yosemite should make special preparation. Those who do not know how to ride should learn; those who know should take a ride every day for a week before starting, so as to be hardened to the saddle. The trip is a hard one, and it can be a very uncomfortable one for those who do not undertake it in the right manner. Both men and women need heavy, thick-soled, calf-skin boots, leather gloves, and stout dress of cheap material. The boots should be well greased with linseed oil thickened with beeswax, as a protection against the water with which the grass is filled every night by the dew. Men who intend to remain long or to climb about much should have duck trowsers. The shirts should be of flannel. Coats are unnecessary. Every lady should have a bloomer dress, or at least a pair of blue drilling pants, and should have the company either of a husband or of another lady. Many ladies ride astride in and near the Valley, and they find it much more comfortable. There is no laundry or laundress at Yosemite, and every tourist washes his own clothes, that is, if they are washed there at all. Ladies who clamber about much usually find their clothes fit only for throwing away by the time they reach Coulterville or Mariposa, and it is well to take a suit that can be thrown away. Clothing should be carried to Coulterville or Mariposa, in a trunk or valise, which can be left there until the return.

....

"Tuolumne Valley, or Hetch-Hetchy,
as it is called by the Indians . . ."

....

Charles F. Hoffmann

"Notes on Hetch-Hetchy Valley," 1868

In the 1860s, as now, most visitors considered "Yosemite" to be Yosemite Valley and nothing else. But for some, especially scientists, geologists, and naturalists, Yosemite was much larger, an ecosystem encompassing hundreds of thousands of acres beyond the valley.

Among these proponents was Charles F. Hoffmann. Born Carl Frederick Hoffmann in Prussia, where he was educated as a civil engineer, he immigrated to the United States in 1857. Known in America as Charles, he was a topographer for Frederick Lander's 1857 Fort Kearney, South Pass, and Honey Lake wagon-road survey. He came to California in 1858 and was recruited by Josiah Whitney to join the California Geological Survey as a topographer. Hoffmann explored and surveyed the Sierra Nevada in 1860–70 and 1873–74. He was a member of the survey team that made the first known ascents of Mount Brewer, Mount Dana, Mount Silliman, and Tower Peak in the Sierra Nevada. Mount Hoffmann in Yosemite National Park is named in his honor. Hoffmann is considered one of the founding fathers of American topographic mapping for his origination of the triangulation technique.

Charles F. Hoffmann later became a mine owner and superintendent and a widely respected mining engineer. Hoffmann toured the world as an influential consultant for mining companies and advisor to governments. He traveled throughout the American West, including Alaska, and internationally, visiting many countries, including Germany, France, England, Russia, Mexico, and Argentina.

In the 1868 *Proceedings of the California Academy of Sciences*, Hoffmann wrote of the Hetch Hetchy Valley as part of the broader Yosemite environment. He conducted the first survey of the valley in 1867. Hetch Hetchy Valley is roughly twenty miles north of Yosemite Valley, would ultimately be incorporated within the national park boundaries, and, since the first nonindigenous visitors arrived in the region in the 1850s, had been considered an equally beautiful but largely unknown "twin" of Yosemite Valley. Hetch Hetchy Valley would become

"Enter These Enchanted Woods, You Who Dare"

the subject of major controversy in the early twentieth century when San Francisco proposed (and ultimately succeeded) in gaining federal approval to build a dam and use the valley as a reservoir.

Tuolumne Valley, or Hetch-Hetchy, as it is called by the Indians (the meaning of this word I was unable to ascertain) is situated on Tuolumne River about fifteen miles in a straight line below Tuolumne Meadows and Soda Springs, and about twelve miles north of Yosemite Valley. Its elevation above the sea is from 3,800 to 3,900 feet, a little less than that of Yosemite. The valley is three miles long running nearly east and west, with but little fall in this distance. Near its center it is cut in two by a low spur of shelving granite coming from the south. The lower part forms a large open meadow with excellent grass; one mile in length, and gradually increasing from ten chains to a little over half a mile in width, and only timbered along the edges. The lower part of this meadow terminates in a very narrow cañon, the hills sloping down to the river at an angle of from 40° to 60°, only leaving a channel from six to ten feet wide; the river in the valley having an average width of about fifty feet. This is the principal cause of the overflow in spring time of the lower part of the valley, and probably also has given rise to the report of there being a large lake in the valley. Below this cañon is another small meadow, with a pond. The upper part of Hetch-Hetchy, east of the granite spur, forms a meadow one and three-fourths miles in length, varying from ten to thirty chains in width, well timbered and affording good grazing. The scenery resembles very much that of the Yosemite, although the bluffs are not as high, nor do they extend as far. On the north side of the valley, opposite the granite spur we first have a perpendicular bluff, the top of which is 1,800 feet above the valley; the talus at the base is about five hundred feet above the valley, leaving a precipice of about 1,300 feet. In the spring when the snows are melting a large creek precipitates itself over the western part of this bluff. I was told that this fall is one of the grandest features of the valley, sending its spray all over its lower portion. It was dry, however, at the time of my visit. The fall is 1,000 feet perpendicular after which it strikes the debris and loses itself among the rocks. About thirty chains further east we come to the Hetch-Hetchy fall; its height above the valley is 1,700 feet. This fall is not perpendicular, although it appears so from the front, as may be seen from the photograph by Mr. Harris. It falls in a series of cascades at an angle of about 70°. At the time of my visit the volume of water was much greater than that of Yosemite fall, and I was told that in the spring its roarings can be heard for miles.

Still further east we have two peaks, shaped very much like "The Three Brothers," in the Yosemite. Their base forms a large, naked and sloping granite wall on the north side of the valley, broken by two timbered shelves, which run horizontally the whole length of the wall. Up to the lower shelf or bend, about eight hundred feet high, the wall, which slopes at an angle of from 45° to 70°, is polished by glaciers, and probably these markings extend still higher up, as on entering the valley the trail followed back of and along a moraine for several miles, the height of which was about 1,200 feet above the valley. The same polish shows itself in places all along the bluffs on both sides, and particularly fine on the granite spur crossing the valley. There is no doubt that the largest branch of the great glacier which originated near Mt. Dana and Mount Lyell, made its way by Soda Springs to this valley. A singular feature of this valley is the total absence of talus or debris at the base of the bluffs, excepting at one place in front of the falls. Another remarkable rock, corresponding with Cathedral Rock in the Yosemite, stands on the south side of the valley, directly opposite Hetch-Hetchy fall; its height is 2,270 feet above the valley. . . .

At the upper end of the valley the river forks, one branch, nearly as large as the main river, coming from near Castle Peak, the main river itself from Soda Springs. About half a

"Enter These Enchanted Woods, You Who Dare"

mile up the main cañon, the river forms some cascades, the highest being about thirty feet.

The valley was first visited, in 1850, by Mr. Joseph Screech, a mountaineer of this region, who found it occupied by Indians. This gentleman informed me that, up to a very recent date, this valley was disputed ground between the Pah Utah Indians from the eastern slope and the Big Creek Indians from the western slope of the Sierras; they had several fights, in which the Pah Utahs proved victorious. The latter still visit the valley every fall to gather acorns, which abound in this locality. Here I may also mention that the Indians speak of a lake of very salt water [Mono Lake], on their trail from here to Castle Peak. Mr. Screech also informed me of the existence of a fall, about a hundred feet high, on the Tuolumne River, about four miles below this valley, and which prevents fish from coming up any higher. The climate is said to be milder in winter than that of the Yosemite Valley, as is also indicated by a larger number of oaks and a great number of *Pinus Sabiniana*. The principal tree of the valley is *Pinus ponderosa*; besides this we have *P. Sabiniana*, Cedar, *Q. Sonomensis*, *Q. crassipocula*; also poplar and cottonwood.

The valley can he reached easily from Big Oak Flat by taking the regular Yosemite trail, by Sprague's Ranch and Big Flume, as far as Mr. Hardin's fence, between south and middle fork of Tuolumne River, about eighteen miles from Big Oak Flat. Here the trail turns off to the left, going to Wade's Meadows or Big Meadows, sometimes called Reservoir Meadows, the distance being about seven miles. From Wade's Ranch the trail crosses the middle fork of Tuolumne and goes to the Hog Ranch [Hogg Ranch], five miles; thence up [the] divide between the middle fork and main river, about two miles, to another little ranch called "The Cañon." From here the trail winds down through rocks for six miles to Tuolumne Cañon. This trail is well blazed, and was made by Mr. Screech and others, for the purpose of driving sheep and cattle to the valley. The whole distance from Big Oak Flat is thirty-eight miles.

Another trail equally good, but a little longer, leaves the Yosemite trail about half a mile beyond the crossing of the south fork, thence crosses the middle fork within about one and a half miles of the south fork crossing, and follows up the divide between the middle fork and the main river, joining the first-named trail at the Hog Ranch.

"Enter These Enchanted Woods, You Who Dare"

7

"All Places That the Eye of Heaven Visits"

Improvements and Irritations, 1870–1889

From 1870 to 1889, Yosemite contended with a new reality but saw old problems persist.

When the Yosemite Valley Grant Act of 1864 brought Yosemite Valley and the Mariposa Grove of Giant Sequoias under the jurisdiction of the State of California, many hoped that the thorny challenges of commercial threats to the extraordinary landscape would disappear, or at least diminish. However, resolution of homesteading claims in the valley took more than a decade. Overgrazing, logging, and mining had severe impacts on the ecosystem adjacent to the Yosemite Valley. Directors of the state's Yosemite Park Commission were often at cross purposes, desirous of environmental protection but also cognizant of the need to promote economic sustainability and enhance the visitor experience. Some suspected the commissioners were clandestine agents of special interests. Critics of the commission called for reform or, better yet, transferring Yosemite Valley and the Mariposa Grove to more trusted federal authority, with expanded boundaries for the park.

The wonders of Yosemite were now widely advertised, and the public's desire to visit grew. However, particularly during the early 1870s, tourists continued to endure lengthy, disagreeable journeys to the park and environs. Roads were being developed or improved, but until 1874 the final twenty miles to the valley had to be traversed on horseback. In the mid-1870s private toll roads extended into the valley, but it still took several days to get to Yosemite from the closest urban areas. Often overlooked is that many of the era's roads were constructed by Chinese crews. In 1873 Chinese laborers built a road from the South Fork of the Merced River to the western boundary of the Mariposa Grove of Giant Sequoias. In the frigid winter of 1874–75, more than 300 Chinese workers crafted a road to carry stagecoaches from the South Fork of the Merced River to Yosemite Valley. In 1883 Chinese workers were instrumental in the construction of the Tioga Road, the 56-mile west-to-east road that bisects Yosemite National Park. Also known as the Great Sierra Wagon Road, the Tioga Road was completed in an astonishing 130 days. Most of the Chinese labor force also worked at the Wawona Hotel, owned and operated by Albert Henry Washburn and his family from 1875 to 1932. In addition to building roads, the Chinese staff, whose community was clustered near the hotel, tended the hotel garden, apple orchard, dairy, and chicken coop and were highly regarded chefs in the hotel kitchen.

Despite improvements to roads and other infrastructure, a Yosemite excursion still largely remained the domain of plucky adventurers. Due to the difficulty in reaching the vast granite temple, wealthier visitors tended to stay for weeks, even months.

The rude lodgings of the 1850s and 1860s were in the next two decades supplemented with a handful of more luxurious accommodations, such as the Wawona Hotel and the Stoneman House Hotel. Sightseers relished the opportunity to patronize the Cosmopolitan Bathhouse and Saloon in the heart of the valley. From 1871 to 1884, grateful Cosmopolitan customers could enjoy hot baths at any hour, tipple at the well-stocked bar, get their hair cut or styled, or play billiards. While camping, hiking, and rock climbing were not yet fashionable activities, fee-based horse and carriage trails were popular. A few intrepid explorers scaled the granite monuments, most notably the supposedly unconquerable Half Dome in 1875.

The small number of Yosemite Valley Indian residents were denigrated, stripped of their humanity, and became bit players in their own country, which often meant being relegated to costumed performances for sightseers.

Tourist visits climbed to a few thousand annually, and some these guests were famous. Transcendentalist icon Ralph Waldo Emerson was a caller, as was huckster par excellence P. T. Barnum. The register of the Cosmopolitan Bathhouse and Saloon included such names as author Rudyard Kipling, newspaper magnate William Randolph Hearst, actress Lillie Langtry, showman Buffalo Bill Cody, Civil War general William Tecumseh Sherman, former U.S. presidents Ulysses S. Grant and Rutherford B. Hayes, and future president James Garfield.

But the rich and famous were not immune from the nuisances all visitors faced—dust, insects, unpredictable weather, the smell of horse manure, and bears. For some tourists, there was an unexpected sense of isolation and claustrophobia.

In this chapter, the selections reflect the jumble of sentiments prevalent from 1870 to 1889. Some excerpts extol the valley's awe-inspiring beauty, while others bemoan the accommodations, the cost, and annoying tourists—some passages do both. Some found Yosemite exhilarating, while others viewed the Yosemite Valley as a granite prison. Some felt that Yosemite had become less a spiritual and geologic refuge, and more a romantic fantasy, a wilderness theme park. All found Yosemite distinctive and deserving of every effort to preserve and protect its standing as an unsurpassed natural cathedral.

"After supper, sat around our camp-fire, smoked our cigarettes, and sang in chorus until 9:30 P.M."

Joseph LeConte

A Journal of Ramblings through the High Sierras, 1870

Joseph LeConte (1823–1901) earned his medical degree in New York and set up a practice in his home state of Georgia but soon discovered that his true calling was geology. LeConte went back to school, studying geology at Harvard, and upon graduation taught natural science, chemistry, and geology at numerous colleges in the South. In 1869 LeConte moved to Berkeley, California, where he joined the faculty of the recently created University of California. He was accompanied by his brother John, a physics professor and future president of the University of California.

In 1870 LeConte embarked on a five-week horseback trip to Yosemite Valley and the High Sierra with a party that included other University of California students and professors. As a result of this excursion and other subsequent visits, this group would soon initiate a campaign to establish today's Yosemite National Park and to promote more recreational use of the Sierra Nevada.

Some of the members of the 1870 expedition were also responsible for urging the founding of the Sierra Club, which appeared on the scene in 1892, with LeConte himself serving as director of the club for several years. A prolific author on a wide array of subjects, LeConte died of a heart attack during a 1901 Sierra Club outing in Yosemite.

In 1903 the Sierra Club built the LeConte Memorial Lodge in his memory. Located in Yosemite Valley, the lodge was renamed the Yosemite Conservation Heritage Center in 2016 after reassessment of Joseph LeConte's white supremacist writings. An unrepentant Confederate and enslaver, LeConte considered Reconstruction indefensible. In his posthumously published *Autobiography of Joseph LeConte* (1903) are frequent negative references to Reconstruction policies, including the statement that "sudden enfranchisement of the negro without qualification was the greatest political crime ever perpetrated by any people, as is now admitted by all thoughtful men."

Despite LeConte's inexcusable racist rantings, he was an early expert focusing on Yosemite and produced commentary that remains a valuable window into what became a standard nineteenth-century manner of sci-

"All Places That the Eye of Heaven Visits"

entific writing about the valley—a mixture of scientific rigor and wistful reverie. In this passage from *A Journal of Ramblings through the High Sierras of California*, LeConte recalls his astonishment at his first glimpse of the Yosemite Valley and his observations on the nature of Sierran granite.

July 30 [1870]

With increasing enthusiasm we pushed on until, about 6 P.M., we reached and climbed Sentinel Dome. This point is 4,500 feet above Yosemite Valley, and 8,500 feet above the sea. The view which here burst upon us, of the valley and the Sierra, it is simply impossible to describe. Sentinel Dome stands on the south margin of Yosemite, near the point where it branches into three cañons. To the left stands El Capitan's massive perpendicular wall; directly in front, and distant about one mile, Yosemite Falls, like a gauzy veil, rippling and waving with a slow, mazy motion; to the right the mighty granite mass of Half Dome lifts itself in solitary grandeur, defying the efforts of the climber; to the extreme right, and a little behind, Nevada Fall, with the Cap of Liberty; in the distance, innumerable peaks of the High Sierra, conspicuous among which are Clouds Rest, Mt. Starr King, Cathedral Peak, etc. We remained on the top of this dome more than an hour, to see the sunset. We were well repaid—such a sunset I never saw; such a sunset, combined with such a view, I had never imagined. The glorious golden and crimson in the west, and the exquisitely delicate diffused rosebloom, tingeing the cloud caps of the Sierra in the east, and the shadows of the grand peaks and domes slowly creeping up the valley! I can never forget the impression. We remained, enjoying this scene, too long to think of going to Glacier Point this evening. We therefore put this off until morning, and returned on our trail about one and a half miles, to a beautiful green meadow (Hawkins had chosen it on his way to Sentinel Dome), and there made camp in a grove of magnificent fir trees (*Abies magnifica*).

July 31 (Sunday)

I got up at peep of day this morning (I am dishwash today), roused the party, started a fire, and in ten minutes tea was ready. All partook heartily of this delicious beverage, and started on foot to see the sunrise from Glacier Point. This point is about one and a half miles from our camp, about 3,200 feet above the valley, and forms the salient angle on the south side, just where the valley divides into three. We had to descend about eight hundred feet to reach it. We arrived just before sunrise. Sunrise from Glacier Point! No one can appreciate it who has not seen it. It was our good fortune to have an exceedingly beautiful sunrise. Rosy-fingered Aurora revealed herself to us, her votaries, more bright and charming and rosy than ever before. But the great charm was the view of the valley and surrounding peaks, in the fresh, cool morning hour and in the rosy light of the rising sun; the bright, warm light on the mountaintops, and the cool shade in the valley. The shadow of the grand Half Dome stretches clear across the valley, while its own "bald, awful head" glitters in the early sunlight. To the right, Vernal and Nevada falls, with their magnificent overhanging peaks, in full view; while directly across, see the ever-rippling, ever-swaying gauzy veil of the Yosemite Falls, reaching from top to bottom of the opposite cliff, 2,600 feet. Below, at a depth of 3,200 feet, the bottom of the valley lies like a garden. There, right under our noses, are the hotels, the orchards, the fields, the meadows (near one of these Hawkins even now selects our future camp), the forests, and through all the Merced River winds its apparently lazy serpentine way. Yonder, up the Tenaya Cañon, nestling close under the shadow of Half Dome, lies Mirror Lake, fast asleep, her polished black surface not yet ruffled by the rising wind. I have heard and read much of this wonderful valley, but I can truly say I have never imagined the grandeur of the reality. After about one and a half hours' rapturous gaze, we returned to camp and breakfasted. . . .

After breakfast we returned to Glacier Point and spent the

"All Places That the Eye of Heaven Visits"

whole of the beautiful Sunday morning in the presence of grand mountains, yawning chasms, and magnificent falls. What could we do better than allow these to preach to us? Was there ever so venerable, majestic, and eloquent a minister of natural religion as the grand old Half Dome? I withdrew myself from the rest of the party and drank in his silent teachings for several hours. . . .

August 2

Started this morning up the valley. As we go, the striking features of Yosemite pass in procession before us. On the left, El Capitan, Three Brothers, Yosemite Falls; on the right, Cathedral Rock, Cathedral Spires, Sentinel Rock.

Cathedral Spires really strongly remind one of a huge cathedral, with two tall, equal spires, five hundred feet high, and several smaller ones. I was reminded of old Trinity [Episcopal Church], in Columbia [South Carolina]. But this was not made with hands, and is over two thousand feet high. . . .

In the afternoon went on up the valley, and again the grand procession commences. On the left, Royal Arches, Washington Column, North Dome; on the right, Sentinel Dome, Glacier Point, Half Dome. We pitched our camp in a magnificent forest, near a grassy meadow (the same Hawkins had selected from Glacier Point yesterday), on the banks of Tenaya Fork, and under the shadow of our venerated preacher and friend, the Half Dome, with also North Dome, Washington Column, and Glacier Point in full view.

After unsaddling and turning loose our horses to graze, and resting a little, we went up the Tenaya Cañon about one and a half miles, to Mirror Lake, and took a swimming bath. The scenery about this lake is truly magnificent.

The cliffs of Yosemite here reach the acme of imposing grandeur. On the south side the broad face of South Dome rises almost from the water, a sheer precipice, near five thousand feet perpendicular; on the north side, North Dome, with its finely rounded head, to an almost equal height. Down the cañon, to the west, the view is blocked by the immense cliffs of Glacier Point and Washington Column; and up the cañon, to the east, the cliffs of the Tenaya Cañon, and Clouds' Rest, and the peaks of the Sierra in the background.

On returning to camp, as we expected to remain here for several days, we carried with us a number of "shakes" (split boards), and constructed a very good table, around which we placed logs for seats. We cooked our supper, sat around our rude board, and enjoyed our meal immensely. After supper, sat around our camp-fire, smoked our cigarettes, and sang in chorus until 9:30 P.M., then rolled ourselves, chrysalis-like, in our blanket cocoons, and lay still until morning. . . .

". . . don't go to Yo Semite."

Olive Logan
"Does It Pay to Visit Yo Semite?," 1870

A common thread in the earliest Yosemite literature is an admission that getting to Yosemite Valley was difficult. Customarily, this acknowledgment was underplayed, simply viewed as the price to be paid to visit the natural wonder.

However, there were exceptions to this rule, and a classic example was an October 1870 magazine article by Olive Logan entitled "Does It Pay to Visit Yo Semite?" The article appeared in *The Galaxy*, a monthly journal that was published from 1866 until 1878, when it merged with the *Atlantic Monthly*. It frequently featured the work of prominent literary figures such as Mark Twain, Walt Whitman, Anthony Trollope, Bret Harte, William Cullen Bryant, and Henry James.

Logan was born in New York in 1839. The daughter of stage performers, she was an actress, playwright, novelist, newspaper correspondent, and lecturer. She was a feminist and spoke throughout the United States in support of women's suffrage. Logan was also a bit of a professional scold, often hurling her sharpest barbs at theatrical targets. She reserved special rancor for the era's popular "leg shows," which she considered exploitative and demeaning to women.

In this excerpt from "Does It Pay to Visit Yo Semite?," Logan does not follow the usual practice of minimizing the hardship of visiting Yosemite but instead makes it her central theme. She rails against the wobbly stagecoach, the dust, the dangerous roads, the poor quality of food and accommodations, and the painful horseback rides. And if that is not enough, Logan finds the Yosemite scenery decidedly underwhelming.

Logan's narrative also includes one of the most odious descriptions of the Native population in all of Yosemite literature. She notes that, as her party approached a Yosemite Indian village, "a vile stench greets us. These filthy wretches found a dead horse yesterday, and are now eating some of its carcass. . . . It will not do to approach these people too closely; they are covered with vermin. . . . The consequence is that the sight of these people so near a pleasure resort is an offence to decency."

I can imagine with what a shout of derision my audacious question will be received by those valiant travellers who have never been to the celebrated Valley; but as I have just returned from my trip *de rigueur* to Yo Semite, and am now, thank fortune, comfortably quartered in a civilized hotel, I think it not unwise to tell a plain, unvarnished tale of what awaits the Yo Semite pilgrim; for of the dozens of persons who have written about Yo Semite, I have never known one who gave anything like an accurate description of the perils and tortures attendant upon the journey thither.

I have said the trip was *de rigueur*. No sooner do you announce to your friends in New York that you are going to California than they immediately cry out, "Ah, then you will see the Yo Semite!" . . .

I must confess it was rather appalling to discover that of the three roads leading to the Valley, even the shortest required two days of staging and one whole day on horseback—before reaching the Earthly Paradise. The Mariposa road is admitted to have fifty miles of horseback trail; the Coulterville twenty-five; that via Hardin's and Chinese Camp only eighteen. I chose the last. . . .

I found that travellers cannot take baggage to Yo Semite. The stages are full of passengers, and have small accommodation for superfluous freight; and when you leave the stage and take to horses, the transportation of baggage is next to impossible. Everything is carried into the Valley on pack-mules, and travellers are frankly told by the agent that a small hand-bag is all that can be taken. "What, no linen—no clean dress? Nothing in the world for two weeks in summer, but a comb and a tooth-brush?" Even so.

At my last breakfast at the Grand Hotel in San Francisco, prior to leaving by rail for Stockton and thence to Yo Semite, there entered the dining room and sat down opposite our party a very distinguished-looking Englishman, who, hearing us talking about Yo Semite, begged our pardons and wanted to know if we were going there. Superfluous question! Doesn't everybody go there? "A terrible trip," said this English gentleman, when I answered in the affirmative, "especially for ladies; and you may take my word for it, it's a trip that *don't pay.*" . . .

I had heard of the dust of California roads, but this surpasses belief. It would be an impossibility for any road in an Eastern State to be so dusty, try as it might; for its soil is nowhere parched with a six months' drought. California ladies have told me that they have seen their husbands come home after stage rides so begrimed with dust that neither the wives of their bosoms nor the mothers who bore them could recognize the wanderers. I tried to talk to my companion in the stage; I was choked by the dust. Conversation was impossible. A fence six feet from the stage window was invisible behind the dust cloud. I put my head gasping out of the window to see the driver. He was gone; so were the horses. The crack of the whip was still heard, and some locomo-

"All Places That the Eye of Heaven Visits"

tive power was impelling us forward; but through the dust who should say what it was? The features of my companions grew indistinguishable through the layers upon layers which gathered upon their once ruddy faces. . . . The wobbling very soon became general, universal, annoying, painful, intolerable, maddening! We had left the few miles of level road which beguile the traveller on leaving Stockton, and were now ascending the foot-hills. And our troubles were but begun. At Chinese Camp some of our passengers got out to go by another route. We also got out, for here we changed stages. We left the decent coach which took us up at Stockton, and were now ensconced in a hard, lumbering, springless, unpainted fiend . . . , and were thumped along at the pace of lunatics over the stony ascent. . . .

At present you are coated with dust, your eyes are smarting, your tongue is clogged, your hair is caked, your limbs are sore, your flesh is inflamed, you want to go home, [a]nd this is only the first day, over the best part of the road, and in the stage. What will it be when it comes to the "trail" and the "pack" and the "horseback" part of it? . . .

Presently the road began to grow worse, then worse; then— "Oh, driver, stop! let me get out and walk! Oh, do go slowly!"—a chorus from inside. The brute, unmindful, tears madly on—jolting over rocks, goading his horses down the hollows only to run up the opposite side at an insane gallop, sending the battered inmates to the roof, where their heads are banged and beaten; around jutting and dangerous precipices, where one inch too near the edge will pitch the stage, crashing through pines, to destruction. . . .

We have not seen the Valley yet. The Valley will repay us for all, the stage-driver says, as he stops to water his horses.

After miles of uncomfortable travel aboard the "lumbering, springless, unpainted fiend" of a stagecoach, Olive Logan and her traveling companions continued on horseback for the final descent into Yosemite Valley.

. . . We mount our steeds—sorry brutes, who look at us

with eyes of sullen reproach. I must confess they are badly treated. Not the slightest politeness is shown even the most aged of them.

At first the change from the stage to the horse is pleasant. At least you can now regulate your own miseries, and need no longer be a poor thing beaten and banged by a merciless stage-driver without remorse. This is your theory. It is groundless. . . .

We are drenched and weary—oh, so weary! We let the reins fall over the horse's neck. He follows the trail of his own free-will, and has such an affectionate regard for the blazes, that he scrubs us up against the trees to our infinite discomfort. . . .

There are only ten miles more of this torture left. At least so we are told by one party; another says there are fifteen. In San Francisco we were told that the whole distance on horseback (of which we have come already considerably more than ten miles) was but eighteen. Doctors and mountaineers disagree. At length an astute person settles it. "It may be eighteen miles measuring as the bird flies, but as *you don't go that way*, you'll find it's about double." No; not being birds, we don't go that way. . . .

And now begins the weary trudge again. Oh, positively we shall never live through it. . . . And so on and on and on we go. Eight miles! It is eighty! At length we reach the precipice which is to conduct us into the Valley. . . .

We do get there at last—all things have an end. But the night has fallen again; we should have reached Hutchings's [Hotel] at noon, but were not able. At any rate, here we are. Our sufferings are at an end now. And to-morrow shall burst upon our enchanted eyes the glorious sight whose beauty is to atone for all. Meantime we are too paralyzed to stir. . . .

The dawn breaks in the morning of the next day, and, shining red as fire through the pine knots of the log-cabin where [James Mason] Hutchings dwells, strikes our leaden eyelids and bids us arise. Reluctantly we do so. This is the end of our wanderings. Here is the great prize to obtain a view of which

"All Places That the Eye of Heaven Visits"

we have come so many weary miles. Now we are to be repaid for all. We make a hurried toilet, and as quickly as our stiffened limbs will permit, we drag out to see the view which shall awe us, shall make us lose our identity, shall cause us to feel as though we were in the spirit land. . . .

And what do we see? Tall rocks, a few tall trees, a high and narrow waterfall, a pretty little river! No more. A lovely natural scene, I grant you; but oh! where in this broad and beautiful land of ours are not lovely natural scenes the rule? Words cannot tell the feeling of cold despair which came over me and all our party as we looked about us. Was it for this we had so suffered! . . .

And then we learn to our dismay, that to see anything more than this in the Valley we have got to mount those unhappy brutes again, and, with Ferguson tagging at our heels at an exorbitant price daily, make trips as dangerous and as perilous, as rocky and as unpleasant in every way as that which with so much difficulty we have just now accomplished! In the house there is neither amusement nor comfort. We are dirty, sick, sore, and miserable, and at night, as we creep heartsick to bed, we can think of nothing but— the Yo Semite Fall, the Bridal Veil, El Capitan, the Cathedral Rocks? *No!* Of the weary distance which lies between us and civilization. . . .

By another day some of us are well enough to mount again and begin our search after Beauty. We find an occasional rattlesnake, unlimited fatigue, and the tombstone of a man who was kicked to death by his horse. The trips are very wearying, the scenery very grand, very beautiful, but we are in no condition to enjoy it. We never get in such condition, and the universal verdict with us is that if every one of the waterfalls in Yo Semite were magnified, every one of its granite domes were an Olympus, if its rivers were the Rhine, and its valley the fairy gardens of Versailles, the sight of it would not repay one for the suffering involved in getting to it. And the plain truth is that nine out of ten who visit Yo Semite think this, but they will not say what they think. . . .

At the end of three days, homesick, and above all physically sick, we conclude to go home. . . .

. . . Spend your money freely in California, for they need it, times being hard, and it is better, more fraternal, to give your money to California than to Europe; go to any of the mountain towns where the railroad stops (the railroad, from end to end, is in splendid condition); but *don't* go to the Geysers, *don't* go to Lake Tahoe, *don't* go to Yo Semite.

"The charm of the wonderful valley
is its cheerfulness and joy."

Anonymous [William Nelson?]
The Yosemite Valley, and the Mammoth
Trees and Geysers of California, 1870

With the completion of the transcontinental railroad in 1869 and road improvements to Yosemite Valley, visitation surged in the 1870s. While the numbers were only in the few thousands annually, tourism greatly increased from the trickle of previous years. As a result, the demand for Yosemite guidebooks also swelled.

Early guidebooks tended to be simple, straightforward inventories with distances, itineraries, and checklists of necessary supplies. But as more and more craved additional information about discussions of Yosemite, the guidebooks of the 1870s offered facts blended with emotional musings. A prime example, circa 1870, was *The Yosemite Valley, and the Mammoth Trees and Geysers of California*, part of a series of illustrated travel guides published by the venerable English publisher Thomas Nelson and Sons, which had been in business since 1798.

Although the fifty-two-page guidebook (including twelve full-color plates) does not list an author, most believe it was written by William Nelson, one of the "sons" of Thomas Nelson and Sons. This is given credence by a footnote on page 32 about a visit to the privately owned Calaveras Grove of Big Trees: "A lady of our party—Mrs. William Nelson, the wife of Mr. W. Nelson, of the well-known British publishing firm of Thomas Nelson and Sons—was allowed by the proprietor of these trees to name one of them after the city of her residence [Edinburgh]."

In this excerpt from *The Yosemite Valley, and the Mammoth Trees and Geysers of California*, the author describes Bridalveil Fall, Yosemite Falls, Lake Ah-Wi-Yah (more commonly known as Mirror Lake), and the lasting imprint made by the "divine atmosphere" of "this Eden land" on the psyche. It is an invigorating fusion of fantasy, practical guidance, and Victorian floridity.

We now begin our exploration of the valley.

The first feature which impresses us is the *Bridal Veil Fall* (the *Pohonó*, or "Spirit of the Evil Wind"), which descends from a height of about 940 feet. Pohonó is an evil spirit of the Indian mythology. The tradition connected with this fall, and with the second peak of the summit west of it, where you may trace the noble head and features of a demi-god in profile, we shall hereafter relate.

The fall itself is the overflow of a stream which flows down a rugged canyon, some twelve or fifteen miles, before it lets itself down from the brink of the cliff in one unbroken sheet of silver, forty feet wide, upon a mass of gigantic boulders.

Its American name is rather happy. For to one viewing it in profile, says [Fitz Hugh] Ludlow, its snowy sheet, broken into the filmy silver lacework of airy spray, and falling entirely free of the brow of the precipice, might well seem the veil worn by Earth at her "granite wedding," millions, it may be, millions of years ago.

On either side of Pohonó the sky-line of the precipice is diversified in the boldest and most striking manner. The fall itself cleaves a deep chasm into the crown of the battlement. To the south-west rises a bold but unnamed rock, 3000 feet in height; and not far distant is *Sentinel Rock*, a "solitary truncate pinnacle," towering to 3300 feet. Nearly opposite soar the three ascending ridges of *Eleachas*, or the *Three Brothers*, the highest attaining to the elevation of 3450 feet.

But . . . the first "object of interest"—to use a hackneyed phrase—which calls for our attention, and, as a matter of course, for our admiration, is

THE YOSEMITE FALLS

Crossing the main stream, which is here about eighty feet wide and five feet deep, we continue along the northern bank, to avoid the marshy flats on the southern, until we reach the ford, where we re-cross the river, under an embowering canopy of oak, maple, and dogwood trees.

As the snow, under the summer sun, is rapidly melting, we ford, not only the main channel, but several smaller streams. Within about a hundred and fifty yards of the fall our progress is interrupted by a succession of large boulders. Therefore we dismount, and, fastening our animals to the nearest saplings, push forward on foot.

We now proceed to climb to the base, or, as nearly as possible to the base, of the great Yosemite Falls, the loftiest cascade or cataract in the world. There are, in fact, *two* falls. . . . The total height of the "sheeted column's perpendicular" is 2548 feet. By some authorities, however, this total is brought up to 2634 feet.

It is difficult to describe the power and majesty of a gigantic waterfall. But the impression made on the mind by the ceaseless rush—by the tumbling waters perpetually flashing and gleaming, roaring and murmuring—by the intuitive feeling that the *motion* before you has never paused since the creation, and *will* never pause until Time shall cease to be,—is almost bewildering. You find yourself at a loss to take in the separate details: the huge wall of granite rising so massively before you; the huge masses of multiform rocks strewn, and scattered, and piled in every direction; the ferns, and wild flowers, and lovely mosses which here and there relieve the harsher features of Nature. All your soul is concentrated on the vastness of the fall, which seems to fill up the entire picture, so that wherever you go you still seem to see the deep glow of the waters, to catch the flash of their diamond spray, to hear the whirr and clash of their endless progress.

It is said that in the winter the spray from the great cataract freezes, and piles up and again freezes, until a hollow pillar is constructed some hundreds of feet in height. Into that pillar the waters pour, and then rebound like rainbow-coloured balls.

In the spring, the rush of the cataract and its thousand voices seem for a moment to be arrested. You hasten to the spot. The floods have undermined this glorious pillar, and made ready to topple it from its elevation. The struggle is brief, but desperate. Suddenly the ice yields, and is shivered, and hurled into the air in a thousand fragments, sparkling and shining with a lustrous gleam, and then falling back into the stream, to be carried away and seen no more. . . .

Lake Ah-Wi-Yah

This is one of the loveliest localities in the valley. You confront the great falls almost with a sense of apprehension and a feeling of undefinable awe: but you look upon this crystal mirror with a sentiment of subdued admiration.

In its sheet of unrippled glass—especially at early morning—it reflects the mountains, 4000 and 5000 feet high, with such a wonderful clearness that you can readily detect the furrows on their brows and the ledges and ravines in their rugged sides. It is not above a couple of acres in extent, but this remarkable translucency gives it a curious *appearance* of vastness. The bases of the mountains all around are fringed with noble trees, which supply in their various foliage a delightful contrast to the azure of the pool beneath. On the north-east a, deep canyon, or gorge, opens wide, to permit the outflow of the north branch of the "River of Mercy," which supplies the lake. . . .

There are excursions enough . . . to occupy the traveller—especially if he carry a sketch-book—for weeks among the beautiful scenes of the valley. Mount your horse early in the morning—or, still better, trust to your own legs—and stroll up and down the marvellous canyon, enjoying the various novel scenes that open up at every step. . . .

The climate is so mild and invigorating that nothing can surpass it. Breathing the air of the Yosemite, a new hope and strength are infused into your life. The charm of the wonderful valley is its cheerfulness and joy. Even the awe-inspiring grandeur and majesty of its features do not overwhelm the sense of its exquisite beauty, its wonderful delicacy, its rich colour, and intense vitality.

"As I recall," says our friend [Charles Brace], "those rides in the fresh morning or dewy noon, that scene of unequalled grandeur and beauty is for ever stamped upon my memory, to remain when all other scenes of earth have passed from remembrance: the pearly-gray and purple precipices, awful in mass, far above one, with deep shadows on their rugged surfaces—dark lines of gigantic archways or fantastic figures drawn clearly upon them—the bright white water dashing over the distant gray tops seen against the dark blue of the unfathomable sky—the heavy shadows over the valley from the mighty peaks—the winding stream and peaceful greensward with gay wild flowers below—the snowy summits of the Sierras far away—and the eternal voice of many waters wherever you walk or rest. This is the Yosemite in memory."

"I invite you join me in a months worship with Nature
in the high temples of the great Sierra Crown."

John Muir
Letter to Ralph Waldo Emerson, 1871

The magnificent Yosemite Valley had been a potent lure for the artistic, the wealthy, and the notable since it received its first nonindigenous visitors in the 1850s. But as Yosemite soared in popularity during the 1870s and access improved, more and more prominent fig-

"All Places That the Eye of Heaven Visits"

ures made the still challenging trek. Dust and discomfort seemed little hindrance to writers, painters, photographers, politicians, and celebrities seeking the Yosemite experience.

During the nineteenth century, thousands of sightseers trod the meadows—captivated by the waterfalls, entranced by the wildflowers, and mesmerized by the granite monoliths. Some were famous, even world famous, but the renowned visitor who generated the most hubbub in the early 1870s was Ralph Waldo Emerson. An essayist, lecturer, poet, philosopher, and leader of the Transcendentalist Movement, he believed in the principles of that movement—the inherent goodness of humanity, appreciation and respect for nature, and the holistic intertwining of people and the environment.

In 1871 Emerson visited California from April 21 to May 22. Born and raised in Boston, Massachusetts, Emerson was an East Coast denizen to the core. But, in spring 1871, sixty-eight-year-old Emerson traveled west on the newly completed transcontinental railroad. His health was in decline, and, while his spirit was willing, his physical condition was often fragile. By 1871 Emerson was, in the words of historian James Brannon in a 2006 article for the University of the Pacific's *John Muir Newsletter*, "by modern standards, . . . a sedentary observer, a car-camper, a relaxed, wine-sipping, cigar smoking viewer from the windows of a plush Pullman train car."

Among the most excited for Emerson's visit to Yosemite was the young and relatively unknown John Muir. The then thirty-three-year-old Muir idolized Ralph Waldo Emerson. In his 1913 autobiography *Stories of My Boyhood and Youth*, John Muir stated that Emerson's 1870 dictum "Hitch your wagon to a star" was a guiding principle in his life. After all, said Muir, "I took Emerson's advice and hitched my dumping-wagon bed to a star" and became a student in the "University of the Wilderness."

Muir wrote to Emerson on May 8, 1871, inviting Emerson to visit him at his Yosemite Valley dwelling and perhaps "join me in a months worship with Nature in the high temples of the great Sierra Crown beyond our holy Yosemite."

Yosemite Valley,

Monday night [May 8, 1871]

Mr. R W Emerson

Dear Sir: I rec'd to-day a letter from Mrs. Prof E Carr [Dr. Ezra Carr was one of Muir's professors at the University of Wisconsin. Carr's wife, Jeanne, was an author and mentor to the young John Muir] of Oakland Cal stating that you were in the Valley & that she expected to see you on your return. Also she promised that she would write you here & send you to me. I was delighted at the thought of meeting you but have just learned that you contemplate leaving the Valley in a day or two.

Now Mr Emerson I do most cordially protest against your going away so soon, & so also I am sure do all your instincts & affinities I trust that you will not "outweary their yearnings." Do not thus drift away with the mob while the spirits of these rocks & waters hail you after long waiting as their kinsman & persuade you to closer communion.

But now if Fate or one of those mongrel & mishappen organizations called parties compel you to leave for the present, I shall hope for some other fullness of time to come for you.

If you will call at Mr. Hutchings mill I will give you as many of Yosemite & high Sierra plants as you wish as specimens.

I invite you join me in a months worship with Nature in the high temples of the great Sierra Crown beyond our holy Yosemite. It will cost you nothing save the time & very little of that for you will be mostly in Eternity.

And now once more, in the name of Mts Dana & Gabb—of the grand glacial hieroglyphics of Tuolumne meadows & Bloody Canon,—In the name of a hundred glacial lakes—of a hundred glacial-daisy-gentian meadows, In the name of a hundred cascades that barbarous visitors never see, In the name of the grand upper forests of Picea amabilis & P. grandis, & in the name of all the spirit creatures of these rocks & of this whole spiritual atmosphere Do not leave us *now*.

With most cordial regards, I am yours in Nature,

John Muir

"Occasionally he rambled among the mountains, and camped out for months, and he urged Mr. Emerson, with an amusing zeal, to stay and go off with him on such a trip."

James Bradley Thayer
A Western Journey with Mr. Emerson, 1884

James Bradley Thayer was a traveling companion of Ralph Waldo Emerson on his 1871 cross-country sojourn and wrote an 1884 memoir of the experience, *A Western Journey with Mr. Emerson*. This excerpt is Thayer's description of Muir's interaction with Emerson.

On the evening of Monday [May 8, 1871] there came an admiring, enthusiastic letter for Mr. Emerson from M. [John Muir], a young man living in the valley, and tending a saw-mill there. He was a Scotchman by birth, who had come to this country at the age of eleven, and was a graduate at Madison University, in Wisconsin. Some friends near San Francisco had written him that Mr. Emerson was coming, and they had also told Mr. Emerson about him. He had read Mr. Emerson's books, but had never seen him, and wrote now with enthusiasm, wishing for an opportunity to come to him. The next morning Mr. Emerson asked my company on horseback for a visit to M. So he mounted his pied mustang, and we rode over, and found M. at the saw-mill alone. He was an interesting young fellow, of real intelligence and character, a botanist mainly, who, after studying a year or two at Madison, had "zigzagged his way," he said, "to the Gulf of Mexico, and at last had found this valley, and had got entangled here,—in love with the mountains and flowers; and he didn't know when he should get away." He had built the saw-mill for Hutchings, and was now working it. He had heretofore tended sheep at times,—even flocks of twenty-five hundred. Occasionally he rambled among the mountains, and camped out for months; and he urged Mr. Emerson, with an amusing zeal, to stay and go off with him on such a trip. He lodged in the saw-mill, and we climbed a ladder to his room. Here he brought out a great many dried specimens of plants which he had collected, and hundreds of his own graceful pencil-sketches of the mountain peaks and forest trees, and gave us the botanical names, and talked of them with enthusiastic interest. All these treasures he poured out before Mr. Emerson, and begged him to accept them. But Mr. Emerson declined; wishing leave, however, to bring his friends to see them. Other calls were interchanged that day and the next; and when we left, two days later, to see the great trees of the Mariposa grove, M. joined our horseback party. . . .

In the morning we were off at eight o'clock for the Mariposa grove. Galen Clark, our landlord, a solid, sensible man from New Hampshire, was the State guardian of the great trees, and now accompanied us, *honoris causa*. It was a sunny and pleasant ride. M. talked of the trees; and we grew learned, and were able to tell a sugar pine from a yellow pine, and to name the silver fir, and the "libocedrus," which is almost our arbor-vitae and second cousin to the great sequoia. By and by M. called out that he saw the sequoias. The general level was now about fifty-five hundred feet above the sea; the

"All Places That the Eye of Heaven Visits"

trees stood a little lower, in a hollow of the mountain. They were "big trees," to be sure; and yet at first they seemed not so very big. We grew curious, and looked about among them for a while; and soon began to discover what company we were in. . . .

We sat down to lunch near a hut, and had a chance to rest and to look about us more quietly. M. protested against our going away so soon: "It is," said he, "as if a photographer should remove his plate before the impression was fully made"; he begged us to stay there and camp with him for the night. After lunch, Mr. Emerson, at Clark's request, chose and named a tree. This had been done by one distinguished person, and another, and a sign put up to commemorate it. Mr. Emerson's tree was not far from the hut; it was a vigorous and handsome one, although not remarkably large, measuring fifty feet in circumference at two and a half feet from the ground. He named it Samoset, after our Plymouth sachem. He had greatly enjoyed the day. "The greatest wonder," said he, "is that we can see these trees and not wonder more."

We were off at about three o'clock, and left M. standing in the forest alone; he was to pass the night there in solitude, and to find his way back to the valley on foot. We had all become greatly interested in him, and hated to leave him. His name has since grown to be well known at the East, through his valuable articles in the magazines.

"When he came into the Valley, I heard the hotel people saying with solemn emphasis, 'Emerson is here.'"

John Muir
Reminiscences of Emerson, 1896 and 1901

The following narrative of John Muir's recollection of his Emerson encounter comes from two sources—a speech Muir gave at Harvard in 1896 and a more comprehensive reminiscence in his 1901 book *Our National Parks*.

I was fortunate in meeting some of the choicest of your Harvard men, and at once recognized them as the best of God's nobles. Emerson, [Louis] Agassiz, [Asa] Gray—these men influenced me more than any others. Yes, the most of my years were spent on the wild side of the continent, invisible, in the forests and mountains. These men were the first to find me and hail me as a brother. First of all, and greatest of all, came Emerson. I was then living in Yosemite Valley as a convenient and grand vestibule of the Sierra from which I could make excursions into the adjacent mountains. I had not much money and was then running a mill that I had built to saw fallen timber for cottages.

When he came into the Valley I heard the hotel people saying with solemn emphasis, "Emerson is here." I was excited as I had never been excited before, and my heart throbbed as if an angel direct from heaven had alighted on the Sierran rocks. But so great was my awe and reverence, I did not dare to go to him or speak to him. I hovered on the outside of the crowd of people that were pressing forward to be introduced to him and shaking hands with him. Then I heard that in three or four days he was going away, and in the course of sheer desperation I wrote him a note and carried it to his hotel telling him that El Capitan and Tissiack demanded him to stay longer.

The next day he inquired for the writer and was directed to the little sawmill. He came to the mill on horseback attended by Mr. Thayer [James Bradley Thayer] and inquired for me. I stepped out and said, "I am Mr. Muir." "Then Mr. Muir must have brought his own letter," said Mr. Thayer and Emerson said, "Why did you not make yourself known last evening? I should have been very glad to have seen you." Then he dismounted and came into the mill. I had a study attached to the gable of the mill, overhanging the stream, into which I invited him, but it was not easy of access, being reached only by a series of sloping planks roughened by slats like a

"All Places That the Eye of Heaven Visits"

hen ladder; but he bravely climbed up and I showed him my collection of plants and sketches drawn from the surrounding mountains which seemed to interest him greatly, and he asked many questions, pumping unconscionably.

He came again and again, and I saw him every day while he remained in the valley, and on leaving I was invited to accompany him as far as the Mariposa Grove of Big Trees. I said, "I'll go, Mr. Emerson, if you will promise to camp with me in the Grove. I'll build a glorious campfire, and the great brown boles of the giant Sequoias will be most impressively lighted up, and the night will be glorious." At this he became enthusiastic like a boy, his sweet perennial smile became still deeper and sweeter, and he said, "Yes, yes, we will camp out, camp out"; and so next day we left Yosemite and rode twenty five miles through the Sierra forests, the noblest on the face of the earth, and he kept me talking all the time, but said little himself. The colossal silver firs, Douglas spruce, Libocedrus and sugar pine, the kings and priests of the conifers of the earth, filled him with awe and delight. When we stopped to eat luncheon he called on different members of the party to tell stories or recite poems, etc., and spoke, as he reclined on the carpet of pine needles, of his student days at Harvard.

Our National Parks

Early in the afternoon, when we reached Clark's Station, I was surprised to see the party dismount. And when I asked if we were not going up into the grove to camp they said: "No; it would never do to lie out in the night air. Mr. Emerson might take cold; and you know, Mr. Muir, that would be a dreadful thing." In vain I urged, that only in homes and hotels were colds caught, that nobody ever was known to take cold camping in these woods, that there was not a single cough or sneeze in all the Sierra. Then I pictured the big climate-changing, inspiring fire I would make, praised the beauty and fragrance of sequoia flame, told how the great trees would stand about us transfigured in the purple light, while the stars looked down between the great domes; ending by urging them to come on and make an immortal Emerson night of it. But the house habit was not to be overcome, nor the strange dread of pure night air, though it is only cooled day air with a little dew in it. So the carpet dust and unknowable reeks were preferred. And to think of this being a Boston choice! Sad commentary on culture and the glorious transcendentalism.

Accustomed to reach whatever place I started for, I was going up the mountain alone to camp, and wait the coming of the party next day. But since Emerson was so soon to vanish, I concluded to stop with him. He hardly spoke a word all the evening, yet it was a great pleasure simply to be near him, warming in the light of his face as at a fire. In the morning we rode up the trail through a noble forest of pine and fir into the famous Mariposa Grove, and stayed an hour or two, mostly in ordinary tourist fashion,—looking at the biggest giants, measuring them with a tape line, riding through prostrate fire-bored trunks, etc., though Mr. Emerson was alone occasionally, sauntering about as if under a spell. As we walked through a fine group, he quoted, "There were giants in those days," recognizing the antiquity of the race. To commemorate his visit, Mr. Galen Clark, the guardian of the grove, selected the finest of the unnamed trees and requested him to give it a name. He named it Samoset, after the New England sachem, as the best that occurred to him.

The poor bit of measured time was soon spent, and while the saddles were being adjusted I again urged Emerson to stay. "You are yourself a sequoia," I said. "Stop and get acquainted with your big brethren." But he was past his prime, and was now as a child in the hands of his affectionate but sadly civilized friends, who seemed as full of old-fashioned conformity as of bold intellectual independence. It was the afternoon of the day and the afternoon of his life, and his course was now westward down all the mountains into the sunset. The party mounted and rode away in wondrous contentment, apparently, tracing the trail through ceanothus and dogwood bushes, around the bases of the big trees, up the slope of the

"All Places That the Eye of Heaven Visits"

sequoia basin, and over the divide. I followed to the edge of the grove. Emerson lingered in the rear of the train, and when he reached the top of the ridge, after all the rest of the party were over and out of sight, he turned his horse, took off his hat and waved me a last good-by. I felt lonely, so sure had I been that Emerson of all men would be the quickest to see the mountains and sing them. Gazing awhile on the spot where he vanished, I sauntered back into the heart of the grove, made a bed of sequoia plumes and ferns by the side of a stream, gathered a store of firewood, and then walked about until sundown. The birds, robins, thrushes, warblers, etc., that had kept out of sight, came about me, now that all was quiet, and made cheer. After sundown I built a great fire, and as usual had it all to myself. And though lonesome for the first time in these forests, I quickly took heart again,— the trees had not gone to Boston, nor the birds; and as I sat by the fire, Emerson was still with me in spirit, though I never again saw him in the flesh.

"Solitude . . . is a sublime mistress, but an intolerable wife."

Ralph Waldo Emerson
Letter to John Muir, 1872

On February 5, 1872, Ralph Waldo Emerson wrote to John Muir, urging him to "leave your mountain tabernacle, [and] bring your ripe fruits so rare and precious into waiting society." The famous man of letters also expressed his hope that Muir would someday pay a visit to his home in Concord, Massachusetts.

But Muir never saw Emerson again. He did travel to Massachusetts years later, and as he wrote in *Our National Parks*, "It was seventeen years after our parting on the Wawona ridge that I stood beside his grave under a pine tree on the hill above Sleepy Hollow. He had gone to higher Sierras, and, as I fancied, was again waving his hand in friendly recognition."

John Muir retained his admiration of Emerson for the rest of his life. In an undated journal entry, Muir wrote, "Emerson was the most serene, majestic, sequoia-like soul I ever met. His smile was as sweet and calm as morning light on mountains. There was a wonderful charm in his presence; his smile, serene eye, his voice, his manner, were all sensed at once by everybody. I felt here was a man I had been seeking. The Sierra, I was sure, wanted to see him, and he must not go before gathering them an interview! A tremendous sincerity was his. He was as sincere as the trees, his eye sincere as the sun."

Concord

5th February, 1872

My Dear Muir:

Here lie your significant cedar flowers on my table, and in another letter; and I will procrastinate no longer. That singular disease of deferring, which kills all my designs, has left a pair of books brought home to send to you months and months ago, still covering their inches on my cabinet, and the letter and letters which should have accompanied, to utter my thanks and lively remembrance, are either unwritten or lost, so I will send this *peccavi*, as a sign of remorse.

I have been far from unthankful—I have everywhere testified to my friends who should also be yours, my happiness in finding you—the right man in the right place—in your mountain tabernacle, and have expected when your guardian angel would pronounce that your probation and sequestration in the solitudes and snows had reached their term, and you were to bring your ripe fruits so rare and precious into waiting society.

I trust you have also had, ere this, your own signals from the upper powers. I know that society in the lump, admired at a distance, shrinks and dissolves,

"All Places That the Eye of Heaven Visits"

when approached, into impracticable or uninteresting individuals, but always with a reserve of a few unspoiled good men, who really give it its halo in the distance. And there are drawbacks also to solitude, who is a sublime mistress, but an intolerable wife. So I pray you to bring to an early close your absolute contracts with any yet unvisited glaciers or volcanoes, roll up your drawings, herbariums and poems, and come to the Atlantic Coast. Here in Cambridge Dr. Gray is at home, and Agassiz will doubtless be, after a month or two, returned from Terra [sic] del Fuego perhaps through San Francisco—or you can come with him. At all events, on your arrival, which I assume as certain, you must find your way to this village, and my house. And when you are tired of our dwarf surroundings, I will show you better people.

With kindest regards Yours

R. W. Emerson

> "Before I could reply, the rash man had leapt down,
> and alighted like a bird on a perch, and grasped a
> bunch of ferns, which he stroked affectionately."

Thérèse Yelverton
Zanita: A Tale of the Yo-semite, 1872

In the early 1870s, encountering the young John Muir in Yosemite was a common occurrence. He was seemingly everywhere, and observers were quick to call attention to his enthusiasm and eccentricities.

Among these onlookers was the equally intriguing Thérèse Yelverton, travel writer and the victim of her scandalous husband, who was a member of the Irish nobility. Born Maria Theresa Longworth, she was the daughter of a wealthy English silk manufacturer and the youngest of six children. Her mother died when Maria Theresa was eight years old, and the young girl was sent to France and educated in a convent. When Maria Theresa was twenty, her father died, and she inherited part of his fortune.

In 1857, after a courtship of several years, she secretly "married" the Rt. Hon. William Charles Yelverton, fourth Viscount Avonmore, and she then began to be called Thérèse Yelverton, Viscountess Avonmore. However, Viscount Avonmore was an Irish Protestant and Thérèse was Catholic, and under British law a marriage between a Protestant and a Catholic conducted by a Catholic priest was not legally recognized. Their "ceremony" had been conducted by a Catholic priest, without witnesses, and no legal vows were exchanged. William insisted the "marriage" be kept secret as well.

In 1858 the Rt. Hon. William Charles Yelverton became involved with Emily Forbes. Despite Thérèse's assertions that she was his wife, Viscount Avonmore wed Emily Forbes, precipitating a series of lawsuits in 1861, known collectively as the Yelverton Case. The Irish courts originally found that the marriage between Thérèse and the viscount was valid. Subsequent appeals, ultimately to the House of Lords, ruled that the first marriage was invalid and that William Yelverton was legally married to Emily Forbes. The case was front-page news, and as Andrea Wulf, a *New York Times* book critic, noted in 2010, Thérèse Yelverton "was alternately vilified and celebrated. . . . Sometimes she was depicted as innocent and pure, at others as a ruthless social climber. After six years of trials and appeals, she finally lost her case. In the process, however, she had become a minor celebrity."

Thérèse Yelverton escaped the spotlight through travel, which she extensively chronicled. In 1870 she spent the summer in Yosemite, became friends with James Mason Hutchings, and met John Muir. She turned her experiences into the 1872 novel entitled *Zanita: A Tale of the Yo-semite*. The work includes thinly veiled depictions of actual people she already knew or those she had met or heard about in Yosemite, including the Hutchings family, Josiah Whitney, Joseph LeConte, and Galen Clark. There was even a character based on the Viscount Avonmore. But the fictionalized figure that received the most notice was Kenmuir, an eye-catching portrayal of John Muir.

In this excerpt from *Zanita*, narrator Sylvia Brown, the novel's representation of Thérèse Yelverton, is being led through Yosemite by her prickly guide Horse-shoe Bill, based on Nathan Bennett "Pike" Phillips, colorful Yosemite denizen, when she spies "a peculiar looking object foreign to the scenery." It is her first glimpse of Kenmuir, or as Horse-shoe Bill bellows in dismay, "It's that darned idiot Kenmuir."

I beheld a chaos of mountain tops and deep chasms, all seemingly thrown inextricably together, and apparently inaccessible. My heart began to fail me as to my further progress, when a peculiar looking object foreign to the scenery caught my eye.

"What on earth is that?" I exclaimed, reining up my not unwilling mustang, and pointing to the singular creature extending itself as though about to take wing from the very verge of a pinnacle overhanging a terrific precipice. "Is it a man, or a tree, or a bird?"

"It's a man, you bet," replied my guide, chuckling. "No tree or shrub as big as my fist ever found footing there. It's that darned idiot Kenmuir, and the sooner he dashes out that rum mixture of his he calls brains the sooner his troubles'll be over, that's my idee."

... We quickly rounded the point, when the singular figure was seen swaying to and fro with extended arms as if moved by the wind, the head thrown back as in swimming, and the long brown hair falling wildly about his face and neck.

The point on which he stood was a smooth jutting rock only a few inches in width, and a stone thrown over it would fall vertically into the valley five thousand feet below. My heart beat fast with horrible dread as my guide coolly explained this fact to me. I hardly dared to fix my eyes upon the figure lest I should see it disappear, or remove them, lest it should be gone when I looked again. In my desperation, I exerted that power of will which is said to convey itself through space without material aid. I strove to communicate with him by intangible force. The charm seemed to work well. He turned quickly towards me, and, with a spring like an antelope, was presently on *terra firma* and approaching us.

"There, you'll have plenty on him now," said Horse-shoe Bill. "He loafs about this here valley gatherin' stocks [sic] and stones, as I may say, to be Scriptural, and praisin' the Lord for makin' of him sech a born fool. Well some folks is easy satisfied!"

As the lithe figure approached, skipping over the rough boulders, poising with the balance of an athlete, or skirting a shelf of rock with the cautious activity of a goat, never losing for a moment the rhythmic motion of his flexile form, I began to think that his attitude on the over-hanging rock might not, after all, have been so chimerical; and my resolve, as to how I should treat this phase of insanity, began to waver very sensibly, and I fell back on that mental rear-guard— good intentions; but when he stood before me with a pleasant "Good day, madam," my perplexity increased ten-fold, for his bright intelligent face revealed no trace of insanity, and his open blue eyes of honest questioning, and glorious auburn hair might have stood as a portrait of the angel Raphael. His figure was about five feet nine, well knit, and bespoke that active grace which only trained muscles can assume.

The guide increased my confusion by exclaiming, "Hallo, Kenmuir! the lady wants to speak to you." . . .

"Can I do anything for you?" asked Kenmuir gently.

"She wants to know what you were doing out on that bloody knob overhanging eternity?"

"Praising God," solemnly replied Kenmuir.

"Thought that would start him," interrupted the guide.

"Praising God, madam, for his mighty works, his glorious earth, and the sublimity of these fleecy clouds, the majesty of that great roaring torrent," pointing to the Nevada, "that leaps from rock to rock in exultant joy, and laves them, and kisses them with caresses of downiest foam. O, no mother ever pressed her child in tenderer embrace, or sung to it in more harmonious melody; and my soul joins in with all this shout of triumphant gladness, this burst of glorious life; this eternity of truth and beauty and joy; rejoices in the gorgeous canopy above us, in the exquisite carpet with which the valley is spread of living, palpitating, breathing splendor. Hearken to the hymn of praise which re-sounds upwards from every tiny sedge, every petal and calyx of myriads and myriads of flowers, all perfect, all replete with the divine impress of Omnipotent power. Shall man alone be silent and callous? Come, madam, let me lead you to Pal-li-li-ma [Overhanging Rock at Glacier Point], the point I have just left, where you can have a more complete view of this miracle of nature, for I am sure you also can worship in this temple of our Lord." . . .

One thought of the maniac shot through my mind, not as a fear, but a souvenir. I looked on the face of Kenmuir, shining with a pure and holy enthusiasm, and it reminded me of the face of a Christ I had seen years ago in some little old Italian village. . . .

I resigned myself cheerfully, and followed his lead to the great projecting rock called the Glacier Point, or Pal-li-li-ma, where I had first seen him, and where there are still traces of ancient glaciers, which he said "are no doubt the instruments the Almighty used in the formation of this valley."

As we proceeded slowly and carefully, my thoughts dwelt with deep interest on the individual in advance of me. Truly his garments had the tatterdemalion style of a Mad Tom. The waist of his trousers was eked out with a grass band; a long flowing sedge rush stuck in the solitary button-hole of his shirt, the sleeves of which were ragged and forlorn, and his shoes appeared to have known hard and troublous times. What if he had been, at some previous period, insane, and still retained the curious mania of believing that human beings might through righteousness float in ambient air?

What if he should insist on our making the experiment this evening together? What would my husband say if he knew all, and saw me here committed to the sole care of this man with the beautiful countenance, and with no other guarantee, in a wilderness of mighty rocks, gigantic trees, and awful precipices, a hundred miles from anywhere! . . .

As we approached the point, Kenmuir said, with a gleeful laugh, "I do not intend to take you out on the overhanging rock, where I was standing, but to a very nice little corner, where you can sit your horse comfortably, unless you really want to dismount."

I thanked him, and, smiling at the arch allusion, said I would remain seated. The scene from Pal-li-li-ma was a marvel of grandeur and sublimity, and fully warranted the lavish enthusiasm of my new friend. Around us vast mountains of granite arose one above another in stupendous proportions, and over them leaped the mighty cataracts with majestic sweep.

"These are the Lord's fountains," said Kenmuir, clasping his hands in the intensity of his delight, "and away up above, elevated amid clouds, are the crests of the God-like peaks covered with eternal snows. These are the reservoirs whence He pours his floods to cheer the earth, to refresh man and beast, to lave every sedge and tiny moss; from those exalted pinnacles flow the source of life, and joy, and supreme bliss to millions of breathing things below; to the dreamy-eyed cattle that you see four thousand feet in the valley beneath us, standing knee-deep in the limpid pool; to the tiny insects that are skimming in ecstatic merriment around every glistening ribbon of water as it falls. Look! and see these silvery threads of water all hurrying down so swiftly, yet so gracefully, to bathe the upturned face of nature, and varnish with new brilliancy her enameled breast. Beyond is the Lord's workshop. With these resistless glaciers he formed a royal road,—from the heights of the topmost Sierras which you now see covered with snow, roseate from the sun's last beams,—into the valley at our feet. Yet all is lovely in form,

"All Places That the Eye of Heaven Visits"

and harmonious in color. Look at that ledge of rock—the hardest of granite—how exquisitely it is tapestried with helianthemum. Would you like a bunch?"

And before I could reply, the rash man had leapt down, and alighted like a bird on a perch, and grasped a bunch of ferns, which he stroked affectionately, and carefully stowed away in the grass cincture, whilst there was but a half foot of rock between him and "etarnity," as the guide expressed it. . . .

"Now," said Kenmuir, "lest you should think I have brought you to this wilderness to make you be food for ghouls and water kelpies, I will point out the spot where you are to spend the night, and as many more as you wish."

I looked round in dismay. "We seem a million miles from anywhere."

"Upwards, yes," he replied,—"but look down, and you will see a yellow spot, surrounded by what appears a few willow sticks, but which are in reality tall pines, with the river winding round like a golden cord,—that is the homestead. We will go down by the trail, which is almost level." . . .

The twilight now had deepened to moonlight. For although we could not see any moon, she had risen, and was taking a ramble behind the cliffs. Yet her light swam over the whole scenery in magic waves, transforming it to the most unearthly vision of weird enchantment. Every notch and projection caught the soft loving light which fell in perfect streams over the mighty Tu-tock-ah-nu-lah, which seemed to have pierced the pale clear blue of the heavens and let out floods of its glistening moonlight.

"Do you not perceive the balmy odors of the pines? They also mark the height and distance of these stupendous adamantine bulwarks. What are the towers of Notre Dame, which they so singularly resemble, compared to these cathedral spires rising in proud majesty three thousand feet with the flying buttresses and ancient caryatides supporting the projecting arches!"

"Yes," I put in. "I believe I see a procession of monks ascending to the great entrance of the church."

"Those are pine-trees two hundred feet high, growing up the ravine. Look at the rich carving and fretwork on the walls, and the tall minarets dazzling in the moon's rays."

"And I hear the *muezzin* calling to prayer."

"That is an owl," answered Kenmuir; "and he says, 'Do! do! oh, do do!' *Do* what, I wonder?"

"Go on," I suggested, "for we have stopped here a full quarter of an hour, and our host will have retired for the night."

"We will wake him up," said Kenmuir, "but he will not be asleep such a night as this, he has too much soul."

"Still we had better move on," I said, recollecting what my former guide had turned back to say in a stage whisper,— "Don't let him stop, or he'll talk till judgement day; and don't let him stoop to pick up any new specimen, or you'll never be through with him for a month."

"Red light streamed through the open Yosemite gateway, brightening the vast, solemn faces of stone."

Clarence King
Mountaineering in the Sierra Nevada, 1872

Born in Rhode Island in 1842, Clarence King graduated from Yale at the tender age of nineteen. Soon after graduation, King became assistant geologist under Josiah Whitney for the California Geological Survey, serving from 1863 to 1866. A year later the twenty-five-year-old King was appointed director of geological and geographical exploration for the Fortieth Parallel Survey. His ten-year expedition explored and surveyed a one-hundred-mile wide swath from eastern Colorado to the California state line. King produced a highly regarded seven-volume report on the exploration: *Geological Survey of the Fortieth Parallel.*

King was meticulously scientific and innovative, stressing laboratory work and introducing the system of contour lines in topography. In 1878 King was appointed the first head of the newly organized western survey department of the U.S. Geological Survey. In 1879 he wrote his most important scientific tome, the eight-hundred-page *Systematic Geology*. But King is much better known for his writing for the general public: his 1872 *Mountaineering in the Sierra Nevada*. King was convinced that he could present the scientific story of the Sierra Nevada without resorting to the romantic rhetoric employed by what King dismissively referred to as "the army of literary travelers." King loved the mountains and hoped that his narrative would lead to increased preservation efforts, but he also feared that his book would promote additional tourism and regional degradation. He was right on both accounts.

Clarence King died in 1901 at age fifty-nine. As a monument to King's influence, a 12,909-foot peak in the Sierra Nevada was named Mount King in his honor.

This selection from *Mountaineering in the Sierra Nevada* presents King's account of his descent into Yosemite Valley during a "blinding fury of snow and wind."

Warmly rolled in our blankets, we suffered little from cold, but the driving sleet and hail very soon bruised our cheeks and eyelids most painfully. It required real effort of will to face the storm, and we very soon learned to take turns in breaking trail. The snow constantly balled upon our animals' feet, and they slid in every direction. Now and then, in descending a sharp slope of granite, the poor creatures would get sliding, and rush to the bottom, their legs stiffened out, and their heads thrust forward in fear. After crossing the Illilluette, which we did at our old ford, we found it very difficult to climb the long, steep hillside; for the mules were quite unable to carry us, obliging us to lead them, and to throw ourselves upon the snow-drifts to break a pathway.

This slope almost wore us out, and when at last we reached its summit, we threw ourselves upon the snow for a rest, but were in such a profuse perspiration that I deemed it unsafe to lie there for a moment, and, getting up again, we mounted the mules and rode slowly on toward open plateaus near great meadows. The snow gradually decreased in depth as we descended upon the plain directly south of the Yosemite. The wind abated somewhat, and there were only occasional snow flurries, between half-hours of tolerable comfort. Constant use of the compass and reference to my little map at length brought us to the Mariposa trail, but not until after eight hours of anxious, exhaustive labor,—anxious from the constant dread of losing our way in the blinding confusion of storm; exhausting, for we had more than half of the way acted as trail-breakers, dragging our frightened and tired brutes after us. The poor creatures instantly recognized the trail, and started in a brisk trot toward Inspiration Point. Suddenly an icy wind swept up the valley, carrying with it a storm of snow and hail. The wind blew with such violence that the whole freight of sleet and ice was carried horizontally with fearful swiftness, cutting the bruised faces of the mules, and giving our own eyelids exquisite torture. The brutes refused to carry us farther. We were obliged to dismount and drive them before us, beating them constantly with clubs.

Fighting our way against this bitter blast, half-blinded by hard, wind-driven snow-crystals, we at last gave up and took refuge in a dense clump of firs which crown the spur by Inspiration Point. Our poor mules cowered under shelter with us, and turned tail to the storm. The fir-trees were solid cones of snow, which now and then unloaded themselves when severely bent by a sudden gust, half burying us in dry, white powder. Wind roared below us in the Yosemite gorge; it blew from the west, rolling up in waves which smote the cliffs and surged on up the valley. While we sat still the drifts began to pile up at our backs; the mules were belly-deep, and our situation began to be serious.

Looking over the cliff-brink we saw but the hurrying snow, and only heard a confused tumult of wind. A steady increase in the severity of the gale made us fear that the trees might crash down over us; so we left the mules and crept cautiously over the edge of the cliff, and ensconced ourselves in a sheltered nook, protected by walls of rock which rose at our back.

We were on the brink of the Yosemite, and but for snow might have looked down three thousand feet. The storm eddied below us, sucking down whirlwinds of snow, and sometimes opening deep rifts,—never enough, however, to disclose more than a few hundred feet of cliffs. . . .

Suddenly there came a lull in the storm; its blinding fury of snow and wind ceased. Overhead, still hurrying eastward, the white bank drove on, unveiling, as it fled, the Yosemite walls, plateau, and every object to the eastward as far as Mount Clark. As yet the valley bottom was obscured by a layer of mist and cloud, which rose to the height of about a thousand feet, submerging cliff-foot and debris pile. Between these strata, the cloud above and the cloud below, every object was in clear, distinct view; the sharp, terrible fronts of precipices, capped with a fresh cover of white, plunged down into the still, gray river of cloud below, their stony surfaces clouded with purple, salmon-color, and bandings of brown,—all hues unnoticeable in every-day lights. Forest, and crag, and plateau, and distant mountain were snow-covered to a uniform whiteness; only the dark gorge beneath us showed the least traces of color. There all was rich, deep, gloomy. Even over the snowy surfaces above there prevailed an almost ashen gray, which reflected itself from the dull, drifting sky. A few torn locks of vapor poured over the cliff-edge at intervals, and crawled down like wreaths of smoke, floating gracefully and losing themselves at last in the bank of cloud which lay upon the bottom of the valley.

On a sudden the whole gray roof rolled away like a scroll, leaving the heavens from west to far east one expanse of pure, warm blue. Setting sunlight smote full upon the stony walls below, and shot over the plateau country, gilding here a snowy forest group, and there a wave-crest of whitened ridge. The whole air sparkled with diamond particles; red light streamed in through the open Yosemite gateway, brightening those vast, solemn faces of stone, and intensifying the deep neutral blue of shadowed alcoves.

The luminous cloud-bank in the east rolled from the last Sierra summit, leaving the whole chain of peaks in broad light, each rocky crest strongly red, the newly fallen snow marbling it over with a soft, deep rose; and wherever a cañon carved itself down their rocky fronts, its course was traceable by a shadowy band of blue. The middle distance glowed with a tint of golden yellow; the broken heights along the cañon-brinks and edges of the cliff in front were of an intense, spotless white. Far below us the cloud stratum melted away, revealing the floor of the valley, whose russet and emerald and brown and red burned in the broad evening sun. It was a marvellous piece of contrasted lights,—the distance so pure, so soft in its rosy warmth, so cool in the depth of its shadowy blue; the foreground strong in fiery orange, or sparkling in absolute whiteness. I enjoyed, too, looking up at the pure, unclouded sky, which now wore an aspect of intense serenity. For half an hour nature seemed in entire repose; not a breath of wind stirred the white, snow-laden shafts of the trees; not a sound of animate creature or the most distant reverberation of waterfall reached us; no film of vapor moved across the tranquil, sapphire sky; absolute quiet reigned until a loud roar proceeding from Capitan turned our eyes in that direction. From the round, dome-like cap of its summit there moved down an avalanche, gathering volume and swiftness as it rushed to the brink, and then, leaping out two or three hundred feet into space, fell, slowly filtering down through the lighted air, like a silver cloud, until within a thousand feet of the earth it floated into the shadow of the cliff and sank to the ground as a faint blue mist. Next the Cathedral snow poured from its lighted summit in resounding avalanches; then the Three Brothers shot off their loads, and afar from the east a deep roar reached us as the whole snow-cover thundered down the flank of Cloud's Rest.

"All Places That the Eye of Heaven Visits"

We were warned by the hour to make all haste, and, driving the poor brutes before us, worked our way down the trail as fast as possible. The light, already pale, left the distant heights in still more glorious contrast. A zone of amber sky rose behind the glowing peaks, and a cold steel-blue plain of snow skirted their bases. Mist slowly gathered again in the gorge below us and overspread the valley floor, shutting it out from our view.

We ran down the zigzag trail until we came to that shelf of bare granite immediately below the final descent into the valley. Here we paused just above the surface of the clouds, which, swept by fitful breezes, rose in swells, floating up and sinking again like waves of the sea. Intense light, more glowing than ever, streamed in upon the upper half of the cliffs, their bases sunken in the purple mist. As the cloud-waves crawled upward in the breeze they here and there touched a red-purple light and fell back again into the shadow.

We watched these effects with greatest interest, and, just as we were about moving on again, a loud burst as of heavy thunder arrested us, sounding as if the very walls were crashing in. We looked, and from the whole brow of Capitan rushed over one huge avalanche, breaking into the finest powder and floating down through orange light, disappearing in the sea of purple cloud beneath us.

"There is here at first a haunting sense of imprisonment, though on a grand scale, of course."

Grace Greenwood
"Eight Days in the Yosemite," 1872

Visitors to Yosemite Valley in the 1870s occasionally expressed a dualistic impression of the majestic mountain cathedral—awe at its extraordinary landscape but a simultaneous sense of confinement, a feeling that the great granite walls were closing in. An archetypal example came from Grace Greenwood in "Eight Days in the

Yosemite," an account of her adventures in the valley. The *New York Times* published this piece on July 27, 1872.

Born Sara Jane Clarke in New York in 1823, she adopted the pseudonym "Grace Greenwood" both in print and in her personal life. Under both her given name and her pen name, Greenwood contributed to many of the prominent journals of her day, but her advocacy of controversial social and political issues often annoyed her publishers. Taking uncompromising stances on the need for prison reform, the abolition of capital punishment, and women's rights, as well as speaking out against war and slavery, Greenwood became a popular writer and lecturer during the Civil War and Reconstruction eras. President Abraham Lincoln dubbed her "Grace Greenwood the Patriot" because of her fundraising efforts for the U.S. Sanitary Commission and her frequent appearances at events sponsored by patriotic organizations.

Greenwood was a pioneering journalist. By the 1870s, she had become the first female reporter on the *New York Times* staff, and, as her 1904 obituary noted, Greenwood "became the first woman Washington correspondent in newspaperdom." Many of her articles focused on what were called "women's issues," such as the wearing of "Bloomers" by women's rights proponents, Susan B. Anthony's demand for women's right to vote, and equal pay for equal work. But some of her articles were pieces commenting on the beauty and bother of traveling in the American West.

In this excerpt from "Eight Days in the Yosemite," Greenwood finds the Yosemite Valley both constricting and exhilarating. Her description of John Muir may be the first reference to the soon-to-be-famous "John of the Mountains" in a national publication.

The Yosemite Falls [is] . . . on the north side of the valley. Of course, from below you can see nothing of the Yosemite Creek. It looks as though it was a cataract from the start,

"All Places That the Eye of Heaven Visits"

born of the sky and the precipice. The roar of this king of the water-falls, in his grandest times, has a singular dual character—there is the eternal monotone, always distinct, though broken in upon by the irregular crash and boom—a sort of gusty thunder. This composite sound, so changing and unchanging, floods and shakes the air, like the roar of the deep sea and the breaking of surf on a rocky shore.

On my first night in the valley the strangeness of my surroundings, a sort of sombre delight that took possession of me, would not let me sleep for several hours. Once I rose and looked out, or tried to look out. The sky was clouded—it seemed to me that the stars drew back from the abyss. It was filled with night and sound. I could not see the mighty rocks that walled us in, but a sense of their shadow was upon me. There was in the awe I felt no element of real dread or fear, but it was thrilled by fantastic terrors. I thought of [Josiah] Whitney's theory of the formation of the great pit, by subsidence. What if it should take another start in the night, and settle a mile or two with us, leaving the rail by which we descended dangling in the air, and the cataracts all spouting away, with no outlet! But in the morning the jolly sun peered down upon us, laughing, as much to say, "There you are, are you?" and the sweet, cool winds dipped down from the pines and the snows, the great fall shouted and danced all the way down his stupendous rocky stairway—the river, and overflowed meadows rippled and flashed with immortal glee. It seems to me that darkness is darker and light lighter in the Yosemite than anywhere else on earth.

Yet, in the midst of its utmost brightness and beauty you are more or less oppressed with a realization of some sudden convulsion of nature that here rent the rocks asunder, that shook the massive mountain till it shook the bottom out; or of the mighty force of drifting, driving glaciers, grinding, carving, just plowing down from the "High Sierra," leaving the stupendous furrow behind them. Somehow you feel that nature has not done with the place yet. Such a grand, abandoned workshop invites her to return. The stage of this great, tragic theatre of the elements waits, perhaps, for some terrible afterpiece. . . .

There is here at first a haunting sense of imprisonment, though on a grand scale, of course. You feel like a magnificent felon, incarcerated in the very fortress of the gods. . . .

I found it impossible to work here, or even to talk fluently or forcibly on what I knew about the Yosemite. . . . I noticed that there were few singing-birds about, and was told by an old guide that they, with most animals, were afraid of the valley. Poetic thoughts and gay fancies seem struck with a like fear. You are for a time mentally unnerved; but you feel that in your powerlessness, you are gaining power; in your silence, more abundant expression. . . .

Among our visitors in the evening was Mr. Muir, the young Scottish mountaineer, student, and enthusiast, who has taken sanctuary in the Yosemite—who stays by the variable valley with remarkable constancy—who adores her alike in the fast, gay Summer life and solemn Autumn glories, in her Winter cold and stillness, and in the passion of her Spring floods and tempests. Not profoundest snows can chill his ardor, not earthquakes can shake his allegiance. Mr. Muir talks with a quiet, quaint humor, and a simple eloquence which are quite delightful. He has a clear, blue eye, a firm, free step and marvelous nerve and endurance. He has the serious air and unconventional ways of a man who has been much with nature in her grand, solitary places. That tourist is fortunate who can have John Muir for a guide in and about the valley. . . .

The Bridal Vail [sic] is my favorite Yosemite cataract. There is for me a tender, retrospective charm to the name. Just opposite to the Bridal Vail is the lovely little trickling cascade, called the Virgin's Tears. Had the sight of the floating, flouting Vail anything to do with that lachrymose condition? We, who reached the Vail, lingered about it for hours—read and slept, botanized, and shouted poetry in each other's ears. When the rainbows came, we went far up into the very heart

"All Places That the Eye of Heaven Visits"

of the splendor. We could have jumped through the radiant hoops like circus-performers. . . .

Glacier Point is on the south side of the valley, 3,700 feet above the meadows. It is the point that gives you the finest comprehensive view of the valley—especially of its upper waterfalls, cañons, and rocks—with vast views of the High Sierra. All the great heights were pointed out to us—Mount Hoffman, Mount Lyell, Mount Dana, Mount Clark, and Mount Starr King. . . .

The vast view from Glacier Point is the despair of poetry and art. Certainly its grandeur can never be compassed by the grandest sweep of human language. Its divine loveliness floats forever before the mind—in smiling, radiant defiance. It is glory that must be seen; it is sublimity that must be felt; it is the "exceeding great reward" that must be toiled for.

"I shouted, 'A living glacier!'"

John Muir
"Living Glaciers of California," 1872

In nineteenth-century Yosemite, climate change was an unknown concept and a worry that lay far ahead in the future. However, one of the earliest scientific studies in Yosemite proved to be a "canary in the coal mine" warning of the future impacts of global warming.

In the early 1870s, John Muir began a systematic inquiry into the features and functions of Yosemite glaciers. Muir was interested in confirming the existence of "living" glaciers and studying their characteristics. With specific focus on two glaciers—on Mount Lyell and Mount Maclure—Muir measured their size and movement. He used the simplest of scientific tools—wooden stakes and careful notation—to determine whether these "snow-banks" exhibited "true glacial motion." It is widely acknowledged that Muir's studies were the first to identify the modern-day existence of glaciers in the Sierra Nevada.

But the story does not end there. The Mount Lyell and Mount Maclure glaciers have been the subject of nearly constant investigation for decades. In 2012 an excellent thesis entitled "Listening to the Trees: Tree Rings, the Little Ice Age, and the Response of Yosemite's Lyell and Maclure Glaciers to Climate Change," by Kali Abel, then a graduate student at the University of Colorado, summarized the effects of climate change on the Lyell and Maclure glaciers. The thesis utilized glacial studies and tree-ring analysis. The results are startling. Since the late 1800s, the Lyell glacier's surface area has decreased 60 percent and its volume has fallen by 95 percent. The Maclure glacier has seen its surface area shrink 47 percent and its volume has declined 90 percent. Later studies, conducted by others, further concluded that the two glaciers had lost nearly 80 percent of their surface area, with 12 percent of the overall reduction occurring between 2012 and 2015. The cause? Abel and other scientists primarily attribute the loss to "thinning," a reduction of glacial thickness due to a variety of factors, including wind, rain, and landslides but also and, most important, rising temperatures, a major component of climate change.

Climate change is a major challenge facing today's Yosemite. And, albeit not realized at the time, scientific consideration of its effects likely began with John Muir sticking five rough-hewn wooden stakes in the Mount Maclure icefield in October 1871.

On one of the yellow days of October, 1871, when I was among the mountains of the "Merced group," following the footprints of the ancient glaciers that once flowed grandly from their ample fountains, reading what I could of their history as written in moraines, cañons, lakes, and carved rocks, I came upon a small stream that was carrying mud of a kind

I had never seen. In a calm place, where the stream widened, I collected some of this mud, and observed that it was entirely mineral in composition, and fine as flour, like the mud from a fine-grit grindstone. Before I had time to reason, I said, "Glacier mud—mountain meal!" Then I observed that this muddy stream issued from a bank of fresh quarried stones and dirt, that was sixty or seventy feet in height. This I at once took to be a moraine. In climbing to the top of it, I was struck with the steepness of its slope, and with its raw, unsettled, plantless, new-born appearance. The slightest touch started blocks of red and black slate, followed by a rattling train of smaller stones and sand, and a cloud of dry dust of mud, the whole moraine being as free from lichens and weather-stains as if dug from the mountain that very day. When I had scrambled to the top of the moraine, I saw what seemed to be a huge snow-bank, four or five hundred yards in length, by half a mile in width. Imbedded in its stained and furrowed surface were stones and dirt like that of which the moraine was built. Dirt-stained lines curved across the snow-bank from side to side, and when I observed that these curved lines coincided with the curved moraine, and that the stones and dirt were most abundant near the bottom of the bank, I shouted, "A living glacier!" . . .

On traversing my new-found glacier, I came to a crevasse, down a wide and jagged portion of which I succeeded in making my way, and discovered that my so-called snow-bank was clear, green ice, and, comparing the form of the basin which it occupied with similar adjacent basins that were empty, I was led to the opinion that this glacier was several hundred feet in depth. Then I went to the "snow-banks" of Mts. Lyell and McClure [the correct spelling is Maclure], and, on examination, was convinced that they also were true glaciers, and that a dozen other snow-banks seen from the summit of Mt. Lyell, crouching in shadow, were glaciers, living as any in the world, and busily engaged in completing that vast work of mountain-making accomplished by their giant relations now dead, which, united and continuous, covered all the range from summit to sea. But, although I was myself thus fully satisfied concerning the real nature of these ice masses, I found that my friends regarded my deductions and statements with distrust; therefore, I determined to collect proofs of the common, measured, arithmetical kind. On the twenty-first of August last, I planted five stakes in the glacier of Mt. McClure, which is situated east of Yosemite Valley, near the summit of the range. Four of these stakes were extended across the glacier, in a straight line, from the east side to a point near the middle of the glacier. The first stake was planted about twenty-five yards from the east bank of the glacier; the second, ninety-four yards; the third, 152, and the fourth, 225 yards. The positions of these stakes were determined by sighting across from bank to bank, past a plumbline, made of a stone and a black horse-hair. On observing my stakes on the sixth of October, or in forty-six days after being planted, I found that stake No. 1 had been carried downstream eleven inches; No. 2, eighteen inches; No. 3, thirty-four, and No. 4, forty-seven inches. As stake No. 4 was near the middle of the glacier, perhaps it was not far from the point of maximum velocity—forty-seven inches in forty-six days, or one inch per day. Stake No. 5 was planted about midway between the head of the glacier and stake No. 4. Its motion I found to be, in forty-six days, forty inches. Thus these ice-masses are seen to possess the true glacial motion.

"The ice in this instance has true glacial motion."

Israel C. Russell

Existing Glaciers of the United States, 1885

In 1885 a U.S. Geological Survey report, prepared under the direction of Israel C. Russell, offered a qualified confirmation of Muir's analysis, noting that while Muir's findings were generally accepted, "the observations on which he based his determinations seem not to have been sufficient to convince all observers."

"All Places That the Eye of Heaven Visits"

Even today, not everyone accepts the reality of a changing climate, no matter the evidence presented. Today the shrinking glaciers of Yosemite are commonly cited as a prime example of the effects of climate change on the national park. In 2021 the National Park Service outlined additional long-term future impacts on Yosemite, especially without significant reductions in global greenhouse gas emissions. The NPS suggested the following: (1) average temperatures in the park may rise by 6.7 to 10.3 degrees Fahrenheit between 2000 and 2100; (2) days per year with temperatures above 90 degrees may quadruple from around twelve in 2016 to forty-eight by 2100; (3) Yosemite is likely to experience extreme storms more often; as well as (4) waning annual snowpack; (5) cessation of flow at waterfalls; (6) increased frequency and intensity of fires; (7) continued glacial thinning; (8) escalating tree death; and (9) undesirable changes in the visitor experience due to heat, lack of water, and smoke.

Although giving precedence to my own observations in describing the glaciers of the High Sierra, I do not wish to ignore the reports of those who have preceded me. The anonymous article on the "Living Glaciers of California" which appeared in the *Overland Monthly* for December, 1872, we have already referred to as being from the pen of Mr. John Muir, and is, so far as known, the first announcement of the existence of glaciers in the Sierra Nevada. Mr. Muir states that in October, 1871, he was among the mountains of the "Merced group" and found a living glacier, with very recent moraines at its foot, from beneath which issued a stream charged with fine mud; further observation revealed dirt-bands, crevasses, and lateral moraines, thus leaving no doubt that the "snow-bank," as it had previously been considered, was an actual glacier. Other similar ice bodies were examined by Mr. Muir on Mount Lyell and Mount McClure [Maclure]; and from the top of Mount Lyell he saw a dozen small glaciers on neighboring peaks.

In August, 1872, Mr. Muir placed five stakes in the glacier on Mount McClure for the purpose of demonstrating that it had true "glacial motion. . . ." These measurements, although not as detailed and perhaps not as accurate as could be desired, are yet sufficient to demonstrate, as claimed by Mr. Muir, that the ice in this instance has true glacial motion. In this example, as in all normal glaciers, the most rapid movement was near the middle of the ice-stream. The Mount McClure Glacier, when visited by Mr. Muir, was approximately half a mile long, and of about the same breadth in the widest part, and was observed to be traversed in the southeast corner by crevasses several hundred yards long but only about a foot wide. The Mount Lyell Glacier, in 1872, is stated to have been about a mile in length by a mile in breadth. Mr. Muir also describes narrow high-grade cañons called "devil's slide," "devil's lanes," etc., which occur about the higher peaks and are frequently occupied by ice. In one of these gorges the ice was found to have a motion of a fraction of an inch per day. It is probable that these small ice-bodies are what we have called "ice-tongues" in describing our observations of last summer. . . .

In connection with the observations[,] Professor [Josiah] Whitney remarks that "it is doubtful whether these residual masses of ice can with propriety be called glaciers." Mr. [Clarence] King also rejected Mr. Muir's observations, as is shown by several emphatic passages in his report of the Exploration of the 40th Parallel, but adds no new information on the subject. From the quotations that have been given it will be seen that the question of the existence of glaciers in the Sierra Nevada has been decided differently by different observers, who perhaps saw the mountains under diverse conditions as regards their snowy covering. In winter the glaciers are buried so deeply beneath accumulations of snow that no one would suspect their existence; it is only late in summer, when the snows have decreased to a minimum, that they are to be seen to the greatest advantage. That Mr. Muir was correct in classing many of the snow masses as

"All Places That the Eye of Heaven Visits"

glaciers is sustained by recent investigation, but the observations on which he based his determinations seem not to have been sufficient to convince all observers.

"Now the valley is a haunt for people who are unprincipled in their treatment of tourists."

John Erastus Lester

The Yo-Semite: Its History, Its Scenery, Its Development, 1873

With increased visitation to Yosemite came a proliferation of complaints as well. Tourists grumbled about poor food, substandard lodging, dust, uncooperative mules, saddle sores, and inflated prices. Sightseers also whined about their fellow travelers, viewing more than a few as unappreciative, unruly, and unsophisticated. But the sharpest criticisms were often reserved for the commercial proprietors in Yosemite Valley, many of whom were regarded as money-grubbing wheeler-dealers exploiting a natural wonder.

In 1872 John Erastus Lester, a Rhode Island lawyer, came west on the transcontinental railroad, which had been completed only three years earlier. Lester was on a personal journey to California, he would write, "in search of health." In the last half of the nineteenth century, California was frequently touted for its salubrious climate and restorative powers, particularly for those suffering from lung ailments, such as tuberculosis.

As part of his Golden State itinerary, Lester visited Yosemite, where he met notable figures such as Galen Clark, James Mason Hutchings, and John Muir. Upon his return to the East Coast in late 1872, Lester presented a paper to the Rhode Island Historical Society on his Yosemite experiences. At the urging of friends and colleagues, Lester self-published his lecture in 1873 as *The Yo-Semite: Its History, Its Scenery, Its Development*. Later in 1873, he expanded his presentation into a book-length manuscript chronicling his trip across country: *The Atlantic to the Pacific: What to See, and How to See It.*

In this selection from *The Yo-Semite: Its History, Its Scenery, Its Development,* Lester describes the Yosemite landscape, catalogs the development of the various hotels in the valley, offers a brief, lawyerly discourse on Yosemite governance, and expresses his disdain for the dubious band callously manipulating Yosemite visitors for profit.

I am aware that my subject seems better fitted for a scientific society, than one, which, like ours, seeks to preserve the recorded facts of the past. But we all love Nature and she addresses us in so varied moods that there is no one, who does not at some time find great pleasure in contemplating her developments. Nowhere probably upon the whole globe, has she given a more sublime and grand development, than in the valley, the surrounding hills and those magnificent waterfalls, which have taken the general name of Yo-Semite. My task then shall be to tell you, what I can, in the brief time allotted me, of the Yo-Semite, the history of its discovery and exploration, its scenery and its future development.

I am also aware, how very far short of satisfaction to myself, as well as to you, I shall come in any attempt to describe the sublimity and grandeur of this scenery; I can only indicate, leaving your imagination to paint a more perfect picture, and trusting that you all may yet behold, as I have, those scenes with your own eyes, and drink in the *inspiration*—the voice of God speaking to us through Nature.

The history of the Yo-Semite is, to a certain extent, the history of California, for in this, culminates all the glories of her magnificent scenery, and to preserve this place, where man is forbidden to build his cities or in great numbers to congregate, as a *sacred* park, she has always labored, aided as far as possible by the Nation in her Legislative Councils. . . .

That range of mountains known as "Sierra Nevada" is limited to California, and extends from Mt. Shasta in the

"All Places That the Eye of Heaven Visits"

north to Tejon pass in the south, a length as estimated of 550 miles. . . .

Within this mountain range is located the Yo-Semite Valley. . . .

Of course . . . early visitors were forced to carry with them a full set of camp equipage, and the condition of the roads and the trails up the mountains made the journey one of hardship and in many places very dangerous. As tourists began to turn their steps towards the valley, persons, whose aim was "to turn a penny" into their pockets, began to try to meet the wants of these travellers. . . .

Several small unfinished buildings are scattered through the valley, used for various purposes, as photographic galleries, telegraph office, a store, &c. The houses and buildings of J. C. Lamon are situated at the upper end of the valley. These comprise the buildings so far erected in the valley, and all of them are rude structures, serving only for a poor protection against storms. . . .

I now come to speak briefly of the development of this famed valley. It will serve us to first see what has been done by Congress and the State of California towards this object. In 1864 Congress enacted that the "Cleft or Gorge" in the Granite Peak of the Sierras, estimated in length fifteen miles, with its various spurs and cañons and one mile back from the edge of the precipice on all sides be granted to the State of California "that the said State shall accept this grant upon the express conditions that the premises shall be held for public use, resort and recreation; shall be inalienable for all time, but leases not exceeding ten years may be granted for portions of said premises." . . . A guardian of the valley, as he is called, was appointed, further surveys made, the roads and trails improved, a map of the valley level completed, and in 1867 a report was made to the Legislature, and further appropriations were asked for, to carry out their plans.

At the time the Commissioners took possession of the valley there were several persons already settled in the valley and many claimants, all of whom the Commissioners proposed to treat liberally. Messrs. Hutchings and Lamon were foremost in their opposition to the Commissioners and persisted in their claims to a fee-simple of 160 acres each. They sought redress in the courts and before the Legislature. . . . At the Legislature of 1867–8 they appeared and pressed their claims with so much tact and energy that a bill was proposed giving them 160 acres each, and so far as votes of the members were needed it became a law. At the Fortieth Congress this bill was presented for ratification, and an act of approval was passed by the House[,] but failed in the Senate. At the second session of the Forty-first Congress a bill was again introduced but failed. Thus matters have rested.

It is no wonder that the press, with almost universal voice, opposed any action of Congress whereby any portion of the valley should be given in fee to any person. Every citizen in the United States has acquired a kind of right in and to this national play ground. It was a shame, yea almost a fraud upon the rights of the people, to thus attempt to set aside a solemn compact entered into by the nation and the State of California. Those discussions are still fresh in your memories and although they resulted in a defeat of the bills proposed in Congress, the partial success of the claimants paralyzed the efforts of the Commissioners, and the natural consequences have flown from this inaction. There might have been long ago a carriage-road built into the valley on the Mariposa side, suitable hotel accommodations might have been provided, trails to the various points of interest could have been made, and all done under the direction of the Commissioners and used by the people under proper restrictions. Now the valley is a haunt for people who are unprincipled in their treatment of tourists. I know of many persons abandoning the trip to the Yo-Semite after reaching San Francisco, upon hearing the story of returned tourists. Cliques and interests combine to make the most money that they can, and these too strong to be opposed, luxuriate in their gains. I would not include all in my indictment, for there are on the road and in the valley gentlemen of high-toned principles, and moral recti-

"All Places That the Eye of Heaven Visits"

tude, but the few are only brought out in fuller relief by the many against whom so many complaints are made.

There are now pending suits involving the collateral questions in the proceedings to procure decisions upon the claims of Mr. Hutchings, but if the Court holds, as it undoubtedly will, to its former rulings, then there need be no fear that any private individual will have in fee any part of that domain, which God himself set apart, and forbade man to build his cities and habitations upon.

> "Hetch Hetchy is one of a magnificent
> brotherhood of Yosemite Valleys."

John Muir
"The Hetch Hetchy Valley," 1873

As awareness of the Yosemite Valley grew during the 1870s, so did recognition of additional extraordinary landforms in the larger Yosemite ecosystem that were not protected by federal or state authority. Preeminent among these was the valley known as Hetch Hetchy, carved by glaciers and the Tuolumne River and situated about twenty miles north of Yosemite Valley.

As difficult as Yosemite Valley was to approach, Hetch Hetchy posed an even greater challenge. It was not routinely visited by nonindigenous observers until the late 1860s. John Muir first visited Hetch Hetchy Valley in November 1871 and was struck by its resemblance to Yosemite Valley, and he later referred to Hetch Hetchy as the "wonderfully exact counterpart" of Yosemite Valley and as the "Tuolumne Yosemite." Muir and others promoted inclusion of Hetch Hetchy Valley as part of an expanded Yosemite protectorate, and eventually Hetch Hetchy would be included in the boundaries of the new Yosemite National Park, established in 1890.

At the turn of the twentieth century, Hetch Hetchy Valley would become embroiled in a controversy that reverberates to the present day. Following the 1906 earthquake and fire, the city of San Francisco became acutely aware of its need for a reliable water source. An abandoned plan to dam the Tuolumne River at the mouth of Hetch Hetchy Valley was revived. Construction of the city-owned O'Shaughnessy Dam and Hetch Hetchy Reservoir was the result. It was built entirely within the confines of Yosemite National Park. Efforts by conservation and National Park advocates to remove the dam and restore the valley to its natural state have been active for decades.

In a letter to the *Boston Weekly Transcript* dated March 1872 but not published until March 25, 1873, John Muir describes his first tour of Hetch Hetchy Valley, in November 1871. Muir's narrative is the beginning of a love affair with the valley that would last the remainder of his life. In 1912, forty years after his initial encounter, John Muir would write in his book *The Yosemite*, "Hetch Hetchy, they say, is a 'low-lying meadow.' On the contrary, it is a high-lying natural landscape garden. . . . 'It is a common minor feature, like thousands of others.' On the contrary, it is a very uncommon feature; after Yosemite, the rarest and in many ways the most important in the National Park."

Hetch Hetchy is one of a magnificent brotherhood of Yosemite Valleys, distant from Yosemite Valley, so-called, eighteen or twenty miles in a northwesterly direction, but by the only trail the distance is not less than forty miles.

In the first week of last November [1871], I set out from here on an excursion of this wonderful valley. . . .

Next morning, after climbing a long timbered slope and crossing a few groove-shaped valleys I came upon the precipitous rim of the great Tuolumne Cañon, a mile or two above Hetch Hetchy. I had explored a few miles of the central portion of this stupendous cañon in one of my former excursions. It is a Yosemite Valley in depth and in width, and is over twenty miles in length, abounding in falls and cascades, and glacial rock forms. Hetch Hetchy is only an expanded lower portion of this vast Yosemite. The view from my first standpoint is one of the very grandest I ever beheld. From the great cañon as a sort of base line, extends a most sublime map of mountains rising gradually higher, dome over dome, crest over crest, to the summit of the range, and the whole glorious engraving is reposed at such an angle that you look full upon its surface near and far. To one unacquainted with the hidden life and tenderness of the high sierra, the first impression is one of intense soul-crushing desolation. Robert Burns described the Scottish Highlands as "a country where savage streams tumble over savage mountains," and nothing but the same (outside) savageness and confusion is apparent here. Castaway heaps of dead, broken mountains outspread, cold and gray, like a storm sky of winter. But, venture to the midst of these bleached mountain bones— dwell with them, and every death taint will disappear, you will find them living joyously, with lakes, and forests, and a thousand flowers, their hardest domes pulsing with life, breathing in atmospheres of beauty and love. . . .

This valley is situated on the main Tuolumne River, just as Yosemite is on the Merced. It is about three miles in length, with a width varying from an eighth to half a mile; most of its surface is level as a lake, and lies at an elevation of 3800 feet above the sea. Its course is mostly from east to west, but it is bent northward in the middle like Yosemite. At the end of the valley the river enters a narrow cañon which cannot devour spring floods sufficiently fast to prevent the lower half of the valley from becoming a lake. Beginning at the west end of the valley where the Hardin trail comes in, the first conspicuous rocks on the right are a group like the Cathedral Rocks of Yosemite, and occupying the same relative position to the valley. . . . In spring a large stream pours over its brow with a clear fall of at least one thousand feet. East of this, on the same side, is the Hetch Hetchy Fall, occupying a position relative to the valley like that of Yosemite Fall. It is about seventeen hundred feet in height, but not in one unbroken fall. It is said to have a much larger body of water than the Yosemite Fall, but at the time of my visit (November), it was nearly dry. The wall of the valley above this fall has two benches fringed with liveoak, which correspond with astonishing minuteness to the benches of the same relative portion of the Yosemite wall. . . .

Thickets of azalea and the brier rose are common and extensive tracts along the edges of the meadows are covered with the common bracken (Pteris aquilina). I measured several specimens of this fern that exceeded eight feet in height, and the fissured walls of the valley, from top to bottom, abound in tufted rock ferns of rare beauty, which we have not space to enumerate. The crystal river glides between sheltering groves of alder and poplar and flowering dogwood. Where there is a few inches of fall it ripples and sparkles songfully, but it flows gently in most places, often with a lingering expression, as if half inclined to become a lake. Many of these river nooks are gloriously bordered with ferns and sedges and drooping willows; some were enlivened with ducks that blended charmingly into the picture, only it seemed wonderful that mountain water, so pure and so light like, could be sufficiently substantial to float a duck.

It is estimated that about 7000 persons have seen Yosemite. If this multitude were to be gathered again, and set down in Hetch Hetchy perhaps less than one percent of the whole number would doubt their being in Yosemite. They would see rocks and waterfalls, meadows and groves, of Yosemite size and kind, and grouped in Yosemite style. Amid so vast an assemblage of sublime mountain forms, only the more calm and careful observers would be able to fix upon special differences. . . .

Tourists who can afford the time ought to visit Hetch Hetchy on their way to or from Yosemite. The trail from Hardin's [a settlement about fifteen miles southwest of Hetch Hetchy] will be found as good as mountain trails usually are, and it certainly is worth while riding a few miles out of a direct course to assure one's self that the world is so rich as to possess at least two Yosemites instead of one.

> "... by dint of pluck, skill, unswerving
> perseverance, and personal daring."

James Mason Hutchings
In the Heart of the Sierras, 1888

Climbing the luminous granite cliffs, towers, and spires of Yosemite Valley has been an aspiration for the bold and, perhaps, reckless. In the earliest decades of non-indigenous visitation, however, the fundamental question became whether it was even possible to ascend these rocks. Experts studied the matter, and most decided that scaling these heights was impossible, especially with the limited tools at hand—namely, rope, hobnail boots, and prayer.

Spectacular but intimidating Half Dome was a particularly desirable goal, but reaching the crown of the soaring granite monolith seemed unachievable. In 1870 Josiah Whitney, the world-renowned scientist and California state geologist, stated that Half Dome "never has been and never will be trodden by human foot" and that the summit of the imposing formation was "perfectly inaccessible."

But there were an audacious few who felt otherwise. After several individuals failed in their attempts to climb Half Dome, on October 12, 1875, George Anderson, a carpenter who lived in a tiny log cabin in Yosemite Valley, accomplished the feat. Once the slippery dome had been successfully topped, the floodgates opened, and within months dozens had scrambled to the summit, including the first woman, Sarah Dutcher, who reached the crest only days after Anderson. Julius Birge, a friend of George Anderson, predicted that Dutcher was "certainly the first and possibly the last woman who made the ascent." He was wrong. Since the mid-1870s, thousands of men, women, and children have climbed Half Dome.

Below is the first of two narratives of scaling Half Dome in 1875. This one details George Anderson's initial climb of Half Dome, as presented by James Mason Hutchings in his 1888 book *In the Heart of the Sierras*.

Until the fall of 1875 the storm-beaten summit of this magnificent landmark was a terra incognita, as it had never been trodden by human feet. In the summer of 1869 three of us set out for the purpose of climbing it, taking the "Indian escape trail" north of Grizzly Peak. There was absolutely no trail whatsoever, as we had to walk on narrow ledges, and hold on with our feet as well as hands, trusting our lives to bushes and jutting points of rock. In some places where the ledges of rock were high, their tops had to be reached by long broken branches of trees, which the Indians used to climb; and, after they were up, cut off the possibility of pursuit from enemies, by pulling up these primitive ladders after them. Not a drop of water could we find. A snow bank increased rather than diminished our terrible thirst. Finally, after many hair-breadth escapes, and not a little fatigue, we reached the top of the lower dome, or eastern shoulder, and were then within four hundred and sixty feet, vertically, of realizing our ambitious hopes. To our dismay, as well as disappointment, we found a great smooth mountain before us, standing at an angle of about 40°, its surface overlaid and overlapped, so to speak, with vast circular granite shingles, about eighteen inches in thickness. There was not a place to set a secure foot upon, or a point that we could clutch with our fingers. The very first sight put every hope to flight of reaching its exalted summit by the means at our command; and, deeming it a simple impossibility, "we surrendered at discretion," and returned without the realization of our ambitious hopes.

Seven years after this an athletic youth informed the writer that he was "going to climb to the top of the Half Dome." I

"All Places That the Eye of Heaven Visits"

quietly suggested that such a feat was among the doubtful things of this life. He was willing to bet any amount that *he* could accomplish it. I informed him that I was not a betting man,—had never made a bet in my life, and was too old to begin now,—but, if he would put a flag upon the only visible pine tree standing there, I would make him a present of twenty dollars, and treat him and his friends to the best champagne dinner that could be provided in Yo Semite. Three days after this he walked past without deigning to stop, or even to look at us,—and there was no flag floating from the top of the Half Dome either!

This honor was reserved for a brave young Scotchman, a native of Montrose, named George G. Anderson, who, by dint of pluck, skill, unswerving perseverance, and personal daring, climbed to its summit; and was the first that ever successfully scaled it. This was accomplished at 3 o'clock P.M. of October 12, 1875.

The knowledge that the feat of climbing this grand mountain had on several occasions been attempted, but never with success, begat in him an irrepressible determination to succeed in such an enterprise. Imbued with this incentive, he made his way to its base; and, looking up its smooth and steeply inclined surface, at once set about the difficult exploit. Finding that he could not keep from sliding with his boots on, he tried it in his stocking feet; but as this did not secure a triumph, he tried it barefooted, and still was unsuccessful. Then he tied sacking upon his feet and legs, but as these did not secure the desired object, he covered it with pitch, obtained from pine trees near; and although this enabled him to adhere firmly to the smooth granite, and effectually prevented him from slipping, a new difficulty presented itself in the great effort required to unstick himself; and which came near proving fatal several times.

Mortified by the failure of all his plans hitherto, yet in no way discouraged, he procured drills and a hammer, with some iron eye-bolts, and drilled a hole in the solid rock; into this he drove a wooden pin, and then an eye-bolt; and after fastening a rope to the bolt, pulled himself up until he could stand upon it; and thence continued that process until he had finally gained the top—a distance of nine hundred and seventy-five feet! All honor, then, to the intrepid and skillful mountaineer, Geo. G. Anderson, who, defying and overcoming all obstacles, and at the peril of his life, accomplished that in which all others had signally failed; and thus became the first to plant his foot upon the exalted crown of the great Half Dome.

His next efforts were directed towards placing and securely fastening a good soft rope to the eye-bolts, so that others could climb up and enjoy the inimitable view, and one that has not its counterpart on earth. Four English gentlemen, then sojourning in the Valley, learning of Mr. Anderson's feat, were induced to follow his intrepid example. A day or two afterwards, Miss S. L. Dutcher, of San Francisco, with the courage of a heroine, accomplished it; and was the first lady that ever stood upon it. In July 1876, Miss L. E. Pershing, of Pittsburg, Pa., the writer, and three others found their way there. In October following, six persons, among them a lady in her sixty-fifth year, and a young girl, thirteen years of age (a daughter of the writer), and two other ladies, climbed it with but little difficulty, after Anderson had provided the way. Since then very many others have daringly pulled themselves up; and enjoyed the exceptionally impressive view obtained thence.

....

"When a mountain is climbed it is said to be conquered—as well say a man is conquered when a fly lights on his head."

....

John Muir
"South Dome," 1875

Only a month after George C. Anderson made the historic first ascent of Half Dome, John Muir made his own climb, not only following in Anderson's footsteps but using his eyebolt holes as well. Having successfully ascended (and descended) the granite hulk, he wrote a newspaper account of how he scaled Half Dome (which Muir calls "South Dome" and "Tissiack"), printed in the *San Francisco Daily Evening Bulletin* on November 18, 1875. Note that the headline and the subheadings were provided by the newspaper and refer to Muir, the *Bulletin*'s "special correspondent," in the third person.

SOUTH DOME: ITS ASCENT BY GEORGE ANDERSON AND JOHN MUIR—

HARD CLIMBING BUT A GLORIOUS VIEW . . .

(From our special correspondent).

Yosemite Valley, November 10, 1875

The Yosemite South Dome is the noblest rock in the Sierra, and George Anderson, an indomitable Scotchman, has made a way to its summit . . . With the exception of [the] conoidal summit of Mount Starr King, and a few minor spires and pinnacles, the South Dome is the only inaccessible rock of the valley, and its inaccessibility is pronounced in very severe and simple terms, leaving no trace of hope for the climber without artificial means. But longing eyes were none the less fixed on its noble brow, and the Anderson way will be eagerly ascended.

The Dome Described

The Dome rises from the level floor of the valley to the height of very nearly a mile. The north side is absolutely vertical from the summit to a depth of about 1,900 feet. On the south it is nearly vertical to as great a depth. The west side presents a very steep and firmly drawn curve from the summit down a thousand feet or more; while on the east, where it is united with the dividing ridge between the great Tenaya and Nevada canyons, the Dome may be easily approached within six or seven hundred feet of the summit, where it rises in a smooth, graceful curve just a few degrees too steep to climb. Nearly all Sierra rocks are accessible on the eastern or upper side, because the glacial force which eroded them out of the solid acted from this direction; but special conditions in the position and structure of the South Dome prevented the formation of the ordinary low grade, and it is this steep upper portion that the plucky Anderson has overcome. John Conway, a resident of the valley, has a flock of small boys who climb smooth rocks like lizards, and some two years ago he sent them up the dome with a rope, hoping they might be able to fasten it with spikes driven into fissures, and thus reach the top. They took the rope in tow and succeeded in making it fast two or three hundred feet above the point ordinarily reached, but finding the upper portion of the curve impracticable without laboriously drilling into the rock, he called down his lizards, thinking himself fortunate in effecting a safe retreat.

Mr. Anderson began with Conway's old rope, part of which still remains in place, and resolutely drilled his way to the top, inserting eyebolts five or six feet apart, and making his rope fast to each in succession, resting his foot on the last bolt while he drilled for the next above. Occasionally some irregularity in the curve or slight foothold would enable him to climb fifteen or twenty feet independently of the rope, which he would pass and begin drilling again, the whole being accomplished in a few days. From this slender beginning he will now proceed to construct a substantial stairway which he hopes to complete in time for next year's travel; and as he is a man of rare energy the thing will surely be done. Then, all may sing "Excelsior" in perfect safety.

Mr. Muir Takes a Walk Up the South Dome

On my return to the valley the other day I immediately hastened to the Dome, not only for the pure pleasure climbing in view, but to see what else I might enjoy and learn. Our first winter storm had bloomed and all the mountains were mantled in fresh snow. I was therefore a little apprehensive of danger from the slipperyness of the rock, Anderson still himself refusing to believe that any one could climb his rope in the condition it was then in. Moreover, the sky was overcast, and solemn snow-clouds began to curl and wreath themselves around the summit of the Dome.... But reflecting that I had matches in my pocket, and that a little fire-wood might be found, I concluded that in case of a dark storm the night could be spent on the Dome without suffering anything worth caring for. I therefore pushed up alone and gained the top without the slightest difficulty. My first view was perfectly glorious. A massive cloud of a pure pearl lustre was arched across the valley, from wall to wall, the one end resting upon El Capitan, the other on Cathedral Rocks, the brown meadows shadowed beneath, with short reaches of the river shimmering in changeful light. Then, as I stood on the tremendous verge overlooking Mirror Lake, a flock of smaller clouds, white as snow, came swiftly from the north, trailing over the dark forests, and arriving on the brink of the valley descended with godlike gestures through Indian Canyon and over the Arches and North Dome, moving rapidly, yet with perfect deliberation. On they came, nearer, nearer, beneath my feet, gathering and massing, and filling the Tenaya abyss. Then the sun shone free, lighting them through and through and painting them with the splendors of the rainbow. It was one of those brooding days that come just between Indian summer and winter, when the clouds are like living creatures. Now and then the Valley appeared all bright and cloudless, with its crystal river meandering through colored meadow and grove, while to the eastward the snowy peaks rose in glorious array, keenly outlined on the pure azure. Then the clouds would come again, wreathing the Dome, and making a darkness like night....

"Conquering" Mountains—Yosemite in Autumn

I have always discouraged as much as possible every project for laddering the South Dome, believing it would be a fine thing to keep this garden untrodden. Now the pines will be carved with the initials of Smith and Jones, and the gardens strewn with tin cans and bottles, but the winter gales will blow most of this rubbish away, and avalanches may strip off the ladders; and then it is some satisfaction to feel assured that no lazy person will ever trample these gardens. When a mountain is climbed it is said to be conquered—as well say a man is conquered when a fly lights on his head. Blue jays have trodden the Dome many a day; so have beetles and chipmunks, and Tissiack will hardly be more conquered, now that man is added to her list of visitors. His louder scream and heavier scrambling will not stir a line of her countenance.

> "My first morning dreams were disturbed by the wail of some venerable spinster who had lost her washrag."

Caroline Nichols Churchill
Over the Purple Hills, or Sketches of Travel in California, 1877

There was never any doubt where Caroline Nichols Churchill stood on an issue. When she visited Yosemite in 1874, Churchill had a scathing opinion about one specific aspect of her stay: annoying and self-centered tourists.

With a reputation for truthfulness and forthrightness, Churchill was an editor, publisher, author, and leading advocate for women's rights in the American West. She also wrote two valuable descriptions of California and the West in the last quarter of the nineteenth century.

Churchill was born in Canada in 1833 and immigrated to the United States in 1846. Briefly married, she was on her own after the untimely death of her husband in 1862. After contracting tuberculosis, Churchill was advised to seek a drier climate. Choosing California, she journeyed westward in 1869. With her health and spirits restored, she plunged into state politics. Incensed by a California bill that would punish and regulate "immoral women," Churchill worked incessantly to defeat the legislation. She was particularly outraged that women would be held accountable for certain immoral activity, while

"All Places That the Eye of Heaven Visits"

men would not be deemed responsible for the same behavior.

The experience made Churchill especially aware of the inequities faced by women in the West. In 1879 Churchill relocated to Denver, Colorado, and began publishing a newspaper called the *Colorado Antelope*. The journal advocated women's suffrage and other feminist causes. In the beginning, Churchill was a lonely voice in the wilderness. Within three years, however, the *Colorado Antelope* had gained in profitability and popularity to the point that it began more frequent publication under a new name, *Queen Bee*. Churchill supported prohibition of alcohol, equal education for women, financial support for women with dependent children, and voting rights. In 1893, partly due to her efforts, women earned the right to vote in Colorado.

Churchill also wrote two entertaining and incisive travel narratives. *Little Sheaves*, a collection of letters describing her trips throughout California and Nevada from 1870 to 1873, was issued in 1874. Her 1877 book, *Over the Purple Hills, or Sketches from Travel in California*, presented an account of Churchill's rail journeys from San Francisco to Lake Tahoe and from Visalia to Placerville, California, in 1874.

The following excerpt from *Over the Purple Hills* offers Churchill's recollections of her visit to Yosemite Valley. She was hoping to refresh her spirits in the Yosemite wonderland and, as she wrote, "enjoy this beautiful scenery in quiet." Instead, Churchill faced an onslaught of maddening and selfish tourists. She begins by recounting the tale of a missing washrag.

At present the hotels of the Yosemite are of bandbox order—cloth and paper, to be sure, answering all the immediate needs of this indulgent climate, but rather generous in the communication of sound. My first morning dreams were disturbed by the wail of some venerable spinster who had lost her washrag. The chambermaid was rallied at five o'clock in the morning, and the din and search kept up with unceasing diligence for one hour. During this time I had heard the word wash-rag pronounced so frequently, that this, with the fatigue of travel, threw me into a laughing hysteric. There was something so utterly ridiculous in hearing the word pronounced so repeatedly, and the absurdity of creating a disturbance for so small a matter, that I came near having what used to be known as a "conniption" fit. In the meantime the poor little chambermaid was vibrating between smiles and tears mentally, and between my room, the other room and the porch personally, all the time wondering what could have become of the unfortunate woman's wash-rag. The smiles were in sympathy with my laughing mood, the tears the cruel sting of unjust accusation, and the bodily movements an uneasy desire to have the stage come and carry off the hapless tourist. The stage came at last, and the woman was torn from the scenes where she had lost her wash-rag and borne reluctantly away. The last sound that I heard from her retreating figure-head was the wail of the wash-rag. In the course of her morning work the chambermaid went into the room, and upon emptying the pitcher gave a faint scream, and called me to come and behold the missing wash-rag. "Stars and stripes!" I exclaimed, "where did you find it?" "In the pitcher," she answered. It was a piece of tufted toweling about a foot square, and striped with red, and when it came sliding out of the pitcher the girl imagined pink snakes, curiosities of tourists, and several things before the real truth flashed upon her. This mystery was solved; "but," said the girl, "I know that lady will think until the day of judgment that I took her wash-rag, unless by some accident she shall hear of this." I lost a package of thread, of spools of cotton and silk, upon this same route—not at this house—enough to have lasted me for ten years; and I am sure that with a warrant I could find them now, but I would rather lose them than run the risk of placing an innocent person under unjust suspicion; besides, there are classes of human beings whose chances to

"All Places That the Eye of Heaven Visits"

compete with others for a livelihood have been so cramped and limited, that they think that they must steal in order to get even, and it is not in my heart to blame them. At the same time I would most assuredly encourage the most rigorous regard for the property of others, as stealing is closely allied to the dreadful crime of murder.

One morning I heard a young girl say, in a whining voice, that she did not want to make the trip on horseback necessary to do the valley, adding that she did not see what people wanted to go scrambling over those rough trails for. I am afraid; should think people could come here and enjoy this beautiful scenery in quiet. But papa had a horse brought, and insisted with a few firm but gentle words, as if accustomed to being obeyed; and every evening when this dainty little miss returned, face flushed with exercise, and so stiff from sitting upon the horse that she could scarcely step, she would call out to those whom she greeted at the hotel, "O, I am so glad that I went; it was so beautiful!" Papa evidently had no idea of going to the trouble and expense of bringing her to this valley, have her lose her interest, and go tamely home without seeing anything. Upon another occasion a very pretty, well dressed family came for a few days, and the wife seemed to be parsimonious. Each morning she had something to say about the extravagance of the trip. The husband would answer. It is a pity, with such an income, that we cannot spend a little money in traveling without such a to do. I do not want to hear another word; not another word. This seemed to settle the matter for another day. But they were a very unhappy couple, in spite of their income; and the children seemed to catch the same spirit—were constantly teasing one another and quarreling.

When you visit the Yosemite for pleasure and put up at a pasteboard hotel, bring as few cares and family jars as you can well get along with, and above all keep quiet while remaining. . . .

I would like a few words to ministers and their families who come to visit this wonder in nature. That in these days of Christian popularity and church prosperity, few are called upon to practice much self-denial at home, and when in this valley it is an excellent time to exercise the Christian graces; and if the beds are not so soft as those you have been accustomed to, just thin[k] of the hymn, "Shall I be carried to the skies on flowery beds of ease," etc., and if you are called upon to eat grass-hoppers and fresh bread, think of an apostle whose meat was locusts and wild honey; and that the beloved founder of Christianity had not a better place to lay his holy head than under the grateful shade of these lofty pines in the Yosemite Valley; and it is very doubtful if the ass which he appropriated was any more spirited than the poor beasts which bore us so laboriously over the rough mountain trail.

"There is no doubt the Indians would be much amused
if they could know what a piece of work we have
made of some of their names."

Stephen Powers
"Yosemite," 1877

As Yosemite Valley gained renown and accessibility, it was not long until aggressive valley promoters and besotted writers and tourists transformed it into a Wilderness Fantasyland—a realm of enchanted rocks, ethereal waterfalls, and ancient, mystical powers. The popular names attached to the natural features echoed this trend of attaching mythology to granite. It was not an accident that a valley waterfall became known as the "Virgin's Tears." Often the designations were corruptions or misinterpretations of the original native names. This did not set well with Stephen Powers, a recognized expert on Native California linguistics who felt that the vibrant Indian languages were being mangled to satisfy a flight of the imagination.

Powers was a journalist by trade. Following service as a Union Army war correspondent during the Civil

"All Places That the Eye of Heaven Visits"

War, he headed west, walking from Ohio to California. From 1871 to 1876, Powers hiked throughout the Golden State and studied the lives, practices, beliefs, myths, legends, and especially the language patterns of Native Californians. In a series of articles for *Overland Monthly* magazine, Powers presented his detailed reports of California's extraordinarily diverse indigenous population. Most notably, Powers categorized Native peoples by linguistic similarities, not purely by geographic location, as others had done.

In 1877, with the guidance and financial support of the Department of the Interior, Powers consolidated his findings into the book *Tribes of California*. It was considered groundbreaking and monumental scholarship. However, Powers did have critics. He dismissed some of the indigenous people as childlike and intellectually deficient. He made errors, which Powers himself readily acknowledged. Many of his language groupings were later found to be invalid or suspect, but as a baseline for future investigation, *Tribes of California* remains an important creation. In 1925 Alfred Kroeber, considered the dean of California anthropology and ethnography in the early twentieth century, perhaps expressed it best when he stated that ethnologists both "writhe and smile" when examining Powers's research. After all, Kroeber continued, "Powers was a journalist by profession and it is true that his ethnology is often of the crudest. Probably the majority of his statements are inaccurate, many are misleading, and a very fair proportion are without any foundation or positively erroneous." Still, Kroeber maintained that *Tribes of California* remained "one of the most remarkable reports ever printed by any government."

In this excerpt from *Tribes of California*, Powers decries how the Native people's appellations for Yosemite Valley landmarks have been twisted into "melodramatic and dime-novel shams." Powers makes reference to the fashionable names as being akin to a page from "Lalla Rookh," an acclaimed 1817 poem by Thomas Moore that is usually described as "Oriental" romance verse set in an extravagant vision of the Persian Empire.

There is no doubt the Indians would be much amused if they could know what a piece of work we have made of some of their names. . . . All California Indian names that have any significance at all must be interpreted on the plainest and most prosaic principles; whereas the great, grim walls of Yosemite have been made by the white man to blossom with aboriginal poetry like a page of "Lalla Rookh." From the "Great Chief of the Valley" and the "Goddess of the Valley" down to the "Virgin Tears" and the "Cataract of Diamonds," the sumptuous imaginations of various discoverers have trailed through that wonderful gorge blazons of mythological and barbarian heraldry of an Oriental gorgeousness. It would be a pity, truly, if the Indians had not succeeded in interpreting more poetically the meanings of the place than our countrymen have done in such bald appellations as "Vernal Fall," "Pigeon Creek," and the like; but whether they did or not, they did not perpetrate the melodramatic and dime-novel shams that have been fathered upon them.

In the first place the aborigines never knew of any such locality as Yosemite Valley. Second, there is not now and there has not been anything in the valley which they call Yosemite. Third, they never called "Old Ephraim" himself Yosemite, nor is there any such a word in the Miwok language.

The valley has always been known to them, and is to this day, when speaking among themselves, as A-wa'-ni. This, it is true, is only the name of one of the ancient villages which it contained; but by prominence it gave its name to the valley, and, in accordance with Indian usage almost everywhere, to the inhabitants of the same. The word "Yosemite" is simply a very beautiful and sonorous corruption of the word for "grizzly bear." On the Stanislaus and north of it the word is *u-zú-mai-ti*; at Little Gap, *o-so'-mai-ti*; in Yosemite itself, *u-zú-mai-ti*; on the South Fork of the Merced, *uh-zú-mai-tuh*.

Mr. J. M. Hutchings, in his "Scenes of Wonder and Curiosity in California," states that the pronunciation on the South Fork is "Yohamite." Now, there is occasionally a kind of cockney in the tribe, who cannot get the letter "h" right. Different Indians will pronounce the word for "wood" *su-sú-eh*, *sú-suh*, *hu-hú-eh*; also, the word for "eye," *hun'-ta, hun'-tum, shun'-ta*. It may have been an Indian of this sort who pronounced the word that way; I never heard it so spoken.

In other portions of California the Indian names have effected such slight lodgment in our atlases that it is seldom worth while to go much out of the way to set them right; but there are so many of them preserved in Yosemite that it is different. Professor Whitney and Mr. Hutchings, in their respective guide-books, state that they derived their catalogues of Indian names from white men. The Indians certainly have a right to be heard in this department at least; and when they differ from the interpreters every right-thinking man will accept the statement of an intelligent aborigine as against a score of Americans. The Indian can very seldom give a connected, philosophical account of his customs and ideas, for which one must depend on men who have observed them; but if he does not know the simple words of his own language, pray who does?

....

"With almost every step, we get a new view—more depth, more valley, more wall, more towering rock."

....

Helen Hunt Jackson
Bits of Travel at Home, 1878

As the 1870s progressed, Yosemite literature developed a persistent theme. Writers extolled the natural splendor but simultaneously disparaged ungrateful tourists who moaned about the low standard of creature comforts. An example is found in the 1878 book *Bits of Travel at Home* by "H.H." (Helen Hunt Jackson).

Born Helen Fiske in 1830 in Massachusetts, she married Captain Edward Hunt in 1852. Sadly, Helen's husband passed away in 1863, and their child died in 1865. Helen Hunt lessened her grief through writing poems and travel articles. In May 1872 she boarded a train with author and close friend Sarah Woolsey for a trip to San Francisco on the still new transcontinental railroad. While in California, she visited Yosemite, which she preferred to call Ah-wah-ne.

Soon after completing her western journey, Helen Hunt contracted a respiratory ailment. Seeking treatment, she wintered in Colorado in 1872. There she met and married William Sharpless Jackson. Subsequently, she was known as "Helen Jackson" or, most commonly, as "Helen Hunt Jackson." However, during her prolific writing career, Helen Hunt Jackson usually published under the pseudonym "H.H."

While Jackson continued to write travel narratives, she turned increasingly to the theme of the mistreatment of Native Americans. In 1881 she wrote *A Century of Dishonor*, a nonfiction examination of the injustices perpetrated against Indians throughout American history. While Jackson promoted justice for Native Americans generally, she was scornful of Yosemite Indians. Jackson described the Awahnichi as "half naked, dirty beyond words," and "too loathsome to be looked at" in *Bits of Travel at Home*.

In 1884 she followed *A Century of Dishonor* with the romantic novel *Ramona*. Set in post–Mexican War Southern California, *Ramona* is an emotional tale of racial discrimination faced by a mixed-race Scottish–Native American girl who has been orphaned. *Ramona* was enormously popular. The novel has been reprinted more than three hundred times and adapted five times into motion pictures and television programs. Many historians believe that the public admiration for the Ramona character influenced the passage of the Dawes Severalty Act of 1887, the first American law to address Native American land rights. At the time, the Dawes Act was considered a humane and forward-looking reform, but current historical scholarship views the act as destructive to Native culture, sovereignty, and identity.

In this passage from *Bits of Travel at Home,* Jackson describes her evocative arrival at "Ah-wah-ne" and her succinct advice for anyone complaining about the accommodations: do Yosemite Valley, and everyone else, a favor and "leave Ah-wah-ne the next day."

AH-WAH-NE! Does not the name vindicate itself at first sight and sound? Shall we ever forgive the Dr. [Lafayette] Bunnell, who, not content with volunteer duty in killing off Indians in the great Merced River Valley, must needs name it the Yosem-i-te, and who adds to his account of his fighting campaigns the following naïve paragraph?

"It is acknowledged that Ah-wah-ne is the old Indian name for the valley, and that Ah-wah-ne-chee is the name of the original occupants; but, as this was discovered by the writer long after he had named the valley, and as it was the wish of every volunteer with whom he conversed that the name Yosemite be retained, he said very little about it. He will only say, in conclusion, that the principal facts are before the public, and that it is for them to decide whether they will retain the name Yo-semite or have some other."

It is easy to do and impossible to undo this species of mischief. No concerted action of "the public," no legislation of repentant authorities, will ever give back to the valley its own melodious name; but I think its true lovers will for ever call it Ah-wah-ne. The name seems to have in its very sound the same subtle blending of solemnity, tenderness, and ineffable joy with which the valley's atmosphere is, filled. Ahwahne! Blessed Ahwahne! . . .

... We set out at three o'clock. Our first sensations were not agreeable. We had seen how steep it looked when horse and rider disappeared over that hill-crest. It felt steeper. To an unaccustomed rider it is not pleasant to sit on a horse whose heels are much higher than his head. One's first impulse is to clutch, to brace, to cling, and to guide the horse. But there is neither comfort nor safety till you leave off doing so. With a perfectly loose rein and every muscle relaxed, sitting as you would sit in a rocking-chair, leaning back when the horse rocks down, leaning forward when he rocks up, and forgetting him altogether, riding down precipices is as comfortable and safe as riding on a turnpike. I do not say that it is altogether easy in the outset to follow these simple directions. But, if you are wise, it soon becomes so, and you look with impatient pity on the obstinacy of women who persist in grasping pommels, and sitting so stark stiff that it seems as if a sudden lurch of the horse must inevitably send them off, before or behind.

The first two miles and a half of the path down the wall of Ah-wah-ne are steep,—so steep that it is best not to try to say how steep. It is a narrow path, zig-zagging down on ledges, among bowlders, through thickets. It is dusty and stony; it comes out suddenly on opens, from which you look over and down thousands, yes, thousands of feet; it plunges into tangles of trees, where a rider must lay his head on the horse's neck to get through, for oaks and pines and firs grow on this precipice; high ceanothus bushes, fragrant with blossom, make wall-like sides to the path, and bend in as if trying to arch it. In some places the rocks are bright with flowers and ferns, which look as if they were holding on for dear life and climbing up: they project so nearly at right angles from the steep surfaces. With almost every step we get a new view,— more depth, more valley, more wall, more towering rock. The small cleared spaces in the valley are vivid light green; they seem sunken like emerald-paved wells among the masses of dark firs and pines, whose tops lie solid and black below us. The opposite wall of the valley looks steeper than the wall we are descending. It seems within stone's throw, or as if we might call across; it is less than a half-mile distant. Its top seems far higher than the point from which we set out; for it lies in full sunshine, and we are in shadow. One waterfall after another comes into view, streaming over its edge like smooth silver bands. . . . It takes an hour to reach the bottom of the wall. As we near it, the opposite wall appears to lift and grow and stretch, till the sky seems pushed higher. Our trail lies along the bank of the river, on sandy stretches of low meadow, shaded by oaks and willows and bordered by alders. Occasionally we come to fields of bowlders and stones, which have broken and rolled down from the walls above; then we pass through green bits of grass-grown land, threaded by little streams, which we ford; then we ride through great groves of pines and firs, two and three hundred feet high. These feel dark and damp, though the ground is sandy, for it is long past sunset here; but the gray spires and domes and pinnacles of the eastern wall of the valley are still bright in sunlight. . . .

What miles they were. Mile by mile the grand rocks, whose shapes and names we already knew, rose up on either hand: The Cathedral Rocks, The Spires, El Capitan, The Three Brothers, The Sentinel. Already the twilight wrapped the western wall. The front of El Capitan looked black; but its upper edge was lined with light, as sometimes a dark cloud will be when the sun is shining behind. The eastern wall was carved and wrought into gigantic forms, which in the lessening light grew more and more fantastic and weird every moment. Bars and beams of sunlight fell, quivered, and vanished on summit after summit, as we passed. At last we heard the sound of waters ahead to the left. Soon we saw the white line, indistinct, waving, ghostly, coming down apparently from the clouds, for it was too dark to see distinctly the lip of a fall two thousand and seven hundred feet up in the air. This was the great Yosemite Fall. Its sound is unlike that of any other fall I have seen. It is not so loud as one would expect, and it is not continuous or even in tone. Listening to it intently, one hears strange rhythmic emphases of under-tone on a much lower key. They are grand. They are like the notes of a gigantic violoncello,—booming, surging, filling full and rounding out the harmony of supernatural music. Sometimes they have an impatient and crashing twist, as if the bow escaped the player's hand; sometimes, for an hour, they are regular and alike, as the beats of a metronome. Men have said that these sounds are made by rocks thundering down under the water. They may be. I would rather not know.

For the last mile before reaching Hutchings's Hotel, the trail is little more than a sandy path, winding in and among huge granite bowlders, under and around oak and pine trees, and over and through little runs and pools, when the Merced River is high. It ends abruptly, in a rough and dusty place, partly cleared of bowlders, partly cleared of trees. Here are four buildings, which stand apparently where they happened to, between the rocks and trees. Three of these make up Hutchings's Hotel. Two of them are cottages, used only for lodgings. One of these is called "The Cottage by the River," and stands closer than is safe to the banks of the Merced; the other is called "The Cottage in the Rocks," and seems half barricaded by granite bowlders. "Oh, Mr. Hutchings!" we exclaimed. "Put us in the 'Cottage by the River.' We can-not be happy anywhere else."

There are no such rooms in Ah-wah-ne as the rooms on the river-side of this little house. This is the back side; and those who wish to see the coming and going of people, the setting-off of saddle-trains, the driving up and down of the laundry wagon, would better take rooms on the front. But he who would like to open his eyes every morning on the full shining of the great Yosemite Fall; to lie in bed, and from his very pillow watch it sway to right and left under moon-light beams, which seem like wands arresting or hastening the motion; to look down into the amber and green Merced, which caresses his very door-sill; to listen at all hours to the

"All Places That the Eye of Heaven Visits"

grand violoncello tones of the mysterious waters,—let him ask, as we did, for back bedrooms in the Cottage by the River.

But if he is disconcerted by the fact that his bedroom floor is of rough pine boards, and his bedroom walls of thin laths, covered with unbleached cotton; that he has neither chair, nor table, nor pitcher; that his washbowl is a shallow tin pan, and that all the water he wants he must dip in a tin pint from a barrel out in the hall; that his bed is a sack stuffed with ferns, his one window has no curtain and his door no key,—let him leave Ah-wah-ne the next day.

"It causes spiders of ice to crawl down one's spine."

Derrick Dodd [Frank Harrison Gassaway]
Summer Saunterings, 1882

By the early 1880s, visitors to Yosemite had written frequently (for more than twenty years, in fact) of the intense, almost transcendent moments of their initial Yosemite encounters and nearly as often of their discomfort in traveling to the valley and their dissatisfaction with the inferior accommodations. But some observers found appeal in the rustic lodgings and interesting, even eccentric, valley residents they met, viewing these as part and parcel of an all-inclusive Yosemite experience.

Frank Harrison Gassaway was a humorist and poet who wrote for several San Francisco newspapers, including the *Examiner*, *Chronicle*, and *Evening Post*. He was usually published under the pseudonym "Derrick Dodd." A native of Virginia and based in Washington DC, he arrived in California in 1880 and soon gained a following for his newspaper columns, which featured short, witty travel narratives reminiscent of Mark Twain's. In 1882 some of these columns were compiled into *Summer Saunterings*, which featured his comments on accommodations, attractions, and transportation throughout California. In later years Gassaway became a critically acclaimed poet and business manager for William Randolph Hearst's flagship newspaper, the *San Francisco Examiner*.

In this passage from *Summer Saunterings*, Dodd (i.e., Gassaway) recalls his visit to the literally hair-raising Glacier Point and presents his recollections of Pike, his "nefarious" trail guide; of James McCauley, the proprietor of the hotel "hashery"; and of the fate of a fearless chicken.

A pleasant peculiarity of sight-seeing in the [Yosemite] valley is the manner in which the passengers of an incoming stage-coach form themselves into a little community of their own, and thenceforward move about with a tacit unanimity. . . . The next morning, therefore, found our original load of thirteen wayfarers mounted on a saddle-train of as many fly-footed, though melancholy-looking horses, and heading up the best trail in the valley in the direction of Glacier Point. Our procession was led by the best-known guide in the valley, named Pike, and whose individuality would merit a place here were it not for a feeling that Bret Harte owns the patent-right for all that description of character writing on the coast. Pike's voice has long ago disappeared into his boots, the result of a cold caught during winter service on the high trails, while, from the effects of a life literally passed in the saddle, his legs have dwindled in like proportion, as well as acquired a most buck-defying outward curve. Pike is as courteous and capable a guide as [a] traveler could wish, however, and possesses only one trait that mars his popularity with male visitors. He always insists on placing the ladies of the party next to himself, at the head of the line, a position claimed as necessary in case of their needing immediate assistance—a plausible theory that does not, however, explain why the prettiest girl in the lot is invariably stationed just in his rear, nor does it account for the fact that said beauty requires her stirrup altered at least once every hundred yards. The distance from the valley-floor to Glacier Point is about three and a half miles by guide and eighteen by tourist measure—two-thirds of it "on end," as John Muir, the geologist, would say. At intervals, the trail zigzags upwards into a series of sharp turns, as continuously recurrent as the rounds of a ladder, and it is a unique sensation to look straight up into the air and behold a series of equestrian statues niched one above the other for a hundred yards over one's head, the whole being capped by a group composed of that nefarious Pike busily absorbed in the forty-first representation of his great

STIRRUP-ADJUSTING ACT.

About midway in our cavalcade that
"Like a wounded snake wound its slow length along."
Rode a Danish scientist, of some three hundred pounds weight, whose ponderous intellectual and physical bulk was such as to cause the animal he rode to groan and stagger at the short turns to the great horror of its rider, and the no less lively apprehension of the next following linesman, who momentarily expected to be swept over the chasm by a human and equine avalanche from above. The slow progress of Danish science operated to materially delay the nethermost section of the procession until an inventive genius, in the extreme rear, telephoned a remedy along the line. One of the party cut a long pole, in the end of which was fixed a hair-pin, in the shape of a goad. By energetically, though secretly, operating this persuader, the corpulent party's steed was urged up the rocky inclines in a manner that made the scientific hair to fairly stand on end.

Two-thirds up the mountain a halt was called on a flat projection, named Union Peak [Union Point], or something equally unsuggestive, in front of which stands what to the writer is by far the most interesting object so far encountered. This is a huge symmetrical rock, called the Agassiz monument [Agassiz Rock]. Shaped exactly like an inverted tenpin, weighing hundreds of tons, and balanced upon its smaller extremity like a club on the fingertip of a juggler, the beholder gazes in breathless expectation that the pressure of the next zephyr will send the toppling mass thundering down the mountain side. At the end of another well-stretched perpendicular mile the party unexpectedly come upon a small hotel, nestling on the cloud-skimmed elevation of Glacier Point. This hashery of the upper deep is kept by a bright, good-humored Irishman named James McCauley, and we would be false to that sentiment of gratitude that lurks even in a tourist's breast did we fail to state that here we enjoyed the best tasting meal we had eaten since leaving 'Frisco, the repast including the two rarest of all dishes on the Pacific Slope—juicy, tender venison, shot from the tavern's back window, and mealy, in fact,

FEATHERY POTATOES.

Let no esthetic Eastern gusher uptilt a contemptuous nose at the prosaic pencil that can turn from such scenery to dwell upon baked potatoes. Let him who has never endured the heartburn attendant upon cheap Mongolian cookery cast the first spud. The soft sponge of time may wipe from our recollection some of the rock-hewn wonders that tower above us as we write, but the tender grace of Jim McCauley's potatoes will desert us only at the grave. Nothing but the want of a good elevator prevents Jim from doing a regular Baldwin Hotel business. Possibly this sincere eulogy is more directly due to the hostess of this aerial caravansary, who, by the way, proudly exhibited a pair of handsome little boys, the only twins ever born in the Yosemite, her maternal satisfaction not seemingly dashed by the ominous thought that the childish gambols of her treasures were to be conducted on the very edge of a five thousand-foot precipice.

And indeed it is something to stop the beatings of a chamois' heart to lean over the iron railing set between two verge-toppling bowlders on the peak's brink, and glance down into the bottomless, awful gulf below. It causes spiders of ice to crawl down one's spine, and the hair of one of the party, whose hat happened to be off, as he bent over the rail, suggested an actor pulling the string of a "fright wig" in a minstrel ghost scene.

As a part of the usual programme, we experimented as to

"All Places That the Eye of Heaven Visits"

the time taken by different objects in reaching the bottom of the cliff. An ordinary stone tossed over remained in sight an incredibly long time, but finally vanished somewhere about the middle distance. A handkerchief with a stone tied in the corner, was visible perhaps a thousand feet deeper, but even a large empty box watched by a field-glass could not be traced to its concussion with the valley floor. Finally, the landlord appeared on the scene, carrying an antique hen under his arm. This, in spite of the terrified ejaculations and entreaties of the ladies, he deliberately threw over the cliff's edge. A rooster might have gone thus to his doom in stoic silence, but the sex of this unfortunate bird asserted itself the moment it started on its awful journey into space. With

AN EAR-PIERCING CACKLE,

that gradually grew fainter as it fell, the poor creature shot downward, now beating the air with ineffectual wings, and now frantically clawing at the very wind, that slanted her first this way and then that, the hapless fowl shot down, down, until it became a mere fluff of feathers no larger than a quail. Then it dwindled to a wren's size, disappeared, then again dotted the sight a moment as a pin's point, and then—it was gone!

After drawing a long breath all round, the women folks pitched into the hen's owner with redoubled zest. But the genial McCauley shook his head knowingly, and replied:

"Don't be alarmed about that chicken, ladies. She's used to it. She goes over that cliff every day during the season."

And, sure enough, on our road back we met the old hen about half up the trail, calmly picking her way home.

....

"... the air is musical with the lullaby of hidden waters ..."

....

Lady Constance Frederica Gordon-Cumming
Granite Crags, 1884

While the majority of Yosemite tourists were from the United States, the perspective of foreign visitors could be particularly interesting, especially if the individual possessed an artist's expert eye or an author's practiced pen. Lady Constance Frederica Gordon-Cumming of Scotland qualified on both accounts.

Lady Gordon-Cumming visited Yosemite in 1877. She planned on staying three days but remained in Yosemite for three months. The child of a wealthy family, Gordon-Cumming was a self-taught painter who was mentored by Sir Edwin Landseer, a favorite artist of Queen Victoria. She traveled the world, often alone, writing of her adventures and painting well-regarded landscapes. Gordon-Cumming visited Australia, New Zealand, Fiji, Tahiti, Hawaii, China, Japan, the United States, and many points in between, including California. During her stay in Yosemite, she made watercolor sketches, many of which were displayed in the valley; that showing is generally regarded as the first art exhibition in Yosemite.

In 1884 the letters of Lady Gordon-Cumming chronicling her tour of California were published as *Granite Crags*. In this selection she paints a vibrant word-picture of one day in May 1877, a day she described as "inexpressibly lovely."

May-day, 1877

When the stars began to pale in the eastern sky, we were astir, and with the earliest ray of dawn set off like true pilgrims bound to drink of some holy spring on May morning. For the first two miles our path lay across the quiet meadows, which as yet are only lightly sprinkled with blossom. We found no cowslips, but washed our faces in Californian May-dew, which we brushed from the fresh young grass and ferns. Soon, they tell me, there will be violets, cowslips, and primroses. We passed by the orchard of the first settler in the valley; his peach and cherry trees were laden with pink and white blossom, his strawberry-beds likewise promising an abundant crop.

"All Places That the Eye of Heaven Visits"

It was a morning of calm beauty, and the massive grey crags all around the valley lay "like sleeping kings" robed in purple gloom, while the pale-yellow light crept up behind them, the tall dark pines forming a belt of deeper hue round their base. . . .

Just at this season, when the snows on the Sierras are beginning to melt, a thousand crystal streams find temporary channels along the high levels till they reach the smooth verge of the crags, and thence leap in white foam, forming temporary falls of exceeding beauty. Three such graceful falls at present overleap the mighty arches, and, in their turn, produce pools and exquisitely clear streams, which thread their devious way through woods and meadows, seeking the river of Mercy.

So the air is musical with the lullaby of hidden waters, and the murmur of the unseen river rippling over its pebbly bed. . . .

We watched by the calm Mirror Lake till the sun had climbed so high in the heavens as to overlook a purple crag, and see its own image in the quiet pool. Then we retraced our way down the wooded canyon till we reached the open valley, now bathed in sunlight. Cloud-shadows floated over the dewy grass-slopes and bare summits of the Sierras, and the sunbeams played on the countless nameless waterfalls, which now veil the crags with a rainbow-tinted, gauze-like film of scattered spray and faint floating mist, swaying with every breath of air. After breakfast the gentlemen started to explore the upper end of the valley, but I preferred a quiet day's sketching beside the peaceful river.

This evening the sun set in a flood of crimson and gold— such a glorious glow as would have dazzled an eagle. It paled to a soft primrose, then ethereal green. Later, the pearly-grey clouds were rose-flushed by an after-glow more vivid than the sunset itself—a rich full carmine, which quickly faded away to the cold, intense blue of a Californian night. It was inexpressibly lovely.

Then the fitful wind rose in gusts—a melancholy moan-

ing wail, vibrating among rocks, forests, and waters, with a
low surging sound—a wild mountain melody.

"... the division between careless
youth and serious manhood."

A. Phimister Proctor

An Ascent of Half Dome in 1884

Throughout its history, a visit to Yosemite has proven
to be a turning point for many. Experiencing the majestic granite cathedral triggered a reexamined life, a spiritual epiphany, a lifelong commitment to environmental
preservation, or simply a renewed appreciation of natural beauty. For two young men in 1884, two days on
Half Dome provided, as one wrote, "the division between
careless youth and serious manhood."

Two artist friends, thirty-year-old Alden Sampson and
twenty-four-year-old Alexander Phimister Proctor, who
preferred to be called "A. Phimister Proctor," were visiting Yosemite Valley when they encountered Guardian
of the Grove Galen Clark. Clark mentioned that the rope
line to Half Dome summit strung by George Anderson in
1875 needed replacement. In the nine years since Anderson's ascent, the rope had disintegrated, and the iron
eyebolts had rusted. On the spot, Sampson and Proctor
decided they were up to the task. However, as Sampson
later recalled, "when we had at last made up our minds
to do so, we quietly reconnoitered the place, and made all
necessary preparations in entire secrecy, so that no one
should have the satisfaction of laughing at us if we failed."

Equipped only with two hundred feet of frayed horse
rope, a meager lunch, and two lemons, the intrepid
pair lit out for Half Dome. Over the next two harrowing
days, Proctor and Sampson reestablished the climbing
line to the top of the massive knob, sometimes barely

clinging to the steep, polished granite incline by their fingertips or their bare feet. Both Sampson and Proctor abandoned rock climbing forever after this scary episode. The two daredevils became business partners, sharing a studio in New York City designed by the famous Gilded Age architectural firm of McKim, Mead & White. Sampson became a respected landscape artist, while Proctor gained an international reputation as a premier sculptor of monumental bronze statues.

Toward the end of his life, Proctor began a memoir. The Sierra Club asked Proctor to recount his Half Dome adventure, and the organization published his recollections in its bulletin in 1946. Proctor's longer autobiography was in rough draft when he died in 1950, at the age of eighty-nine. In 1971 Proctor's reminiscences were edited and issued as *Sculptor in Buckskin: An Autobiography by Alexander Phimister Proctor*.

The selection that follows is Proctor's retelling of his 1884 ascent of Half Dome with Sampson, as it appeared in *Sculptor in Buckskin*.

Late in 1883, after a good summer and fall of sketching at Grand Lake and Flat Top Mountain [Colorado], I pointed my horses' heads toward Denver. I had taken a studio on Laramie Street preparatory to a winter's work of engraving and painting and was about ready to put out my shingle when Alden Sampson, my New York artist friend, dropped in. He was planning a sketching and hunting trip and invited me to join him. Since it was December, the Rockies were out of the question and Mexico was infested with bandits in those days. We finally decided on California. Loaded with sketching and hunting outfits, we boarded the Santa Fe train for Los Angeles.

In those days, Los Angeles was a picturesque semi-Mexican town. Its streets were ankle deep in mud. We stayed at a hotel with a patio filled with tropical fruits and flowers, a striking contrast for us who had just come out of the Rockies where the snow was several feet deep.

We bought five horses: Spider, Buck, Pinto, Pink and Rattlesnake. As soon as we assembled our paraphernalia, we left Los Angeles, spending our first night in Pasadena, and decided to go up the Wilson Trail until the rainy season was over.

Shortly after leaving Pasadena, we found out that our ponies were neither pack horses nor mountain animals. Not being used to the top loads, they fell over with the least provocation. The trail ran along the ridge of a hogback, and the falling was equally good on either side. They took turns flopping off the trail and rolling down the slopes. Once they all went over in chorus, doing a free-for-all rough-and-tumble for fifty feet. Since none of them could get up with his pack on, we had to unpack each pony, lead him up to the trail and then carry the equipment up the steep mountainside, just to re-pack for another fall. . . .

In spite of our prize pack horses, in six months we safely traveled fifteen hundred miles through California to Yosemite. One day Sampson and I were standing on Hanging Rock at the top of Glacier Point, gazing down into wonderful Yosemite Valley.

"Yes, sir," came a voice next to us, "it's over three thousand feet from this 'ere point down inter that valley, an' ye can spit clear to the bottom in one spit!"

Turning, I saw a fine old man with long fuzzy hair and whiskers standing at Sampson's side. He proved to be no less a person than the valley's oldest inhabitant, Galen Clark, who pointed out to us all the interesting places to visit from where we stood, including Half Dome.

As we looked at the peak, Clark told us how a sailor named Anderson had put a rope on the top fifteen hundred feet of Half Dome and charged a dollar to anyone who wanted to make the ascent. Anderson had died several years before and a snowslide the previous winter had torn down the cable. Since then many parties had attempted to scale the mountain and replace the rope, but all had failed and now the valley

"All Places That the Eye of Heaven Visits"

was waiting for a group of Swiss climbers to do the trick. My blood tingled, and I decided right then that no Swiss would do the job until after I had at least given it a try. Sampson felt the same way.

We camped half a mile from Glacier Point for some days, enjoying the wonderful views and riding around the valley. Finally we set up camp in Little Yosemite, the nearest approach to Half Dome. A day or so later we were standing at the bottom pitch of Half Dome. The only side that looked remotely possible to climb appeared to be as smooth as writing paper. At our feet lay the remains of the sailor's rope cable.

As we studied the face of the mountain, we saw how Anderson had accomplished his work. He had climbed the steep grade as far as he could go, using the slightest toe hold. Then, when he could go no farther, he reached up and drilled a six inch hole into which he worked a half-inch-diameter bolt, whose end was bent into a ring. This pin stuck out from the rock about two inches. When a pin was well secured in the granite, he attached the cable to the ring with a smaller rope. His cable had been fashioned by stringing together a number of bale ropes until the diameter was about three inches. To keep the cable from tangling, he bound it every foot with heavy twine.

Wherever it was possible to climb (and he was a master at that game), he took advantage of the toe holds. When the rock became too smooth and steep, he put in another pin, fastening the cable as he went. Anderson had built a cabin at the nearest spring, a mile away where he had lived and kept a forge for making the bolts.

Sampson and I returned to camp after our tour of inspection, to prepare to tackle Half Dome in the morning. We gathered all the pack and picket ropes that we could spare, and both of us looked forward to the attempt with considerable excitement. We intended to use the sailor's cable, fastening it to the pins with our rope.

Early the next morning we started the ascent, climbing the first couple of hundred feet and hauling up and fastening our rope and the cable. We tried every expedient we could think of to negotiate the smooth, steep rock, but no matter how hard we tried we kept slipping back. Forty feet or so above our heads a rock jutted out. If we only reach it! But there was no way. Fortunately, we had not given anyone a hint of our intentions, and no one but ourselves would know if we failed. That was some comfort but a mighty small one.

"I'll lasso it!" I yelled. Luckily I was a pretty fair hand with the lariat. Tying a loop on a lash rope, I made a throw. After several false pitches, I finally got the range. The knot caught in a crack of the rock and stuck. It didn't look too secure to us, but I started up the steep slope, supporting my weight on the rope. Just before I could grab the projection, the knot slipped down and I slid twenty feet. While I was collecting my scattered nerves, Sampson climbed up and secured the cable. I soon followed.

We found that the slide not only had carried away almost all of the sailor's cable but had also torn out most of the iron pins and loosened several of those remaining. Wherever a number of pins were missing, the only way to reach the next one was by lassoing it and pulling ourselves up to it with the rope. Some of the remaining pins had been bent over and were difficult to rope. Often my loop would slip over the ring twenty times before it caught, even though the throws were good. Some of the pins pulled out as soon as I put my weight on the rope.

I discarded my shoes, a poor set of hobnails. When I reached a pin, I would hook my big toe over it, then straighten myself up slowly, always leaning against the stone wall. The only way I could get my toe over the pin was to double up like a jackknife, put my toe on the fingers by which I was holding the pin, and when I was balanced, all doubled up, pull my fingers out from under my toe.

By noon we had reached the only ledge on the mountainside where we could rest, and there we ate lunch. The ledge

"All Places That the Eye of Heaven Visits"

was all of six inches wide and we were able to push a leg down in it and rest without holding on. By the end of the first day we had made about half the distance. Just before sunset, we slid down the cable, mounted our horses and rode to camp. My feet were mighty sore, and to tell the truth I looked at that mountain with a heap of dread, though I didn't let on. Later I found that Sampson was scared too but since I showed no fear, neither did he.

Bright and early the next morning we were back at the starting place with all the rope we possessed. The ascent was easy as far as our cable reached, although pulling the spare rope up after us was work. But then our trouble began— everything slipped off the minute we let go. We had to lean against the mountain every minute, and it always seemed trying to push us away.

Early in the day my right glove got away from me and went sliding down the mountain. That made changing my weight from fingers to toe much more painful. By then we had reached a place where there were a few rough surfaces. It was Sampson's turn to go ahead, since my bare feet would not cling unless I had some support. Using whatever fing- erholds he could find, he at last reached a ledge which went up from his level. Clinging to small cracks in the rock, he worked a piece of bail rope from his pocket and tied it to a small shrub just above him. Then, putting just enough weight on the rope to keep it from slipping, he inched along until the angle was too great and he had to let go of the rope. Then he worked himself to a little hump, cupped his hand over it, and clung there for several minutes to get his breath. Climb- ing up several yards more to a safe spot, he fastened the rope and I pulled up to him.

From there on the surface was deadly smooth. There were few pins and I had to go ahead with the lasso. About 150 feet above where I took the lead, I clung by my big toe to one pin and lay against the steep granite trying to rope the next one. A wind was blowing, which made roping difficult, but finally the rope caught. I put my weight on it, and it held. Then, just as I was about to let go of my toehold, I gave another yank and out came the roped pin!

Luck was with me, for the next pin was only five feet above the one that had pulled out. After half an hour of throwing, the loop finally caught on the pin, and I made my way up to it and fastened the cable.

The next pin was the worst of all. It was thirty-five feet above me on a small ledge. It seemed next to impossible to make that rope fly up those extra perpendicular feet. When the loop finally settled over the pin and stayed, Sampson and I both yelled! I crawled up on my knees. Taking hold of the pin with my fingers, I wormed myself over it, got my toe over my fingers and pulled my fingers free, losing considerable skin in the process. As I rested on the tiny ledge, leaning against the sloping granite, that hellish old mountain seemed more determined than ever to push me off.

The next pin, which was a long way above me, was still wrapped with a bundle of Anderson's broken cable. The wind had come up again and time and time again my loop dropped over the pin only to slide off.

Finally, my leg began to tremble from standing so long in one position. I had to go down or fall off the mountain[;] below me the rock face bulged out. To the right it drifted toward Little Yosemite, three thousand feet down. To the left it dropped eight thousand feet into the main valley. If I slipped, there wasn't much doubt which way I'd go. If there had been anything to hang onto, I could have backed off over the ledge, twist myself out into space, and slide down the cable to a place where I could rest.

By the time we finally reached the top of Half Dome, the sun was low. The valley spread out below us in all its blue, hazy beauty. We sat for a while enjoying the setting sun and then built a fire, in view of the whole valley, to let people know that Half Dome had again been conquered, Reluctantly, we left one of the grandest views in the world, slid down the cable, and reached the safety of the ground just at dark.

The next day we learned that our innocent beacon on the

"All Places That the Eye of Heaven Visits"

peak the night before had disrupted the whole valley. From the valley floor people had watched the fire, which had burned for hours since we had built it near a dead stump. Apparently they thought it was a distress signal. One watcher, a New Yorker, offered a hundred dollars to any guide who would hurry up the trail to the bottom of the cliff to assure us of early relief in the morning. There were no takers.

Later in the day we met James M. Hutchings, superintendent of the valley, on his way up to rescue us. Relieved to find us safe, he thanked us for what we had done and promised to put up a permanent cable before taking down our ropes. . . .

Great experiences in a young man's life can produce important changes in the direction he will take. Those days on Half Dome were for me the division between careless youth and serious manhood.

> "*Any* extortion, incivility, misrepresentation,
> or the riding on unsafe animals, should be promptly
> reported at the Guardian's Office."

Lewis Stornoway [George G. MacKenzie]
"Maximum Rates for Transportation," 1888

Transportation in Yosemite was always predicated on two important factors—comfort and cost. Despite concerted efforts to improve accessibility and mitigate discomfort, traveling in Yosemite remained bumpy, dusty, and generally aggravating throughout the nineteenth century. It was also expensive. Once you were secluded in what Lady Gordon-Cumming dubbed the "wonderful granite prison," you were at the mercy of the sightseeing concessionaires, and, although the fees were somewhat regulated by the state's Yosemite commissioners until the establishment of Yosemite National Park in 1890, tourists paid through the nose for saddle horses and carriages.

In his 1888 guidebook, *Yosemite: Where to Go and What to Do*, Lewis Stornoway detailed transportation costs in the Yosemite region. "Lewis Stornoway" was the pseudonym of George G. MacKenzie. MacKenzie, who was born in New York but whose parents had emigrated from Scotland, published under his clever pseudonym as a tribute to his parents' heritage—Stornoway is a village on the Scottish Isle of Lewis. George MacKenzie also wrote for the *Century Magazine*, advocating better management of Yosemite. In 1898, when the federal government ordered the military units responsible for protecting and patrolling Yosemite out of the park and into service during the Spanish-American War, MacKenzie was a member of the armed civilian security force that replaced the soldiers.

Prices charged for Yosemite transportation were set by form of conveyance and per person. Distance covered was a central consideration. Some trips or tours could be shorter than two miles, while others could be thirty to forty miles one way. And all were pricey, which becomes obvious when the prices are viewed in comparison with modern dollar equivalents (presented in table 1). Stornoway's guidebook provides price data for conveyance by saddle horse and by carriage in 1888; the tabular format has been provided here for the reader's convenience.

Table 1. 1888 dollars versus 2020 equivalent

1888 dollars	Equivalent 2020 amount	1888 dollars	Equivalent 2020 amount
$1	$27	$3.50	$95
$1.25	$34	$3.75	$102
$1.50	$41	$4	$108
$2	$54	$5	$135
$2.25	$61	$15	$409
$2.50	$68	$25	$682

Source: created by the author.

"All Places That the Eye of Heaven Visits"

Maximum Rates for Transportation

The following rates for transportation in and about the Valley have been established by the Board of Commissioners:

SADDLE HORSES.

From	Route to	Amount
Valley	Glacier Point and Sentinel Dome, and return, direct, same day	$3.00
Valley	Glacier Point, Sentinel Dome, and Fissures, and return, direct, same day	$3.75
Valley	Glacier Point, Sentinel Dome, and Fissures, passing night at Glacier Point	$3.00
Valley	Glacier Point, Sentinel Dome, Nevada Fall, and Casa Nevada, passing night at Casa Nevada	$3.00
Valley	Glacier Point, Sentinel Dome, Nevada Fall, Vernal Fall and thence to Valley same day	$4.00
Glacier Point	Valley direct	$2.00
Glacier Point	Sentinel Dome, Nevada Fall, and Casa Nevada, passing night at Casa Nevada	$2.00
Glacier Point	Sentinel Dome, Nevada Fall, Vernal Fall, and thence to Valley same day	$2.00
Valley	Summits, Vernal, and Nevada Falls, direct, and return to Valley same day	$3.00
Valley	Glacier Point by Casa Nevada, passing night at Glacier Point,	$3.00
Valley	Summits, Vernal, and Nevada Falls, Sentinel Dome, Glacier Point, and thence to Valley same day	$4.00
Valley	Cloud's Rest and return to Casa Nevada	$3.00
Valley	Cloud's Rest and return to Valley same day	$5.00
Casa Nevada	Cloud's Rest and return to Casa Nevada or Valley same day	$3.00
Casa Nevada	Valley direct	$2.00
Casa Nevada	Nevada Fall, Sentinel Dome, and Glacier Point, passing night at Glacier Point	$2.00

Valley	Nevada Fall, Sentinel Dome, Glacier Point, and Valley same day	$3.00
	Upper Yosemite Fall, Eagle Peak, and return	$3.00
	Charge for Guide (including horse), when furnished	$3.00
	Saddle horses, on level of Valley, per day	$2.50

1. The above charges do not include feed for horses when passing night at Casa Nevada or Glacier Point.

2. Where Valley is specified as starting point, the above rates prevail from any hotel in Valley, or from the foot of any trail.

3. Any shortening of above trips, without proportionate reduction of rates, shall be at the option of those hiring horses.

4. Trips other than those above specified shall be subject to special arrangement between letter and hirer.

CARRIAGES.

From	Route to	Amount
Hotels	Mirror Lake and return, direct	$1.00
Hotels	Mirror Lake and return by Tissaack Avenue	$1.25
Hotels	Mirror Lake and return to foot of Trail, to Vernal and Nevada Falls	$1.00
Hotels	Bridal Veil Fall and return, direct	$1.00
Hotels	Pohono Bridge, down either side of Valley, and return on opposite side, stopping at Yosemite and Bridal Veil Falls	$1.50
Hotels	Cascade Falls, down either side of Valley, and return on opposite side, stopping at Yosemite and Bridal Veil Falls	$2.25
Hotels	Artist Point and return, direct, stopping at Bridal Veil Fall	$2.00

Hotels	New Inspiration Point and return, direct, stopping at Bridal Veil Fall	$2.00
	Grand Round Drive, including Yosemite and Bridal Veil Falls, excluding Lake and Cascades	$2.50
	Grand Round Drive, including Yosemite and Bridal Veil Falls, Lake, and Cascades	$3.50

1. When the value of the seats hired in any vehicle shall exceed $15 for a two-horse team, or $25 for a four-horse team, *for any trip* in the above schedule, the persons hiring the seats shall have the privilege of paying no more than the aggregate sums of $15 and $25 *per trip* for a two-horse and four-horse team, respectively.

2. If saddle horses should be substituted for any of the above carriage trips carriage rates will apply to each horse. In no case shall the *per diem* charge of $2.50 for each saddle horse, on level of Valley, be exceeded.

Any excess of the above rates, as well as *any* extortion, incivility, misrepresentation, or the riding of unsafe animals, should be promptly reported at the Guardian's office.

8

"An Intelligent and Generous Policy
towards the Yosemite"

Trepidation and Transformation, 1890–1899

In 1890 Yosemite as we know it today began to take shape.

After years of advocacy calling for an expanded park, on October 1, 1890, Congress passed legislation establishing Yosemite National Park, which brought nearly twelve hundred square miles of territory surrounding the Yosemite Valley under federal control. The new national park (the third in the nation's history) was huge, about twenty-five times the size of San Francisco, but it did not include the Yosemite Valley and Mariposa Grove of Giant Sequoias, which remained under California's jurisdiction as provided in the Yosemite Valley Grant Act of 1864.

The U.S. Army was tasked with patrolling the new federal zone. Units of cavalry and infantry patrolled the national park. Most famously, African American troops known as the Buffalo Soldiers served in Yosemite. For the most part, the army considered the soldiers' duty to be nonmilitary, as their responsibilities primarily involved ejecting sheepherders from park grounds, repairing tourist damage, and removing illegal advertising signs. The military received praise for their efficiency and for projecting a positive image of federal authority in the region.

In the 1890s, access was enhanced with transportation improvements. The government purchased sections of private toll roads. Accommodations were upgraded, the food was of better quality, and the visitor experience was generally more enjoyable.

But concerns remained as the nineteenth century ended. What would be the relationship between the state-controlled

Yosemite Valley and the much larger federal domain? How would administration of the Yosemite National Park evolve? Should Yosemite Valley and the Mariposa Grove be incorporated into the national park? Was California's Yosemite Park Commission up to the task of effectively managing the Yosemite Valley, the superstar of the broader Yosemite province? Since it still could be a stressful to visit Yosemite, how could the journey be improved? Given that more national parks were being created, should a federal agency be formed to collectively oversee the national parks?

Answers would be provided in the early years of the twentieth century. In 1906 California ceded control of the Yosemite Valley and Mariposa Grove of Giant Sequoias to the federal government. In 1907 a railroad line would be extended to El Portal, on the western boundary of the national park. The U.S. Army would continue to manage Yosemite National Park until 1914. Then, in 1916, the National Park Service was created.

The long and twisting road of nineteenth-century Yosemite history had seen the fabled wonderland pass from isolated Native homeland to battlefield to revered natural temple and artistic inspiration to symbol of American majesty to administrative controversy and governmental wrangling to environmental icon and crown jewel of the national parks.

But the story of Yosemite was not over. Additional trials and tribulations would arise in the twentieth century. But through it all would be the eternal sunrise of Yosemite, inviting us to return and forever warming our souls.

....

"... the most phenomenal of the national pleasure grounds ... treated on principles of forestry which would disgrace a picnic ground."

....

Century Magazine
"Amateur Management of the Yosemite Scenery," 1890

As the 1890s dawned in Yosemite, there was continuing uneasiness over the management, or, more precisely, the mismanagement of the Yosemite Valley Grant. Yosemite advocates and defenders were grateful that the environs, through state government oversight, had escaped the specter of a Niagara Falls–like carnival in the valley, but they were troubled by the apparent incompetence and lack of vision exhibited by the state's Yosemite Park Commission.

Most notable among the skeptics was John Muir, who as early as 1876 had spotlighted the California legislature's noticeable indifference to the state's rapacious forestry practices. In the 1880s, Muir focused on the destruction of natural resources in the Yosemite region, especially by uncontrolled livestock grazing in the high country. Ironically, Muir, a former shepherd, was most alarmed by the damage caused by sheep, which Muir venomously dubbed "hoofed locusts." John Muir called for, at the very least, reform of the Yosemite Park Commission and, even more desirable, stripping state jurisdiction from Yosemite and placing the region under federal control, which Muir considered more capable and harmonious.

In 1889 John Muir took Robert Underwood Johnson, editor of *Century Magazine*, to Yosemite's Tuolumne Meadows to observe how sheep were destructively altering the landscape and to campaign for federal Yosemite authority. Inspired, Johnson commissioned Muir to write two articles in 1890 for *Century Magazine* detailing his vision of a "Yosemite National Park." The articles—"The Treasures of the Yosemite" (August 1890) and "Features of the Proposed Yosemite National Park" (September 1890)—were instrumental in guiding the U.S. Congress to the October 1, 1890, passage of "An Act to Set Apart Certain Tracts of Land in the State of California as Forest Reservations," which would thereby establish Yosemite National Park.

Johnson and *Century Magazine* eagerly supported the Yosemite National Park concept. Through a series of

editorials and articles, the magazine became the leading voice criticizing the Yosemite Park Commission
and endorsing federal protection and jurisdiction for
Yosemite.

In the September 1890 editorial "Amateur Management
of the Yosemite Scenery," the magazine rails against the
Yosemite Park Commission and the "lamentable condition of affairs in the valley" that it had wrought. Specifically, the editorial targets the commission's wrongheaded
forestry policies and "a scheme to uproot and destroy the
undergrowth, brush, and trees of the last forty years" to
foster fire suppression—an action, the article opines, that
demonstrates preference for the "axman" over the natural
wonders of Yosemite. The commentary concludes with a
warning that the "conflagration" that endangers Yosemite will not arise from an unattended campfire but from
a bungling and oblivious Yosemite Park Commission.

The articles by Mr. John Muir in the present and preceding
numbers of *The Century* on the Yosemite Valley and the proposed National Park will have failed of their natural effect
if, in addition to exciting the wonder of the reader at the
unique beauty of waterfall and cliff effectively portrayed in
Mr. Muir's picturesque descriptions, they do not also stimu-
late the pride of Californians to an active interest in the better
discharge of the trust assumed by the State in its acceptance
of the Yosemite grant.

Mr. Muir shows abundantly how desirable it is to reserve
for public use, under national supervision, contiguous lands,
only less rich in natural wonders than the Yosemite. The
reservation is not only desirable for its intrinsic value, but
also because incidentally it will attract attention to the valley itself, and especially to the dangers to which it is exposed
from the lack of skill and knowledge in the commission which
should be its most intelligent guardian. On this point Mr.
Muir, who in California is recognized as the best authority
on matters relating to the Sierra, adds his testimony to that

of many other unprejudiced observers and lovers of the valley. He says:

> Ax and plow, hogs and horses, have long been and are still busy in Yosemite's gardens and groves. All that is accessible and destructible is being rapidly destroyed—more rapidly than in any other Yosemite in the Sierra, though this is the only one that is under the special protection of the Government. And by far the greater part of this destruction of the fineness of wildness is of a kind that can claim no right relationship with that which necessarily follows use.

One might multiply testimony as to the injury already done to the floor of the valley were not the later boards' lack of respect for the plainest principles of the treatment of landscape already notorious in California through testimony before an investigating committee of the California legislature—testimony abundantly supported by photographs of the injury done.

These later sins of commission might long ago have been avoided were it not for the sins of omission of earlier boards. Mr. Frederick Law Olmsted, the distinguished landscape forester, and a member of the first Yosemite Commission, was once officially invited to suggest a plan for making the valley available to the public. Mr. Olmsted's suggestions contemplated as little alteration to the natural growth as would be consistent with a public use which would not impair the sentiment of wildness and grandeur characteristic of the valley. His suggestions, however, though formally presented, were not only not adopted, but were never even printed in full. Had these been followed, visitors to the Yosemite in the past few years would not annually have seen the spectacle of the most phenomenal of the national pleasure grounds ignorantly hewed and hacked, sordidly plowed and fenced, and otherwise treated on principles of forestry which would disgrace a picnic ground.

Following Mr. Olmsted, another distinguished member of the first board, Prof. J. D. Whitney of Harvard University, for several years State Geologist of California, made further efforts to place the valley under systematic and proper supervision. Of his success Professor Whitney has lately written:

> As chairman of the executive committee of the Yosemite Commission for several years, thwarted in every effort to carry out liberal, honest, and Christian ideas in regard to the management of the valley, finding my path blocked at all times by legislatures and courts, I have no confidence that anything could or would be gained by making any further conveyance of United States property to the State of California. If the Yosemite could be taken from the State and made a national reservation I should have some hope that some good might be accomplished. I have no idea that the State will ever manage the matter as it ought to be, and I should regret to see the limits of the grant extended.

A member of the present commission made very clear the issue between the friends and the enemies of reform when he said that he would rather have the advice of a Yosemite road-maker in the improvement of the valley than that of Mr. Frederick Law Olmsted. Since the Yosemite is unique among pleasure grounds, it is at one time assumed by this commissioner that Mr. Olmsted would make the valley a marvel of potted plants, and at another time that his love of wildness would lead him to import decayed and picturesque tree trunks; the fact being that no member of the commission has shown any conception of the principles upon which the modern treatment of nature in making it available to man is professionally carried on. The protest of the friends of reform is clear enough, and is not capable of being mistaken. It is simply that the Yosemite Valley is too great a work of nature to be marred by the intrusion of farming operations or of artificial effects.

Judging from the published reports of the meeting of the Yosemite Commission in the valley in June of the present year, steps are now being taken to put into operation a scheme to uproot and destroy the undergrowth, brush, and trees of the last forty years—a policy which Mr. Olmsted has declared would result, if carried out, in "a calamity to the civilized world." It is difficult to believe the commission, sincere in the exaggerated fear of a conflagration in Yosemite, which is given as the reason for this policy; for, as the reader will see by reference to the illustrations of Mr. Muir's article in *The Century* for August, there has been permitted a pernicious system of trimming up the young conifers to so consider-able a height as to destroy the beauty of the trees, while the dry brush and the lopped limbs have been left lying upon the ground, where the writer of this article saw them in June, 1889. Assuming the danger from fire to be an actual one, it would seem to be better to spend one's energies in pre-venting the beginning of a conflagration than to destroy the beauty of the valley by cutting out what at most would be but a small part of the combustible material. But even if it were necessary to make extensive alterations by means of the ax, does this lessen to any degree the necessity for expert knowledge in the operation? Members of the commission have publicly discussed the matter as though the question to be considered were the stoutness of the axman, and not the effect of his work to the eye. After this, the qualifications of the "experienced foresters" whom they expect to consult in their avowed policy of slaughtering the young growth in the valley may easily be imagined; they are certainly not such as will commend themselves to the respect and confidence of the public.

So far *The Century* has confined its protest against Yosem-ite management in this matter solely to the lack of expert supervision of the scenery. As to the causes which lie behind, and have for years preceded, the lamentable condition of affairs in the valley, Californians have every reason to be intelligent. It is devoutly to be hoped for the good name of the State that it will not be necessary to transfer to the halls of Congress the scandals of California's Capitol. If this shall not be necessary, it will probably be due to the fact that the next legislature of the State will be awakened to a sense of its responsibility in the matter. Meanwhile it is easy to see that the fire which endangers the Yosemite is not so much the unextinguished embers of the wandering camper as the all-consuming flame of politics, which nowhere burns with a fiercer or more withering heat than in the noble State of California.

> "These duties were entirely new to me
> and I had no idea what they were."

Captain Abram Epperson (A. E.) Wood
"Report of the Acting Superintendent of Yosemite National Park," 1891

On October 1, 1890, Congress passed legislation that established Yosemite National Park. Although California retained jurisdiction over Yosemite Valley and the Mariposa Grove of Giant Sequoias, the new park vastly expanded the territory subject to federal government supervision. The problem was that the act did not provide for management or security protection for the national park. Secretary of the Interior John W. Noble drew upon precedent to offer a solution. The U.S. Army had been tasked with patrolling Yellowstone National Park, so Secretary Noble asked President Benjamin Harrison in December 1890 to have soldiers assigned to Yosemite National Park "to prevent timber cutting, sheep herding, trespassing, or spoliation in particular." On April 6, 1891, Troop I of the Fourth Cavalry, stationed at the Presidio, the army post in San Francisco, was authorized to patrol the park. Its commander was Captain Abram Epperson (A. E.) Wood.

Wood faced a daunting task. The boundaries of Yosemite National Park were not marked; occasionally destructive and unregulated camping and tourism were prevalent; and trespassing was common, particularly by cattle grazers and sheepherders.

When Captain Wood and 250 troops arrived in May 1891, he established Camp Wawona on the southern edge of the park as a base of operations. He thus became the first acting superintendent of Yosemite National Park. Wood used tactics that had proven successful in Yellowstone, even though the geography and circumstances were quite different in Yosemite. For example, to address trespassing by shepherds, Troop I of the Fourth Cavalry arrested the sheepherders, separated them from their flocks, evicted them, and dispersed their herds on the opposite side of the park. Although of questionable legality, these forceful actions cured the trespassing problem until shepherds thwarted these procedures several years later.

Captain Wood's tenure as acting superintendent of Yosemite National Park was short-lived. He died of cancer in 1894. Camp Wawona was renamed Camp A. E. Wood in his memory and Mount Wood, a thirteen-thousand-foot peak just outside the eastern boundary of Yosemite National Park, was named in his honor in 1894.

The following excerpts from Captain Wood's initial 1891 report to Secretary of the Interior Noble detail the obstacles Wood faced and the exasperating fact that he did not have any official guidance as to how to proceed.

Camp near Wawona, Mariposa County, Cal.,

August 31, 1891.

The Secretary of the Interior:

Sir: In accordance with your letter of July 28, I have the honor to submit the following report of the condition of affairs and of the management of the Yosemite National Park since it has been under my supervision during the fiscal year ending June 30, 1891.

Soon after the department commander had designated Troop I, Fourth Cavalry, as the guard for the Yosemite

"An Intelligent and Generous Policy"

National Park, I procured an order to visit the park for the purpose of examining the ground and selecting a suitable place for a camp.

I arrived here with the troop May 17, established the camp, reported by letter to the Secretary of the Interior for orders, instructions, and suggestions, and immediately commenced examining into the situation.

These duties were entirely new to me and I had no idea of what they were. I managed to procure a copy of the regulations of the Yosemite National Park, from which I learned that trespassing of stock or persons would not be permitted. I wrote to the Department for copies of these regulations. I also wrote to the War Department for copies of maps of Wheeler's survey of this section of California. In the mean time I purchased a small township map of the Park which was printed in San Francisco. This is very defective topographically, but I was enabled by it and such information as I could get from the old mountaineers to approximately locate the boundaries of the park.

The lands within the boundaries of this park have been used as a grazing ground by the cattle and sheep owners for many years, and in order to begin what in this country is called a "square deal" with them I wrote a letter to every stock owner whose name and address I could learn in middle and southern California, notifying them that it was my duty to keep all stock off this reservation, and asking them as law-abiding citizens to use due diligence towards keeping their stock away, thereby aiding me in the execution of the will of Congress. When at a later date I received the regulations of the park, I distributed them freely and inclosed them in letters to about twenty post-offices in the four adjacent counties, requesting the postmasters to tack them up in a conspicuous place in their respective post-offices.

The cattle owners have generally tried to observe the law, but there are many small holders living in the vicinity of the park who are too poor to hire a herder, and whose old stock will drift up the various cañons leading into the park as the feed in the foothills gets poor. This stock has given some trouble this year, but most of the owners have told me that they would dispose of such stock before the snows melt next year.

The last days of May the sheep commenced their annual migrations to the mountain grazing grounds, and by the 10th of June there were fully 60,000 of them close to the southern and at least 30,000 near the western boundaries of the park. These sheep are owned in the San Joaquin Valley and on the coast. They are organized into bands of from 2,000 to 3,000, each band having a regular outfit of from three to five herders and their dogs, with pack animals as a supply train. These herders and many of the owners are foreigners—mostly Portuguese, with a few Chilians, French, and Mexicans. They have carried things with a high hand and have "bulldozed" the poor squatters among these mountains for years. It was no unusual thing for the herder to open the fence and let his sheep into the squatter's small field, where they would eat up everything.

As these bands approached I kept patrols along the border with instructions to warn the chief herders that it was against the law to trespass upon the reservation. All of them knew just as well as we did about where the boundary lines were located, but I did not wish to take severe measures until a repeated or willful trespass was committed.

In one or two instances, where ignorance of the boundary was advanced as an excuse for trespass, the herders were directed to remove their sheep and not repeat the offense. . . .

The sheep herders knew all this, but thought that I did not, so three or four bands moved into these townships and commenced grazing. This convinced me that I had to adopt some plan of action that would thoroughly frighten the owners as well as the herders, or my men and horses would be worn out by perpetually scouring these almost

"An Intelligent and Generous Policy"

impassable mountains, and even then, as soon as our backs were turned the herds would be slipped in and grazed until another patrol came along.

I knew that any measures which I might adopt that would rid the mountains of these vandals would be popular, for they are hated by the inhabitants of these regions with a hatred that surpasses belief. . . .

The wagon roads which enter this park are three in number. They are all toll roads, and are owned by incorporated companies.

The only road entering from the south is the best and by far is of the greatest importance. . . .

There are two roads which enter the park from the west, the most southerly being the road from Coulterville to the Yosemite Valley. It is in very good repair and traverses about 25 miles of the park. It is known as the Coulterville and Yosemite Turnpike. . . . The remaining road enters the park in township 1 south, range 19 east, and leads from Milton, a railroad station to the Yosemite Valley. It is kept in fair repair. It is known as the Big Oak Flat road. . . .

There are about 35 Indians living within the boundaries of this park. They are the remnants of the Yosemite tribe, and have inhabited the Yosemite Valley and neighboring country longer than their traditions go back. They dress similarly to the whites, and some of them are quite intelligent. In summer they gain a livelihood by fishing, chopping wood, putting up hay, washing, and laboring about the hotels. In winter they hunt and do placer mining and such odd jobs as they can get.

Like all of their kind, they, with but few exceptions, will get drunk whenever they can get the liquor, but they are more steadfast than the white man, in that they will never betray the man who gets the liquor for them.

They have petitioned the Congress for an appropriation of $1,000,000. But if left to themselves I can not see how this money would make them happier or improve their condition. A few designing whites would have the most of it in a short time, and it would beget homicide and crime among the Indians themselves. . . .

Recommendations

The boundary lines are not well marked. They are simply neighborhood traditions. Thus far I have not had time to hunt the township corners or in any manner mark the boundaries, even if I could find them.

An appropriation for the purpose of establishing these boundaries is respectfully recommended.

I have devoted much time and thought to the subject of the boundaries of this national park, and after a careful examination of the ground I find that there are natural boundaries for the most of it. I hope I will not be considered over-officious if I state and recommend what, in my judgment, are the best boundaries. . . .

Such a boundary line will include all the natural wonders, excluding none whatever. It excludes about all the mining country on the east and nearly all in the southwest. It takes in all the immense forests worth mentioning that is now within the park. It excludes all the old agricultural districts . . . and it excludes a barren, rocky waste north of the Tuolumne River. It excludes no timber, the shade of which would keep the snows from melting until late in the season, and it includes the only portion of country that furnishes a reason for a national park. . . .

The limited time in which I have to write this report necessarily excludes smaller details, which I will forward in a supplemental report at the end of the season. I have mentioned only those subjects which I conceived would be of aid to the Secretary in his annual report.

Very respectfully, your obedient servant,

A. E. Wood, Captain Fourth Cavalry,

Acting Superintendent Yosemite National Park.

"An Intelligent and Generous Policy"

> "We do not wish to part with our last remnant of territory for merely the enrichment of a few adventurous white men."

Petition to the Senators and Representatives of the Congress of the United States in the Behalf of the Remnants of the Former Tribes of the Yosemite Indians Praying for Aid and Assistance

Letter of Petition to Interior Secretary John W. Noble, 1891

In 1891 members of the remaining Yosemite Native community submitted a petition to the U.S. Congress addressing injustices they claimed to have suffered at the hands of the Anglo-American regulators of the Yosemite region. Despite the document's outward appearance of diplomatic propriety, the petition was a scathing indictment of the California and federal administration of Yosemite. The missive complained that the valley was not being protected as a park, as promised, but converted to officially sanctioned hay production and cattle grazing. The petition charged that policies allowing extensive grazing and fishing impeded Native traditions, such as acorn gathering and hunting. These practices, the document continued, threatened the continuing presence and survival of the indigenous population within Yosemite.

The Yosemite Indians, specifically the Awahnichi, who had never signed any treaty with the State of California or the U.S. government, offered a solution. They requested restitution of $1 million for their economic and cultural losses, in return for which they would convey any rights and titles to the Yosemite environs to the respective governments. Acting Superintendent of the Yosemite National Park A. E. Wood was generally sympathetic to the indigenous population, but, in his 1891 report to the secretary of the interior, Wood recommended their request be denied. He stated, "I can not see how this money would make them happier or improve their condition. A few designing whites would have the most of it in a short time, and it would beget homicide and crime among the Indians themselves." Predictably, the petition was indeed denied.

The writer of the petition is a matter of speculation. Historians feel that the petition was approved and signed but not written by Yosemite's indigenous people. The author is generally believed to be Charles Dorman Robinson, award-winning landscape artist and summertime resident of Yosemite Valley for twenty-four years. As Mark Spence has noted in his excellent essay "Dispossessing the Wilderness: Yosemite Indians and the National Park Ideal, 1864–1930," the 1891 petition has similar wording to that used by Robinson in his 1889 testimony in support of an investigation of the Yosemite Park Commission conducted by the California State Assembly. Most historians concur that the evidence points to Robinson as the source of the petition.

To his excellency,

The President of the United States and to the Congress of the United States

Your Honors:

We, the undersigned chiefs and head men of the existing remnants of the tribes of the Yo-Semite, the Mono and the Piute Indians, who hold claims upon that gorge in the Sierra Nevada Mountains known as the Yosemite Valley, and the lands around and about it, by virtue of direct descent from the aforenamed tribes, who were inhabitants of that valley and said territory at the time when it was so unjustifiably conquered and taken from our fathers by the whites, do utter, petition and pray your Excellency and your honorable bodies in Congress assembled to hear, deliberate upon, and give us relief, for the following reasons to wit:

1st. In all of the difficulties, disagreements, quarrels, and violences which sprang up between our fathers and the whites of their days, the first causes can invariably be traced to the overbearing tyranny and oppression of the white gold hunters, who had and who were continually usurping our territory. Those causes were briefly as follows: The white gold hunters brought among us drunkenness, lying, murder, forcible violation of our women, cheating, gambling, and wrongful appropriation of our lands for their own selfish uses. We have been made aware that at this period there was no harmonious system of laws or bonds of restraint operating to check the lawlessness or violence of these bands of adventurous and desperate white men, who had sought our shores in search of gold, and little or nothing could be expected of them as remuneration for our lands; nor could punishment be inflicted upon them by laws which, if existing, remained in the main unenforced: yet in after years, when the long list of oppressions and outrages to which our fathers were forced to submit at the hands of the whites had long ended by the slaughter and dispersal of our tribes, no notice was taken of the few who remained, and who from then until now have continued to travel to and fro, poorly-clad paupers and unwelcome guests, silently the objects of curiosity or contemptuous pity to the throngs of strangers who yearly gather in this our own land and heritage. We are compelled to daily and hourly witness the further and continual encroachments of a few white men in this our valley. The gradual destruction of its trees, the occupancy of every foot of its territory by bands of grazing horses and cattle, the decimation of the fish in the river, the destruction of every means of support for ourselves and families by the rapacious acts of the whites, in the building of their hotels and operating of their stage lines, which must shortly result in the total exclusion of the remaining remnants of our tribes from this our beloved valley, which has been ours from time beyond our faintest traditions, and which we still claim. Therefore, in support of our petition, we beg leave to offer the following reasons for our prayer:

1st. We, as Indians and survivors of the aforenamed tribes, declare that we were unfairly and unjustly deprived of our possessions in land, made to labor in the interest of the whites for no recompense, subjected to continual brutality, wrong, and outrage at the hands of the whites, and were gradually driven from our homes into strange localities by their action, and that our few retaliatory acts were feeble and deserving of no notice, in comparison to the gross injustices and outrages that we were continually subjected to. And we respectfully call your attention to the official report of Maj. Gen. Thomas J. Green to Gov. Peter H. Burnett, dated May 25, 1850, (page 769, Journals of the Legis. of Cal. for 1851); Brig. Gen. Thomas B. Eastland's report to Gov. Burnett, June 15th, 1850, (page 770, Ibid); letters of Gen. Eastland to Gov. McDougal (page 770, Ibid), and various others. If we were in the wrong the punishment we have suffered and the war indemnity which our fathers were forced to pay—their all and their lives besides—is in monstrous disproportion to the damage they inflicted, however just they may have deemed the provocation.

2d. The action of the Mariposa Battalion towards our chief at that time, Tenaya, and his tribe was wantonly unjust and outrageous. Our only quarrel with the whites then was owing to our determination not to go upon a reservation being established on the Fresno, and give up to the whites this magnificent valley, which was to us reservation and all that we desired and that for a few paltry blankets, gewgaws and indifferent supplies of rations, that might be furnished us or not, at the discretion of any appointed Indian Agent. Our fathers had the sorrow to see their tribe conquered, their dignified and honored chief Tenaya led out by a halter, like a beast, into a green field to eat grass, amid the wonder and laughter of our pursuers; and his youngest son shot dead

"An Intelligent and Generous Policy"

for no other reason than that he had tried to escape the unjust thralldom of our persecutors. For proof of these statements, you are referred to Dr. Bunnell's History of the Discovery of the Yosemite. He was himself attached to this battalion, and was an eye witness to all the facts related. Those who were left of our fathers were taken with their chief, however, to the reservation on the Fresno, from which place hunger and destitution finally forced them to run away; after which, we have been informed, the reservation was broken up, having shed disgrace upon all connected with its management.

3d. From that time up to the present the remnants of the various bands formerly in possession of the valley have earned a scanty livelihood by hunting, fishing, etc. There has never been a cause of complaint against the descendants of the old Yo Semites, neither have they broken the peace or indulged in warfares of any kind; they have silently been witness to the usurpation of their lands and valley; they have never been provided for in any way by the Government of either the State or the United States. The wisdom of their action in quietly escaping from the Fresno reservation was justified by the bad management of that reservation, which finally led to its being abolished by the United States Government. Now we, the last remnant of the once great Yosemite tribe, and also those from the Mono and Piutes tribes who have claims here, see that the time is fast approaching when we must all abandon this, our valley, together, for the following reasons. White men have come into this valley to make money only. They have continually disobeyed the laws which were made for the government of this valley by the Washington Government. Those laws declared that this valley should be kept as a reservation and park for the white people forever but the head men appointed to govern this valley by the State Government do not obey those laws; instead, they have given control of the lands of the entire valley into the hands of a few whites, who only wish to make money here, and care neither for the laws nor the Indians. Those white men have fenced the valley all up with wire fences, with sharp barbs all along the wire, close together; it is divided off into fields, many of which are ploughed up by the white men to raise grain and hay to feed their own horses upon, and the Indians are forbidden to walk across their own fields by reason of this farming; the other fields are filled with the horses and cattle of these white men, as many as 125 horses, and sometimes 40 head or more of cattle being at large in these fields; all of the tender roots, berries and the few nuts that formed the sustenance of the Indians are trampled down and torn up by the roots, or eaten and broken off in this way by these few white men's horses and cattle. If the Indians have two or three horses they must starve, for there are no fields left for them to run in, neither can the strange whites, who came in wagons to look at the great rocks in the valley, find food for their horses, by reason of these wire fences of these few white men. Where there are no fences, the valley is cut up completely by dusty, sandy roads, leading from the hotels of whites in every direction. The head men of the whites also order their workmen to cut away the trees in every direction, and destroy the shade and beauty of the valley, so that they may have more room to plough and raise hay to sell to strangers, and to plant in gardens and build their houses upon.

Every once in a while the State Government changes its head men, and every new lot turn away from their homes more and more of the old resident whites, whom we have known so long, and young, strong and hungry looking new faces come in their places. All seem to come only to hunt money. Why the old ones are turned away we do not know, but when they are sent away their houses are torn down, and new ones are built for these new men to live in. This does not seem to us to be right, neither do we believe the great Washington Government wants this wonderful valley to be ploughed up into a hay farm, or its fine forest

"An Intelligent and Generous Policy"

trees to be cut down and destroyed for the pleasure of those whites who seem to be afraid of and to hate trees. This is not the way in which we treated this park when we had it; and we know that these white headmen often say that the Indians were the only ones who knew how to take care of Yosemite. We have heard that the white men in the valley intend to plough up nearly all of the open and level portion of the valley, to raise hay upon, and it will only be a short time before they will tell the Indians that they must go away and not come back any more. Now, in this valley grow all the things that we can rely upon for our winter supplies, and we cannot go away from here to gather acorns and nuts, or to hunt game, without trespassing upon some other Indians' ground and causing trouble; besides, we do not wish to leave this valley if we can help it, though as it is governed now in the interest of only a few white people, and for them to make money in, we do not see that we can possibly stay here much longer, for every year these few whites reach out for more, more, and drive us slowly further back. We have already been told by the former chief of the whites in this valley, that we must go away from here and stay away; but we say this valley was not given to us by our fathers for a day, or a year, but for all time. The whites are too numerous and powerful for us. We willingly keep the peace, we have no desire to do otherwise, but it is with an uneasiness that we see the time approaching when we must leave this spot which has been the home of our people from time immemorial. Therefore we pray our head white father at Washington and his Great Council to consider the following things, viz:

First. Soon after this valley was taken away from us by the whites, the great Washington Council gave it to all the white American people for a pleasure ground, a park, where they might come and see the great rocks and waterfalls, and enjoy themselves.

Now it seems to us that the laws imposed upon the head men of this valley by the Washington Government are being wilfully disregarded, and that Yosemite is no longer a State or National Park, but merely a hay-farm and cattle range.

Second. The valley is almost entirely fenced in, mostly with barbed wire. There are no walks for pleasure. There are horses and cattle in every field. There are nine fenced-off fields within a space of two miles or less, at this upper end of the valley, and consequently the People's Park is a thing of the past. It has now resolved itself into a private institution, making only a show and pretence of being a public benefit and is supported by the State in this condition. Consequently, as we have been wronged and robbed [of] this valley in the first place by the whites, and has been turned by them into a place for their own benefit, and has been withheld from us for 37 years and we have received not one iota of remuneration for our natural rights and interests therein at any time and as we see we must relinquish all our possessions here soon, and go among strange tribes and in strange places to live, and as we are sufficiently civilized to understand the ways of the whites, and conform in a measure to their habits and customs, we pray you, our great White Chief, and you, the great Washington Council, to give us for our just claims upon this Yosemite Valley, and our surrounding claims so violently and wrongfully wrested from us without either cause or provocation, out of the abundance of your great wealth, for the future support of ourselves and our descendants, one million of dollars, United States gold coin; for which consideration we will forever bargain and convey all our natural right and title to Yosemite Valley and our surrounding claims.

We know that Indians far away in your country have received indemnities in this way for lands forcibly taken from them and other wrongs inflicted upon them by whites in former times; and also that the whites constantly receive such indemnifications for losses sustained at the hands of Indians. Therefore, we hope in justice that you,

"An Intelligent and Generous Policy"

the Great White Chief, and you of the Great White Council of this Nation, at Washington, may hear with wide open ears, and grant our prayer; also, in case that you declare justly and favorably for us in our great need, suffering under this condition of great wrong and poverty, we desire to be heard, and have a voice in the Council which shall appoint the men who are to receive the indemnity money for us, as we do not wish to part with our last remnant of territory for merely the enrichment of a few adventurous white men. Here we place our marks as opposite our names, the Chiefs and head men of the petitioning remnants of the former Yosemite tribes with our principal women and children.

YOSEMITE INDIANS.

Te-he-he or Capt. Henry.

Cha-muk or Lancisco.

Mu-mu or Capt. Dick.

Sung-ok or John (Capt. Dick's son).

Chich-ka or John Lawrence.

Hick-ah or Peter Hilliard.

Wit-ta-ra-bee or Tom Hutchings.

Low-a or "Bill."

Bu-lok or "Bullock."

Chor-cha or "Austin."

Chre-cra or "Mike."

Hul-i-na or "Capt. Reuben."

Una-moy-na or "Capt. John."

or "Scipio."

"Cary."

"Johnny Brown."

"Charley Bill."

Su-pan-chee or "Capt. Paul."

Car ra-nee or "Pedro."

Chee-tee or "Jim."

"Wilson."

"Willie Wilson."

Meme-lem or "Melquita."

Pancho or "Jack."

Cha-muk or "Louie."

Ha-tam-e-we-ah or "Nancey."

"Billy Stanley."

MONO-YOSEMITES.

Shi-ban-nah or "Capt. John." (Head Chief of the Mono
Piutes)

Bos-seek

Chen-na-pee

Tor-tah-hock-a-mah

Pah-aw-zack or "Jim."

YOSEMITE INDIANS. WOMEN.

Pa-ma-ha or "Callipene."

Y-mu-sa or "Betsey."

Yo-ne-pa or "Mary Ann."

Chen-na-chu or "Susey Lawrence."

Shu-wi-o-nee or "Jenny."

Why-to-ne

To-nee-pa or "Mary."

"Dulcy."

"Caledonia."

Awl-kim

"Julia Ann."

"Cosey."

"An Intelligent and Generous Policy"

"Louisa."

"Susey."

"Yusey."

"Nancy."

"Lucy."

"Old Lucy."

Chi-nee

Wil-la-pum or "Co-qui."

And many others.

....

"Yosemite Fall could be maintained either by damming the
creek or by turning a portion of the waters of Tuolumne River
into its bed through a flume about 20 miles long."

....

Allen Kelly
"Restoration of Yosemite Waterfalls," 1892

Yosemite National Park was established in October 1890.
The park was predicated on the idea that the federal
government would leave the natural attributes of the
park untouched as much as possible. Some felt that that
this preservation ethos harmed economic interests and
impeded any development of the area for the betterment
of tourism and society in general. Among the latter was
Anthony Caminetti, a member of the U.S. House of Representatives whose district included the Yosemite region.

In February 1892, Caminetti introduced H.R. 5764,
legislation designed to protect mining, livestock, and
timber enterprises by reducing the size of Yosemite
National Park. The legislation also requested authori-
zation for the federal government to "pay for surveys of
reservoir sites in the mountains surrounding Yosemite
Valley, with a view to storing water in the streams that
supply the numerous falls." The so-called Caminetti Bill

would be a major impetus to the founding of the Sierra Club in May 1892 and instigated the club's first preservation crusade.

In "Restoration of Yosemite Waterfalls," a July 16, 1892, article for *Harper's Weekly*, Allen Kelly, head forester for the State of California, supported Caminetti's reservoir concept. Although the bill was mostly in support of using Yosemite watersheds to provide water for irrigation, Kelly specifically argued in favor of a reliable water source (i.e., reservoirs and flumes) to keep Yosemite waterfalls flowing during the drier months of summer and fall. Such construction, Kelly claimed, would afford "added beauty and attractiveness of the Yosemite Park, as well as in utilitarian benefit to the people of a great State."

The Caminetti Bill would ultimately die in committee. The bill's history offers an early case study in the tension between proponents of preservation versus development of national park lands, a tension that persists to the present day. This battle of beliefs reached a zenith in the controversy over hydroelectric infrastructure in Hetch Hetchy Valley in the early twentieth century.

In establishing the Yosemite National Park, a reservation of 1500 square miles surrounding the Yosemite Valley grant, Congress sought to protect the water-sheds of the Merced and Tuolumne rivers, and preserve such a flow of water throughout the year as would insure an adequate supply for the falls that add so much to the charm and attractiveness of scenery in the valley. Incidentally, the protection of the water-shed is a practical benefit to the State of California, in the preservation of forests and the storage of water for irrigation. For more than a quarter of a century the tract now included within the lines of the Park has been the summer grazing-ground for wandering herds of cattle and flocks of sheep, and for several years past more than 100,000 sheep have been pastured upon this portion of the public domain.

The irresponsible and usually ignorant men who herd the great bands of sheep in the mountains have no concern for anything but feed, and neither know nor care what damage they do to the forests and streams. It is their custom, when they leave the mountains in the fall, to start innumerable fires in the brush, and as everything is dry as tinder after the long hot California summer, these fires not only sweep away the undergrowth and kill the saplings, but scorch and eventually top-kill the larger forest-trees. The tender green shoots and seedlings that come up in the spring are eaten by the sheep, and renewal of forest growth is thereby prevented. It is unnecessary to point out the effect thereof upon the water supply. New York's experience with the Adirondack forests and the water-shed of the Hudson has been a public lesson on that subject.

United States troops were employed last year, and will be this year, in keeping sheep and cattle out of the Park, and the beneficial effects of the protection are already apparent. Last year there were no forest fires in the Park, and in the course of an examination of the great fir timber belt, made under the directions of the State Board of Forestry, I noticed that a thick growth of seedlings had sprung up on mountain slopes usually kept bare and barren by the sheep.

But while the protection now afforded will prevent further injury to the forests, it will require many years to restore them to their original condition; and meanwhile the larger trees will die and fall, the winter snows will be left exposed to the sun, the water will be wasted in spring floods, and the streams will run dry, or nearly so, in August. It is obvious that the natural conservation of water supply must be supplemented by artificial storage, and preliminary steps to that end have been taken in Congress.

Congressman [Anthony] Caminetti, of California, who is actively and intelligently interested in forestry and the preservation of streams, has asked for an appropriation to pay for surveys of reservoir sites in the mountains surrounding the Yosemite Valley, with a view to storing water in the streams that supply the numerous falls.

Under existing conditions, the waterfalls of Yosemite Valley are seen at their best in June, and after that rapidly diminish, and disappear entirely during the season when the valley is otherwise most attractive. The Yosemite Fall, where the water of a large creek takes a plunge of almost half a mile downward from the crest of the valley wall, is one of the most famous features of Yosemite scenery; but at the time of year when tourists from abroad find it most convenient to visit the valley there is no waterfall, only a discolored streak on the dry face of the cliff.

Bridal Veil Fall, a lacelike ribbon nearly 900 feet long, iridescent with rainbow hues its whole length, becomes a mere trickling film over the rocks. The vast volume of Nevada Fall, that plunges in a broad sheet of foam 600 feet downward into a roaring, seething caldron, and fills all the cañon with spray, dwindles to an insignificant dribble in October; and when its waters come to the precipice that makes Vernal Fall—perhaps the most beautiful of all the Yosemite cataracts—there is scarcely so much of them as would flow from a street hydrant.

The Sentinel Fall (3270 feet), Widow's Tears, and a dozen or twenty other spring falls and cascades, vanish utterly early in the summer, and leave no trace.

Yosemite Fall could be maintained either by damming the creek or by turning a portion of the waters of Tuolumne River into its bed through a flume about 20 miles long. A dam 100 yards in length across the mouth of Little Yosemite Valley would store plenty of water for Nevada and Vernal falls, and a supply for the Bridal Veil could be secured by making a reservoir of the meadows along the creek.

Mirror Lake, a beautiful little sheet of water, a perfect mirror of the mountains, at the mouth of Tenaya Cañon, becomes an unsightly pool of mud when the flow of water ceases in the creek. A dam 1400 feet long at Lake Tenaya, eight miles distant and much higher in the mountains, would not only

"An Intelligent and Generous Policy"

keep Mirror Lake full, but would store a vast amount of water for the Merced that would be precious as gold to the irrigation districts of the plains.

Chilnualna Falls, near Wawona, in the southern part of the National Park, a series of seven cataracts and cascades, are as beautiful as any of the waterfalls in the valley itself—in many respects even more lovely and interesting—and in any other part of the world would be the Mecca of innumerable summer pilgrims. The blight of deforestation has fallen upon Chilnualna, and can be removed only by the building of storage reservoirs or the turning of other waters into the bed of its parent stream.

It will cost a great deal of money to carry out the contemplated scheme of restoration, but in added beauty and attractiveness of the Yosemite Park, as well as in utilitarian benefit to the people of a great State, the work will be well worth the expense.

ALLEN KELLY,
Head Forester of California

"If we keep our heads in the clouds
let our feet rest on solid ground."

San Francisco Call
"To Save Yosemite," 1892

In May 1892, partly in response to the recently introduced Caminetti Bill authorizing reduction in the size of Yosemite National Park, the Sierra Club was founded. However, it was not a knee-jerk, overnight development. As early as 1889, *Century Magazine* editor Robert Underwood Johnson had urged John Muir to form an organization to focus on protecting the Sierra Nevada. From small, preliminary gatherings, held in places such as the artist William Keith's San Francisco apartment, the framework of what came to be called the Sierra Club emerged.

In 1892 the association was formalized by Muir, University of California botanist Willis Linn Jepson, and attorney Warren Olney. They modeled the Sierra Club after the Appalachian Mountain Club, founded in 1876 by Boston academics and forest enthusiasts. Officers, charter members, and supporters of the new Sierra Club included Robert Underwood Johnson; William Keith; prominent topographer Willard Drake Johnson; geologist Joseph LeConte; David Starr Jordan, president of Stanford University; Dr. J. T. McLean, a physician and public health officer for Alameda, California; William H. Beatty, chief justice of California; Yosemite innkeeper and tourism booster James Mason Hutchings; German language professor Joachim Henry Senger; Guardian of the Grove Galen Clark; Andrew Hallidie, developer of the San Francisco's cable car system; and Muir's eleven-year-old daughter Wanda. John Muir was elected president of the Sierra Club, a position he held until his death in 1914.

In November 1892, the Sierra Club held its first semi-annual general meeting in San Francisco. The primary focus of the meeting was to draft a response in opposition to the Caminetti Bill. Muir was unable to attend this initial meeting. On November 20, 1892, the *San Francisco Call* reported on the assembly.

To Save Yosemite

The Boundaries Must Not be Curtailed

So says the Sierra Club

Resolutions Adopted Opposing the Caminetti Bill and Favoring the Paddock Measure

The Sierra Club has decided unanimously against Congressman Caminetti's bill restricting the boundaries of the Yosemite National Park.

It was expected that the Congressman would be present at the first semi-annual general meeting of the club, held in the lecture-room of the Academy of Sciences building last

"An Intelligent and Generous Policy"

night to explain the reason why he wants the boundaries of the park curtailed, but it was announced by Vice-President Olney that he was unavoidably absent owing to sickness in his family.

Chief Justice Beatty was to have presided, but was detained at Sacramento, and in the absence of President Muir Mr. Olney took the chair.

In his opening remarks the chairman said that Congressman Caminetti was in favor of the objects of the club and forest reservation, and would oppose any scheme for the sale of forest land. He referred to [Nebraska] Senator [Algernon] Paddock's bill to provide for the establishment, protection and administration of public forest reservations, which had been introduced in the Senate, and that a committee of the club had been appointed to wait upon Senator Morgan of Baltimore [Senator "Morgan" of Baltimore is probably Senator Arthur P. Gorman of Maryland], who was expected here shortly, with the object of getting his support to the bill.

"If the club," he concluded, "will put forth an effort and act unitedly it can lead public sentiment in the setting apart of large tracts of forest lands for the benefit of the people," [Applause.]

Professor Arms, secretary, explained the features of the Paddock bill, which are, in effect, that a commission be appointed by the Government who will have the appointment of officers to take charge of forests and have the power of withdrawing from sale lands found to be timber rather than farming land.

Professor Sanger [Senger] moved that the directors of the club be authorized and directed to prepare a memorial to Congress supporting the general features of the Paddock bill, which was adopted unanimously.

Dr. J. T. McLean of Alameda thought that the memorial should be signed by the people of the State as well.

The chairman said it would be taken for granted that the action of the club would be accepted as the action of the people of the State. . . .

The chairman, by the aid of a large map of the National Park, explained what the Caminetti bill proposed to do. The proposed reductions were marked in red lines. He said that in talking with Caminetti he had stated he had no objection to have the bill amended so as to allow all that part of the park at the head of the Tuolumne River to remain.

J. M. Hutchings said the boundary line must remain on the crest of the Sierras, but he saw no objection to the two and a half sections to the southwest being excluded, as they were occupied by miners and small farmers. It would be a sad thing for California if the sheepherders were allowed to wander wantonly through the reservation. The last time he was there he saw nineteen fires in different places that had been started by these herders. The watersheds and the groves of sequoia trees must be preserved. There were only two of these groves now, and he remembered the time when there were twenty.

Dr. J. T. McLean said he had been more or less associated with the Yosemite Valley since 1867. For several years the residents had been anxious for the segregation of the domain so as to preserve the watersheds supplying the water to the wonderful falls, and all were delighted when, on October 1, 1890, Congress set apart the national park.

"Why anybody should think," said the doctor, "of curtailing the park now I cannot conceive. It should rather be extended. [Applause.] The whole western slope of the Sierras should be made a reservation and preserved for the enjoyment of all. [Applause.]

"The Paddock bill will come near doing what ought to be done—namely, to segregate from the public domain all forest reservations. One of its important features is the preservation of the water flows. What would our foothills be if it were not for the water flowing from these watersheds? Deforestation will devastate instead of gladden our foothills and valleys.

"Caminetti is a capable and intelligent man, but he has made an unfortunate mistake in this matter. [Applause.]

"An Intelligent and Generous Policy"

The summit of the Sierras should, by all means, be the eastern boundary of the park. The glaciers are the sources of the San Joaquin River, and it is fed by smaller streams. It is all that is necessary for horticultural and agricultural purposes in the foothills and San Joaquin Valley. We need these streams. [Applause.]

"We want the western slope; we want all of these townships. We ought to leave it to the action of the Paddock bill to take out whatever is not necessary for park purposes. But Caminetti's bill takes out the North Tuolumne region, the very part that must not be taken out.

"A new grove of sequoias had been discovered in Placer County and the Secretary of the Interior has sent a special agent to segregate the land surrounding it and have it preserved. From that I believes [sic] that Secretary Noble would be amenable to reason in regard to preserving the sequoia groves in the southwestern part of the park."

He objected strongly to excluding the two and a half sections to the southwest, or any portion of the park. "Let it go out," he said, "that the park must stay as it is in the interests not only of California but of the whole world; let us keep it; endeavor to get more." [Applause.]

He concluded by moving the following resolution, which was adopted unanimously amid great applause: "That the directors of the club be instructed to prepare a memorial to Congress opposing any restrictions to the boundaries of the Yosemite National Park as established by act of Congress." . . .

Professor Le Conte was called upon by the chairman to make a few remarks. On stepping upon the platform the venerable geologist was greeted with great applause. He said, referring to the book of Rev. Dr. Warren, president of the university at Boston, on the Garden of Eden, that a portion of the garden had been left stranded on its way back to the North Pole in the midst of the Sierras, and the club was trying to preserve it.

"It will not last long if we don't," said the professor. "As a geologist I deeply sympathize with the club. Alpine exploration has been the very nursery of geology.

"The tendency of civilization is to lead us further and further and farther away from physical nature. Let us not lose our hold on lower nature. If we keep our heads in the clouds let our feet rest on solid ground. This club helps to develop the type of true, noble manhood.

"Mother earth is kinder to Californians than to those who live in the East. It gives strength, life and vigor to sleep upon her bosom. The cares and pressure of life are in danger of strangling us unless from time to time we come in contact with mother earth.

"The sight of the Yosemite Valley always fills me with joy such as no other place on earth has the power to do. It is not alone for its beautiful scenery, but from the renewed health and life I obtain by contact with nature.

"The greatest riches of California are in her magnificent forests and scenery, and she has the climate adapted to their enjoyment in the fullest extent.

"No part of the reservation must be given up, but we must strive for the reservation of all the forests and magnificent scenery of the Sierra Nevada." [Great applause.]

This closed the proceedings and the chairman declared the meeting adjourned.

....

> "A large majority of the people would be in favor
> of letting the government of the Yosemite Valley
> revert to the National Government."

....

Special Land Inspector Major Eugene F. Weigel
Report to Secretary of the Interior James W. Noble, 1892

In 1892 Secretary of the Interior James W. Noble was increasingly concerned about the quality of transportation in and around Yosemite. Secretary Noble asked several of his agents to investigate the condition and practices of private toll roads and the convenience for and

"An Intelligent and Generous Policy"

usage of roads by the visiting public. Among the agents dispatched was Special Land Inspector Eugene F. Weigel. Noble also detailed Weigel "to make investigation concerning the condition of affairs in Yosemite Valley."

On October 3, 1892, Weigel reported his findings to Secretary Noble.

Eugene F. Weigel's career was mostly in public administration. A Civil War Union Army veteran, Weigel was secretary of state for Missouri from 1871 to 1875. He was the first commissioner of parks in St. Louis, serving from 1877 to 1886. Weigel was an early member and served as adjutant general of the Grand Army of the Republic, a fraternal organization for Civil War veterans that had been founded in 1866. After his stint as special land inspector for the Department of the Interior, Weigel was commissioned to write a special report entitled "Beer: History and Advancement of the Art of Brewing" for the World's Columbian Exposition of 1893, the world's fair held in Chicago.

A good deal of underbrushing had been done near the Stoneman House in Yosemite Valley and around the stables of the Transportation Company by direction of the State commissioners, under the supervision of Galen Clark, the guardian. Mr. Clark was formerly one of the commissioners, and although 78 years old is still active, and appears to be an educated, honorable man. He took me around to the places where the clearing had been done for the purpose of lessening the danger of fires, and which, it is true, at times partook of the nature of a mutilation of natural beauty.

Guardian Clark was free to confess that he was no scientific landscaper, and that he carried out the orders of the board to the best of his ability. He said that he had frequently importuned the commissioners to employ some expert landscape engineer to thoroughly study the valley and make a systematic plan of improvements that might be carried out in the course of several years, but all to no avail. It is certainly true that the young pines and underbrush are too thick in places and need a judicious thinning out, and the dead and decaying trees should all be removed. To my inquiry, Mr. Clark replied that it was not designed to carry this work on any further down the valley, and that it certainly was not intended to clear any more ground for meadows or planting.

More drives and pedestrian walks are needed, and the roads in the valley should be sprinkled. Many of the old, unsightly buildings should be removed, and whenever a new building of any kind is needed it should in outward appearance conform to the requirements of park surroundings.

For the kind of accommodations furnished the charges of the hotels are rather high, and the charges for stabling, teaming, or hire of vehicles or saddle animals in the park are beyond all reason.

To judge by the utterances of individuals here, as well as in Merced, Mariposa, and Fresno counties, a large majority of the people would be in favor of letting the government of the Yosemite Valley revert to the National Government. I have been informed by different parties that an effort will be made in the next assembly to accomplish this object. To the ordinary traveler the toll-roads in and outside of the park are very annoying, and the free road to be built up to the valley, from Merced this winter, will be hailed with delight, besides possessing the advantage of enabling the tourist to visit the valley all the year round. It will reach Yosemite Valley on easy grades via Mariposa, and attain no high altitudes, so that it can be kept open all winter.

Besides acquiring all the toll-roads within the limits of the Yosemite National Park, the National Government should endeavor to secure by purchase the rights and claims of all private individuals within the boundaries of the park (except that portion in the southwest corner which you have recommended to be released), but especially all timber or agricultural claims. It is terribly demoralizing to the visitors of this

"An Intelligent and Generous Policy"

national park to pass through a tract of land 12 miles within the limits of the park, between Wawona and the Yosemite Valley, where a heartless vandal is even now chopping down magnificent pines 4 and 5 feet in diameter and between 100 and 200 feet high, merely for the purpose of cutting out a section of 20 or 30 feet from which to make shakes. The main road runs right through this place.

Although Wawona may be the best place for headquarters of the troop of cavalry, stationed in the park for its protection, yet it is on the extreme southern boundary of the park, from whence only a limited circle can be readily patrolled. I would respectfully suggest that one-half of the troop be ordered to establish a camp somewhere near the center of the park, on the Tioga road, next year, from where it can much more readily control the larger portion of the park. Mr. [Charles Dorman] Robinson, an artist, informed me that a fire recently had burned for two weeks around the Tuolumne grove of big trees, badly burning one of them before the soldiers came up to put it out.

The Southern Pacific Railroad Company, in conjunction with the Yosemite Stage and Transportation Company (headquarters at Wawona), is doing everything in its power to discourage travel into the Yosemite Valley except by its route, via Raymond. Although they advertise four different routes . . . , they all lead over Raymond, and anyone desiring to take routes 3 or 4 will be talked out of it by being told that the roads are very rough and dangerous.

This, together with the exorbitant prices charged for everything, really makes the Yosemite National Park inaccessible except to persons of ample time and means. The free road to be built this winter from Merced will undoubtedly be provided with a good stage line, which will carry passengers at reasonable rates.

An electric road to and even into this park would not be very objectionable, as there is no game to be scared away, as in the case of Yellowstone Park.

San Francisco Call
"Valley Vandals," 1893

When Yosemite National Park was established in 1890, Yosemite Valley and the Mariposa Grove of Giant Sequoias remained under state jurisdiction by the terms of the Yosemite Valley Grant Act of 1864. For years prior to that, however, there was criticism of the slipshod and seemingly shady management of the Yosemite Valley by the state's Yosemite Park Commission.

The most persistent critic was Charles Dorman Robinson. Robinson was an acclaimed landscape artist who was in summer residence in Yosemite Valley for more than twenty years. In 1889 he led the public effort to compel the state legislature to investigate the questionable actions of the Yosemite Park Commission. Robinson is believed to have been the author of a petition from the Yosemite Native population to the U.S. Congress seeking mitigation of the indigenous population's economic and social losses in the valley, mostly caused by the ineptitude and corruption of the Yosemite Park Commission.

Robinson was a curmudgeon and outspoken to a fault. In the late nineteenth century, he strikingly represented a vision held by increasing numbers of people that ceding control of Yosemite Valley to the federal government was essential to ensuring that Yosemite Valley would become, in Robinson's words, "a pleasure-ground for all mankind."

On New Year's Day 1893, the *San Francisco Call* published a remarkable interview with Robinson about the failings of the Yosemite Park Commission and its allies. As the *Call* chronicled the conversation with this most "adoring worshiper" of Yosemite, which was conducted in Robinson's "picturesquely trashy studio on Montgomery street," Robinson did not hold back. As the *Call* reported, he was "fiery with indignation or sarcastically contemptuous." Additionally, in a massive understatement, the newspaper noted that Robinson "thinks that a lot of farmers, politicians and hotel-keepers are trying to improve the Almighty's masterpiece and he doesn't like their efforts."

Valley Vandals.

Give Yosemite to the Government.

Artist Robinson's Advice.

Men Who Think That They Can Improve the Almighty's Landscape Gardening.

Yosemite Valley is the hobby of C. D. Robinson, the landscape painter, as everybody knows!

Outraged Yosemite, despoiled, denuded, disheveled and scarred by vandals, is a theme for which he is always loaded. He may be expected one of these days to paint an allegorical picture of Yosemite a weeping captive among the Philistines.

Nature receives into that great cathedral no more adoring worshiper than Mr. Robinson, and there comes out of it no one crying "shame" so loudly and cursing so deeply the unholy hands of the sextons there. He thinks that a lot of farmers, politicians and hotel-keepers are trying to improve the Almighty's masterpiece and he doesn't like their efforts.

It was Mr. Robinson who instituted the legislative investigation of Yosemite affairs in 1889. He has contributed matter to the *Century Magazine*, critical of the way the big scenic attraction is managed.

He talked to a *Call* reporter yesterday about his remedy for the valley's ills and misfortunes, which is to turn it over to the Federal Government, which gave it in trust to the State.

While he was talking he was bustling about his picturesquely trashy studio on Montgomery street and digging into piles of photographs for graphic illustrations of what he described.

He has a little over 3000 photographs taken in and about

Yosemite Valley, and when he displays some of them he grows fiery with indignation or sarcastically contemptuous.

"I expect that something will be done by Congress about Yosemite Valley this winter," he said. "I have been in favor of placing the park in the hands of the [Federal] Government ever since 1884, when J. M. [James Mason] Hutchings was retired as guardian of the valley and it began to be run in private interests, as has been done ever since.

"If that were done the entire park would be in the hands of absolute experts who have taste, judgment and discretion in matters of that kind.

"Now, there is not a square rod of the Yosemite region for thirty miles about that is not as familiar to me as your old clothes are to you.

"Why, the place has been my home for fourteen years or more. I have spent most of my time there, every summer. This last summer I was there during July and September, returning to the city in October.

"Yes, I know what has been done in the valley during the past summer. About all the improvement that has been effected has been to destroy the timber. They have cleared out what they called a 'jungle' at the upper end of the valley, and now it looks like a man with the hair shaved off one side of his face. Here are some of the 'jungles' they have cleared out."

In illustration Mr. Robinson produced a series of photographs of magnificent clumps of ferns, great masses of wild azaleas and picturesque groups of trees and shrubbery, all of striking beauty, and with grand canyon walls, rocks and forests in the background.

Then he displayed some pictures of plowed land and hay-fields.

"That is the way they improve the 'jungles,'" he went on. "That shrubbery is the beauty of the valley floor. Nature's landscape gardening there has always been conceded to be unique and perfect. That underbrush is asserted by botanists to contain some of the finest shrubbery on the face of the earth, and years ago one botanist found in it 400 species absolutely new to the science. . . .

"An unsightly fence of poles, boards and barbed wire has been moved back three rods along one of the drives, but it ought to be removed entirely. It was done at the desire of [George] Fiske, the photographer. For years it has been impossible for a photographer or a painter to get a view of the grandeur of the Yosemite Valley without finding an infernal fence or telegraph or telephone wires in front of him somewhere. This was a good move as far as it went.

"I saw it stated recently in praise of the present commissioners that they were making the valley look less like a ramshackle ranch.

"In 1889 I was denounced up hill and down for saying that that was just what the valley looked like. Now it is practically admitted by the same influences that scored me in 1889. . . .

"They are talking about building fascines [long bundles of wooden sticks] in the Merced River to 'protect' its banks.

"The Merced River is one of the most beautiful streams on the face of the earth, and now they propose to build stone wails, turn it into a ditch, and make it look like the river Seine in Paris.

"Look at these views of the river. What do you think of protecting with stone walls such spots as those?

"Then they propose to take out the cobblestone bars in the river. The cobblestone bars are not good enough for the Yosemite Commission, but they seem, to be good enough for the Almighty, who has been doing the work so far.

"They have decided to tear out Clark's dam that was built at the mouth of Mirror Lake in 1889 to raise the water. There were bars in the lake, and with their usual sapiency, instead of digging the bars out they decided to raise the water. Now the lake has filled up with the deposits, and all the beautiful trees and shrubbery that used to surround its edges have been killed by the rising water. There are oak and pine trees that had been growing 430 years there undisturbed that are now unsightly stumps, and the lake looks like a milldam in a forest. But they don't know any better.

"J. M. Hutchings did more with the $25,000 under his control in 1880 and 1881 than has been done with all the money the State has appropriated since. . . .

"If the Government had control it would be ready to spend money to make it a pleasure-ground for all mankind, instead of a private farm. The United States would spend more money than the State does and in a far more judicious way. The place would be advertised more widely, and it would be run under a more broad-gauge and liberal policy. It would make the roads leading into the valley free and there would be more of them.

"Mariposa County has been trying for years to get a free road into the valley, but this stage company has always successfully fought it off on one pretext or another. Their toll-road and stage-line monopoly is quite profitable. The fare by stage for the round trip between Raymond and the valley is said to be $40, and the distance is 130 miles. Between Visalia and Moore and Smith's Mills, a round-trip distance of 110 miles, the fare by stage is $7.

"The Government has made all around the valley the largest public park in the world and the valley should be incorporated with it. The terms of the grant to the State have been violated in every clause. This statement can easily be substantiated and the sooner the National Government regains control the better.

"An article recently appeared in a morning contemporary, evidently contributed to that journal by order of the 'powers that be,' which we hear of so often in Yosemite. This effusion was highly eulogistic of the ignorant mischief that is and has been for the last three years going on in the valley under those national as well as State inflictions yclept [so-called] 'Boards of Commissioners.'

"The total incapacity of all such bodies of public nuisances is nowhere more strikingly exemplified than in the management of the Yosemite for the last ten years, to go back no further.

"An Intelligent and Generous Policy"

"It has degenerated into the most pitiful scandal that has ever afflicted much-wronged California. It is not necessary to seek interviews with individuals regarding this matter. Only let a person or persons of right feeling and taste, good judgment and discrimination visit Yosemite, and that wonderful spot, the crown jewel at present in California's gorgeous diadem of scenic glories and wonders, will tell more in its mute appeal against the disgrace and scarification to which it is being subjected at the bands of this official conclave of dilettantes and ignoramuses than could volumes of the choicest rhetoric. Its condition to the eye is sufficient to declare the outrages to which it is being subjected.

"Well, what is at the bottom of it all I'll tell you—more boodle. Said one of the sharpest men who was ever on the board to me several days ago, 'Robinson, if they ever refuse to give appropriations to the Yosemite Commission that body will dissolve like a morning mist.'

"That's the matter in a nutshell. Every dollar that is appropriated for the use of the valley is now used to its detriment, with but a few trifling exceptions.

"Wholesale evictions have been the rule, and now there are but four persons left of the old valley pioneers who are holding privileges under this railroad board.

"All of the valley business has been through the agency of this railroad stage line absorbed by them, aided by the obsequious obedience of their ordained and appointed commission.

"They are now preparing to jump the State for another big sack to aid the schemes of the Stoneman House ring, and to be used as a farther bar and hindrance against the people of the State who supply the 'sinews,' i.e., the much-despised 'camper,' who does not bleed in their hostelry, or to their illegally protected livery monopoly to the tune of $10 per diem.

"You can say, additionally, that there is lots more of the same kind of material just where this came from, all of which I would like to see proved false before unbiased witnesses. As to the 'investigation' of 1889, it was a clear case of taking a case to Hades, where the devil was judge; and still if the ring is satisfied with the printed outcome I have nothing to complain of—nothing at all."

"It is getting there that is the difficulty."

James M. Carson
"The Yosemite in Winter," 1892

By the 1890s, Yosemite had been a desirable tourist destination for forty years. There had been improvements in roads, most of which were privately owned, and accommodations, which, in the estimation of visitors, ranged from modest to commendable, but traveling to the breathtaking region was still demanding. One of the stronger arguments made by proponents of transferring control of the Yosemite Valley from state to federal administration was to improve accessibility and remove substandard commercial lodging.

With this public park gaining in popularity as the years passed, most wished that Yosemite would become easier to visit, but the trials of the journey remained challenging. Potential transportation solutions were complicated and bewildering. Bottom line—traveling to Yosemite was daunting, and it appeared that would remain the case for years to come unless there was significant policy reformation.

In December 1892, author James M. Carson wrote "The Yosemite in Winter," a thoughtful meditation on the valley in the grips of chill midwinter. In the conclusion of his article, Carson addressed the dichotomy of the Yosemite experience in the nineteenth century: no one regrets the encounter, but practically everyone loathes the physical trek. As Carson succinctly observed, "It is getting there that is the difficulty."

From the time when winter sets in to the return of spring the forty or fifty residents of Yosemite may be regarded as

"An Intelligent and Generous Policy"

voluntary prisoners therein. Communication with the outside world is closed to all but the hardiest mountaineers; the
stage lines are blockaded with snow, and casual visitors so
seldom make their way into the valley, under the difficulties
which Mr. [James Mason] Hutchings faced alone, that their
arrival during the winter months is no more frequent than
angels' visits. Once within the valley, however, none of the
discomfort is found that may have been expected. Residence
therein, without the summer sun and without the summer
tourist rushing from scene to scene with hasty impetuos-
ity and superficial observation, is no hardship. Good cheer
and comfortable lodging greet you; instead of heat and dust
and rush with disquiet and excitement all around you, you
find repose and a season for contemplation, while sublime
views and glorious sights, not seen elsewhere, contribute
their spectacular wonders for your entertainment. When to
these great factors of human happiness are added pleasant
company and intellectual conversation, the visitor will find
that there is nothing to regret in a sojourn in the Yosemite
during the winter. It is getting there that is the difficulty.

Let us make the trip with Mr. Allen Kelly [head forester
of California], who paid the valley a visit last winter, leaving
Raymond February 28th. Riding to Grant's Springs at the foot
of Chowchilla mountain, a distance of twenty-five miles, on
the following day he left the stage road and reached Ferguson's ranch by way of Snow Creek. Then he proceeded on a
mountain trail in company with Hiram Branson, who carries the mail up the Merced River, for a distance of thirty
miles. "Between Ferguson's and the south fork of the Merced
is a high ridge that forms the westerly wall of Devil's Gulch,
one of the deepest, roughest, most inaccessible gorges of
the Sierras. The road to Hite's Cove winds down this ridge
and from some of the turns, where the road is but a shelf
on the mountain side, one can look almost straight downward about 2,000 feet into the dark gorge where the grizzly's reign is undisputed and undisturbed by man." The trail
down the mountain ends at Hite's Cove, and from the river

bank abruptly begins to climb the mountain, zigzaging over rocks and through low brush to a height of over 4,000 feet on to a ridge so narrow that "a horse cannot stand transversely upon it." From the summit of this "hog's-back" Mr. Kelly could see the Merced's "foam-white ribbon of water" 2,500 feet below, and it seemed as if he could toss a stone from each hand, one into the main river and the other into its southern branch. The scenery was stupendous.

When the trail strikes the bottom of the cañon, it follows up the course of the river along the line of the projected free road from Mariposa to Yosemite. It was neither an easy nor a safe task to cross the Merced. Half a mile above Ward's place there is a ford, but a dangerous one and too pregnant with disaster to be available in winter time. Just below it a wire cable has been stretched across the river and the venturesome traveler had to pull himself to the opposite side, hand over hand, seated on a six-inch plank slung from the cable on trolleys. Then the horses were driven across the ford and Mr. Kelly was within an ace of losing his animal which was nearly swept away by the impetuous current.

Continuing along the trail they found it bad and dangerous. Skirting on smooth shelving ledges along the brinks of cliffs where a slip meant death to man and horse, and passing a huge storm-rent and weather-rifted granite cliff that overhangs the trail and ever threatens with a downpour of rocks and bowlders, they pursued their way for twenty miles, and then struck the Coulterville road just outside the Yosemite grant; thence a good wagon road led them into the valley. Speaking of that overhanging cliff with its oft-repeated slides of granite slabs and disintegrated masses of rock, an old mountaineer said: "I don't want anybody to speak above a whisper in that place, because I think the ghost of an echo would start some of those loose rocks. I never crossed there yet without finding new rocks on the trail, and I don't think it would take much of a blast to bring that whole mountain side down into the Cañon, dam the Merced River and make a lake of the Yosemite Valley."

"An Intelligent and Generous Policy"

There was but little snow in the valley when they entered it, and they proceeded without difficulty; but there are times when the mail-carrier is obliged to leave his horse near the entrance and continue his journey for eight or ten miles on snowshoes. But these spells of heavy weather do not last. In the valley the snow rarely lies deep for any length of time, except in isolated places that protect it from the liquefying effect of sun and weather.

Few, very few, of the numerous visitors to Yosemite see it in all the phases of its thousand glories even in the summer time. The impressions carried away by most tourists are general and common to the majority. Following beaten tracks under similar conditions of season and weather, and under like circumstances of transportation and hurry, the same routine of views and emotions is followed by all. It is only those exceptional individuals, whose enthusiasm carries them off the hackneyed highway of the sight-seer, that behold nature under other than ordinary aspects; and the few who face the discomforts of a journey to Yosemite through the snow have their reward in being spectators to some of the most sublime sights that Nature, in her prodigality of phenomena, is in the habit of exhibiting.

> "The troopers are constantly kept busy in removing
> the marks of the tourist and the advertiser."

Captain John A. Lockwood
"Uncle Sam's Troopers in the National
Parks of California," 1899

An often forgotten aspect of Yosemite history in the late nineteenth century is that the U.S. Army managed, patrolled, and protected the parklands for twenty-two years, from 1891 until 1913.

When Yosemite National Park was established in 1890, the legislation did not provide for administration. However, the history of Yellowstone National Park provided a solution. When Yellowstone was founded in 1872, the park did not have management and protective services. After more than ten years of nonexistent supervision, Congress passed H.R. 7595 in 1883, which authorized military oversight of Yellowstone. In 1900 Congress passed a bill that rectified some lingering legal questions and clearly specified the role and obligations of the military in national parks.

In 1891, following this precedent, Secretary of the Interior John W. Noble requested a military presence in Yosemite National Park. Despite initially lukewarm support, the request was granted, and the first U.S. Army troops arrived in Yosemite in 1891. The soldiers were officers and troopers from the Fourth Cavalry, stationed at the Presidio, in San Francisco. The commanding officer was designated as "Acting Superintendent of Yosemite National Park."

Every summer the U.S. Army dispatched cavalry to patrol the park. Units of the Twenty-Fourth Infantry, Third Artillery, First Cavalry, Fourth Cavalry, Sixth Cavalry, Ninth Cavalry, and Fifteenth Cavalry served tours in Yosemite. Most famously, African American troopers, the "Buffalo Soldiers," of the Twenty-Fourth Infantry and Ninth Cavalry, were stationed in the national park in 1899, 1903, and 1904.

The soldiers did not relish the duty. Many considered their posting to be unmilitary and done purely out of government penny-pinching. Troops found their off hours in Yosemite boring compared to the bright lights of San Francisco. But not all troopers disliked their stint in Yosemite, and a few became park rangers upon leaving the service.

In 1899 Captain John A. Lockwood wrote of the cavalry's experiences and accomplishments in California's national parks in an article for the *Overland Monthly*. Lockwood chronicled the army's service in Sequoia National Park, General Grant National Park, and Yosem-

"An Intelligent and Generous Policy"

ite National Park. In this excerpt, Captain Lockwood
describes the journey from San Francisco and the troopers' responsibilities in Yosemite.

It was an ideal morning in early May at the Presidio of San
Francisco. The four troops of cavalry, two hundred odd men
strong, had been ordered some weeks before to move out on
this particular day toward their summer camps, over three
hundred miles away, in Southeastern California. The day
arrived and men and horses were ready.

There was no unusual hurry or confusion. All had been
carefully planned and arranged for beforehand. "Boots and
Saddles" and "The Assembly" were sounded, and the men
saddled, bridled, led out, and prepared to mount, as if for drill,
instead of for an absence of six or seven months. The pack-
mules were more refractory. It took a packer no less skilled
in handling a mule than the veteran, Dennis, who learned
his art under General Crook, to drive the disgusted little animals with their unusual burdens into the rear of the column
and keep them there. The last farewells were said, the band,
whose sweet strains the cavalrymen would not hear again
for many months, played "The Girl I Left Behind Me," the
troopers swung into the saddle, and the command was off.

Winding up the hilly road which flanks the reservation
on the east, the column moved along at a walk. First the
field and staff, then "K" troop, with its coal-black horses, the
troop officers riding at ease at the head, then the three other
troops, followed by a dozen or more four-mule army wagons
with their white canvas covers, and finally the troublesome
pack-mules, followed and hurried along by the packers, civil-
ians, and soldiers. . . . [T]he troop dogs began to make their
appearance. They had been lying low and avoiding arrest and
the pound and the other bugbears of dogdom, until, danger
apparently passed, the dogs' best friend, the trooper, turned
his charge loose. . . .

The San Joaquin Valley took five days to cross. It is always
hot, dusty, and alkaline, or else it is cold, muddy, and rainy,

according to seasons. The dogs before mentioned as not visible at all when we left the Presidio, by the time we were three or four days out, had taken unto themselves other dogs, and when the sun-baked plain of the San Joaquin was reached, the original number had certainly doubled,—all different in appearance, in bark, and in capacity to hunt; for they chased, with tireless activity, the fleet cottontail or the frightened jack rabbit, disturbed in their haunts by the march of our column. It was rare indeed when a dog actually caught a rabbit; but when that did happen, the men became as excited as the dogs over the great event. . . .

The permanent camp of the cavalry troop detailed to patrol the Yosemite reservation is about a mile from the well-known Wawona Hotel, on the north side of the Merced River. The famous Yosemite Valley is some twenty-five miles beyond this camp, and the celebrated Wawona grove of big trees is some eight miles distant from the camp.

The old story of bad roads repeats itself in the less traveled districts of the Yosemite reservation. The Tioga road has been neglected until it is no longer passable for wagons; yet if kept in repair, this road would connect with others, over which could be made a tour of the park extending over one hundred miles, and diversified with some of the finest scenery in the world. This road, such as it is, leads to the summit, almost, of the Sierra,—Tioga Pass,—at an altitude of nine thousand feet. There are easy trails from here to two other elevations,—Mount Lyell on the summit of the grand Sierra, and Mount Conness, whence the ascent to the very summit can be reached in ten miles over a good saddle trail. Here the altitude is thirteen thousand feet, and commands one of the grandest views in the world. Both the main road and the side trails lead through a veritable Eden, and should, by all means, be kept in good condition. The panorama unfolded along this Tioga wagon road defies description. It skirts Mount Hoffman and Mount Dana. It touches the shore of Lake Tenaya, with the ten-lake country within easy distance. Countless wild and beautiful mountain torrents

"An Intelligent and Generous Policy"

cross its path in the wake of glacial meadows. It is skirted by plateaus of luxuriant grasses and multi-hued flowers. The original cost of this road is roughly estimated to have been sixty thousand dollars. A few hundred dollars a year would keep it in good repair.

In the Yosemite, some of the troopers are constantly kept busy in removing the marks of the tourist and the advertiser. All appeals to public favor which can be made on bits of wood and tin and muslin are destroyed almost as soon as created. It is not so easy to obliterate the defacements made on rocks and trees. But while sometimes the tourist is a vandal, more often he appreciates the work of the blue-coats, and is glad to meet the soldierly looking columns of troopers riding over the trails, or to come across them in out of the way nooks and mountain recesses. At times, a prospector, a legacy from '49, will follow the trail of a soldier detail, and usually manages to over-take "Uncle Sam's" boys just at meal-time; for the wearer of brass buttons is proverbially generous and ready to share his last crust with the hungry wayfarer. An officer told me that last summer he went to make his monthly inspection of General Grant Park and found that the detail of men there was living upon half rations. Investigation developed the fact that a dead-broke prospector was camping with them and had been there, a self-invited guest, for two weeks; consequently, the entire detail was reduced to half rations, and bacon, potatoes, and hard-bread, at that.

The troopers, at times, are obliged to arrest all sorts and conditions of men. A well-known society man of San Francisco, in search of novel sensations, made a trip through the Yosemite Park alone, on foot. As his garb and mode of progression was unusual, he found himself much annoyed by inquisitive tourists, whom he met, stopping him and asking him questions; so he pretended to be deaf and dumb, and replied to all questions by using the deaf and dumb alphabet as he strode along. A well-meaning trooper endeavored to arrest him as a lunatic at large, when the member of the four hundred suddenly found his voice.

The national parks suffer serious injury from fires; and these are of frequent occurrence, either from accident, from the carelessness of persons camping, or from the design of sheep-men. Aside from the destruction of the trees, it is of great importance that the yearly deposit of dry leaves and cones, and other woodland accumulation, should not be burned away in spots. This accumulation is a natural coverlet, designed by nature to prevent a too rapid surface drainage and evaporation by the winds. This great forest floor or carpet thus increases, and in a great degree, equalizes the water supply; and the principal object of the great forest reserves in California is the regulation and preservation of this water supply.

Late in September, the sheep, having been driven back down to the plains, and the tourist no longer finding life in the mountains desirable, the work of the soldier-guardians of the park becomes much easier, and by November of each year, the guard is withdrawn for the winter, snow and ice forming a no less impenetrable barrier to depredators than the bayonets of the soldiers.

"There, on a crag a yard square, he stood and saw a vision as no one, elsewhere, ever did."

Charles A. Bailey
"The Vantage Point of Yosemite," 1899

By 1899 Yosemite had become a known commodity. Now a more easily accessible tourist destination, the national park was in the throes of determining its future path. Questions as to administrative jurisdiction, the quality of the visitor experience, and ease of transportation were the primary concerns. But one constant remained, the same constant that had defined Yosemite from the beginning—the extraordinary landforms of the Yosemite Valley. And the valley could still yield surprises. For years there had been a desire to locate a single spot in Yosemite from which the four major waterfalls could be

"An Intelligent and Generous Policy"

observed. The waterfalls are Vernal Fall, Nevada Fall, Yosemite Falls, and Illilouette Fall.

In June 1897 the long-sought viewpoint was located following an ascent of the southern shoulder of Half Dome, below Grizzly Peak, by three intrepid climbers—Charles A. Bailey, Walter E. Magee, and Warren Cheney of Berkeley. All three were Sierra Club members, and Bailey named the site "Sierra Point" in honor of the club. The name still stands today.

In the April 1899 edition of *Sunset Magazine*, Bailey described the discovery of Sierra Point by a mysterious figure identified only as "He." There is little doubt that "He" is Bailey himself.

His article, entitled "The Vantage Point of Yosemite," is more than simply a climber's journal; it is also a reverential tribute to the enduring power and majesty of the granite cathedral of Yosemite Valley at the end of the nineteenth century.

Bailey was no stranger to Yosemite. A successful real estate magnate in Alameda County, Bailey spent business breaks climbing and hiking in Yosemite. He devoted sixteen summers to roaming the splendid canyon of the Merced River. On June 5, 1905, while climbing west of El Capitan, Bailey slipped from a cliff ledge and fell to his death. Some historians consider Bailey to be the first known climbing fatality in Yosemite.

Should he see Yosemite with a good understanding?

He said he would if he could. He entered its portals. A river was lifted up and dropped its radiant waters down, delicately spread and woven.

Across from it was a great rock that he could not measure aright with what he had, and he saw that his rule and yard stick and understanding were all too small.

And he took for his measuring rod a golden reed of a hundred feet. And the radiant dropping river was nine times its length and the rock was thirty-three times.

And he saw that there were other dropping rivers and running waters, and other rocks, and they were in and about a great rent in the mountains, and the plan of their arrangement was superb and mighty.

And he took his golden reed and with it he measured among the rocks and mountains and dropping rivers for the best horizontal plane and the best point of view, that his eyes might see and his understanding be opened.

And he climbed a lifted rock and it was ten times the measure of his golden reed and of his meager rule a thousand times.

And above him a lifted river was dropped down as never other river was, and beside him was a trench, dug in the solid rock by its leapings and swirlings, and at its end the river plunged.

And the dropping river was sixteen times the measure of his golden reed, the leapings in the trench were six times and the plunge at its end was four times.

All the droppings and leapings and plungings of the uplifted river were twenty-six hundred times his meager rule, and he did not understand the full measure thereof.

And he climbed to another high perched rock on the same horizontal plane, and from there he saw other rivers, and they dropped three times. And all the droppings of the rivers were five times, and rocks rose up and hid the rivers one from the other.

And he diligently searched for what he wanted. And it was not along the upmost rim from El Capitan to Tenaya Canyon. And it was not from the Leaning Tower to Sentinel Rock, or along all the high perimeter of Glacier Point, or by the edge of Panorama Wall from Illilouette to the Nevada.

It was not from the heights of Eagle Peak, Yosemite Point or Lost Arrow, or from Washington Column, North Dome or Basket Dome. Nor was it from the towering height of Half Dome, or from Liberty Cap or Mt. Broderick.

From Grizzly Peak were beheld the rivers, and they dropped

four times. But nowhere could be seen the rivers dropping five times.

And he took his golden reed and he leveled and measured among the rocks and rivers in and about the great rent for the best plane and angle of vision. And it led him to the great flankings of Half Dome, and down to where it was the least and the end and the buttress where the rivers met.

There, on a crag a yard square, he stood and saw a vision as no one, elsewhere, ever did.

The rivers dropped five times. Encompassed by waters and walls and monuments he was shut in. And the crag was lifted up. By his golden reed it was ten times, and by his meager rule a thousand times. He peered down and a horse was as a grasshopper and the stature of a man was as an inch. And he saw that all his life his eyes were lifted to a plane five times the measure of his meager rule and they should be lifted a thousand times.

The falling waters were about him. Nearest and eastward was the Vernal in the great curve. Its width was the measure of his golden reed and its setting was monumental and unequaled.

Above and beyond was the graceful and exuberant Nevada.

Mounting upward and southward was the rugged canyon of the Illilouette, with its falls in profile, beside the pines, near its upper end.

To the westward were the Upper and Lower Yosemite, dropping down the great cliffs. And he saw that where he stood was the converging point of vision of the five great waterfalls of Yosemite, and that no other place was. And there were mighty steps in the great rent in the mountains, down which the rivers fell, and the best horizontal plane was between the steps.

And the Royal Arches were lifted to the same plane; below were the Lower Yosemite and the Vernal, above were the Upper Yosemite, Nevada and Illilouette.

Waterfalls were below him and waterfalls were above, and

down a thousand times the measure of his meager rule were the Happy Isles and the rivers joined in one.

Behind was the sprawling upward sweep of Grizzly Peak, and flanking Vernal and Nevada were the granite monuments of Liberty Cap and Mt. Broderick.

Before were the massive walls and buttresses that would bear up a Popocatepetl.

And the measure of the falling waters were:

Feet

Upper Yosemite Falls	1,600
Lower Yosemite Falls	400
Vernal Falls	350
Nevada Falls	600
Illilouette Falls	400
	———
	3,350

And the stretch of all the falling waters that he saw from that single standpoint were three thousand three hundred times the measure of his meager rule, and were the measure of the granite wall that rose before him.

And his vantage point was lifted up, yet it was crouched among the shadows of the mighty and there were gathered the leaping, singing rivers, and the yawning canyons and the uplifted walls, and he looked down and up and around, and his understanding was opened. And he saw that he was on the best horizontal plane and at the converging point of vision, and his conceptions grew, and he was better prepared to see.

And he went to Inspiration Point and saw the grandeur and beauty of the entrance to Yosemite and a glimpse beyond.

And he went to Glacier Point and the canyons were opened before him, and he saw their depths and wealth of waters and monuments. And he went to Clouds' Rest, and in grand array the mountains were around.

And he toiled up the trail beside the Yosemite River, that drops as no other river does, and looked up and down the great gorge from Yosemite Point and Eagle Peak.

And he saw that the best points of observation of Yosemite were five:

1. Inspiration Point.

2. Sierra Point (or Point of Vantage).

3. Glacier Point.

4. Clouds' Rest.

5. Yosemite Falls and Eagle Peak.

And the five points should be taken in their order and the eyes be opened to see.

One should enter Yosemite by Inspiration Point, and the rest may be seen in four days.

And he said he would understand that single rock at the gate.

And he sought among the world's seven highest structures, each supreme in its kind.

Feet

	Feet
Highest Pyramid, Cheops	450
Highest Hotel, de Ville Brussels	364
Highest Cathedral, Strassburg	468
Highest Statue, Statue of Liberty	329
Highest Chimney, Glasgow	460
Highest Monument, Washington	555
And above all places the Tower of Babel, built to reach heaven	680
	———
	3,306

And the reach of them all is but the span of El Capitan, that stands at the portal a colossal greeting and farewell.

Epilogue

As the nineteenth century ended, it was natural that society simultaneously reminisced about days gone by and dreamed of the future. For students of Yosemite, there was much that had changed in the previous decades but just as much that was enduring.

In the previous hundred years, the extraordinary granite gorge had seen a whirling kaleidoscope of pestilence, war, deceit, conceit, hullabaloo, bitching, heroism, romanticism, intolerance, ignorance, incompetence, reverence, and escapism. Turn-of-the century observers fretted over what was yet to come, what would be lost, and what could be gained.

But dwarfing these earthly anxieties was the seemingly eternal valley of the Ah-wah'-nee. Although altered by relentless geologic and environmental transformation, Yosemite remained a marvel of polished stone, graced by the nimble dance of the waters and the easy sweep of zephyrs and birdsong. Yosemite endured as a glorious tapestry of time immemorial embroidered with the broad smiles of the enchanted. It is "incomparable," John Muir wrote in 1912, suggesting that "no temple made with hands can compare with Yosemite." It was, he wrote "as if into this one mountain mansion Nature had gathered her choicest treasures, to draw her lovers into close and confiding communion with her."

But, even in wonderland, change is inevitable. The symbolic dawn of the twentieth century, perhaps the birth of a new age, came on June 24, 1900, when Oliver Lippincott and Edward E. Russell piloted the first automobile to enter Yosemite National Park. The vehicle was a Locomobile, a two-cylinder steam-powered car that was unreliable and had the unfortunate tendency to catch fire. It was more novelty than practical transport. The car startled visitors and animals alike. Lippincott noted, "At night the mere sight of the Locomobile's headlights and the sound of its shrill electric bell were sufficient to secure its right of way of every other vehicle, for horses were willing to jump over the bank or climb a tree to make way for us." While Lippincott suspected that what he referred to as an "unassuming little machine" might alter access to Yosemite to some degree, he concluded that "whatever the new type of conveyance, it cannot detract from the sublimity of the great valley or lessen the majesty of the eternal hills."

Lippincott was correct about the undying virtues of the Yosemite Valley but incorrect that the automobile would prove mostly unobtrusive. The Yosemite of yore—a realm of horses, pack mules, and buggies—would yield to the internal combustion engine. It dramatically improved access to the valley and accommodated a flood of cars, and the thousands of annual visitors multiplied into millions. Long lines at the entrance gates became standard, infrastructure was strained, and auto exhaust drifted through the valley. The newest Yosemite memory, as indelible as the first glimpse of Half Dome but deeply aggravating, became fighting for a parking space. And Yosemite would never be the same. For better or worse, a new Yosemite emerged.

In the modern Yosemite, the past quickly acquired a patina of quaintness and innocence, with the troubling and contemptible relegated to the shadows. But nineteenth-century Yosemite was neither old-fashioned nor simple; it was a complicated microcosm of then-current worldly affairs and a prognosticator of the future. The incidents and disputes of that era inform the contentious issues of today. The tensions that arose between the Native population and the newly dominant Anglo-American culture foreshadowed moments of racial reckoning in the United States. The clashes over federal versus state jurisdiction of wild lands is an ongoing engagement. The friction between environmental preservation and conservation policies was and remains intense. The clashes over utilizing public lands as a potential commercial resource or maintaining them as an untouched spiritual refuge were and often remain heated. The Yosemite of today can learn much from the Yosemite of yesteryear.

The gifts and guiding principles of the valley of the Ahwah'-nee are manifold—emotional discovery, environmental consciousness and commitment, innovative policy strategies, physical challenge, and temporary escape from daily burdens. These have always been waiting for us in the breathtaking granite temple.

What have we learned, what can we learn, from Yosemite, nature's mountain mansion?

SOURCE ACKNOWLEDGMENTS

Excerpts from William H. Brewer's *Up and Down California in 1860–1864: The Journal of William H. Brewer* (Berkeley: University of California Press, 2003) are used by permission of the University of California Press.

Excerpts from Kathleen L. Hull's *Pestilence and Persistence: Yosemite Indian Demography and Culture in Colonial California* (Berkeley: University of California Press, 2009) are used by permission of the University of California Press.

Excerpts from Jean-Nicolas Perlot's *Gold Seeker: Adventures of a Belgian Argonaut during the Gold Rush Years* (New Haven: Yale University Press, 1998) are used by permission of the Yale University Press.

Excerpts from Alexander Phimister Proctor's *Sculptor in Buckskin: An Autobiography by Alexander Phimister Proctor* (Norman: University of Oklahoma Press, 1971) are used by permission of the University of Oklahoma Press.

Excerpts from Mark Spence's "Dispossessing the Wilderness: Yosemite Indians and the National Park Idea, 1864–1930," *Pacific Historical Review* 65, no. 1 (1996): 27–59, are used by permission of the University of California Press.

SOURCES

Preface

Adams, Ansel. Quoted in *"The Incomparable Valley"* (catalog). Yosemite CA: Ansel Adams Gallery.

Greenwood, Grace [Sara Jane Clarke Lippincott]. "Eight Days in the Yosemite." *New York Times*, July 27, 1872.

Hutchings, James Mason. *Scenes of Wonder and Curiosity in California*. San Francisco: Hutchings and Rosenfeld, 1860.

Logan, Olive. "Does It Pay to Visit Yo Semite?" *The Galaxy* 10, no. 4 (1870): 498–509.

Muir, John. *The Yosemite*. New York: Century Company, 1912.

Sanders, Sue A. [Susan Augusta Pike Sanders]. *A Journey to, on, and from the "Golden Shore."* Delevan IL: Delevan Times Printing Office, 1887.

Zwinger, Ann. *Yosemite: Valley of Thunder*. San Diego: Tehabi Books, 1996.

1. The Soul of the Ah-wah'-nee

Clark, Galen. *Indians of the Yosemite Valley and Vicinity: Their History, Customs and Traditions*. Yosemite Valley CA: Galen Clark, 1904.

Five Views: An Ethnic Historic Site Survey for California. Sacramento: California Department of Parks and Recreation, Office of Historic Preservation, December 1988.

Godfrey, Elizabeth H. *Yosemite Indians: Yesterday and Today*. Yosemite CA: Elizabeth H. Godfrey, 1941. Originally published in *Yosemite Nature Notes* 20, no. 7 (1941): 49–72.

Heizer, Robert F. *The Destruction of California Indians*. Lincoln: University of Nebraska Press, 1974.

Hull, Kathleen L. *Pestilence and Persistence: Yosemite Indian Demography and Culture in Colonial California*. Berkeley: University of California Press, 2009.

Merriam, C. [Clinton] Hart. "Indian Village and Camp Sites in Yosemite Valley." *Sierra Club Bulletin* 10, no. 2 (1917): 202–9.

Perlot, Jean-Nicolas. *Gold Seeker: Adventures of a Belgian Argonaut during the Gold Rush Years*. New Haven: Yale University Press, 1998. Perlot's

351

memoir was originally published as *Chercour d'or: Vie et aventures d'un enfant de l'Ardenne* [Gold seeker: Life and adventures of a child of the Ardennes]. Paris: F. Bruck Arlon, 1897.

Russell, Carl P. [Parcher]. *One Hundred Years in Yosemite: The Story of a Great Park and Its Friends*. Berkeley: University of California Press, 1947.

Spence, Mark. "Dispossessing the Wilderness: Yosemite Indians and the National Park Idea, 1864–1930." *Pacific Historical Review* 65, no. 1 (1996): 27–59. Spence's article was expanded into a book and published as *Dispossessing the Wilderness: Indian Removal and the Making of the National Parks*. Oxford: Oxford University Press, 1999.

Voices of the People: Traditional Associated Tribes of Yosemite National Park. San Francisco and El Portal CA: Yosemite Conservancy, 2021.

2. "Earth's Undecaying Monuments"

The chapter title comes from Nathaniel Hawthorne, "Sketches from Memory: The Notch of the White Mountains," in *Mosses from an Old Manse*, vol. 2 (Boston: Ticknor and Fields, 1865).

Adams, Ansel. *The Portfolios of Ansel Adams*. Introduction by John Szarkowski. Boston: New York Graphic Society, 1977.

Muir, John. "Studies in the Sierra, No. 1." *Overland Monthly* 12, no. 5 (1874): 393–403.

——— . "Yosemite Glaciers." *New York Tribune*, December 5, 1871.

Whitney, Josiah D. *The Yosemite Book: A Description of the Yosemite Valley and the Adjacent Region of the Sierra Nevada, and of the Big Trees of California, Illustrated by Maps and Photographs*. New York: Julius Bien, 1868. Although the publication date is 1868, this book was not released until 1869.

3. "The Blood-Swollen God"

The chapter title comes from Stephen Crane, *The Red Badge of Courage* (New York: D. Appleton & Company, 1895).

Boling, John. Letters to the editor. *San Francisco Daily Alta California*, June 12, 1851, and June 14, 1851.

Bunnell, Lafayette Houghton. *Discovery of the Yosemite and the Indian War of 1851, Which Led to That Event*. Chicago: Fleming H. Revell Co., 1880.

Burnett, Peter H. "Governor's Annual Message to the Legislature, January 7, 1851." *Journals of the Legislature of the State of California at Its Second Session*. San Jose CA: Eugene Casserly, State Printer, 1851.

Fletcher, Thomas C. *Paiute, Prospector, Pioneer: The Bodie–Mono Lake Area in the Nineteenth Century*. Lee Vining CA: Artemisia Press, 1987. Includes reports from Lieutenant Tredwell Moore.

Garrett, Gary E. "The Destruction of the Indian of Mendocino County, 1856–1860." Master's thesis, California State University, Sacramento, 1969.

"The Indian Expedition" (letter from "M"). *San Francisco Daily Alta California*, April 23, 1851.

Johnston, Adam, Indian Agent. Letter to Luke Lea, Commissioner of Indian Affairs, March 7, 1851. From U.S. Senate Executive Document #4, 33rd Congress, Special Session, Serial Set 688, March 17, 1853.

Lewis, Albert. "Review Work: The California Diary of General E. D. Townsend, by Malcolm Edwards." *Southern California Quarterly* 53, no. 4 (1971): 358–60.

Mariposa Gazette. "Captain Boling Dies—Discoverer of Yosemite," June 17, 1864.

Palmer, Theodore G. Letter to his father, January 16, 1851, concerning the Mariposa Indian War of 1851. Originally published in chapter 2 of Lafayette Houghton Bunnell, *Discovery of the Yosemite and the Indian War of 1851, Which Led to That Event*. Chicago: Fleming H. Revell Co., 1880.

Russell, Carl P. [Parcher]. "Early Years in Yosemite." *California Historical Society Quarterly* 5, no. 4 (1926): 328–41.

Russell, Carl Parcher. *One Hundred Years in Yosemite: The Story of a Great Park and Its Friends.* Berkeley: University of California Press, 1947.

San Francisco Daily Alta California. "The Indian War." March 17, 1851.

Wozencraft, O. M. [Oliver Meredith]. "To the People Living and Trading among the Indians in the State of California." *Annual Report of the Commissioner of Indian Affairs*, 32nd Congress, 1st Session, 1851, 229–31. Washington DC: printed for the Office of the Commissioner of Indian Affairs by Gideon and Co., 1851.

4. "The Lark at Heaven's Gate Sings"

The chapter title comes from William Shakespeare, *Cymbeline*, 2.3.22.

Ayres, Thomas A. [Almond]. "A Trip to the Yohamite Valley." *San Francisco Daily Alta California*, August 6, 1856.

Baer, Warren. "A Trip to the Yosemite Falls." *Mariposa Democrat*, August 5, 1856.

Bunnell, Lafayette Houghton. *Discovery of the Yosemite and the Indian War of 1851, Which Led to That Event*, chapter 2. Chicago: Fleming H. Revell Co., 1880.

Country Gentleman. "The Yo-hem-i-ty Valley and Falls," October 8, 1856.

Greeley, Horace. *An Overland Journey from New York to San Francisco in the Summer of 1859.* New York: C. M. Saxton, Barker & Co., 1860.

Hutchings, James Mason. "California for Waterfalls!" *San Francisco Daily California Chronicle*, August 18, 1855.

———. "The Great Yo-Semite Valley." *Hutchings' California Magazine* 4, no. 40 (1859): 145–61.

———. *In the Heart of the Sierras.* Oakland and Yosemite Valley CA: Pacific Press and Publishing and Old Cabin, Yosemite Valley, 1888.

Hutchings's California Magazine 4, no. 40 (October 1859): 184. This article reprinted from the *Mariposa Star* includes a list of the "Necessaries of Life" for a trip to Yosemite.

Lawrence, James H. [Henry]. "Discovery of the Nevada Fall." *Overland Monthly* 2nd ser., 4, no. 22 (1884): 360–71.

Mariposa Gazette. "The Yo Semity Valley," October 11, 1855. Reprinted in the *Stockton San Joaquin Republican*, October 16, 1855.

Richards, T. [Thomas] Addison. *Appletons' Illustrated Hand-Book of American Travel*. New York: D. Appleton and Co., 1857.

5. "Sermons in Stone"

The chapter title comes from John Muir, "The Yosemite National Park," *Atlantic Monthly* 84 (August 1899): 145–52.

"An Act to Set Apart a Certain Tract of Land in the State of California as a Forest Reservation." *United States Statutes at Large*, vol. 26, chap. 1263, 650–52.

Hine, Robert V., and John Mack Faragher. *Frontiers: A Short History of the American West*. New Haven: Yale University Press, 2007.

Muir, John. "In the Yo-Semite: Holidays among the Rocks." *New York Weekly Tribune*, March 13, 1872.

———. *The Mountains of California*. New York: Century Co., 1894.

———. *My First Summer in the Sierra*. Boston and New York: Houghton Mifflin, 1911.

———. "The Treasures of the Yosemite." *Century Magazine* 40, no. 4 (1890): 483–500.

———. "Yosemite in Spring." *New York Tribune*, July 11, 1872.

Wolfe, Linnie Marsh. *Son of the Wilderness: The Life of John Muir*. New York: Knopf, 1946. Recipient of the 1946 Pulitzer Prize for Biography/Autobiography.

6. "Enter These Enchanted Woods"

The chapter title comes from George Meredith, "The Woods of Westermain," in *Poems and Lyrics of the Joy of Earth* (London: Macmillan, 1883), 1–27.

An Act of June 30, 1864, 38th Congress, 1st Session, Public Law 159, 13 STAT 325, Authorizing a Grant to the State of California of the "Yo-Semite Valley," and of the Land Embracing the "Mariposa Big Tree Grove."

Act of the Legislature of the State of California, Approved March 3, 1905, Regranting to the United States of America the Yosemite Valley and the land embracing the "Mariposa Big Tree Grove." *Statutes of California* (1905), 54.

An Act to Set Apart Certain Tracts of Land in the State of California as Forest Reservations [H.R. 12187]. 1890, *U.S. Statutes at Large*, vol. 26, chap. 1263, 650–52. Sections 1 and 2 of this act concern Yosemite National Park, while section 3 establishes General Grant National Park (now part of Kings Canyon National Park) and a portion of Sequoia National Park.

Bird, Isabella. *The Englishwoman in America*. London: John Murray, 1856.

Bowles, Samuel. *Across the Continent: A Summer's Journey to the Rocky Mountains, the Mormons, and the Pacific States, with Speaker Colfax. By Samuel Bowles, Editor of the Springfield (Mass.) Republican.* Springfield MA: Samuel Bowles & Company, 1865.

Brewer, William H. *Up and Down California in 1860–1864: The Journal of William H. Brewer.* Berkeley: University of California Press, 2003.

Conness, Senator John. *Congressional Globe*, Senate, 38th Congress, 1st Session, May 17, 1864, 2300–2301.

Hittell, John Shertzer. *Yosemite: Its Wonders and Its Beauties; With Information Adapted to the Wants of Tourists About to Visit the Valley.* San Francisco: H. H. Bancroft & Company, 1868.

Hoffmann, Charles Frederick. "Notes on Hetch-Hetchy Valley." *Proceedings of the California Academy of Sciences*, vols. 3–4 (1863–67), 368–70. San Francisco: California Academy of Sciences, 1868.

Joint Resolution Accepting the recession by the State of California of the Yosemite Valley Grant and the Mariposa Big Tree Grove in the Yosemite National Park. 1905, *U.S. Statutes at Large*, vol. 33, part 1, Resolution No. 30, 1286 [S.J.R. 115; Public Resolution No. 29].

Joint Resolution Accepting the recession by the State of California of the Yosemite Valley Grant and the Mariposa Big Tree Grove, and including the same, together with fractional sections five and six, township five south, range twenty-two east, Mount Diablo meridian, California, within the metes and bounds of the Yosemite National Park, and changing the boundaries thereof. 1906, *U.S. Statutes at Large*, vol. 34, part 1, Resolution No. 27, 831–32 [H.J.R. 118; Public Resolution No. 27].

King, Reverend Thomas Starr. "A Vacation among the Sierras, No. 6." *Boston Evening Transcript*, January 26, 1861.

Ludlow, Fitz Hugh. *The Hasheesh Eater.* New York: Harper and Brothers, 1857.
——— . "Seven Weeks in the Yo-Semite." *Atlantic Monthly* 13, no. 80 (June 1864): 739–54.

Olmsted, Frederick Law. "Draft of the Preliminary Report upon the Yosemite and the Big Tree Grove, 1865." Frederick Law Olmsted Papers, Digital ID: amvrm-vm02, Library of Congress, Washington DC. The Library of Congress has a digital copy of a draft of the report in the hand of Henry Perkins, Olmsted's secretary, and images of a typewritten transcript of the report produced in the twentieth century. A hybrid version mixing the 1865 report and Olmsted's 1868 *New York Evening Post* letter, entitled "The Great American Park of the Yosemite," was published as "The Yosemite Valley and the Mariposa Big Tree: A Preliminary Report," in *Landscape Architecture* 43, no. 1 (1952): 12–25. Also reprinted as *Yosemite and the Mariposa Grove: A Preliminary Report, 1865.* Yosemite National Park CA: Yosemite Association, 1993.

———. "The Great American Park of the Yosemite." *New York Evening Post,* June 18, 1868. Also reprinted in the *Sacramento Daily Union,* July 29, 1868.

"Review: *Across the Continent: A Summer's Journey to the Rocky Mountains, the Mormons, and the Pacific States, with Speaker Colfax by Samuel Bowles.*" *North American Review* 102, no. 211 (April 1866): 619–23. The *North American Review* was published in Boston, Massachusetts, from 1815 to 1940. Since 1964, it has been published by the University of Northern Iowa in Cedar Falls, Iowa.

San Francisco Call. "The Yosemite Muddle," July 1, 1905.

Twain, Mark [Samuel Clemens]. *The Innocents Abroad, or The New Pilgrims' Progress.* Hartford CT: American Publishing Company, 1869.

———. "Letter from 'Mark Twain,' No. 24." *San Francisco Daily Alta California,* August 4, 1867. Review of Albert Bierstadt's *The Domes of the Yosemite.*

7. "All Places That the Eye of Heaven Visits"

The chapter title comes from William Shakespeare, *Richard II,* 1:3:275.

Anonymous [probably William Nelson]. *The Yosemite Valley, and the Mammoth Trees and Geysers of California—Nelson's Pictorial Guide-books.* New York: T. Nelson and Sons, [1870?].

Badè, William Frederick. *The Life and Letters of John Muir.* Vol. 1. Boston: Houghton Mifflin, 1924. Letter from John Muir to Ralph Waldo Emerson, May 8, 1871, and letter from Emerson to Muir, February 5, 1872, are in chapter 8.

Brannon, James. "Radical Transcendentalism: Emerson, Muir and the Experience of Nature." *John Muir Newsletter* 16, no. 1 (2005–6): 1, 4–6.

Chan, Yenyen F. "Interpreting the Contributions of Chinese Immigrants in Yosemite National Park's History." *George Wright Forum* 34, no. 3 (2017): 299–307.

Churchill, Caroline Nichols. *Over the Purple Hills, or Sketches from Travel in California.* Chicago: Hazlitt & Reed, 1877.

Crosby, Anthony, and Nick Scrattish. *Historic Structure Report, Design and Installation of a Fire Detection and Suppression System: Wawona Hotel, Yosemite National Park, California.* Ann Arbor: University of Michigan Publishing Library, 1983.

Dodd, Derrick [Frank Harrison Gassaway]. *Summer Saunterings.* San Francisco: Francis, Valentine & Co., 1882.

Gordon Cumming, C. F. [Lady Constance Frederica Gordon-Cumming]. *Granite Crags.* Edinburgh and London: William Blackwood & Sons, 1884. Reprinted as *Granite Crags of California* in 1886 and 1888. The title page lists the author's surname as "Gordon Cumming," which is how the family name was commonly presented; however, Lady Constance preferred to use the hyphenated version of "Gordon-Cumming" in her daily life.

Greene, Linda W. *Yosemite: The Park and Its Resources*. Yosemite CA: U.S. Department of the Interior, National Park Service, 1987.

Greenwood, Grace [Sara Jane Clarke Lippincott]. "Eight Days in the Yosemite." *New York Times*, July 27, 1872.

Guerra, Stephanie. "Piecing Together the Past: Chinese Immigrants in Yosemite." *Yosemite Science* 1, no. 1 (2011): 14–16.

H.H. [Helen Hunt Jackson]. *Bits of Travel at Home*. Boston: Roberts Brothers, 1878.

Historic American Engineering Record (HAER). *Wawona Road Yosemite National Park HAER No. CA-148*. Yosemite CA: U.S. Department of the Interior, National Park Service, 1991.

Hutchings, James Mason. *In the Heart of the Sierras*. Oakland CA: Pacific Press Publishing, 1888.

King, Clarence. *Mountaineering in the Sierra Nevada*. Boston: James Osgood & Co., 1872. *Mountaineering in the Sierra Nevada* was originally published as a series of articles in the *Atlantic Monthly* from May to December 1871. The book was revised and reprinted by Charles Scribner's Sons in 1902.

Kroeber, A. L. [Alfred Louis]. *Handbook of the Indians of California*. Bulletin 78, Bureau of American Ethnology of the Smithsonian Institution. Washington DC: Government Printing Office, 1925.

LeConte, Joseph. *The Autobiography of Joseph LeConte*. New York: D. Appleton and Company, 1903.

———. *A Journal of Ramblings through the High Sierras of California by the "University Excursion Party."* San Francisco: Francis & Valentine, 1875. Reprinted several times by the Sierra Club and the Yosemite Association.

Lester, John Erastus. *The Atlantic to the Pacific: What to See and How to See It*. Boston: Shepard and Gill, 1873.

———. *The Yo-Semite: Its History, Its Scenery, Its Development*. Providence RI: printed for John Erastus Lester by Providence Press Company, 1873.

Logan, Olive. "Does It Pay to Visit Yo Semite?" *The Galaxy* 10, no. 4 (1870): 498–509.

Muir, John. "The Hetch Hetchy Valley." *Boston Weekly Transcript*, March 25, 1873.

———. *John of the Mountains: The Unpublished Journals of John Muir*. Edited by Linnie Marsh Wolfe. Madison: University of Wisconsin Press, 1979.

———. "Living Glaciers of California." *Overland Monthly* 9, no. 6 (1872).

———. *Our National Parks*. Boston: Houghton Mifflin, 1901.

———. "South Dome." *San Francisco Daily Evening Bulletin*, November 18, 1875.

———. *Stories of My Boyhood and Youth*. Boston: Houghton Mifflin, 1913.

———. *The Yosemite*. New York: Century Company, 1912.

Powers, Stephen. *Tribes of California*. Published in *Contributions to North American Ethnology*, vol. 3, Department of the Interior, United States

Geographical and Geological Survey of the Rocky Mountain Region, J[ohn] W[esley] Powell, in charge. Washington DC: Government Printing Office, 1877. Reprinted by the University of California Press, 1976. The chapter on Yosemite was first published in "The California Indians: No. VII—The Meewocs," *Overland Monthly* 10, no. 4 (1873): 322–33.

Proctor, A. Phimister. "An Ascent of Half Dome." *Sierra Club Bulletin* 31, no. 7 (1946): 1–9.

Proctor, Alexander Phimister. *Sculptor in Buckskin: An Autobiography by Alexander Phimister Proctor.* Norman: University of Oklahoma Press, 1971.

Reynolds, Annie, and Albert Gordon. *Stage to Yosemite: Recollections of Wawona's Albert Gordon.* El Portal CA: Big Tree Books, 1994.

Russell, Carl P. *One Hundred Years in Yosemite.* Yosemite National Park CA: Yosemite Association, 1959.

Russell, Israel C. *Existing Glaciers of the United States.* Washington DC: U.S. Geological Survey, 1885.

San Francisco Chronicle. "Death Calls for Aged Author," April 21, 1904. Obituary of Grace Greenwood.

Sargent, Shirley. "Wawona's Yesterdays." *Yosemite* 40, no. 4 (November 30, 1961): 64–105. *Yosemite* was a quarterly journal published by the Yosemite Natural History Association and the Yosemite Association from 1922 to 1962 and from 1970 to 2010.

Sargent, Shirley. *Galen Clark: Yosemite's Guardian.* Yosemite CA: Flying Spur Press, 2008.

——— . *Yosemite's Historic Wawona.* Yosemite CA: Flying Spur Press, 2008.

Stornoway, Lewis [George G. (Gordon) MacKenzie]. *Yosemite: Where to Go and What to Do.* San Francisco: C. A. Murdock & Co., 1888.

Thayer, James Bradley. *A Western Journey with Mr. Emerson.* Boston: Little, Brown, 1884.

Wawona Hotel Complex Yosemite National Park Cultural Landscape Report, Part 1 and Part 2. National Park Service, Yosemite National Park Delaware North Companies Parks and Resorts at Yosemite, Inc., August 2012.

Wulf, Andrea. "He's Not That into You." *New York Times*, April 2, 2010. Review of Chloë Schama, *Wild Romance: A Victorian Story of Marriage, a Trial, and a Self-Made Woman.* New York: Walker and Company Books, 2010.

Yelverton, Thérèse (Viscountess Avonmore). *Zanita: A Tale of the Yo-semite.* New York: Hurd and Houghton, 1872.

8. "An Intelligent and Generous Policy"

The chapter title comes from "The Care of the Yosemite Valley," *Century Magazine*, January 1890, 474–75, an editorial decrying the poor management of the Yosemite Valley by the California Yosemite Park Commission and calling for federal control of the valley.

Bailey, Charles A. "The Vantage Point of Yosemite." *Sunset Magazine* 2, no. 6 (1899): 121–24.

Caminetti Bill (H.R. 5764). *Journal of the House of Representatives of the United States of America*, 52nd Congress, 1st Session, vol. 52, issue 1 (February 9, 1892), 124. The text of the bill can also be found in *Congressional Record*, vol. 23, part 2 (1892), 295, 1042.

Carson, James M. "The Yosemite in Winter." *Californian Illustrated Magazine* 3, no. 1 (December 1892): 138–45.

Castillo, Edward D. "Petition to Congress on Behalf of the Yosemite Indians." *Journal of California Anthropology* 5, no. 2 (1978): 271–77.

Century Magazine. "Amateur Management of the Yosemite Scenery," 40, no. 5 (September 1890): 797–98.

"General Correspondence Relating to Yosemite National Park." 1890–1907. Part I: Secretary of the Interior John W. Noble to President of the U.S. Benjamin Harrison, December 4, 1890. Letters Sent, Record Group 79, National Archives, Washington DC.

Greene, Linda Wedel. *Yosemite: Its Park and Its Resources: A History of the Discovery, Management, and Physical Development of Yosemite National Park, California.* 3 vols. Washington DC: United States Department of the Interior, National Park Service, September 1987. Volumes 1 and 2 consist of a historical narrative.

Kelly, Allen. "Restoration of Yosemite Waterfalls." *Harper's Weekly* 36 (July 16, 1892): 678.

Lockwood, Captain John A. "Uncle Sam's Troopers in the National Parks of California." *Overland Monthly* 23, no. 196 (April 1899): 356–68.

Muir, John. "Features of the Proposed Yosemite National Park." *Century Magazine* 40, no. 5 (September 1890): 656–67.

———. "The Treasures of the Yosemite." *Century Magazine* 40, no. 4 (August 1890): 483–500.

Noble, James W. [Willock]. *Reports of the Secretary of the Interior Relative to Yosemite Park.* Washington DC: Government Printing Office, 1893. A report by the special land inspector Major Eugene F. Weigel to Secretary of the Interior James W. Noble, October 3, 1892, is found on pages 6–7.

"Petition to the Senators and Representatives of the Congress of the United States in the Behalf of the Remnants of the Former Tribes of the Yosemite Indians Praying for Aid and Assistance." The original petition is in Letters Received by the Office of the Secretary of the Interior Relating to National Parks, 1872–1907 (Yosemite), Record Group 79, National Archives, Washington DC. Reprinted in Edward D. Castillo, "Petition to Congress on Behalf of the Yosemite Indians," *Journal of California Anthropology* 5, no. 2 (1978): 271–77.

Runte, Alfred. *Yosemite—The Embattled Wilderness.* Lincoln: University of Nebraska Press, 1990.

San Francisco Call. "To Save Yosemite," November 20, 1892.

———. "Valley Vandals," January 1, 1893.

Spence, Mark. "Dispossessing the Wilderness: Yosemite Indians and the National Park Idea, 1864–1930." *Pacific Historical Review* 65, no. 1 (1996): 27–59.

Wood, Captain A. E. [Abram Epperson]. "Report of the Acting Superintendent of Yosemite National Park." *United States Congressional Serial Set,* issue 2935 (1891): 659–66.

Epilogue

Currey, Lloyd W., and Dennis G. Kruska. *Bibliography of Yosemite, the Central and Southern High Sierra, and the Big Trees, 1839–1900.* Los Angeles: Dawson's Book Shop; Palo Alto CA: William P. Wreden, 1992.

Farquhar, Francis P. *Yosemite, the Big Trees, and the High Sierra: A Selective Bibliography.* Berkeley and Los Angeles: University of California Press, 1948.

Johnston, Hank. *Yosemite's Yesterdays.* Yosemite CA: Flying Spur Press, 2014. Description of Oliver Lippincott and the Locomobile.

Muir, John. *The Yosemite.* New York: Century Company, 1912.

Scott, Amy, ed. *Art of an American Icon: Yosemite.* Los Angeles: Autry National Center in association with the University of California Press, 2006.

Williams [California] Farmer. "An Automobile's Success," June 30, 1900. An account of the first automobile in Yosemite Valley.